MW00643693

MANAGEMENT PRINCIPLES
FOR CHRISTIAN SCHOOLS
2nd Edition

JAMES W. DEUINK
BRIAN A. CARRUTHERS

JOURNEYFORTH
Greenville, South Carolina

Library of Congress Cataloging –in-Publication Data
Deuink, James W.
  Management principles for Christian schools / James W. Deuink and Brian
A. Carruthers. — 2nd ed.
     p. cm.
  Rev. ed. of: Effective Christian school management. 1982.
  Summary: "Presents a biblical, practical model for Christian education"—
Provided by publisher.
  Includes bibliographical references.
  ISBN-13: 978-1-59166-803-9 (perfect bound pbk. : alk. paper)
  1. Church schools—United States—Administration. I. Carruthers, Brian
A., 1962- II. Deuink, James W. Effective Christian school management.
III. Title.
  LC377.D38 2008
  371.071'068—dc22

                                                              2007043235e

Management Principles for Christian Schools
James W. Deuink (EdD) and Brian A. Carruthers (EdD)

Design by Nathan Hutcheon
Page layout by Kelley Moore
Edited by Debbie L. Parker

© 2008 by BJU Press
Greenville, South Carolina 29614
JourneyForth Books is a division of BJU Press

ISBN 978-1-59166-803-9

15 14 13 12 11 10 9 8 7 6 5 4 3 2 1

CONTENTS

Appendixes

Bibliography

List of Figures

PREFACE

This work, initially coauthored by James Deuink and Carl Herbster, had its beginning as *Effective Christian School Management* in 1982. At the time it was the most comprehensive book of its kind. It was followed in 1985 by *Christian School Finance* and *The Ministry of the Christian School Guidance Counselor* as the need for more specific information in these two areas of Christian education was recognized.

In 1986 Dr. Herbster and Dr. Deuink again collaborated and the second edition of *Effective Christian School Management* was released. In 1996 Dr. Deuink brought *Effective Christian School Management* and *Christian School Finance* under one cover as *Management Principles for Christian Schools*, a more comprehensive work. It was subsequently revised again in 2001. Now it is time for this work to be updated again.

Dr. Deuink has now retired as dean of the School of Education at Bob Jones University. Brian Carruthers was appointed to take his place in May of this year. Dr. Carruthers and Dr. Deuink have collaborated in this second edition of *Management Principles for Christian Schools.*

In the twenty-five years since *Effective Christian School Management* was first published, many changes have occurred in the Christian school movement. The Devil has fought our schools on every imaginable front. In spite of the challenges, God has seen fit to preserve the Christian school movement and it continues to meet great needs of children around the world.

Many of the changes we have seen recently are technological in nature. While they make it possible to provide instruction to more children, and sometimes to do it more efficiently, there is a danger that we risk losing some of what has made our movement so effective. We have known for a long time that the personal interaction of a born-again teacher with the students has been a key component in seeing desired spiritual changes. Much of the technology we are being encouraged to adopt weakens the link between the teacher and the student. We must be careful we do not surrender the most important components of the process of education for financial savings and efficiency. It was the personal ministry of the Lord Jesus, His disciples, and the apostles that turned the world upside down.

In the beginning years of our movement, unreasonable expectations were advanced as reasons to start Christian schools. Well-intentioned leaders suggested that Christian schools could solve problems we now recognize can only be solved by individuals surrendering hearts and lives to the will and purpose of God. No system or program can guarantee the accomplishment of either our will or God's in the lives of our children. This can happen only when individuals quietly and humbly acknowledge God as Savior, acknowledge His right as their Lord to choose for them, and freely submit to the leading of His Spirit. Since we were wrong in our expectations for Christian schools, does that mean they are not needed? Certainly not.

Christian schools exist primarily to provide the opportunity for the seeds of God's Word to be presented to young people in an environment where everything encourages their acceptance. Consequently, the faith of our children can be nurtured and strengthened before Satan has an opportunity to uproot and destroy it.

In the early years of the Christian school movement, we made another mistake. We assumed that placing our children in a totally Christian environment would in itself insure their salvation and the personal development of spiritual maturity. We were, of course, wrong on this count. We forgot that even Adam and Eve, living in the perfect environment of the Garden of Eden and free of a sin nature, still had a free will they chose to exercise against God. Consequently, as we reevaluate Christian schools in the twenty-first century, let us not forget our continuing responsibility not only to provide the opportunity for our children to know God and His will for their lives but also to recognize the importance of our own example before them. We cannot expect our children to have a stronger, more enduring faith in God than we demonstrate before them. Neither can we expect them to have a more tender heart toward the wooing of His Spirit than we demonstrate before them.

Christian schools, then, represent only one piece of the puzzle parents attempt to solve in rearing their children to honor God. But it is a very important piece.

As Christian educators read this edition of *Management Principles for Christian Schools*, our prayer is that it will help them develop Christian schools that will provide security and nurture in the faith.

The purpose of this book continues to have a threefold thrust: (1) as a textbook for college courses in educational leadership, (2) as a practical day-to-day guide for direction to Christian school administrators, pastors, and school board members, and (3) as a help to Christians desiring to start a Christian school ministry.

James W. Deuink
Brian A. Carruthers
Fall 2007

CHAPTER 1

HISTORICAL PERSPECTIVE

For inquire, I pray thee, of the former age, and prepare thyself to the search of their fathers: (For we are but of yesterday,
and know nothing, because our days upon earth are a shadow:)
Shall not they teach thee, and tell thee, and utter words out of
their heart?

Job 8:8–10

For whatsoever things were written aforetime were written
for our learning, that we through patience and comfort of the
scriptures might have hope.

Romans 15:4

It would be difficult, if not impossible, to understand the problems facing Christian education today without some familiarity with the development of both private and public education in our country. Because
current attitudes and concerns in education, particularly in the Christian
community, are the products of a constantly changing educational environment throughout our history, school administrators need a sound
historical perspective of the Christian school movement.[1]

COLONIAL EDUCATION

Common Emphasis

The earliest schools in America were religious in character. Most of them
used the Bible as the foundation of the curriculum and taught the academic subjects from the framework of a Christian interpretation of Scripture. In fact, education often existed for the express purpose of teaching
young people how to read so that they could read the Bible. One of the
more prominent examples of this religious purpose was The Old Deluder
Satan Act, passed by the General Court of Massachusetts in 1647. Ac-
knowledging that a purpose of Satan is to keep men from knowledge,

---

[1]Information Note. See *A History of Christian Education,* Vols. 1 & 2, for a comprehensive review of Christian education from the time of Christ to the present.

that act provided for the instruction of youth in order to thwart him. It required that all towns of fifty or more householders appoint someone to teach children to read and write. The teacher was to be paid either by the parents or by the residents of the town collectively.

The religious emphasis of the colonial schools is also clearly evident in their textbooks. The *New England Primer*, for example, contained rhymes with religious teachings such as "In Adam's fall we sinned all" and "Zacchaeus he climbed the tree, his Lord to see."

Religion permeated every area of colonial life. The following quotations from colonial leaders and legal documents evidence this pervasive religious perspective:

> It is the right as well as the duty of all men in society, publicly, and at stated seasons, to worship the Supreme Being, the great Creator and Preserver of the universe. (Massachusetts Bill of Rights, 1780)

> I have lived, Sir, a long time, and the longer I live, the more convincing proof I see of the truth—that God governs in the affairs of men. (Benjamin Franklin, in Federal Convention, 1787)

> Of all the dispositions and habits which lead to political prosperity, religion and morality are indispensable supports. . . . Let it simply be asked where is the security for property, for reputation, for life if the sense of religious obligation deserts the oaths which are the instruments of investigation in Courts of Justice. . . . 'Tis substantially true, that virtue or morality is a necessary spring of popular government. (George Washington, Farewell Address, 1796)

> They [the American people] were bound by the laws of God, which they all, and by the laws of the Gospel, which they nearly all, acknowledged as the rules of their conduct. (John Quincy Adams, Secretary of State Orations, July 4, 1821)

Distinctions

Colonial America was actually three distinctly different regions: the Southern Colonies, the Middle Colonies, and the New England Colonies. Each of these sections was to some degree unique. The South, largely an agrarian economy, developed much of the leadership that was to provide the early direction for our country. With the exception of those in metropolitan areas, most families lived considerable distances from one another. This isolation did not lend itself to the development of schools like those found in the Middle and New England Colonies. In the South, education was more a private and individual matter, and the religious influence was not as strong as it was in the North. The Anglican Church, the dominant religious force in the Southern Colonies, did not instill in its membership that same religious fervor found in the prevalent religious groups in other sections of the colonies. Though it provided education for poorer children on a charity basis, it did not seem to be interested in providing schooling for all. Children of wealthy landowners were usually taught by private tutors.

In the Middle Colonies religious direction came from several different denominations, the Quakers and Dutch Reformed among the most prominent. Practical education, based firmly on religious beliefs, was the primary emphasis. Although there was considerable interest in education in the Middle Colonies, its development was retarded by the diversity of the population. More than any of the other sections of the New World, the Middle Colonies were settled by immigrants from widely different backgrounds in the Old World. Because of the differences in religious affiliations, traditions, political theories, and languages, the development of education was made much more difficult in this region than it was in the other two.

Education in New England was dominated by the influence of the Puritans. New England had two types of schools: the primary schools, providing the earliest instruction for boys and occasionally girls; and the Latin grammar schools, patterned after the Latin schools of Europe. The primary schools, supported by the parents of the students, were normally held in the homes of the teachers. Although they are usually credited with emphasizing reading and writing, actually they often deemphasized writing to emphasize reading, considered important for religious instruction. The Latin grammar schools basically followed a classical curriculum with a heavy emphasis on religious instruction. As might be expected, the Latin grammar schools catered to the needs of the wealthier class.

Despite regional distinctions, education throughout the colonial period was predominantly private and strongly religious. Though the denominational emphasis, the quality of instruction, and the length of study varied from region to region, education nevertheless served a primarily religious purpose.

THE RISE OF PUBLIC EDUCATION

As time went on, communities expressed more and more interest in making education available to all children. Proponents of this idea could be found in all three regions of the country, though Massachusetts, not surprisingly, was the leading supporter of a public system of education. Even there, James G. Carter noted in 1826 that only a small percentage of children had an opportunity to attend school. In 1837 Carter himself was instrumental in establishing the first effective State Board of Education in the United States. Horace Mann (1796–1859) became the first secretary of the newly formed board on June 30 of that same year.

Some religious leaders preached against the idea of a state-directed education. A. A. Hodge (1823–86) more than one hundred years ago said:

> It is capable of exact demonstration that if every party in the State has the right of excluding from the public schools whatever he does not believe to be true, then he that believes most must give way to him that believes absolutely nothing, no matter in how small a minority the atheists or the agnostics may be. It is self-evident that on this scheme, if it is consistently and persistently carried out in all parts of the country, the United States system of national popular education will be the most efficient and wide instrument for the propagation of Atheism which the world has ever seen.

> It is no answer to say that the deficiency of the national system of education in this regard will be adequately supplied by the activities of the Christian churches. No court would admit in excuse for the

diffusion of poison the plea that the poisoner knew of another agent actively employed in diffusing an antidote. . . .

I am sure as I am of the fact of Christ's reign that a comprehensive and centralized system of national education, separated from religion, as is now commonly proposed, will prove the most appalling enginery for the propagation of anti-Christian and atheistic unbelief, and of anti-social nihilistic ethics, individual, social and political, which this sin-rent world has ever seen. . . .

However, public schools initially attracted parental support, not only because they were ostensibly free but also because they appeared to be as spiritual in their overall curriculum and instruction as the private schools they were supplanting. Many of the same teachers taught in them; many of the same textbooks were used. But public schools, though based largely on generally accepted moral principles, were never based on a Christian philosophy.

Because Horace Mann was a distinctly religious person, some observers of his plan for education in this country were less suspicious of his views than they might have been otherwise. Education, rather than Jesus Christ, had come to be viewed by some as the means for society's salvation. Mann shared that belief, having been influenced by a number of religious faiths; he eventually became a practicing Unitarian, with an educational philosophy based largely on his beliefs in the doctrine of the perfectibility of man. This tenet provided the impetus for the development of an educational system designed to cure America of all its ills. Mann's views have been summarized as follows:

As against the Calvinist conception of man as sinner, man is good; as against the doctrine of man's responsibility and accountability to God, of life as a stewardship, the non-biblical conception of natural rights as introduced into education. The pupil is therefore a person with rights rather than responsibilities. Instead of being accountable to God, parents, teachers, and society, the pupil can assert that God, parents, teachers, and society are responsible to him. (Rushdoony, 1963, 23)

THE DECLINE OF PUBLIC EDUCATION

Various evolutionists and humanists like Charles Darwin (1809–82) and John Dewey (1859–1952) subtly made their impact on instruction in public schools. Though Darwin is not known as an educational theorist or philosopher, his evolutionary theories influenced education indirectly through men like Dewey, who applied them to aspects of child development and theories of learning. The theory of evolution suggested that life was progressing from a lower state to a higher one, from simplicity to complexity, from lesser value to greater. Dewey saw in this a "principle of continuity and change" that would be useful in education.

Dewey encouraged belief in moral principles, but not for spiritual reasons:

> The one thing needful is that we recognize that moral principles are real in the same sense in which other forces are real; that they are inherent in community life, and in the running machinery of the individual. If we can secure a genuine faith in this fact, we shall have secured the only condition which is finally necessary in order to get from our educational system all the effectiveness there is in it. The teacher who operates in this faith will find every subject, every method of instruction, every incident of school life pregnant with ethical life. (Boydston, 1972, 83)

As head of the Education Department at Columbia University and a prolific writer, Dewey was in a unique position to influence the nation's public school educators. Consequently, his profound philosophical influence pervaded educational practice much more quickly than might have been possible otherwise. However, not until the Supreme Court decisions in the 1960s, when prayer and Bible reading in the public schools were virtually banned, did conservative Christians awake to the gradual but drastic changes in the nation's schools.

The impact of the Supreme Court decisions was much broader than the specific matters with which they dealt: the reading of Scripture and the recitation of prayers. These decisions established a basis for gradual elimination of anything religious from the schools. Before this time many Christians had worked as teachers in our nation's public schools, feeling the same freedom to discuss their religious convictions in the presentations of their subject matter as the teacher in the next room felt to teach his secular views. Though the Supreme Court decisions did not deal with the teaching of other subject matter in accordance with one's personal convictions, it had a chilling effect on religious expression in any form. Soon groups like the American Civil Liberties Union began to challenge the propriety of religiously oriented holiday celebrations, such as plays, programs, and nativity scenes.

As Christian teachers began to feel intimidated, many of them withdrawing into a shell, humanist teachers became bolder in their atheistic teaching. As a result, moral (that is, Bible-based) conduct and discipline in the nation's public schools declined rapidly. Christian parents became concerned about the teaching of evolution, the increased availability of illegal drugs, sexual promiscuity, vandalism, violence, and a general breakdown of order in the schools. Many of these parents began seeking alternatives to escape the perceived evils of the public system they had supported for years.

Many Christians continue to teach in our public schools; some even have a moderately effective influence there. There is, however, much difference between teaching in a public school in order to have a godly influence on others and using the public schools as a means of education for our children.

THE INFLUENCE OF
PUBLIC EDUCATION IN THE COMMUNITY

Public education is so deeply ingrained in the fabric of our society that it is likely to be the dominant form of education in the foreseeable future. Since 1900, 90 percent of the children attending school have attended public schools. Consequently, the general public does not have either an intellectual or philosophical understanding of private education in general, or Christian education in particular. Their natural response is to see Christian schools as inferior to public education if not something of a threat to public schools. Recent support for government financing of choice in education, including the right to choose a private religious school, in lieu of a public school, has increased this hostility.

The American public generally believes that public education is necessary, that we could not continue to develop and prosper as a nation without it. That view, however, is not universally held. One of the most eloquent of the opponents to this position is Dr. Samuel Blumenfeld. Blumenfeld says that the necessity of public education is an idea promoted by the educational establishment (Blumenfeld, 1981). In fact, he says public education is supported in this country by six myths:

1. The first myth is that public education is a great democratic institution fundamental to America's prosperity and well-being.

2. The second myth is that public education is necessary as the great equalizer in our society, bringing together children from different ethnic, social, racial, and religious groups and molding them into homogenized "Americans"—which we are all supposed to want to be. Included in this myth is the notion that public education, because of our separation of church and state, is ideologically neutral and preaches no religious doctrine.

3. The third myth is that it provides the best possible education because we are the best possible country spending the most possible money.

4. The fourth myth is that the neighborhood school with its cadre of dedicated teachers and administrators belongs to the community and is answerable to it through an elected school board.

5. The fifth myth is that our society cannot survive without it, that is, public education and all the people who run it.

6. The sixth myth is that all men are created equal and that government as the great equalizer is the most benevolent dispenser of human goodness, generosity, and justice on earth. (pp. 1–2)

While not everyone would concur in all of his points, most supporters of private education would agree that most of his points are accurate representations of the views of the education establishment.

Blumenfeld (1981) further contends that a recognition of these myths supporting public education is only part of understanding public education. He suggests that there are six components of the institution of public education that must also be understood:

1. The physical existence of the public school is evident in every community. It represents a landmark recognized by all the citizens in the community. It is frequently the center of social activity in the community. The facility and educational resources represent a continuing visual reminder of the existence of the public school.

2. Public education is money. Public education is one of the largest items in the federal budget and the budget of the respective states. Employees of public schools represent a significant economic impact in every community.

3. Public education is political power. The National Education Association and its state affiliates are among the largest and most powerful political lobbies in America.

4. Public education is a complex legal structure. The system not only requires the expenditure of enormous sums of money but also the laws and regulations supporting the system restrict the freedom of every parent in the nation. The educational establishment not only directs the activities of public schools but also casts a shadow over all private educational activities and homeschools as well.

5. Public education is a process intended to mold every American child into an American adult. The present system of public education reflects the changing perception of what constitutes an American adult. The current graduate of the public schools has less cognitive knowledge and developmental skills and a much different set of values than his predecessor of the previous generation.

6. The public school is an instrument of public policy. A major role of the American public educator is to implement whatever the current public policy happens to be. Since 90 percent of the nation's children are educated in public schools, and the public school establishment influences, to some degree, the education of all children educated in the private sector, the impact of public education on the thinking of American young people and adults is pervasive. (pp. 3–8)

Public education is built on a foundation of shifting values. As the values of this nation have shifted, the emphasis of public education has shifted. Some would even say that public education has had a great deal to do with those shifts in values. Christian education, on the other hand, is built on the unchanging principles of the Word of God. In the early years of public education, those values paralleled one another sufficiently to convince most of the Christian community that public schools could do a satisfactory job of educating their children. That is not the view of many Christian parents today.

The Rise of the Christian School Movement

Prior to 1960 there were relatively few Christian schools in existence. Those that did exist were mostly independent schools, frequently referred to as "parent-society" schools. They were established as a direct result of God-fearing parents who recognized the spiritual needs of their children. Such schools were generally organized, owned, operated, and financed by the parents and had no connection with a local church or any other organization that would provide substantial, long-term financial support. Since 1960 most Christian schools have been associated directly with a local church. The school is viewed by the pastor and congregation as an integral ministry of that local church. Some of these schools are separately incorporated, but most of them operate under the corporate umbrella of a church.

During the 1960s and 1970s our nation experienced a steep decline in moral standards. This moral decline was given impetus by the judicial system when the United States Supreme Court outlawed prayer and Bible reading in the public schools. To be fair, it must be acknowledged that the court did not change the direction of the nation; their decisions merely reflected the mood of the country. These factors caused an increasing number of Christians to examine the type of education that their children were receiving in the public schools. Fundamental pastors began to preach and teach about the inherently religious nature of education. Laymen also began to search the Scriptures to discern what God had to say about education. The result was that many became convinced that they had to provide an alternative to secular education, an alternative that would enable them to provide an education consistent with biblical standards for their children. This alternative became the modern Christian day school, and thousands began to spring up across America. Some have estimated that during certain periods of this rapid growth, as many as two or three schools were organized per day.

Unfortunately, this rapid growth was not conducive to the careful development of a sound philosophical base for many of the schools. The initial widespread acceptance of the Christian school movement caused unfounded feelings of security and caused us to overlook inadequacies. During the 1980s we experienced some decline in the popularity of the Christian school. Many schools had faced serious financial problems and other internal difficulties that challenged their commitment to the cause. A number of schools experienced significant declines in enrollment, and others closed their doors. Relatively few new Christian schools were started. During this period homeschooling became an attractive option for many Christian parents who had become disenchanted by the failure of Christian schools to meet their needs. Many parents with school-age children who had to make decisions concerning their schooling for the first time chose to homeschool their children.

By the end of the decade of the 1980s we saw a renewal of interest in Christian schools, the good schools began to grow again, and there was considerable interest in starting new schools. This trend was carried over into the 1990s. Though the growth of Christian schools is not currently as frenzied as it was in the 1970s, the better schools are once again growing and new schools started. The homeschool movement also continues to grow and will probably continue to be the educational choice for many Christian parents. Christian schools must take this movement into consideration in their plans for the future.

Christian schools are as necessary in the twenty-first century as they were when the modern Christian movement was launched. Unfortunately, in recent years, fundamental churches have demonstrated less commitment to Christian schools than in the past. Much of the growth in the movement is occurring in those churches representing the evangelical Christian community. Even more distressing is the trend evidenced in some of our oldest schools to minimize their Christian distinctives in order to become more appealing to a broader Christian community.

PHILOSOPHICAL CONSIDERATIONS

The rapid growth of the Christian school movement resulted in many pragmatic decisions and their negative impact continues to haunt us today. Among the most basic of these considerations is "Who is primarily responsible for Christian education?" The answer to this question will establish our perspective and will determine how we approach every aspect of Christian education.

Is the State Responsible for the Child's Education?

Some have said that the state is responsible for a child's education. However, if the state bears the financial burden of a child's education, it should also be permitted to choose the curriculum the child will use and to establish the standards for those who will teach him. This leads to a more serious problem. We cannot deny the inherently religious nature of education, for our belief system will inevitably influence what we teach and how we teach it. Since the state must represent all its citizens, whose religion will it choose to establish as the basis for education? An honest look at our culture in America will assure us that the choice would not be biblical Christianity.

Is the Church Responsible for the Child's Education?

This question is more difficult to answer, and it is one on which not all Christian educators will agree. There would be few who would dispute the fact that the church has a responsibility to educate. The Great Commission states that we are to "go . . . and teach all nations." This command refers to *spiritual discipleship.*

The church is responsible to lead others to Christ and then to use God's Word to instruct them in doctrine and righteousness. Many passages support this command. It would be difficult, however, to find scriptural support for the position that the church is equally responsible for a *general academic education.* What text, for example, states that the church should provide instruction in algebra, history, English, science, technology, or law? After examining the Scriptures, we must conclude that the church does not appear to have primary responsibility in this area.

Are Parents Responsible for the Child's Education?

Scripture teaches that children are the responsibility of the parents. They have a stewardship responsibility before God that has never been rescinded. Educating their children is part of that responsibility. The following passages support this concept, and more specifically, establish the father as the one primarily responsible for this duty.

- Deuteronomy 6:6–9

- Psalm 78:1–8

- Psalm 127:3–5

- Proverbs 19:27

- Proverbs 22:6

- Ephesians 6:1–4

This does not imply the necessity of direct parental involvement in all aspects of the educational process. Some who homeschool their children do so because they have become convinced that it is the only way they can satisfy God's expectations for the education of their children. I would contend that, while a father cannot delegate his responsibility for the task of rearing his children, the Scripture does not forbid him from delegating authority to others to help him with this task. This is true whether he delegates this authority to his wife, his other children, a tutor, or an institution. For example, when a father employs a tutor to teach his children, he is responsible for the actions of the tutor and the effect that these actions have on his children. The father is also responsible to pay the tutor for his services (Jer. 22:13; Luke 10:7). Likewise, if the teaching authority is delegated to an institution, the father retains the responsibility for the effect that the school has on his child and for seeing that the school is paid for the service that it renders in training his child.

Unfortunately, it seems difficult for some Christian parents and Christian leaders to accept this principle. Why is this true? Children have a wide range of needs. They need clothing, food, shelter, medical attention, and many other basic provisions. If Christian parents see the necessity of providing these things, why do they find it difficult to accept the responsibility to provide education as well? The problem may result from reasoning like the following: "Our tax dollars support public education. Why should we pay a 'double tax' for the privilege of having our children in a Christian school?" Such reasoning leads to the assumption that another ought to bear the primary responsibility for this financial burden. Is this, however, a valid assumption?

There appears to be no scriptural prohibition of government financing Christian work; in fact, there are even limited examples in Scripture of the government's providing finances and materials to support God's work. In the early history of this nation there was limited government assistance for Christian work. Unfortunately, as the nation has adopted an increasingly secular purpose, government aid has come to be seen as a violation of the mystical principle of separation of church and state. Even tax exemption has come to be viewed as aid that can be withdrawn when even the religious purposes of an institution become at odds with the purposes of the state. Consequently, it seems wise for Christian ministries and Christian parents that value their freedom to plan to pay their own way.

It cannot be denied that providing a quality Christian education is a financial burden. Nor should it be denied that to rear children to love and serve God through the secular program of the public school system is virtually impossible. However, the fact that it is a heavy financial burden does not imply that it should be assumed by another. The fact remains that the parents will be held responsible to God for how their children are educated, and they must do whatever is necessary to insure that their children are educated according to biblical standards. Part of the burden we assume when we bring children into the world is to insure that they are properly educated. God has promised to supply all our needs, and if Christian education is a need, He will supply that too (Phil. 4:19).

Our country is listed among the richest nations in the world. Few families could honestly say they do not have the resources to provide their children with a quality Christian education. The problem is that the typical Christian family has become so consumed with the materialism of the age that the financial obligations they have assumed do not leave them sufficient resources to pay for the education their children deserve.

To assert that the parents are primarily responsible for the education of their children is not to say that others cannot choose to help them. But there is a considerable difference between soliciting help for parents and stating that the state or church or some other person is primarily responsible for the Christian education of somebody else's children. When church members, staff members, and others in the Christian community are encouraged to sacrifice and financially support Christian education, it must be with the clear understanding that they are voluntarily assuming a portion of the parents' burden. Those outside the family should not be expected to bear the primary burden of financing Christian education. Understanding this basic philosophy will help Christian schools resolve current problems and avoid future pitfalls.

Another potential problem for Christian schools today is the effort to revise the curriculum of public schools to make them more palatable to some Christian groups. While there is certainly nothing wrong with concerned Christians seeking to make improvements in the public schools, this effort will not result in an educational program that is God honoring. Neither a Christian school financed in part or whole by a secular state nor a public school with a "moral" curriculum can develop Christlikeness in students. Because Christian education is inherently religious, the schools that espouse a biblical philosophy must be free of all government control, both financial and academic.

There are two philosophical bases used in determining who should attend a Christian school. One view holds that Christian schools exist primarily for the edification of children from Christian homes. The other position says that the Christian school should be used to develop a student body that can provide opportunities for evangelism. Many well-meaning Christian schools offer enrollment to any who come, hoping that once students are enrolled, the influence of the school will overpower their sinful nature and bring them to salvation. Evangelism, however, is not the basic purpose of Christian education, and attempting to operate a school on such a premise has almost always kept the school from successfully developing Christlikeness in those students who have enrolled to receive a Christian education. Schools that have admissions policies based on edification typically are the ones most successful in seeing the development of Christlikeness in their student body.

CHAPTER 2

PHILOSOPHY OF CHRISTIAN SCHOOL MANAGEMENT

Seest thou a man diligent in his business? he shall stand before kings; he shall not stand before mean men.

Proverbs 22:29

Not slothful in business; fervent in spirit; serving the Lord.

Romans 12:11

The word *philosophy* comes from Greek words meaning "love of wisdom." Since the time of the Garden of Eden, man has wanted to be wise and has striven to know all truth (Gen. 3:5). In searching for the truth, each individual develops a system of values and beliefs that guides his every action. This system is his philosophy of life.

The Christian must develop his philosophy by studying God's Truth—the Bible (John 17:17). The apostle Paul warns us not to be spoiled by the philosophies of this world—philosophies such as situation ethics, humanism, and materialism (Col. 2:8). He defines a Christian philosophy as one that follows after Christ and not after the world because in Christ "are hid all the treasures of wisdom and knowledge" (Col. 2:3). The Christian's philosophy must be based on the Lord Jesus Christ as He is revealed in the Scriptures. An individual whose system of values and beliefs is determined by any source other than God's Word is susceptible to worldly influences and error.

THE PURPOSE OF CHRISTIAN EDUCATION

Although the Bible does not mention the Christian school, it says much about the education of young people. God makes it plain that His will for all Christians is that they "be perfect, throughly furnished unto all good works" (2 Tim. 3:17). To accomplish this task, God gives men various gifts "for the perfecting of the saints, for the work of the ministry, for the edifying of the body of Christ: till we all come in the unity of the faith, and of the knowledge of the Son of God, unto a perfect man, unto the measure of the stature of the fulness of Christ" (Eph. 4:12–13). These verses describe the goal of Christian education: to help create in every young person the likeness of Christ. Christian education should develop Christians whose activities in this life anticipate their eventual conformity to the image of Christ (Rom. 8:29).

THE RESPONSIBILITY FOR CHRISTIAN EDUCATION

Christian education should take place first and foremost in the Christian home. In the Old Testament, parents are commanded to "teach [God's Word] diligently unto [their] children" (Deut. 6:7). In the New Testament, parents are commanded to "bring them up in the nurture and admonition of the Lord" (Eph. 6:4). These commands are directed to Christian parents, who bear ultimate responsibility for the success or failure of their children's education.

Another institution with God-given responsibilities for education is the church. In the Great Commission Jesus tells His church—all Christians—to go and disciple "all nations, baptizing them in the name of the Father, and of the Son, and of the Holy Ghost: teaching them to observe all things whatsoever I have commanded you" (Matt. 28:19–20). Notice the order in which the Great Commission was given. First, we are to make disciples. A prerequisite to discipling is evangelism; a person must be won to Christ before he can be discipled. Second, we are to baptize these converts. Third, we are to teach them everything that Christ commanded the apostles. Christians are to win the lost to Christ and *then* teach them regardless of their age.

In our generation the Christian school has been established as an arm of the home and, usually, of the church. It has accepted responsibility for reinforcing the biblical teachings of the home and church. It operates *in loco parentis* (in the place of the parents). The Christian school does not relieve parents of the ultimate responsibility for the education of children. However, the goal of the Christian school should be the goal of Christian parents: making the student Christlike.

WHY HAVE A CHRISTIAN SCHOOL?

In the United States, compulsory education laws require all educable children to attend school. Since as Christian citizens we are to be subject unto the higher powers (Rom 13:1), Christian parents must make sure that their children go to school during the appropriate years for the required number of days. The government has established public schools to help parents fulfill this attendance requirement. However, public schools today are secular. Some would even say they are anti-God. Their goal is to make students worldly—to make them conform to the mores of society. This goal is in complete contradiction to God's goal. Scripture commands, "Be not conformed to this world but be ye transformed by the renewing of your mind" (Rom. 12:2). As the goals of secular schools have become increasingly contrary to the goals of Christian education, new schools that meet the requirements of the attendance laws and also allow parents to guide their children toward being conformed to the image of Christ have become necessary.

This, then, is the reason for the Christian school—not to get students away from drug abuse, poor academics, poor discipline, or racial integration. The Christian school has been established to allow parents to obey God's command to give their children a Christian education and at the same time to obey the law of the land. No matter how secular schools may improve academically, Christian parents will continue to turn to the Christian school to obtain Christian education since the goals of secular education are contrary to the will of God.

WHAT ABOUT HOMESCHOOLS?

Just a few years ago this question would not have been part of the Christian education equation. Now it is. Home education has become an increasingly important option for parents who want their children to receive a Christian education. As committed as one may be to the provision of Christian education through a conventional Christian school, not all parents have that opportunity. Not all parents that have that opportunity believe the conventional schools available to them will do as good a job as they can by educating their children at home. Fortunately, all state compulsory attendance laws are broad enough to allow parents that option.

Some Christian schools have been slow to accept the homeschool movement. Some have even refused to accept into their schools any children that have been homeschooled. They have developed negative attitudes toward homeschooling, in part because they resent the rejection by homeschool families of conventional Christian schooling. They have sometimes had experiences with homeschool families that have not provided a quality education for their children. However, to refuse to help homeschool families when they turn to them for aid is neither wise nor in the true spirit of Christianity.

Christian schools must recognize that the same freedom they desire to operate their schools is also due homeschool families who prefer to be in complete charge of the education of their children. They should view helping homeschool families with the same enthusiasm as they would opportunities to help children coming to them from public schools, secular private schools, and other Christian schools.

Friction has developed between conventional Christian schools and homeschool parents because some parents have asked for services and privileges without being willing to pay for them. Such requests, of course, are not reasonable, for someone must pay for all the services offered by the Christian school. Some difficulties have also arisen when homeschool families have wanted their children to participate in extracurricular activities offered by Christian schools. To date, Christian schools have been generally unwilling to permit this. Homeschool families need to understand that Christian schools have the same right to limit participation in their programs as homeschoolers have to educate their children on their own. Public schools have been challenged by homeschoolers for selective services, and some courts have been supportive of their requests. This changing legal picture may suggest some need for Christian schools to reexamine their own policies carefully.

A better understanding of one another, and of each other's needs and objectives, will hopefully lead to a better relationship between conventional Christian schools and homeschool families. There is no reason for animosity to exist between them.

THE DIFFERENCE BETWEEN CHRISTIAN EDUCATION AND THE CHRISTIAN SCHOOL

Christian education and the Christian school are not the same. Christian education is the process of helping our students become conformed to the image of Christ. The Christian school is a place designed to give students a large part of their Christian education. We generally say that Christian education begins at salvation and continues until death. That, however, is not altogether true in the broadest sense of Christian education. For the Christian family, preparation for Christian education actually should begin before the child is born as plans are made for his conformity to Christ. In the years before he is born again, Christian education is used to prepare the child for the moment he recognizes his personal need of salvation and that his need can be met only in Christ.

Typically, Christian day schools begin with four- or five-year kindergarten and stop at the twelfth grade. Some, however, incorporate full daycare programs into their educational programs. A few include some form of postsecondary education such as a Bible institute or Bible college.

Many people falsely assume that once a child is in a Christian school he will automatically obtain a Christian education. Unfortunately, that is not true. No matter how good a school is, it cannot guarantee how a child will respond to the opportunity of obtaining a Christian education. Not all schools that are called "Christian" produce students conformed to the image of Christ. A school that does not have as its goal the development of Christlike character in its students is not truly a Christian school. On the other hand, it is possible for a child to obtain a Christian education without ever attending a Christian school. In many cases the children of missionaries and evangelists never attend a Christian school; they become conformed to the image of the Lord Jesus Christ through the training they receive at home. Since attending a Christian school does not guarantee a Christian education, and since a Christian education does not require a Christian school, the two terms are not synonymous and should not be used interchangeably.

FIGURE 2.1

No Christian education taking place in a Christian school

A PROCESS

Christian Education

A PLACE

Christian School

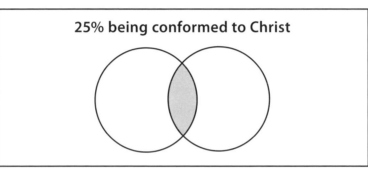

25% being conformed to Christ

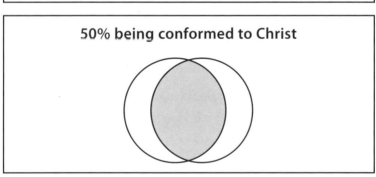

50% being conformed to Christ

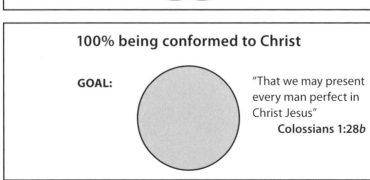

100% being conformed to Christ

GOAL:

"That we may present every man perfect in Christ Jesus"
Colossians 1:28b

Figure 2.1 presents the problem faced by Christian schools in America today. Everything within the circle labeled "Christian education" represents the Christian education taking place in the lives of young people. Everything in the circle labeled "Christian school" represents the students attending a Christian school. The first rectangle, where the two circles never meet, represents a Christian school with no Christian education taking place. The circles in the second rectangle intersect so that 25 percent of the young people in the Christian school are obtaining a Christian education. However, 75 percent failure is never satisfactory. The next rectangle represents a school with 50 percent of its students being conformed to the image of Christ. Still we should not be satisfied. The leadership of the Christian school should never be content until 100 percent of the school's students are becoming more like Jesus Christ (Col. 1:28).

It is understood that this is the ultimate goal and one that will not be reached as long as we are here on this earth. We should work toward this goal, however, just as we should work toward the goal God has given us of being perfect, even though we can reach neither goal until we meet Him face to face (1 John 3:2).

THE RECIPIENT OF CHRISTIAN EDUCATION

Christian education, properly considered, is for Christians and the children of Christians. "As education in general begins with physical birth, Christian education properly begins with spiritual rebirth" (Horton, 1992, 4). The unsaved person cannot be conformed to the image of Christ because "the natural man receiveth not the things of the Spirit of God: for they are foolishness unto him: neither can he know them, because they are spiritually discerned" (1 Cor. 2:14). The unregenerate person cannot be expected to conform his life to Christ's commandments since he does not have the Holy Spirit to teach him all truth (John 14:26; 16:13). Without the Teacher, there can be no education.

To say that Christian education is only for Christians is not to say that the Christian school is only for Christian young people. The Christian school is designed to help Christian parents, usually members of local fundamentalist churches train young people for the Lord. Many of the children from these homes, especially those in the lower grades, may not yet have come to salvation. In addition, some of the junior and senior high students who profess to be saved really are not. For these reasons, it is very important that the Christian school give clear biblical teaching on salvation so that these young people can become "wise unto salvation through faith which is in Christ Jesus" (2 Tim. 3:15). It is obvious that evangelism must take place in the Christian school. However, the school should not be designed primarily for evangelism; it should be designed for the education of Christians. Unless the student body of a school is predominantly Christian, the school cannot be considered a Christian school.

FINANCES

Christian education is primarily the responsibility of parents (Deut. 6:7; Eph. 6:4). When others operate educational institutions, they do so to provide a service to parents. Consequently, parents are primarily responsible for paying for the educational program provided for their children.

The institutions providing education for others typically determine in advance that a portion of the operation of the school will be assumed by the institution. This is done by finding other sources of revenue that will enable it to provide education to children at less than its actual cost. This approach qualifies the school as a ministry. The cost that remains is then to be paid by the parents of the children served. Typically it is passed on to them in the form of tuition and fees.

Each family must pay its fair share, or the cost of educating its children becomes a greater burden for either the institution or other parents. Consequently, parents who are unwilling or unable to pay their share of the expense of operating the school must either assume the responsibility of finding other sources of revenue, or they must be denied access to the school.

Although it is a ministry, the Christian school has a responsibility to operate as a responsible business, maintaining appropriate accountability to its constituents and the government. Its business must be conducted in a manner that is acceptable and that does not bring reproach upon itself or the Lord Jesus Christ.

TEACHING AND LEARNING

Instruction in a Christian school should prepare students to function in life's activities and to pursue further academic training—in most cases, college. Bob Jones Sr. said we must teach students "not only how to make a living but also how to live." Each subject should be presented from a biblical point of view and made applicable to the student's Christian life, developing in him Christlikeness.

The Christian school must teach every subject in such a way as to help students learn principles that they can apply in life's situations, forcing them to think and not merely memorize. Students who simply learn facts and never learn to apply them are not developing biblical wisdom. Wisdom, the ability to use facts, is what God wants us to seek (Prov. 4:5–7). It is not enough for the Christian school to teach students how to memorize. In order to educate young people properly, administrators and teachers should teach students to apply the things that they learn to everyday situations.

Not every servant of the Lord will need the same educational background. However, since school personnel do not know what God's plan may be for a particular student, they should, as a general principle, encourage every student to seek as much education as he can reasonably assimilate.

CURRICULUM

In the broadest sense, curriculum means the planned program of the school. For a Christian school this includes the spiritual, academic, and extracurricular program. The school program should include everything possible to achieve the goals of the school and conscientiously eliminate anything that hinders the attainment of those goals.

The educational goal of the school is to insure that each student has the opportunity to develop spiritually, intellectually, physically, and socially (Luke 2:52) in the image of Jesus Christ (Rom. 8:29). Consequently, the foundation stone of the curriculum is the Word of God. The Bible will be supplemented with other textbooks that will aid the school in its overall educational goals. These textbooks must be selected carefully to insure that while seeking the child's intellectual development, the school is not undermining his spiritual development (Hadik, 1984). Truth must always be measured by the absolute standard of the Bible.

The Bible must be taught as an academic subject with regular instruction from a qualified teacher. Teachers should hold students accountable by means of homework and examinations. Grades should be given as in any other subject. Chapel must be an important part of the curriculum, which, together with the Bible classes, will result in the students being challenged concerning their accountability to God and developing in their knowledge of Him and His Word.

The academic curriculum of the Christian school must include all academic subjects generally taught at each grade level offered by the school. It is important that courses be offered at the appropriate level and in proper sequence. Each course must be supported by a qualified teacher and proper, educational resources.

The extracurricular program of the school should offer as many opportunities for the spiritual, cultural, physical, and social development of its students as its constituents can support. They should be age appropriate and balanced in their provisions for all areas and for both genders.

STUDENTS

The best way to maintain a predominantly Christian student body consistent with the goals stated above is to have a restrictive admissions policy. Restricting students on the basis of religion is permissible for Christian schools under current law. They must however, be consistent in the basis on which they discriminate. The Christian school should limit enrollment primarily to Christian young people or to those from Christian homes. Since the Christian school is designed for Christian young people, the majority of the students should be recruited from fundamentalist churches in the area. Parents who want their children to develop Christlike character should be encouraged to enroll their children.

However, unsaved parents of unsaved young people should not be so encouraged unless they truly desire that their children be saved and conformed to the image of Christ. Many unsaved parents desire only the high academic standards and discipline that the Christian school offers and not the training in godliness that the school exists to provide. Some are attracted to the Christian school only because of the opportunity to obtain a quality education for their children at a modest cost.

Christian schools with an edification philosophy typically do not want to graduate a student who is not a born-again Christian. Consequently, if a school decides to permit the enrollment of some unsaved young people from homes where both parents are unsaved, it should generally be limited to cases where the family appears genuinely receptive to the gospel. As a rule, these enrollments should be restricted to the elementary and junior high school years. The response of these children and their parents to presentations of the gospel should be carefully observed. Those who are not saved by grade nine should not be permitted to re-enroll. It is generally unwise to knowingly accept unsaved students in grades ten and above from homes where their parents are unsaved. Few Christian schools would admit an unsaved student in his senior year.

PERSONNEL

All the people involved in a Christian school ministry must have high spiritual and academic qualifications. Every staff member must be a born-again Christian whose life evidences the fruit of the Spirit (Gal. 5:22–23) and testifies to the students of the grace of God. No matter what the position—be it teacher, coach, bus driver, or custodian—every person involved in the Christian school must first of all have a living relationship with the Lord Jesus Christ. The teaching staff must be prepared academically as well since the faculty determines the quality of the education offered (Luke 6:40). Because teachers wield such influence, their spiritual and academic qualifications cannot and should not be minimized. A Christian school will never be any better than its people.

Beyond these qualifications, it is especially important that each employee have a servant's heart (Matt. 20:27), that each be willing to give of himself rather than be concerned about what he will receive for himself. This attribute is not easily acquired. It is easier to train a teacher to be effective in the classroom than to help him cultivate a servant's heart.

SUPERVISION OF INSTRUCTION

Every school that claims to offer Christian education has a stewardship responsibility before God (Rom. 14:12) to assure parents enrolling their children in the school that the kind of education actually delivered is that which it advertises. The activities that are most likely to permanently influence the children are those resulting from their interaction with the professional staff at the school.

What the teacher teaches and how the teacher behaves are equally important in the process of educating children (Col. 3:23). Supervision then must take into consideration not only what goes on in the classroom but also the public and private life of the staff (Exod. 39:43; Rom. 13:1, 4).

BEHAVIORAL STANDARDS

The Christian school should have behavioral standards consistent with biblical principles and designed to help young people develop Christlike character. An important principle applicable to Christian schools is that God wants young people to possess self-control (2 Pet. 1:6), which is developed during the application of external control (Prov. 3:11–12; Heb. 12:11). Students should expect not only to behave themselves in an orderly and controlled fashion but also to incur disciplinary measures when they do not live up to the standards set by the school. Those who consistently violate the behavioral standards of the school must be excluded so that they do not negatively influence the rest of the students (1 Cor. 5:7).

Every standard of conduct set up by the Christian school should have a biblical basis. Though there may not be an explicit command in Scripture for every standard of behavior, the school administrator should be able to justify each standard as an application of a biblical principle (e.g., respect for property, respect for authority, avoidance of any appearance of evil).

Students should be taught the biblical principle as well as the standard of behavior so that they can learn to live by principles, not just by rules.

ACADEMIC STANDARDS

To be Christlike, a student must increase "in wisdom and stature, and in favour with God and man" (Luke 2:52). Children can be trained spiritually, physically, and socially in the home or local church, but it is very difficult for the local church to give proper academic instruction without special preparation. Personnel trained in various academic areas are not usually teaching academic subject matter in the church, nor are most parents equipped to teach every academic subject. For most children, therefore, the Christian school is the best institution to teach the academic material necessary for young people in the twenty-first century. The Christian school should not neglect the spiritual, physical, and social areas of development, but it must especially stress academics since this area will probably not be fully developed any-where else.

In order to operate a Christian school effectively and efficiently, the school's leader must have a practical biblical philosophy by which he determines his course of action. He must be willing to sacrifice conven-ience, financial gain, and even large numbers of students if methods for obtaining these things conflict with clear scriptural principles.

When evaluating students, Christian schools must resist modern trends that make it difficult to measure a child's progress. Traditional grading schemes served the educational establishment well for years be-cause they communicated student progress in ways in which students and parents could understand. At the same time, Christian schools should not necessarily reject approaches to evaluating and reporting stu-dent progress just because they are new or different.

PHYSICAL PLANT, FACILITIES, AND EQUIPMENT

The physical environment and facilities have the potential to enhance learning and the testimony of an institution. The Master Teacher did not have the benefit of a permanent building or media support for His earthly ministry, yet it was effective. Our constituents, nevertheless, base their expectations on those things generally available.

Christian schools should provide their educational programs in facilities that are consistent with those in general use by those they serve. Equipment and other modern resources should be provided as the finances of the ministry enable them. Furthermore, physical facilities and equipment should be maintained in good condition because their appearance and serviceability are part of the school's testimony.

STATEMENT OF MANAGEMENT PHILOSOPHY

To insure consistency in its operation, each Christian school should develop its own statement of management philosophy. One to three well-written paragraphs on each of the following subjects will usually be sufficient:

- Purpose of the school

- Finances

- Curriculum

- Admissions policy

- Personnel

- Supervision of instruction

- Behavior standards

- Academic standards

- Physical plant, facilities, and equipment

BJU Press began publishing a series of philosophy statements in 1978 to provide guidance to Christian school personnel in the development of their schools. This series is available in one volume: *Christian Education: Its Mandate and Mission.* This book would be a valuable addition to the professional library of every pastor and Christian educator. See also Appendix A for a Christian philosophy of education from an administrator's perspective.

CHAPTER 3

STARTING A CHRISTIAN SCHOOL

The simple believeth every word: but the prudent man looketh well to his going.

Proverbs 14:15

Therefore whosoever heareth these sayings of mine, and doeth them, I will liken him unto a wise man, which built his house upon a rock.

Matthew 7:24

For which of you, intending to build a tower, sitteth not down first, and counteth the cost, whether he have sufficient to finish it? Lest haply, after he hath laid the foundation, and is not able to finish it, all that behold it begin to mock him, saying, This man began to build, and was not able to finish.

Luke 14:28–30

This entire book will be of benefit to those planning a new Christian school. This chapter is intended to focus specifically on some of the important steps and to provide some direction as to the sequence of events the planning should follow.

Appendix B gives twenty-six characteristics of a good Christian school. These guidelines should help in establishing the direction of a new school.

It is not an easy task to start a Christian school. In the past some have thought that all they had to do was buy certain textbooks and procedure manuals and follow them explicitly. However, this approach has been less than adequate in establishing schools that give a quality Christian education. It is important for those who are considering starting a Christian school to take the proper steps.

The first thing anyone must do is to ask himself the question "Why do I want to start a school ministry?" Some poor reasons for starting a Christian school are these:

1. Because other churches have Christian schools

2. Because I want the prestige or the profit

3. Because some people in the community do not like the public school system

4. Because of the serious discipline problems in the public schools

5. Because of poor academics in the public schools

It is important for all concerned to spend much time in prayer in order to make sure that it is God Who wants the Christian school started. Nowhere in Scripture does God command that Christian schools be started. Nowhere in Scripture does God command every church to have its own Christian school. However, He does mandate that Christian parents give their children a Christian education. Since all states have a compulsory attendance law, it becomes necessary for parents who want to give their children a Christian education to find a satisfactory alternative to public education. This is the only biblical reason for starting a Christian school—to provide children an opportunity for a Christian education.

A Christian school allows parents to fulfill the command of God to educate their children according to biblical principles and to obey the laws of the land at the same time. God wants Christian schools so that Christian education can take place. This does not mean, however, that every church must have a Christian school. Too many times a church decides to start a Christian school although there is another Christ-honoring school in the same town. People should prayerfully consider whether to start a Christian school in a town where there are one or two other good Christian schools.

After it has been decided that a Christian school should be started, the people must be taught a biblical philosophy of Christian education. It is not enough for a Christian leader to desire Christian education for his own children. Everyone (church members and others) must know the biblical reasons for Christian education. They should review the information presented in chapter 2 of this book so that they understand the basis for Christian education. There is no sense in trying to start a

Christian school if those involved do not understand why they are doing what they are doing.

Once the biblical philosophy of Christian education is thoroughly ingrained, a leader should organize the people to make plans for the school ministry. If the school ministry will be part of a local church, it is advantageous for the church board initially to operate as a school board. If the church board is large, then several members of the church board may be appointed or elected to serve on a school committee to formulate plans for implementing the Christian school. If the school will be an independent work, then several Christian leaders in the community should be formed into a school board that will make policy decisions. If possible, some board or committee members should be knowledgeable in educational practices and procedures. They must also meet qualifications set forth in Figure 4.3 of this book.

PRIORITIES OF THE CHRISTIAN SCHOOL

In formulating plans for the Christian school, board members must keep in mind certain priorities, which include the following.

Philosophy

First and foremost, the philosophy of the Christian school must always be biblical. It may not be necessary to write a formal philosophy statement the first year of a school's operation, especially if the board makes use of preexisting written philosophies from established Christian schools that the school is using as models. However, leaders of a new Christian school must thoroughly understand and espouse a proper, biblical philosophy of education on which to base every decision that they make and as the criterion for choosing every person whom they hire. For this reason the philosophy must be clear, concise, and communicable.

People

Once the philosophy is set in the minds of the board members, they must hire a staff. Chapter 17 suggests guidelines for the selection and recruitment of a staff. Those starting a Christian school must realize that their school will be only as good as the people whom they hire. They must make sure that their staff members espouse the same philosophy as the board members and that they are qualified to teach the grades and/or subjects that will be required of them. It is impossible to have a quality Christian school without quality people.

Program

The leaders and staff of the school must also put together an educational program—the nuts-and-bolts, day-to-day operating procedures of the Christian school that will facilitate teaching and learning. The program includes such things as curriculum, textbooks, scheduling, and finances. Those starting Christian schools with quality people in their organization will usually be able to put together a quality program. It does not pay to forego hiring quality people in order to spend more money on a program that somebody else recommends. Since every school is somewhat unique, every program must be geared to the specific area of the country, the type of students, and other situations found in the community in which the school will be established.

Plant

The last priority in establishing and maintaining the Christian school is the school plant, or facilities. This is not to say that facilities are not important; however, they are not the most important. Many times when a school is being established as part of the ministry of the local church, the church facilities can be adapted to house the school activities. The board should contact the city's fire and/or building inspector and request him to inspect the facilities to be used for the school. He will then make suggestions for improvements if any are needed. If the leaders of the school ministry will work graciously with the inspector, they will usually find that he is reasonable in trying to protect the students who will be attending the Christian school. The new school should attempt to make the facilities conform as much as possible to the standards presented in chapter 15 for the ideal classroom situation. Though the facilities will not be perfect, the board should regularly implement steps to upgrade them. There is never a reason for the

Christian school to be messy or cluttered; even if the facility is not new, it should always be neat and clean.

STEPS IN ESTABLISHING A SCHOOL

Research

After the school board members have thoroughly established their priorities in beginning a Christian school, they must decide either to do the research needed to start the school's program or to hire a trained, preferably experienced, administrator who will bring recommendations to them for their approval. Another option is to employ a Christian school administrator to serve as a consultant to provide guidance in the initial planning stage. The latter procedure is usually preferable. This person may be somebody already in the local church or Christian school organization, or he may be a faculty member at a Christian college who has a proper biblical philosophy of Christian education and a desire to serve the Lord by helping new schools get established.

Probably the first contact this person will need to make is with the local superintendent of public schools. Sometimes we Christians believe this person to be our enemy. However, Christian school personnel can foster a good, healthy relationship with him. Perhaps someone in the local church knows the superintendent personally and can make contact for the school board or administrator. The superintendent can explain the state requirements on the operation of a school. He may even be willing to provide a year-old manual on state requirements for school operation. One should also find out from the superintendent how he desires the Christian school to report students who are transferring from the public school to the Christian school or vice versa. Many states mandate that private schools make annual reports of their enrollment. A good initial contact with the superintendent of public schools can be of benefit for many years to come.

The Christian school should also contact the state department of education to determine the state requirements for private schools. Because every state is different, the Christian school should have a copy of specific laws for its state. It should also contact the county health department to find out the immunization and other health requirements of its particular county. Certain reporting may be required of the Christian school and it should be done faithfully. If food services are to be offered, these will also come under the jurisdiction of the health department. As stated previously, the Christian school should give all due consideration to meeting health requirements established by the government.

Every Christian school should have legal counsel to help in the incorporation and application for tax exemption as a nonprofit organization. It should have a good lawyer, knowledgeable in the issues facing Christian schools today, with whom the administrator has established a relationship so that he may be called upon in time of need. In addition, there are a number of publications that deal with legal problems the Christian school is likely to face. (See bibliography.) The school should also establish a relationship with a CPA familiar with government regulations for private nonprofit schools.

Determining the Size and Grade Levels to Be Offered

The next step is to determine how many grades to offer in the first year of operation. It is tempting to start everything at once; yet many schools that have tried to start a complete program of kindergarten through twelfth grade in the first year have regretted it later. Often the best way to start the school is with either two classes (kindergarten and first grade), or four classes (kindergarten through third grade). The second year the rest of the elementary program can be added. Beyond that, a grade may be added every year until the school has all twelve grades. In a small community, however, a church that does not anticipate a large enrollment may feel a burden to offer Christian education to all the children of its members. With competent personnel and sound materials that combine group instruction with independent study, a school can successfully combine two or more grades in a classroom and still offer quality schooling to the families.

Once the board members determine what grades to offer the first year, they may design a survey to distribute to members of the church and other interested Christian parents to determine how many children will be attending the Christian school. Certainly it would be unwise to start a Christian school if there is no demand for it. The leaders may find from the survey that they need to spend more time teaching parents the importance of Christian education before starting the school. Postponing the opening for a year or more may benefit the school in the long run by insuring the support of the people. By telling the school leaders how many students they can expect the first year, the survey provides information necessary for planning financial matters and hiring staff. The survey is a very important tool and should be distributed before teachers are hired or a program is established.

Personnel

After determining the number of classes to offer, the school must hire teaching staff. (See chapter 17.) Naturally, the better the teachers, the better the school. Prepackaged curriculum taught by novices are one alternative to public education, but only in the short run, if ever. Biblical teaching always puts an emphasis on the teacher (Luke 6:40). Those starting Christian schools will be tempted to take the short, easy way out by buying such prepackaged curriculum and letting anyone teach them; however, that system will not give the quality Christian education that parents desire. Only with quality people will the Christian school have a quality program.

Textbooks

A Christian school that hires quality teachers is also hiring a wealth of background information and knowledge that can be helpful in selecting textbooks and other educational materials. The school board should allow the educational personnel to make these decisions, within certain guidelines. For example, the materials in a Christian school should give preeminence to Jesus Christ and salvation by grace. Second, the materials should integrate biblical principles into every subject. A Christian school textbook should not simply teach an academic discipline; it should also teach principles that will help conform the student to the image of Christ. Third, the materials must give sufficient priority to the understanding of subject matter rather than simply the rote memorization of facts. Too many Christian schools spend the majority of their time drilling students on factual material rather than teaching how to apply to life what they have learned. Of course, it is impossible for students to apply what they do not understand. For this reason, textbooks and other materials used in the Christian school must emphasize understanding. We have reached the point where it is no longer necessary to use secular textbooks in the Christian school. Quality Christian textbooks and resources are available in all academic disciplines in all grade levels.

Curriculum

In setting up its curriculum, a school with a small enrollment may consider using one of various independent-study programs developed to allow students to teach themselves by working through program textbooks at their own rate. This type is attractive to small schools because all ages can be in the same classroom working on their own individual material at the same time, with less operating cost than a conventional classroom setup.

Even though the independent-study school has these advantages, it lacks many of the requirements for successfully training all young people. One of the biggest pitfalls is that a teacher is not controlling the classroom experience. The teacher is the most important element in the child's Christian school experience. He is responsible to direct the class and to teach the subject matter, integrating faith and learning so that true Christian education takes place. The teacher influences the lives of students through his own Christian walk. He, not the program, is the key.

Another pitfall of the independent-study program is that the students miss out on interaction with other students in the classroom. They miss being motivated by peers who are achieving. If a student is not self-motivated or has good reading skills in the independent-study program, he may fall behind in his work.

Other problems with the independent-study program are that students do not develop listening and note-taking skills since they do not have to listen to a teacher to distinguish between essential and nonessential material. As a supplement, an independent-study program does have advantages and can be used effectively in the Christian school, but it is too weak to be the only system a new Christian school uses.

After hiring personnel and choosing materials, the board or administrator may want to visit other successful Christian schools to gain ideas from them. Those starting new schools can also request the help of outside experts who thoroughly understand Christian education.

Finances

Schools are expensive to start, and a great deal of money must be spent before any income will be received. Once a school is operating, it will receive registration fees and tuition payments to cover operating expenses. However, to cover some initial expenses, the church may begin by taking a special offering. With proper teaching, many people will be convinced of the necessity of Christian education and will be willing to help the Christian school by giving financially. It is important to impress upon people that their school offering should be over and above their regular tithes. People who give to the school ministry feel they are a part of the ministry. Once the board is convinced that it will have the funds necessary to begin a school, it should establish a budget for at least one year. Planning the first year's expenses is very difficult. There are a number of initial expenses that will not continue to occur. It is difficult to know how many students will enroll the first year, so estimating income is harder.

Many Christians have gotten the idea in the past few years that starting a Christian school is a simple matter. The information presented here should convince them that this is not the case. In essence, it takes time, money, expertise, and—above all—God's blessing to start a Christ-honoring Christian school. There are no shortcuts. Every detail must be cared for. Yet nothing can be more Christ-honoring than a ministry effectively educating Christian young people to live for Christ.

CHAPTER 4

ORGANIZATIONAL STRUCTURE

Let all things be done decently and in order.

1 Corinthians 14:40

Obey them that have the rule over you, and submit yourselves: for they watch for your souls, as they that must give account, that they may do it with joy, and not with grief: for that is unprofitable for you.

Hebrews 13:17

From the perspective of organization, there are three basic types of Christian schools: the independent school, the church-school, and the independent church-school (organized separately from the church, yet wholly owned and controlled by it). Until recent years, when Christian schools have faced repeated attacks in the courts, Christian educators and church leaders had given little thought to the organizational structure of their schools. Persecution, however, has prompted them to examine this area more closely.

TYPES OF SCHOOLS

Independent School

Until the surge in the growth of the Christian school movement in the 1960s, most schools were organized as independent, parent-oriented schools; that is, they were conceived, developed, financed, and controlled primarily by groups of parents interested in the training of their children. Such schools function independently of any other institution.

Almost without exception these schools are organized as nonprofit educational institutions. As a result they enjoy a number of benefits that work for their stability and growth. Since gifts to them are tax deductible, it is easy to develop the donor constituency essential for their development and survival. Furthermore, they are not required to pay corporate income taxes, real estate taxes, federal excise tax on gasoline, or state sales taxes in most states. These factors work together to present the most favorable income and expense picture possible.

Independent schools are operated by boards that are usually dominated by parents. The success of the independent school varies with the quality of the board, the administration, and the overall support of the parents. However, the parental support often fluctuates greatly as the conditions that precipitated the school's organization change. For example, the election of a liberal public school board may have given impetus to parental support for a Christian school, while an eventual return to a conservative board with conservative practices may then erode that support. Christian schools also flourish in a sound economic climate but sometimes founder as the economy declines. Because the number of independent Christian schools has not increased appreciably in the last few years, while the number of church-schools has, the relative importance of the independent school has lessened considerably.

Independent schools will have two things to consider that the church-school does not have to consider:

1. They must formally apply for recognition of exempt status with the Internal Revenue Service if they choose to operate as a tax-exempt entity.

2. Independent schools are required to pay unemployment taxes on all employees. This is not a requirement of church-school employees except in the state of Oregon.

Church-School

Most Christian schools established since the mid-1970s have been organized as part of the local church, partially because much of the concern for Christian education has come from within the church. Many Christian educators became convinced that Christian education is a mandate to the church and thus must be part of the church. In any case, although Scripture clearly commands parents to educate their children (Eph. 6:4), the church may be the most logical institution to assist the parent in educating his child. The church-school also offers a practical advantage over the independent school since the church already has a bookkeeping system, a legal structure, a staff, and a physical facility that is used little during the daytime from Monday through Saturday. The same benefits of tax exemption that accrue to the independent school apply equally to the church-school. Because the Internal Revenue Service automatically recognizes a church as tax-exempt so long as basic criteria are observed, a church-school is not required to file separately for the recognition of exempt status.

Independent Church-School

A few church-schools have been organized as separate legal entities. However, a number that were originally organized in this manner have since dissolved their charters and gone under the corporate umbrella of the church. The passage of time may prove that this change in practice was a mistake.

In the 1970s the Internal Revenue Service promulgated some very strict guidelines that they sought to impose on private schools with regard to their admissions policies. Many Christian educators saw dissolving their schools' corporate charters and operating them as integral ministries of the church as a means of escaping this scrutiny. The Internal Revenue Service responded to this move by implementing new regulations that imposed the same standards on church-schools. Unfortunately, additional regulations followed that placed churches under stricter oversight than they had ever experienced before.

During the same period of time, many Christian schools became entangled with government agencies and regulatory bodies at the federal, state, and local levels. These groups did not want to recognize the distinction between the independent school maintaining its own legal identity and the church that was operating a school as part of its ministry. Consequently, additional burdens were imposed on the church that were intended to be applied only to schools.

In the years to come, we would probably be better off if all Christian schools were incorporated separately. This would not in any way inconvenience churches that operate schools. They could still exercise the same degree of control over them as they do over schools that share their legal identity. However, it would permit them to hold the schools at arm's length and allow them to accept government regulations over the school that they would consider unacceptable for the church.

It may be best for all new schools to be organized as separate legal entities. Churches with existing schools should consider restructuring their schools to give them their own legal identity. This can be done without surrendering any control over them.

The nature and objectives of the school dictate organizational policy and, consequently, structure. Basic organizational structure of the Christian school differs little from its public school counterpart. A typical structure appears in Figure 4.1.

FIGURE 4.1

ORGANIZATIONAL STRUCTURE

Independent School/
Independent Church-School

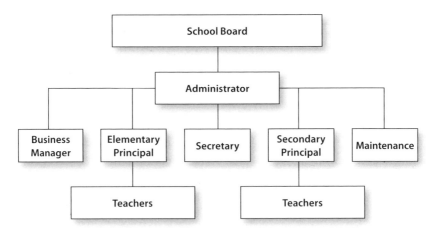

Church-School

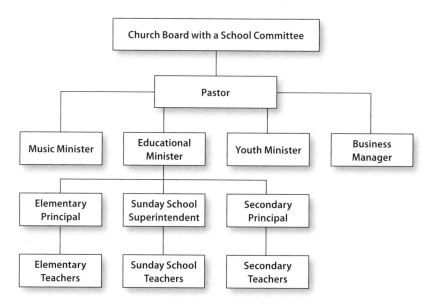

Church-Related School

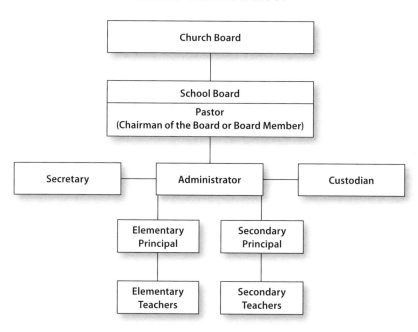

Small Christian School

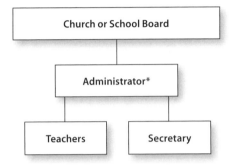

* This position could be assumed by the pastor in a church-school even though it is more desirable to have an administrator who also has some teaching responsibilities.

LEVELS OF LEADERSHIP

Some church-schools have no school board at all. They operate the school through an administrator who is responsible directly to the pastor and/ or the church board. This arrangement places on the pastor and administrator a great deal of responsibility that they are not always prepared to handle. It is generally a better practice to have the decision-making power in the hands of several rather than just a few.

School Board

The independent school will usually elect a board from its constituents or supporters in accordance with the specifications contained in its constitution and bylaws or charter. However, almost without exception, the board members of the church-school or the independent church-school will be elected from the membership of the church. Prominent Christian legal experts suggest that to do otherwise raises potentially serious questions about the genuineness of the conviction for a thoroughly Christian church-school. Some churches have chosen to make the school board a committee selected from their deacons or elders, emphasizing the spiritual imperatives of Christian education. Other churches make the qualifications for school board members the same as those for the office of deacon or elder. In so doing they place the same emphasis on spiritual qualifications while making the offices separate. It is imperative to remember that the school board is in authority over all school employees; consequently, their spiritual qualifications must be at least equal to those required of school employees.

Perhaps one of the most hotly debated qualifications for school board membership is whether those with school-age children must have them enrolled in the school. Some schools require board members to enroll their children for two reasons: (1) they would be keenly interested in the quality of the school and aware of problems, and (2) to have their children enrolled elsewhere would bring into question their commitment to a Christian philosophy of education. Others take the opposite position, forbidding board members to have children enrolled. Such schools prefer to avoid potential difficulties with lack of objectivity in dealing with situations in which the children of board members are disciplined or injured.

The school board functions in essentially the same capacity as the board of directors in a corporation. Figure 4.2 presents the responsibilities of the school board.

FIGURE 4.2

DUTIES OF THE CHRISTIAN SCHOOL BOARD

1. Hold title to any property owned by the corporation (In a church-school this function will be performed by the church board of trustees.)

2. Employ personnel (In many schools this responsibility is delegated to the school administrator, who employs personnel for positions approved by the board under employment guidelines established by the board.)

3. Enter into contracts

4. Develop policy and approve policy with the guidance of the school administrator

5. Supervise the management of the financial resources

6. Formulate a master plan for the development of the ministry with the guidance of the school administrator

---

Regardless of the school's organizational structure, those to be elected to the school board should meet the qualifications listed in Figure 4.3.

FIGURE 4.3

QUALIFICATIONS FOR BOARD MEMBERS

1. Exemplary Christian testimony

2. Be a member of the sponsoring church (for church-schools and independent church-schools)

3. Have demonstrated leadership ability

4. Have an aptitude or special area of knowledge that will contribute to the work of the board

5. Be in harmony with the purposes and objectives of the school

6. Have sufficient time to invest in the work of the board

7. Have a strong commitment to Christian school education (Those who have children of school age should be required to have them enrolled in the school.)

Parents or congregations elect board members and establish their terms of office by a variety of methods, often with all members standing for election at the same time and reelection permitted indefinitely. Although there is probably no one best arrangement, Figure 4.4 lists some factors that should influence the election and terms of office for board members.

FIGURE 4.4

FACTORS CONCERNING THE TERM OF OFFICE

1. Three- to four-year terms provide sufficient time to become familiar with the ministry and to make meaningful contributions.

2. Election to unrestricted numbers of terms can lead to a "strong board" unresponsive to the concerns of others.

3. Election of board members should be staggered to avoid having a completely new board at one time.

School boards traditionally elect several officers: president, vice president, secretary, and treasurer. Their terms of office can vary with the length of a board member's term or can simply be limited to one year. Assuming that the board members are all capable leaders, reelecting officers annually gives all members an opportunity to participate in the leadership of the board.

It is often good to divide responsibilities among the board members by forming committees. Appropriate committees include curriculum, finances, public relations, building and grounds, transportation, and personnel. Although committees do not make final decisions in any matter, they are sometimes able to discuss issues of concern in greater detail than the entire board could.

Frequency of board meetings is a matter of preference, governed to some extent by the degree of the board's involvement in the details of the school's operation and by its size. A Christian school with an experienced administrator requires fewer board meetings. However, since board members have the legal responsibility for the school, they must be kept abreast of the day-to-day affairs. Certainly they should meet at least quarterly; for larger schools, a monthly meeting would be more appropriate. During times of the year when the budget is being prepared, it would not be unusual for the board to meet even weekly for a brief period of time. Of course, the administrator will normally be interacting with the pastor on a daily basis.

A major function of the school board is to develop policy. Unfortunately, most Christian school boards develop policy only as it is needed. To serve their intended purpose, policies need to be developed far in advance of their need. Without clear, written policies communicated to all concerned, there is no consistent direction for the school and its administration. If such a school ever achieves its objectives, it will do so only accidentally, and probably no one will ever realize that the objectives have been met.

Administrator

The key person in every organization is its leader. In private schools the title of administrator, principal, and headmaster are often used interchangeably. In larger schools the overall school leader is most often referred to as the administrator. In such a school there may be a high school principal and an elementary school principal. Other schools may call their lead administrator the principal and use the title vice-principal for those who serve under him. For sake of simplicity, the term *administrator* will be used in this book to refer to the school leader. The choice of this leader can determine the success or failure of the ministry.

In a church-school, the administrator is often considered a member of the pastoral staff, and in many instances, he is ordained and has responsibilities for other church ministries as he serves under the senior pastor. For this reason, most Christian schools that are church-related hire men for the position of administrator. Consequently, the administrator of the Christian school should first of all be a spiritual man who meets the basic prerequisites outlined in 1 Timothy 3 and other passages of Scripture dealing with the leadership of the church. The ministry of the Christian school as such is not mentioned in the Bible; but since it is an important spiritual ministry, using the qualifications for pastor and deacon is appropriate.

The question of the appropriateness of hiring a woman to serve as the school administrator is often raised. Many women possess the natural ability to lead an educational institution, and many also possess the general spiritual and academic qualifications for the position. A number of women have served admirably as school administrators. The question that each church-related institution must resolve on its own is how the administrator is to relate to the pastoral staff. If in your church the school administrator does not have to be a member of the pastoral staff, there is no reason a woman cannot serve in this capacity if she meets the other criteria established for the position. In an independent school there is no reason not to consider a woman for the position.

Among the qualifications outlined in 1 Timothy 3 that are especially important in selecting an administrator are those dealing with his family. In this day of little emphasis on the importance of the family, it is especially essential that those who serve as role models for our children be free of character flaws that would likely encourage young people to lower their personal standards. A Christian school administrator, therefore, should not be divorced or married to a divorcée. Preferably, he should be married. If his children are still living at home, they must set an example worthy of the students at his school. His wife, while not necessarily involved directly in the school work, must show a vital interest in the ministry. His personal finances must be in order so that they will not be an offense to the businessmen in the community.

In addition to spiritual qualifications, the school administrator must have professional competence. First Timothy 3:6 calls attention to the fact that there is a danger in giving responsibility to a novice. This is a frequent error in the Christian school ministry. Because Christian educational facilities have increased rapidly, there has been a shortage of leaders. In their haste to fill a position, administrators have too often placed people in positions for which they are not trained. Although it is possible for a man to develop skills and knowledge while on the job, it is dangerous and foolish to assume that he will become something entirely different from what he was at the time he was hired.

The Christian school administrator should have academic training in education—preferably a master's degree in educational administration or leadership. However, many men with different training have been very successful school leaders, and they should not be overlooked. Every administrator should have at least a bachelor's degree in Bible or some academic area, preferably education. How high the standards must be maintained in your school depends somewhat on the academic preparation of the teaching staff, the age of the school, and the expectations of the community in which the school is located. As the leader of the Christian school, the administrator must not embarrass himself, the school, or the Lord (2 Tim. 2:15).

It is desirable to employ administrators with experience. Some excellent Christian school administrators were former public school principals who late in life responded to God's call to the Christian school ministry. Good school administrators have also come from the ranks of business. Many teachers leave education and go into business, later returning to serve God as Christian school administrators. The experience in business is often very helpful in Christian school administration.

An important factor to consider in evaluating an applicant's experience is his record as an administrator. Employers are often reluctant to be completely candid about a former employee's performance, particularly if he held a responsible position. If a prospect's former work was not satisfactory, it is important to consider very carefully why it was not satisfactory and determine whether he would likely have the same kind of problem in your school. An applicant with several unsatisfactory employment situations should not be given serious consideration.

Another source of administrators is the faculty of the school. A wise administrator will appreciate the need for additional leaders within the movement and will seek to train those on his staff who have the potential to be developed for future responsibility. In many cases, when the Lord moves the school's administrator on to another school, there is someone on the scene to step into his shoes. The same criteria used to judge new employees should be applied to existing staff members. Other things being equal, however, a current staff member offers definite advantages.

The specific needs and characteristics of the school play an important part in evaluating applicants. A new school may need a more experienced administrator than an older, well-established school that is operating smoothly. A small elementary school needs a different type of person from that needed by a school of nine hundred with all twelve grades and kindergarten. A rural community needs a different type of administrator from that needed by a school located in a large metropolitan area.

Small schools often expect their administrator to teach full-time and also handle all administrative duties. This approach is not recommended; however, if there is no alternative, the administrator should be paid more than the normal teaching or administrative salary because he will have to spend many more hours on the job than someone with a regular workload. Figure 4.5 provides a general list of the responsibilities of the administrator.

FIGURE 4.5

DUTIES OF AN ADMINISTRATOR

The role of the administrator of a Christian school is multifaceted. While his student body will, in most cases, be much smaller than that of his public school counterpart, the range of duties that will comprise his responsibilities may be much broader. Formal preparation for this position is very important. In a church-related school, these duties are carried out under the authority of the pastor and/or the school board. The typical administrator will have responsibility for the following activities in most Christian schools:

1. Development and implementation of educational philosophy
2. Development and implementation of educational policy
3. Development and implementation of the curriculum
4. Development of the budget
5. Supervision of the financial resources
6. Recruitment and selection of professional staff
7. Recruitment and selection of support staff
8. Orientation of staff
9. Recruitment and selection of pupils
10. Supervision of the instructional program
11. Supervision of pupil personnel services
12. Administration and supervision of discipline
13. Staff development
14. Supervision of the transportation program
15. Development and maintenance of the physical facilities
16. School/community relations

The job description for the administrator will also dictate some of the characteristics sought in the applicant. In some schools the administrator is responsible only for those things directly related to instruction. In other schools he supervises instruction, business, personnel, maintenance and operations, and transportation. What will be expected of the administrator will have a major impact on the type of person sought. Schools that do not have job descriptions for administrators invite serious misunderstanding. They will also find it nearly impossible to agree on the person to hire.

The best prospects for the position of administrator can usually be found by reviewing the school faculty or by advising the various executive directors of the state Christian school organizations of your need. Utilization of the placement services offered by such organizations as the American Association of Christian Schools and the placement services of the Christian colleges that offer graduate programs in educational administration or leadership provides information on new prospects.

One word of caution is in order. Schools should not steal administrators, or teachers for that matter, from other Christian schools. It is generally considered to be unethical to contact employees under contract to another institution, unless they personally have made it known that they are available. If you feel led to contact a person who is already employed at another school about a vacancy at your school, you should request that school's permission to talk with him. In most cases the most appropriate person to contact first is the pastor of the church.

How does a school find an administrator? The decision should be bathed in prayer, of course. God is able to work in ways that are beyond us; He can and will touch hearts of people we do not even know. In order for schools to interview candidates for administrative positions, careful preparation is needed.

Figure 4.6 provides a list of steps that should be taken as a school seeks a new administrator.

FIGURE 4.6

SELECTING THE CHRISTIAN SCHOOL ADMINISTRATOR

1. Develop a job description.
2. Identify personal characteristics you expect in a candidate (spiritual, academic preparation, and experience).
3. Determine the total financial package (salary, fringe benefits, relocation expenses, and so forth).
4. Publicize the availability of the position as widely as possible.
5. Review your present professional staff for possible candidates.
6. Determine the information you will need from candidates to make an employment decision.

7. Establish a procedure for screening applicants.

8. Determine the format of the interviews.

9. Review prospective candidates to determine which ones will be invited for interviews.

10. Schedule interviews.

11. Make the employment decision.

12. Advise unsuccessful candidates of your decision.

Pastor

The pastor of a church that sponsors a Christian school should assume essentially the same leadership role in the church-school as he does in the rest of the church ministry. Some pastors assume low-key roles in their churches, while others are strong and very direct in their leadership. Their influence should be much the same in relation to their schools. The pastor should be a voting member of the school board. In many church-related schools, the pastor of the church is designated the permanent chairman of the board. In other church-schools the pastor is designated the superintendent of the school to clarify his administrative role over the school. Whatever role the church wants the pastor to have with regard to its school, the role should be clearly specified in the church constitution and bylaws so that no misunderstanding will occur.

The pastor's leadership will be felt most keenly in his relationship to the school board and the school administrator. The pastor of a church with a Christian school must provide leadership essential to the maintenance and balance of the educational activities within the overall church ministry that is consistent with the central purpose of the church. The various ministries, and personnel responsible for them, cannot be allowed to operate in a manner that puts them in competition with one another. The overall activity of the church-school must complement the testimony of Christ through the local church. Effective leadership on the part of the pastor is absolutely essential to realize this objective. The pastor, however, must exercise caution not to micromanage the administrator.

The pastor's involvement in the church-school is an important one. Since it is easy for professionally trained educators to get sidetracked from the spiritual essentials of the school, the pastor's responsibility is to maintain the proper spiritual course and to strive to keep a consistent balance between the spiritual and academic concerns.

Although pastors are generally well trained in spiritual matters, few have formal training in education. Pastors need to take advantage of every opportunity to become more knowledgeable concerning academic affairs by attending and participating in activities in Christian school conventions and associational meetings, reading good books, participating in in-service training sessions conducted for teachers, and taking course work in school administration at a good Christian college.

The pastor also plays an important part in keeping conflicts between the church and the school at a minimum. Many important school activities compete with church activities for time in a student's schedule. A pastor must give considerable attention to maintaining an appropriate balance before these conflicts become serious. The pastor must maintain close contact with the activities of the school and take every opportunity to inform the church of the school's activities. The pastor should be the school's number one cheerleader!

The structure of the Christian school is important, but no one structure is best for all situations. A Christian school must be carefully organized, not only to insure that it meets its objectives but also (in the case of a church-school) to insure that it does not compete with other ministries to the detriment of the whole church.

CHAPTER 5

FINANCING EDUCATION IN AMERICA

Render therefore unto Caesar the things which are Caesar's;
and unto God the things that are God's.

Matthew 22:21

Let every soul be subject unto the higher powers. For there is
no power but of God: the powers that be are ordained of God.
Whosoever therefore resisteth the power, resisteth the ordinance
of God. . . . Wherefore ye must needs be subject, not only for
wrath, but also for conscience sake. For this cause pay ye tribute also: for they are God's ministers . . . render therefore to all
their dues: tribute to whom tribute is due.

Romans 13:1–2, 5–7

M uch of what we do in Christian education follows the traditional
pattern established over the years by public and private schools. If
we are to appreciate fully the attitudes and concerns of secular educators
about the Christian school movement, we need a working knowledge of
the development of these educational systems.

To understand public and private education during the early history
of our country, one must realize that the clear distinction we now have
between public and private education did not exist then. There was a
unique blend of public and private monies and governance supporting
these educational programs.

Before we begin our historical examination, it may be wise to define public and private education. *Public education* may be defined as
an educational system owned and financed by the government. *Private
education* may be defined as an educational system owned and financed
by an individual or an organization. This is not to say that private institutions never receive government aid, but government funds are not
their primary means of support. However, the more that private schools
accept public money, the less private these schools become. It should also

be noted that private education includes both religious and nonsectarian schools. These definitions become more important when discussing the legal aspects of educational development.

EARLY YEARS (1642–1776)

A thorough review of education during the colonial era is beyond the scope of this book. However, a brief overview of the colonists' approach will help us understand some foundational ideas that still affect the financing of today's educational systems.

Public financing of education in America goes back at least to 1642. In that year, the General Court of Massachusetts passed a law that required the following:

> Certain chosen men of each town [were] to ascertain from time to time, if parents were attending to their educational duties: if the children were being trained in learning and labor and other employments . . . profitable to the state; and if children were being taught to read and understand the principles of religion and the capital laws of the country and empowered them to impose fines on those who refused to render such accounts to them when required. (Cubberly, 1920, 364)

Education historians note that this was the first time an English-speaking people required that children be taught to read. It turned out, however, that this legislation was not enough to meet the colonists' objectives. Consequently, the General Court passed a new law in 1647. This law required the following:

1. That every town having 50 householders shall at once appoint a teacher of reading and writing and provide for his wages in such a manner as the town might determine; and,

2. That every town having 100 householders must provide a grammar school to fit youths for the university, under penalty of 5 pounds (afterward raised to 20 pounds) for failure to do so. (Cubberly, 1920, 365)

This legislation came to be known as The Old Deluder Satan Act because its primary purpose was to hinder Satan in his attempt to keep people ignorant of the Scriptures. Schools to teach children to read and write were, therefore, a necessity.

This New England legislation was the first legal basis for a public school system in Massachusetts, and it is noteworthy for establishing the following foundational ideas:

1. It set the precedent for the authority of the state to establish educational requirements.

2. It gave local governments authority to levy taxes to assist in financing both elementary and secondary schools.

3. It showed that if the state requires an educational program to be provided, it must also provide a means for financing that program if it is to become available. (Johns, Morphet, and Alexander, 1983, 2)

This legislation had a great effect on the other colonies, particularly in New England. By 1720 Connecticut, Maine, New Hampshire, and Vermont had passed similar legislation.

The Middle Colonies had a private educational system. They relied on various churches rather than the government to finance education. These churches established their own parochial schools and financed their programs by charging the parents fees according to the number of children enrolled in the school.

In the Southern Colonies education was largely limited to the wealthy. These colonies chose to pattern their educational system after England's. In England the schools were either supported by the Church of England (which the Southern Colonies also supported) or were private, nonsectarian schools. Tutors were also used by many of the plantation owners where the distances between families made the establishment of a school impractical. There were a few private schools supported by religious organizations that were founded to provide education for the poor. The Society for the Propagation of the Gospel in Foreign Parts was one of the better known.

MIDDLE YEARS (1776–1900)

Despite the early New England legislation, widespread support for public education was slow to take hold in America. This, however, was not due to a lack of support from influential politicians. Prominent leaders such as Henry Barnard, James Carter, Benjamin Franklin, Thomas Jefferson, Horace Mann, and Thaddeus Stevens were leaders of this period who fought for free education for the common man. Still, in the early nineteenth century, government support was generally limited to the elementary grades.

In 1874 the financing of public high schools received considerable impetus from the Kalamazoo decision. In this case, the supreme court of Michigan upheld the concept of tax support for public high schools. Though this decision greatly influenced the development of public schools, it did not mean that tax-supported schools were generally available to all students. Walter Page reported that in 1890 26 percent of the white population of North Carolina could neither read nor write (Page, 1952). In 1900 only 8 percent of the students between fourteen and seventeen years of age were enrolled in high school, and public high schools were not available to many rural families even as late as 1920. It was not until the mid-1950s that the state of Georgia expanded its high school program to include twelve grades statewide. However, the groundwork of tax support for public education was well established by the beginning of the twentieth century.

RECENT YEARS (1900 TO PRESENT)

By 1925 the majority of schools were public schools, and an adverse attitude began to emerge toward private schools. This attitude is better understood when we examine closely the financial basis for the public school system. You will recall that we defined public education as a system of education *owned* and *financed* by the government. Once we understand the development of the public school's financial system, we will begin to understand why there is an increasing antagonism toward private education.

Initially, public schools were financed with local funds. As their needs grew, however, these funds were supplemented first with state revenues and later with federal revenues. By examining Figure 5.1, you will notice the rapid change in dependency for financial support from local to state and federal funding.

FIGURE 5.1

TRENDS IN SOURCES OF PUBLIC SCHOOL REVENUE BY LEVEL OF GOVERNMENT

Year	Federal Percent	State Percent	Local Percent
1919/20	0.3	16.5	83.2
1929/30	0.4	16.9	82.7
1939/40	1.8	30.3	67.9
1949/50	2.9	39.8	57.3
1959/60	4.4	39.1	56.5
1969/70	8.0	39.9	52.1
1979/80	9.8	46.8	43.4
1989/90	6.1	47.1	46.8
1999/00	7.3	49.5	43.2

Source: Digest of Education Statistics, 2005, Washington, D.C. (http://nces.ed.gov/programs/digest/d05/tables/dt05_152.asp)

This change in the source of funding has been accompanied by a drastic change in control of the schools. The federal government, through the Department of Education, exerts influence over every facet of public school education. Considerable pressure is put on local schools through the funding process. The penalty for being in noncompliance with federal regulations is loss of funding. Public schools were once dominated by the neighborhood in enrollment and control, but now the neighborhood is not dominant in its control. At the present time, the influence of the federal government on public education is at least as great as, if not greater than, the state—with the local school board having the least control. Figure 5.2 shows the flow of funds in a typical public school district. As this figure illustrates, the degree of control exercised by the individual levels of government is not in proportion to the level of funding each provides. In fact, many public educators would agree that the degree of control exercised—by the federal government in particular—far exceeds the value of its financial support.

FIGURE 5.2

GREENVILLE (S.C.) COUNTY SCHOOLS— 2005 BUDGET FIGURES

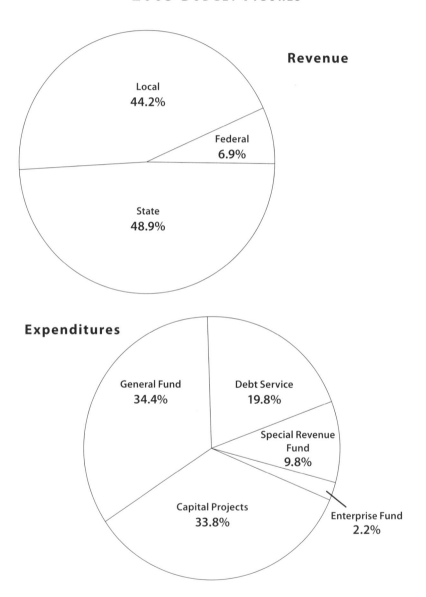

Revenue

Local
44.2%

Federal
6.9%

State
48.9%

Expenditures

General Fund
34.4%

Debt Service
19.8%

Special Revenue
Fund
9.8%

Capital Projects
33.8%

Enterprise Fund
2.2%

Source: http://www.greenville.k12.sc.us/district/support/finance/budget4.asp

The local funds for public schools are derived largely from property taxes—the taxation of all real estate property and any improvements to the property within a district. The value of the property is known as the tax base. This tax base, of course, excludes property belonging to tax-exempt organizations. These property taxes are controlled by local governments. Often the school district will establish the amount of revenue needed, and then the local government will establish the tax rate necessary to generate that amount. In recent times, many school districts have sought authority to control the tax rate on property taxes to give them more direct control over local revenues available to them. Of course, the local government is limited in raising revenues by the willingness of the voters to support the local program. The following formula is commonly used when determining the tax rate:

$$\frac{\text{Amount of Tax Revenue to Be Raised}}{\text{Tax Base (assessed value of property)}} = \text{Rate}$$

State support of public education is generated by sales or "use" taxes and by individual and/or corporate income taxes. The federal government, relying primarily on individual and corporate income taxes, also targets funds for education. The executive and legislative branches, through the budget process, determine the contributions to education at both the state and federal levels. The state contribution to public education normally follows a well-established plan and is thus fairly consistent from year to year. These general education revenues allocated by the state governments are usually related in some way to the enrollment or the average daily attendance within each district. Federal aid to education is far less consistent than state aid. The federal aid to education is more like a political football, and much of the funds now allocated are targeted for specific programs. There is considerable pressure from political conservatives to change this process to provide for block grants of federal money that can be used at the discretion of the state department of education or the local school system.

There has been a great deal of controversy recently concerning how public education is funded. The year-by-year changes in average expenditure per pupil in average daily attendance is reported in Figure 5.3. The concern is that many inequities exist from state to state and within the individual states from district to district.

FIGURE 5.3

PUBLIC ELEMENTARY AND SECONDARY EXPENDITURES PER PUPIL 1980 TO 2003

	Average per Pupil Year Expenditure in ADA
1980	$2,272
1990	$4,980
1991	$5,258
1992	$5,421
1993	$5,584
1994	$5,767
1995	$5,989
1996	$6,147
1997	$6,393
1998	$6,676
1999	$7,013
2000	$7,394
2001	$7,904
2002	$8,259
2003	$8,600

Source: Digest of Education Statistics Tables and Figures, 2005
http://nces.ed.gov/programs/digest/d05/tables/dt05_162.asp

Vast differences in the tax bases often exist between various school districts within a state. The funding practices currently followed by most states do little to eliminate these differences. Consequently, very rich and very poor districts are often found within the state, and such discrepancies result in significant differences in the quality of education offered. The statewide differences are illustrated by Figure 5.4. Within each state the same range of differences exists between individual school districts. The entire financing programs of several states have recently been found to be unconstitutional, and new ways of funding public schools are being considered. The most common approach being considered is some means to eliminate dependence on local property taxes. At least in some states, serious consideration is being given to the elimination of property taxes with funding coming primarily from the states. A negative perspective causing concern about this approach is that this move will probably result in even less local control of public schools.

FIGURE 5.4

PER PUPIL EXPENDITURE BY STATE IN 2003/2004

Public Elementary and Secondary Schools

State	Average per Pupil State Expenditure in ADA
Alabama	$6,953
Alaska	$11,432
Arizona	$5,595
Arkansas	$6,663
California	$7,860
Colorado	$8,651
Connecticut	$12,394
Delaware	$10,347
District of Columbia	$14,621
Florida	$7,181
Georgia	$8,671
Hawaii	$9,019
Idaho	$6,779
Illinois	$10,866

State	Average per Pupil State Expenditure in ADA
Indiana	$9,138
Iowa	$7,696
Kansas	$8,189
Kentucky	$8,298
Louisiana	$7,840
Maine	$10,961
Maryland	$9,824
Massachusetts	$11,445
Michigan	$9,416
Minnesota	$9,513
Mississippi	$6,556
Missouri	$7,548
Montana	$8,631
Nebraska	$7,947
Nevada	$6,177
New Hampshire	$9,902
New Jersey	$11,847
New Mexico	$8,772
New York	$12,408
North Carolina	$7,511
North Dakota	$7,112
Ohio	$10,102
Oklahoma	$6,405
Oregon	$8,575
Pennsylvania	$9,949
Rhode Island	$10,976

State	Average per Pupil State Expenditure in ADA
South Carolina	$7,395
South Dakota	$7,611
Tennessee	$6,983
Texas	$7,698
Utah	$5,556
Vermont	$12,157
Virginia	$9,401
Washington	$7,904
West Virginia	$9,509
Wisconsin	$10,293
Wyoming	$10,413

Source: US Census Bureau, 2007
http://www.census.gov/prod/2006pubs/smadb/smadb-06tablea.pdf

How does this financial basis affect private schools? You will remember from Figure 5.1 the growing dependence of public schools on state and federal funds. In 1999/00 the average school district was receiving 49.5 percent of its revenue from the state. Almost without exception the amount of money a school receives from the state is based upon average daily attendance. While the number of students lost to an individual public school is usually small, when this loss is viewed on a districtwide basis, such a loss can be significant.

The extent of this financial impact may be better understood by examining the effects of adding just one small private school in a particular district (Figure 5.5). For example, suppose a school offering kindergarten through sixth grade opened with an enrollment of 250 students its first year. The second year the school expanded through grade twelve and had an enrollment of 400.

FIGURE 5.5

REDUCTION OF PUBLIC SCHOOL FUNDS
BECAUSE OF PRIVATE SCHOOL ENROLLMENT

Average Expenditures per Pupil per Year	$8,600
Revenue Lost First Year School Operated	(250~x~$4,300) $1,075,000
Revenue Lost Second Year School Operated	(400~x~$4,300) $1,720,000
Total Revenue Lost in First Two Years School Operated	$2,795,000

In the first two years of a new Christian school's operation the local district would lose $1.5 million in revenue with virtually no opportunity to reduce its own expenditures.

Even though financial consequences for the public school system exist, we must do what is necessary for the preservation of our children and their preparation for the future. Perhaps an understanding of how our schools affect the local public schools financially will, however, make us more understanding of their reluctance to see our schools established and expanded.

From our review of the historical development of education, we noted that in 1825 public schools were supported by only a few. By 1925 the overwhelming majority of students enrolled in school were in public schools. During that one-hundred-year span there was a gradual but definite shift away from private education in favor of public education, and in 1925 the first major test case against private education erupted in Oregon.

LEGAL PROBLEMS AFFECTING THE
FINANCING OF PRIVATE EDUCATION

The secularization of America and the secular attitudes developing are perhaps best illustrated in this first legal battle between the Roman Catholic church, private military academies, and the state of Oregon

(*Pierce v. Society of Sisters*). The state had passed legislation requiring all normal children between the ages of eight and sixteen to attend public schools. There was a substantial Roman Catholic population in the state at the time, and it had developed a number of parochial schools. These schools had neither sought nor desired state funding. They simply desired to have the freedom to operate their private schools to be consistent with their consciences. Consequently, these schools along with some independent military academies challenged the state legislature. The case made its way through the court system, and in 1925 the United States Supreme Court ruled that such legislation had the capacity to impair greatly and perhaps destroy the nonpublic schools and diminish the value of their property; thus, the legislation was unconstitutional.

In this initial test case, the courts ruled in favor of private schools. However, the following review of succeeding cases will show that the gradual shift in perspective is evident in the historical development of the judicial system. The opposition of the federal government against private schools is increasing, and unfortunately these schools can no longer rely on judicial support. An examination of the following court decisions may help those currently seeking government financial assistance to understand the pitfalls of seeking such aid. This case review will not be exhaustive, but it will represent those cases that have established important legal precedents.

Five years after *Pierce v. Society of Sisters*, another case (*Cochran v. Louisiana State Board of Education*) reached the Supreme Court. The state of Louisiana had enacted legislation providing free textbooks for all children within the state, regardless of where they attended school. This law was attacked as a violation of the Fourteenth Amendment. Opponents of the law claimed that providing textbooks for private school children was actually taking property through taxation for nonpublic purposes. The court disagreed, stating that it was the children who benefited from the legislation, not the schools. This 1930 court ruling established the "child-benefit theory," which for a number of years served as a test of the constitutionality of aid to private schools.

The next major test of public financing of private education came in 1947. The New Jersey legislation authorized local districts to make provisions for transportation of children to and from school. One local district, rather than provide transportation, decided to reimburse children within the district for the funds they spent on bus fare. This legislation excluded children attending private schools that were operating on a for-profit basis. However, those children who attended private schools operating on a nonprofit basis were reimbursed. A taxpayer challenged the constitutionality of spending public revenues to transport children to private sectarian schools (*Everson v. Board of Education*). The United States Supreme Court upheld that a program financing transportation for the students attending sectarian schools was constitutional when included in the program of reimbursement for children attending public schools.

Support for various kinds of assistance for private schools increased during the 1960s and 1970s because of the intense pressure to integrate public schools. Included in these efforts were free textbooks, either as an outright gift, as a loan, or in the form of funds to purchase them; transportation; salary supplements; funds to purchase services from the public schools; equipment and facility loans; and various forms of tax breaks for parents who sent their children to private schools. Subtler forms of aid included the sale of property, surplus buildings, and equipment at ridiculously low prices. Such attempts to support private education precipitated several court cases.

In 1968 a New York statute required local districts to lend textbooks to private schools free of charge for grades seven through twelve. A local school board challenged the legislation, but the Supreme Court ruled in favor of the private schools (*Board of Education v. Allen*). The court argued that providing textbooks for public and private schools alike was constitutional.

In 1970 the court ruled in a case that did not directly involve education but later had serious legal implications for nonprofit religious schools. New York City, as is typical of most municipalities, offered property-tax exemption to nonprofit religious, educational, and charitable institutions A real estate owner challenged the exemption, stating that such exemption forced him to be an unwilling contributor to all tax-exempt organizations. The Supreme Court disagreed, ruling that the government had not actually taken revenues and given them to these organizations but had simply chosen not to tax their property. This case, known as *Walz v. Tax Commission,* upheld the long tradition of exemption for religious and charitable organizations. The case also established another important principle—the principle of avoiding the entanglement of government and religion. In this instance the principle of separation of church and state served as a protection for the private schools. The time would come, however, when the same principle would be used as an excuse for refusing support to private education.

The following year brought another battle (*Lemon v. Kurtzman, Early v. Dicenso,* 1971). The battle began because both Pennsylvania and Rhode Island had initiated plans to improve the overall quality of education in their respective states. A Pennsylvania statute authorized the state to reimburse private schools for their expenditures for teachers' salaries, textbooks, and instructional materials for secular instruction. The same year in Rhode Island, a law was passed that provided salary supplements to attract better private-school teachers. Though both of these legislative plans carried restrictive provisions, the goal was the same in each case—to provide significant financial assistance to sectarian and nonsectarian private schools. The Supreme Court's ruling in these cases marked a turning point in the judicial attitude toward financial aid to private schools. It is interesting to note that the court used the *Walz* decision—in which it had ruled in favor of private schools—to support its decision to rule against the private schools. The court argued that excessive government entanglement would be required to monitor the provisions of the legislation; thus, the principle of the separation of church and state would be violated.

Following this decision, Pennsylvania passed new legislation. This time the court sought to provide financial aid directly to parents of children enrolled in private schools. In 1973 the Supreme Court ruled that this legislation was also unconstitutional (*Sloan v. Lemon*). In this instance the court argued that the state had selected a special group of its citizens to receive a unique benefit and that its purpose was to "advance religion."

In another 1973 case, however, the courts permitted reimbursement for certain specified services. In the *Lemon v. Kurtzman* case, commonly referred to as *Lemon II,* the court ruled that reimbursement was appropriate because the legislation had avoided excessive entanglement. Since only specified secular services were involved, no establishment of religion occurred.

Two major court decisions handed down in May of 1983—*Regan v. Taxation with Representation* and *Bob Jones University v. United States*—have the potential for significant long-term impact on Christian schools. These cases deal specifically with the attack of the Internal Revenue Service on tax-exempt organizations and are thus pertinent to a new issue Christian educators must now face. These cases will be discussed in chapter 6 because they bear directly on the tax exemption of private schools.

Grove City College, an independent Presbyterian college in Pennsylvania, and Hillsdale College, a private college in Michigan that was originally founded by Freewill Baptists and currently operates as an independent, both found government aid to students a threat to their independence. In 1984 the Supreme Court ruled (*Grove City College v. Bell*) that Grove City College was a recipient of federal funds because its students received federal grants and guaranteed loans. This decision, of course, also impacted the Hillsdale College case dealing with the same issues. An attempt to remedy the problem in Congress also failed.

In 1994 a private, parochial school in Alexandria, Virginia, faced the loss of its school lunch program, sponsored by the U.S. Department of

Agriculture, because it claimed it could not meet the needs of children requiring special education. St. Stephens and St. Agnes School had enrolled a kindergarten child with attention deficit disorder with hyperactivity. After working with the child for one year, they determined they were not able to meet his special educational needs, and reenrollment for the following year was denied. The child's parents sued the school for reinstatement and $50,000 in damages. Rather than lose the freedom to make administrative decisions concerning the school's admissions policy, the school decided to withdraw from the school lunch program and return thousands of dollars of materials and equipment received from the local school district that were purchased with money received from the U.S. Department of Education.

As a result of this controversy a number of other private schools in Virginia withdrew from the school lunch program. A survey of its membership conducted by the National Association of Independent Schools found that, in order to retain their independence, two-thirds of its 930 member schools did not accept various forms of federal funding to which they are entitled.

The court rulings of recent years have shown that government support of private sectarian education is unpredictable at best. Christian educators who rely on government funds to support their schools are relying on an uncertain source. Legislation providing assistance is always subject to challenge. Schools receiving aid risk careful government scrutiny of their procedures and challenges to their ministries that could be avoided by remaining financially independent. Furthermore, school officials face the threat of having to defend the "secular" nature of the part of their school program that receives aid. What Christian school administrator would want to be placed in the position of having to defend the idea that a portion of his program was merely secular rather than spiritual? Perhaps even worse is that a school that becomes dependent on government funds is in danger of unscriptural compromise to retain those funds.

The government has demonstrated that it will not finance what it cannot supervise, regulate, or control. We hope no one is naive enough to believe that the government will provide funds without some strings attached. The freedom to operate our schools in accordance with our conscience is more important than any amount of financial aid.

CHAPTER 6

FOR PROFIT OR NOT FOR PROFIT?

For which of you, intending to build a tower, sitteth not down first, and counteth the cost.

Luke 14:28

Historically, all levels of government have recognized certain types of organizations as exempt from taxation. They have done so in appreciation of the services these organizations provide to the general public, services that would otherwise possibly have to be provided at government expense. Traditionally, private schools have been among those recognized as eligible for tax exemption. This tax exemption was valuable for two reasons: (1) those who contributed to the schools would often benefit from doing so by a reduction of their own tax liability, and (2) the schools did not have to pay taxes on their incomes or on the value of their assets.

Initially, to be recognized as tax-exempt, an organization simply had to verify that it was organized exclusively for an approved exempt purpose. In more recent years tax exemption has been associated with public policy. Only organizations deemed to be operating in a manner consistent with well-established public policy may be recognized as worthy of this benefit.

In *Walz v. Tax Commission* (1970) the U.S. Supreme Court recognized the constitutionality of tax exemption for religious organizations when the property was "used exclusively for religious worship." The court reasoned that "few concepts are more deeply embedded in the fabric of our national life" from the colonial period of our history than tax exemption for religious institutions. The decision clearly specified that no government sponsorship occurred because tax exemption "does not transfer part of its [government] revenue to churches but simply abstains from demanding that the church support the state."

Unfortunately, there is a growing number in our society who are unwilling to accept the tax-exempt status of any organization whose activities they happen to dislike. Civil rights groups in particular have, under the guise of racial discrimination, succeeded in placing restrictions on tax exemption that traditionally would not have been considered. Unfortunately, the government has placed its stamp of approval on these proceedings by taking the position that tax exemption is a type of government aid to the institution that receives it. This was a new position, one that reversed the position previously upheld in the *Walz* case, which was verbalized for the first time by the U.S. Supreme Court in *Regan v. Taxation with Representation* (1983). The court took another giant step the following day in *Bob Jones University v. United States* (1983) when it added conformity to public policy as a condition of qualifying for tax exemption. See chapter 26 for a more detailed discussion of court cases and their impact on private schools.

These changing attitudes have caused some private school educators to reexamine tax exemption for private schools, particularly private religious schools. Even some church-schools are no longer operating on a nonprofit basis. Some have voluntarily chosen to change their status; others have been forced to do so by the Internal Revenue Service (IRS) because the schools were unwilling to change policies the IRS considered in violation of federal public policy.

WHAT IS THE GOVERNMENT'S ATTITUDE CONCERNING TAX EXEMPTION FOR PRIVATE SCHOOLS?

November 30, 1970, is significant because on this date the IRS sent its first notice to all known tax-exempt private schools, inquiring about racial restrictions in the schools' admissions policies. This inquiry was the first instance of using the IRS and the tax system as a means of advancing social policies. Reams of regulations and several court cases have followed this initial action. The IRS has now given a definitive policy outlining the requirements that will be imposed on all private schools desiring federal tax exemption. (See Publication 557, Tax-Exempt Status for Your Organization, March 2005.)

HOW DOES THIS ATTITUDE AFFECT PRIVATE SCHOOLS?

The *Regan* and *Bob Jones University* decisions and those that preceded them resulted in federal support for present IRS policies that prohibit any form of racial discrimination as they define it in any part of a school program, for any reason. These rulings have opened the door for using other civil rights legislation as a means of further restricting tax exemption. Some educational institutions sensing the likelihood of this action have already changed their internal policies. For example, in 1984 the University of Washington prohibited student organizations from excluding members or refusing to employ personnel on the basis of race, color, creed, religion, age, sex, national origin, handicap, sexual orientation, or status as a disabled veteran or Vietnam era veteran. This policy, of course prohibits a Baptist or a Catholic student organization from limiting membership or employment to those of its religious faith.

Kamehameha School in Hawaii faced the threat of losing its right to discriminate on the basis of religion in 1993 because of issues tied to the 1964 Civil Rights Act. The school was founded in the nineteenth century as a private Protestant school. The endowment providing continuing funding for the school had been given by Bernice Pauahi Bishop. She stipulated that the school must always employ Protestant teachers. When the school refused to employ a non-Protestant as a part-time language teacher because of her religion, the Equal Employment Opportunity Commission filed suit (*Kamehameha v. EEOC*) charging the school with illegal discrimination on the basis of religion. They claimed the school had ceased to be a distinctly religious school and was not entitled to the exemption permitting discrimination on the basis of religion. The ninth circuit court agreed. When the U.S. Supreme Court refused to hear the case on appeal, it affirmed the circuit court's decision. While this decision involved the EEOC rather than the IRS, the school could face a public policy that could ultimately cost it its tax exemption unless it revises its policies.

The IRS is one of a growing number of government agencies that are refusing to accept the Christian school as an integral part of the church ministry. Its publications say, "examples of organizations considered to be integrated auxiliaries of a church . . . [include] a religious school (such as a seminary). . . . However, schools of a general academic nature are not considered integrated auxiliaries since their activities can serve as the basis for exemptions, even if they are not affiliated with a church." (See Publication 557, Tax-Exempt Status for Your Organization, March 2005.) As a concession, schools below the college level are, for the time, exempt from annual filing requirements.

Many Christian schools that had originally been organized as separate institutions were, as a matter of perceived protection, brought under the umbrella of a local church during the 1970s. Unfortunately, it seems that this action did not serve to protect schools but rather to jeopardize the whole church. The presence of the school within the organizational structure of the church, in some instances, has brought the entire ministry under government scrutiny. Some churches have already been audited by the IRS as a result of the existence of their school ministry. Some churches have even lost their tax-exempt status because the school did not meet the IRS's racially nondiscriminatory admissions and internal policies standards and the church was unwilling to change them to conform to IRS expectations.

How rapidly the changes in government policies will occur, how vigorously they will be enforced, and what effect they will have on our ministries are difficult to project. It is important, however, that Christian leaders recognize that this benefit, long taken for granted as a constitutionally protected privilege, can no longer be taken for granted. Organizations that are now tax-exempt must seriously plan for the possibility of operating without tax exemption.

WHAT SHOULD BE DONE?

We are not suggesting that Christian schools currently exempt from federal income taxes should surrender that exemption. Nor are we saying that new schools should not apply for exemption. From both a legal and a constitutional perspective, lawyers agree that our ministries are entitled to these exemptions. We are advocating that all Christian educators be well informed on IRS policies and that they carefully weigh the possible future hazards the tax-exempt status may bring to the school. This is just one more reason that it might be best for all Christian schools to have their own legal identity. Then if the school loses its tax exemption, the exemption of the church would not necessarily be in jeopardy.

Important Responsibilities

Schools that choose to operate as tax-exempt organizations should be aware of their responsibilities. It is optional for churches to file for formal recognition of an exempt status. However, the IRS suggests that some churches may find it helpful to apply formally for this exemption. Conversations with IRS personnel have revealed that this may be especially valuable to independent churches that are not identified with a traditional denomination that has a well-established history.

Congress did not see fit to define the church; it just said that churches were to be exempt. Unfortunately, the IRS has not been content to accept the decision of Congress; it has taken upon itself to define what is and what is not a church for purposes of tax exemption. In 1979 the IRS published a list of fourteen characteristics (see Publication 557) it proposed to use to determine whether a church was in fact a church. That list created such a furor that the next revision of the publication omitted the fourteen points; however, the IRS did retain the right to determine what is and what is not a church. Subsequently, these fourteen points found their way back into IRS guidelines (Figure 6.1). A quick review of these points will demonstrate their subjectivity and general inadequacy to delineate between bona fide churches and sham organizations that profit from loopholes in the tax structure.

Of great concern to Christians is the fact that the IRS has been used as an instrument of social engineering. In 1970 the IRS declared that discriminating on the basis of race in admissions policies was a violation of federal public policy. Schools that continued such discrimination were faced with the loss of their tax-exempt status. In 1975 the IRS ruled that its policy applied to all schools, including those operated as part of a church. Failure of the church-schools to adopt acceptable policies would result in the loss of tax exemption for the church. In 1978 the IRS announced proposed rules that would have extended the arm of the IRS into virtually every internal policy of schools, including church-schools, under the guise of regulating the admissions policies. Particularly devastating was the IRS's assumption that the suspect organization was guilty until proven innocent. This procedure and a similar revision announced in 1979 were set aside after extensive lobbying by concerned Christians all over the country.

FIGURE 6.1

INTERNAL REVENUE SERVICE CRITERIA
TO DEFINE CHURCHES

1. A distinct legal existence
2. A recognized creed and form of worship
3. A definite and distinct ecclesiastical government
4. A formal code of doctrine and discipline
5. A distinct religious history
6. A membership not associated with any other church or denomination
7. An organization of ordained ministers
8. Ordained ministers selected after completing prescribed courses of study
9. A literature of its own
10. Established places of worship
11. Regular congregations
12. Regular religious services
13. Sunday schools for the religious instruction of the young
14. Schools for the preparation of its ministers

Independent schools must file separately for recognition of the exempt status on Form 1023, Application for Recognition of Exemption Under Section 501(c)(3) of the Internal Revenue Code (Department of the Treasury, Internal Revenue Service, June 2006). This filing must be made within fifteen months of the inception of the organization if it is to be treated as exempt for the entire period of its existence. Schools applying for recognition of tax exemption will be asked to provide the following information:

1. The racial composition of the student body and of the faculty and administrative staff as of the current academic year

2. The amount of scholarship and loan funds, if any, awarded to the students enrolled and the racial composition of students who have received such awards

3. A list of the school's incorporators, founders, board members, and donors of land or buildings, whether individuals or organizations

4. A statement indicating whether any of the organizations described in item (3) above have an objective of maintaining segregated public or private school education at the time the application is filed and, if so, a statement indicating whether any of the individuals described in item (3) are officers or active members of such organizations at the time the application is filed

5. The year the school was organized

6. The public school district and county in which the school is located

Private schools have specific record-keeping requirements that must be available for IRS review upon demand. (See Publication 557, Tax-Exempt Status for Your Organization, March 2005.) They must maintain the following:

1. Records indicating the racial composition of the student body, faculty, and administrative staff for each academic year

2. Records sufficient to document that scholarship and other financial assistance is awarded on a racially nondiscriminatory basis

3. Copies of all materials used by or on behalf of the school to solicit contributions

4. Copies of all brochures, catalogs, and advertising dealing with student admissions, programs, and scholarships

Both independent schools and church-related schools must certify annually that they operate in a racially nondiscriminatory manner. (See Publication 557, Tax-Exempt Status for Your Organization, March 2005.) Independent schools must certify this on their annual information return (Form 990), and church-related schools must certify this with Form 5578, Annual Certification of Racial Nondiscrimination for a Private School Exempt from Federal Income Tax.

The IRS occasionally requires churches to submit to detailed internal audits, which some are strenuously resisting. The supposed purpose is to determine if an organization claiming to be a church is in fact a church as defined by the IRS. The courts have already ruled that the IRS has the authority to make audits and, in at least one instance, have ordered a bank to give agents the financial records of the church.

An extremely dangerous legal philosophy utilized currently is the idea that in those cases where constitutional amendments appear to contradict one another, the more recent amendment takes precedence. For years the Bill of Rights was considered as much a part of the Constitution as the seven original articles themselves. An example of the new thinking is found once again in the IRS attitude toward the Sixteenth Amendment, which established the income tax. The organization's position is that since the Sixteenth Amendment does not contain an exemption for churches, the exemption currently in force is simply a statute. Traditionally, Americans have believed that the First Amendment prohibited the government from taxing the church.

Before making a decision about being a tax-exempt or for-profit school, individuals responsible for the decision would be wise to discuss their options with an attorney and/or CPA well acquainted with regulations applying to tax-exempt organizations, particularly churches and schools.

CHAPTER 7

FUNDING CHRISTIAN EDUCATION

> For which of you, intending to build a tower, sitteth not down first, and counteth the cost, whether he have sufficient to finish it? Lest haply, after he hath laid the foundation, and is not able to finish it, all that behold it begin to mock him, Saying, this man began to build, and was not able to finish.
>
> **Luke 14:28–30**

One of the grim realities of Christian education is that it is expensive. The small size of the typical school works against its economical operation. Consequently, a well-planned financial program is essential. To establish such a program, administrators and pastors must first be aware of their available resources. At present there are six primary sources of revenue available to Christian schools:

1. Tuition and fees common to all students

2. Fees for special activities common to all students participating

3. Gifts

4. Church supplements

5. Fundraising projects (other than gifts)

6. Government assistance (all levels)

TUITION AND REGULAR FEES

The most common and certainly the largest single source of income for most private schools is tuition. Tuition is charged to the parents of children attending the school and usually provides for teachers' salaries, general personnel expenses, instructional materials and equipment, general maintenance and operational costs, building and ground maintenance, expansion programs, and similar expenses for services used by all students.

In addition to the general tuition, private schools have also traditionally had specific fees to cover basic administrative costs associated with
student recruitment and reenrollment. These fees include application
fees (often referred to as enrollment, reenrollment, or matriculation fees)
and book rental or supply fees.

FEES FOR SPECIAL ACTIVITIES

Certain services and activities offered by the Christian school are relevant only to certain students. For example, not all students use the
school's transportation and food services. Nor do all students use the lab
equipment and the computers. Instruction in art, music, and physical
education usually also apply to only a few students. Generally only those
who participate in these activities and use these services are charged for
them. Some schools also charge special fees for those participating in extracurricular activities or, instead of special charges, require that students
provide their own uniforms and/or equipment. Such charges for special
activities are normally made on a one-time, first-of-the-year basis. Some
charges are made on a semester-by-semester basis. This is especially true
if the fee is a substantial amount.

GIFTS

Virtually all Christian schools receive some gift income, but for most the
amount is not a significant portion of their budget. The amount received
varies, depending largely on the school leaders' attitudes toward gift income—primarily the pastor's in a church-school and the administrator's
in an independent school.

Generally it is easier to obtain gifts for special school projects rather
than for support of the general budget. For example, parents, other relatives of students, and friends of the school, who would not necessarily
make general undesignated gifts, may readily give funds for a new building, for new library books, or for new science laboratory equipment.

Gift income could also be considered as a source of income for scholarships for needy families. Few Christian schools have a parent constituency so affluent that there are no needy families in their ranks. Many

Christian school administrators struggle each year with how to handle families who are unable to meet their financial obligations to the school. These funds should not come from a school's general revenues. If these funds are used for scholarships, the school is forcing parents to subsidize the tuition and fees of other students. A good solution is scholarship or tuition loan funds obtained from other sources. Supporters of the school can often be successfully encouraged to give to programs designed to aid needy families. Generally, independent schools are more successful in raising scholarship funds. Church-schools might consider including scholarships in its benevolence funding in the regular budget, at least for its own families.

Most Christian schools are church-schools. These schools usually do not have large gift incomes. It is not because they have no need of gifts or because they deliberately discourage such giving. The reason is that it is difficult to generate gifts for the school without having a negative effect on the other church programs that are dependent solely on gift income. The pastor must give clear direction in this area. Of course, those who benefit from the church-school should be encouraged to support the school financially. It may be possible to develop gift support over a period of time, but to do so will require patience and hard work.

Failure to recognize the value of gifts to the school is shortsightedness on the part of parents. Tuition and fees are not deductible for income tax purposes; gifts to a nonprofit organization are deductible. Schools that generate substantial gift incomes are in a position to charge appreciably less tuition. School administrators would be wise to point out this advantage to school parents. Unfortunately, few parents have yet been convinced of the long-term value of supporting the school through gifts. Consequently, church-school leaders should recognize that gift income will not likely be a significant portion of the church-school's budget.

Unlike the church-school, the independent school has a greater need and a greater freedom to pursue gift income. Such schools usually have a broader and more loyal constituency than the local church-schools. Alumni of independent schools seem to retain more of an attachment to their school, and this loyal attitude shows itself in greater financial support.

CHURCH SUPPLEMENTS

Christian schools are frequently the recipients of aid from local churches in the community, either the church actually sponsoring the school or churches in the community sending substantial numbers of students to the school. Though sometimes this support is given in cash, oftentimes it is given in less tangible forms. The following are a few examples of less tangible support: free facilities or greatly reduced rental rates; free or subsidized utilities and maintenance; and custodial, secretarial, or other personnel help at no charge or at substantially reduced rates.

There are many appropriate ways in which the local church can aid the Christian school. Those that can afford to do so should plan to include the school in their regular budget and designate a specific amount of the support the school can count on receiving throughout the year. This approach is not inconsistent with the position taken in chapter 2. Though the primary responsibility of Christian education rests with the parents, it is not inappropriate for the church to financially supplement the program. Indeed, it may be argued that the church has some responsibility to assist in the education of young people (Matt. 28:19–20), especially since the goal of Christian education is to conform students to the image of Christ. Such education involves indoctrinating young people in the Christian faith and teaching them essential facts that will help them develop suitable values.

The role of the church, however, must be a secondary role and should be carefully planned. Many churches make significant contributions to the school each year out of necessity. For example, when a school is without resources and in debt at the end of a year, the church may feel compelled to assume the debt for the sake of testimony. This is not what is meant by church supplements.

It is only logical for churches that have a school as part of their ministry to make a regular contribution to its support. In fact, it would be difficult to support the position that the school is part of its ministry if the church has no part in the financial support. How much support the church gives to its school is dependent on many factors. Several of them will be examined here.

The level of appropriate support depends somewhat on the age, the size, and the overall financial stability of the church. Few churches would want a Christian school to become the only part or even the most significant part of their overall ministry. Church leaders must, therefore, see that church supplements do not become the financial foundation of the school. Of necessity, a new school will normally require more support from the sponsoring church at the outset. In this case the church should carefully assess the needs of the new school and make the necessary sacrifice to get the ministry launched. As the school grows, however, the financial responsibility should be shifted primarily to the parents.

Some churches may decide that one of their major emphases will be Christian education and will thus determine to continue making a major investment in the school even after it has stabilized. Nothing is wrong with this approach if it is the result of careful deliberation and is a church-wide commitment.

Another approach some have taken is to operate the school on a tuition-free basis. This idea was quite popular for a time, but its practical application has many difficulties. The idea is based on the assumption that if the church is going to operate the school, it should operate it as it operates any other program. They reason that if the church does not charge for other ministries, it should not charge for the school. In many cases these churches calculate their cost in providing education and then ask the parents to contribute at least that amount to the church over and above their regular church giving. Some review church records regularly to insure that contributions at least match educational costs. Parents who are not contributing at least the minimum requested may be asked to withdraw their children.

One problem with this approach is that the IRS frowns on tuition-free schools. Initially the IRS viewed this arrangement as tuition laundering and refused to recognize the parents' gifts until the amount exceeded the value of the education received. The IRS has agreed to consider these plans on an individual basis and make individual rulings on their acceptability. Any church-school desiring to operate on a tax-exempt basis with no tuition would be wise to contact the District Director of Internal Revenue and ask for specific guidance. Only when strict and narrowly interpreted rules are followed is this procedure acceptable. If the premise is accepted that education is primarily the responsibility of the parents, this approach would not seem to be tenable.

The independent school and the church-school have a somewhat different relationship with the local church. Since the church does have a role in Christian education, it is entirely appropriate for local churches whose memberships are served by an independent school, or several schools, to have a regular part in their support. The support may be direct aid as regular cash gifts, or it may be given as services or facilities even as is typically done with church-related schools.

Many independent schools are housed in churches that consider it a part of their ministry to provide facilities to the independent school without charge or at considerably reduced rent. Likewise, utilities may be provided by the host church, church buses may be used for transportation, members of the church staff may be made available to the school without charge, and so on. Churches whose members are served by independent schools should consider having a substantial investment in the ministry of the independent school.

FUNDRAISING

Another major source of revenue for some Christian schools is fundraising, that is, selling a product or service for a profit. Schools of five to six hundred students have been known to make more than $50,000 in a single fundraising effort. This amount is obviously not the average, but it is exemplary of the potential that fundraising holds for those willing to discipline themselves to the task.

Christian leaders should recognize, however, that fundraising can have a negative effect on the school during the activity. A serious fundraising effort is both demanding and time consuming for faculty, parents, and students. The benefits to be gained must be weighed in terms of their real cost, not just net cash after expenses. Some fundraising efforts can even be life threatening. For example, a middle Georgia church-school conducted a jog-a-thon. The pastor, who was in late middle age and not in good physical condition, felt compelled to take a lead in the activity. He overexerted, had a heart attack, and nearly died. The money gained would hardly have been worth this pastor's life.

Carefully planned, well-managed fundraising activities can be successful and can result in greatly needed funds for the school. Students may also profit by working together toward a common goal. Likewise, fundraising can often unify the faculty, staff, parents, and students in a way not experienced previously. For some schools it seems to be the best way to obtain large sums of money in a short period of time.

There are several reputable fundraising companies that specialize in directing school programs. An excellent selection of products and services are available for use in Christian-school fundraising that do not in any way compromise the testimony of church or school. If you decide to use this method of raising funds, choose an established firm that has a good track record for working with Christian schools. Check their references carefully.

Another significant factor to consider is how the money that is raised will be used. Most Christian leaders see a difference between raising money for some student activity, like a senior trip, and raising money to pay teachers salaries or to retire old debts. Many who would object to fundraising for the general budget would not object to helping with student-oriented activities.

Another type of fundraising activity emphasizes various programs that encourage people to give money to the school. Frankly, this straightforward approach to fundraising is the most practical. The object of fundraising is always money. However, some schools attempt to hide that objective behind a scheme to offer a product or service for a fee. Usually the product or service is greatly overpriced, but people overlook that because of the cause. Why not simply state the need and ask people to give the money you need in exchange for a tax-deductible receipt? If parents considered the actual cost of many of the fundraising activities they have supported, they would realize giving a cash gift would be much more beneficial to the school and less strain on the family. When large sums of money are needed for major capital projects, there are fundraising companies available to help the school put together an efficient capital campaign. Well-planned banquets for the specific purpose of raising money have been very effective for some schools.

One other essential consideration when planning a fundraising activity is the position of the pastor and the congregation toward such a project. Fundraising poses convictional problems for some, especially when the school is a ministry of a local church. These objections cannot be taken lightly. If fundraising is considered a revenue producer in your school, be certain to give the matter of convictions thorough consideration before entering into it. Not only should the convictions of the pastor, the school's leaders, and the congregation be considered but also the attitudes of the entire school constituency.

GOVERNMENT ASSISTANCE

In preceding chapters the issue of receiving direct government aid for Christian schools was discussed. For the last several years, however, there has been increasing pressure to provide government aid indirectly through the parents of children attending private schools. Frustrated by the myriad of legal difficulties associated with direct aid to schools, various groups have sought to relieve this financial burden by providing assistance directly to the parents. It would be difficult to assess the consensus on the issue because it changes frequently, depending on the specific characteristics of the legislation under consideration. Tuition tax credits and vouchers are two of the most frequently considered methods of providing this assistance.

Under a voucher plan, usually the state government provides a voucher, in effect a negotiable instrument of a specified value that can be used to "purchase" education at the school of the parent's choice. Under the tuition-tax-credit approach, either the state or the federal government would allow an income tax credit to the parents up to an agreed maximum per child to offset the tuition expense incurred in sending their children to a private school or a public school requiring payments. The plan seems innocent enough. Many sincere Christian leaders believe it should be possible to enable parents of private school children to receive relief in some form. And indeed it is reasonable to assume that position. The secular mind is not reasonable, however. The lessons of recent history are clear. The government cannot be relied on to finance private schools, particularly religious schools, without conditions unacceptable to fundamentalist, Bible-believing Christians. The government's previous actions confirm that whatever one gets, whatever form it comes in, it is not worth it. There is no free lunch!

The following excerpt from *The Baltimore Sun*, August 19, 1975, reported in the American Association of Christian Colleges' newsletter, illustrates the point effectively.

> Westminster's Western Maryland College permanently has removed all religious symbols, including crosses from atop its chapels, and has agreed to strict quotas that limit the number of Methodists on its board and teaching staff as part of settling a suit which disputed its right to get public support.
>
> The college, which formally was supported by the United Methodist Church, also has agreed "neither to sponsor nor conduct any religious services," to "remain totally neutral as to the spiritual development (in a religious sense) of its students" and not to include prayers, religious hymns or sermons in its graduation exercises.

These stipulations are part of a settlement the college made in April with the American Civil Liberties Union and Americans United for Separation of Church and State which ended three years of litigation over the college's right to get public funds.

> The two organizations maintained in the suit that Western Maryland, contrary to its contention that it severed its ties with the Methodist church, was a church-related college and should not receive public funding.

As much as we would like to see parents have an opportunity to get back some of the tax dollars they have paid for education at the private school of their choice, we do not believe government will ever permit funding of private religious schools on a long-term basis while retaining their religious distinctives. The long-term risk to our ministries is not worth the short-term gain.

CHAPTER 8

FINANCIAL MANAGEMENT

Woe unto him that buildeth his house by unrighteousness, and
his chambers by wrong; that useth his neighbor's service without wages, and giveth him not for his work.

Jeremiah 22:13

Moreover it is required in stewards, that a man be found
faithful.

1 Corinthians 4:2

It is our Christian duty to conduct the business aspect of our ministries
properly. The apostle Paul in Romans 12:11 warned believers not to be
slothful in business and the writer of Proverbs commended those who
were diligent in business (Prov. 22:29). But these are not the only passages that encourage us to be careful stewards over what God has given
us. There are twenty-seven other references to the word *business* in the
Bible. The principles in these passages confirm that how we handle our
financial affairs is an important part of our testimony.

FINANCIAL PRIORITIES

The purpose of nonprofit organizations is to serve rather than to profit.
The emphasis is not on saving money but on efficiently using the resources available to meet the total needs of the organization. In a school,
the students are the greatest concern. Schools exist for the benefit of the
students. Consequently, such groups must establish financial priorities
that will enable them to meet the needs of the students in the most effective and cost-efficient manner. Peter Drucker emphasizes this point in
the following statement:

> A managed expense budget is the area in which a business makes its
> real decisions on its objectives. No business can do everything. Even if
> it has the money, it will never have enough good people. It has to set
> priorities. . . . Setting priorities is risky. For whatever does not receive
> priority is, in effect, abandoned. There is no formula for making the

decision, but it has to be made, and the mechanism for making it is the budget. (Drucker, 1974, 119)

Drucker goes on to say that *posteriorities* are even more important than priorities. Posteriorities are those things we choose not to do or choose not to do immediately. Identifying posteriorities and sticking to them is more difficult than establishing and pursuing priorities. Posteriorities, however, are the key to effective administration.

To establish both priorities and posteriorities, we must have a thorough knowledge of the following:

1. The purpose of the ministry

2. The personnel required to conduct the ministry effectively

3. The material needs of the personnel employed

4. The resources that are required to conduct the ministry effectively

5. The resources of those responsible for financing the ministry

There is no magic formula to offer those who are responsible for establishing the final budget of a school. It is a difficult task even for the most conscientious administrator. The needs are great and the resources are limited. An understanding of the following expense areas may help an administrator to discern what God would have him do in these specific circumstances:

1. Personnel

2. Instructional program

3. Extracurricular activities

4. Physical facilities and equipment

5. Ancillary services

6. Capital improvements

Personnel

People are the real keys to success in any organization. Do not try to save money by hiring unqualified personnel. Hire the people with the training and the experience necessary to do the job. Then honor God by providing for their needs. Pay them a salary that enables them to maintain the quality of testimony you expect and provide them with reasonable employee benefits. People are our most valuable asset. Never forget "that material things come and go. They get 'used up' or 'worn out.' People stay" (Debruyn, 1976, 98).

Instructional Program

Every school has a limited amount of money to spend on instructional resources—textbooks, teacher supplies, and equipment. The dollar amount involved in these decisions is only a small portion of the typical Christian school's annual budget. However, these decisions are fundamental.

Textbooks should be selected on the basis of content, not cost. Some Christian schools elect to use secular textbooks because they are cheaper. Such schools mistakenly believe that Christian publishers are out to make profits. The truth is, however, that secular publishers can charge less because their market is much larger. A secular publisher will initially run several hundred thousand copies of a new book. The sale of these books easily covers the high costs involved in producing the book. On the other hand, the Christian publisher must cover production costs with an initial run of only a few thousand. Even with a staff working at "ministry" wages, the Christian publisher cannot financially compete with secular publishers. This fact aside, however, we must realize that money "saved" on secular textbooks is false economy. If our primary objective is to educate children for the least amount of money, we can leave them in the public schools.

Christian schools also need modern, well-maintained equipment that is readily available to teachers. We need to be cautious, however, about spending large sums of money on things that may soon become obsolete. This is a special concern with high-technology equipment such as computers and software. Advances are occurring so rapidly that even specialists are having difficulty keeping abreast of them. When purchasing such equipment, seek the counsel of others but avoid making decisions primarily on the opinions of those who have a commission depending on the decision made. They find it difficult to be totally objective. Focus on those things teachers actually need and will use. Educators do not need the very best or latest models of everything but rather need thorough preparation to do their jobs well. Christian schools should be modern and up-to-date in all areas that make a contribution to student needs, but they must remain old-fashioned in those areas where modernization threatens our philosophy or financial security.

Teachers should not be expected to purchase their own supplies. It is the school's responsibility to provide for quality instructional supplies in sufficient quantity to meet the needs of each teacher. We cannot convince parents that we are interested in quality education if the teacher-prepared materials that children take home are not legible because of poor equipment or supplies.

Extracurricular Activities

Extracurricular activities are an integral component of any school. The decision of whether to have them has already been made. It would be nearly impossible to operate any school without some provision for the extracurricular needs of its student body given the expectations of parents in our society. The decision involves what extracurricular activities will be provided and how much of the school's financial resources should be allocated to them. Unless the administration makes the correct decision, the school will inevitably commit itself to a more aggressive program than the parents are willing to support, and the school will find itself in the position of funding a disproportionate amount of the extracurricular program from its general operating revenues. There must be a good balance of opportunities for spiritual, athletic, and fine arts activities. Opportunities for involvement for both boys and girls must be provided that are consistent with the level of interest manifested and the willingness of the parents to support them.

Physical Facilities and Equipment

Education was taking place long before the first school building was designed. Some of history's most famous teachers taught without benefit of a classroom. Many of them taught under the shade of a tree or on the steps of a public building, and our Lord even taught from a borrowed boat. Even though buildings are not essential to the educational process, they have become inseparably linked to our modern educational system. And, like it or not, meeting public expectations is a major part of our testimony.

Testimony and utility are two factors we must consider in planning our facilities. Our buildings should be designed to fit the community and the site selected. They must also be serviceable. The durability, the maintenance, and the age level of those using the facility are basic considerations. Minor price cutting at the construction stage is rarely economical in the long run. To cut back at this initial stage will mean only more immediate and costly repairs.

The library is one specific educational facility that is often given little or no consideration by Christian schools. The tighter the overall budget, the more likely it is to be pushed into the background. Many Christian schools have no library or a library woefully inadequate for the student body that is enrolled. Appropriate books and materials are as important to a school as desks are to a classroom. The presence of a public library in proximity to the Christian school does not eliminate the need for a library. Public libraries do not carry the type of books or periodicals needed to support the Christian school curriculum.

The science laboratory is also an important component of a school's facility that is overlooked. No high school curriculum is complete without provision for laboratory science courses such as biology, chemistry, and physics.

Christian schools also need computer laboratories. Some schools attempt to meet their needs by having computers strategically located throughout the schools in their regular classrooms. However, even a school of modest size will find it is unable to serve its student population adequately without a lab that permits students to receive instruction on the computers as a group.

The school buildings, equipment, and grounds must be well maintained to conserve the investment of God's money that has been made in them. A maintenance program should be adequately funded so that these important components of your ministry are maintained in a manner that insures their serviceability and protects the testimony of your ministry.

Ancillary Services

Two ancillary services commonly offered by Christian schools are transportation and food service. Neither service is required for quality Christian education, and it would be wise to consider operating without them.

Transportation should be considered only where substantial numbers of students could not attend the school without a bus program. Churches with bus ministries do have the opportunity of spreading the investment in equipment over two ministries, and for them, offering this service may be more feasible. A hot-lunch program should not be offered unless the school constituency consents to pay the total cost of the program.

A third ancillary service becoming increasingly popular with Christian schools is a bookstore. A school bookstore can facilitate the purchase of textbooks and supplies for students. It can also be expanded to meet the needs of the church congregation.

Capital Improvement

Capital expenditures are those funds used for improving, replacing, or expanding facilities and major items of equipment. Since these expenditures will be discussed in detail in a later chapter, we will simply state here that money should be set aside regularly for these expenses. Schools often fail in this regard. Administrators are tempted to use such money for more "pressing" needs. However, failure to provide funds for capital improvement will inevitably bring financial strain in the long run.

BUDGETING

The budget reflects an organization's priorities. Responsibility for establishing priorities should be given to those who are acquainted with the educational process and who have the courage to make decisions in the best interest of the ministry. These decisions establish the course for the school both now and in the future.

Consequently, those who have the authority to determine the final budget will, to a great extent, determine the success or the failure of each ministry.

Every organization should have a financial plan that realistically details projected income and expenses. The Christian school is no exception. The U.S. Office of Education defines a budget in the following manner:

> A school budget is an official statement of the anticipated revenues and expenditures of the school district for a definite period. Through the budget the board of education, the school administration, and the people in the community reach agreement on the financing of the educational program. In other words, the annual budget is the educational plan of a school district for a school year expressed in dollars and cents. (Adams et al, 1967, 37)

A budget will assist the school in maintaining maximum utility of its financial resources. Properly prepared, the Christian school budget is a realistic projection of both anticipated income and anticipated expenses over a specified period of time, usually one academic year. It is not uncommon for larger schools to develop financial projections for up to five-year periods.

There are several different types of budgets designed to meet the unique needs of varying kinds of organizations. Three of the most common approaches to budgeting are known as the following: incremental budgeting, program budgeting, and zero-base budgeting (Vargo, *Church Guide to Planning and Budgeting*, 1995).

Incremental budgeting, sometimes referred to as line-item or traditional budgeting, is based on a review of historical data. This is probably the most common approach to budgeting in Christian work. One of the basic assumptions is that what has been done in the past is essentially what should be done in the future. Numbers are adjusted to reflect the uniqueness of the new year's activities and to cover the cost of inflation.

Program budgeting focuses on the various activities of the organization and provides a logical way for those who are most knowledgeable about the activities to have planning input. This approach is more likely to be influenced by appropriate consideration of goals and objectives unique to that component of the organization.

Zero-base budgeting gained some popularity as a result of the emphasis of former president Jimmy Carter. Zero-base budgeting requires the justification of each item in the budget every year. Unless the item can be justified, it is not funded. One of the disadvantages to zero-base budgeting is the time and expense required to prepare the budget each year.

Which approach to budgeting will be best for your organization? The choice must be determined by a careful consideration of the nature of your organization and its strengths and weaknesses. No one approach is best for everyone. Nor is it necessary to limit yourself to just one approach. Good points from each can be utilized to formulate your own budget process.

To assist the organization in reaching its objectives, the budget must be flexible; it is not a straitjacket. There are good reasons for modifying and, in some cases, even setting aside the most carefully prepared budget. Remember that the primary purpose in the budget process is to reconcile an organization's resources and needs. Since there are almost always more needs than apparent resources, the budget process becomes one of establishing priorities. Those responsible for preparing the budget are remiss in their duties if they fail to make budget decisions based upon the capability of the requested items to fulfill instructional objectives. Lay people in the church, often unaccustomed to thinking in these terms, will need an explanation.

Formats

The purpose of an accounting system is to provide the data necessary to manage the financial resources of the organization and to provide basic information to others who require it. A chart of accounts enables the organization to organize its income and expenses in logical units so that the information is useful. Individual schools may need to make some adjustments to make this format useful to them.

Figures 8.1 and 8.2 provide a listing of account descriptions that may be used as a format for the budget and the school accounting system. (See Appendix C for further explanation.) Figure 8.1 shows how to summarize anticipated receipts and disbursements by major headings. Figure 8.2 provides the detailed breakdown for disbursements under each of these headings. Though this plan was developed for a church-school, it could easily be modified to meet the needs of the independent school.

FIGURE 8.1

CHART OF ACCOUNTS FOR INCOME
AND A SUMMARY OF EXPENSES

Income

001   Tuition, fees, and other charges for student services

002   Unearned tuition, fees, and other charges for student services

003   Food service

004   Interest

005   Sales of promotional material

006   Loan proceeds

007   Sales of school assets

008   Gifts and pledges

009   Athletic activities

010   Fine arts activities

011   Yearbook

012   Other student activities

015   Total income

Expenses

030   Administration

040   Instruction

050   Extracurricular activities

060   Maintenance and operation

070   Food service

080   Transportation

090   Fixed charges

100   Capital outlay

110   Debt service

120   Depreciation (for those on an accrual accounting basis)

150   Total expenses

FIGURE 8.2

EXPENDITURES DETAILED

016	Payroll	051	Payroll
017	Administrative travel	052	Maintenance of buildings
018	Legal service	053	Maintenance of equipment
019	Office expense	054	Utilities
020	Advertising	056	M & O equipment
021	Promotional materials	**060**	**Maintenance and operation**
022	Recruiting		
023	Office equipment	061	Payroll
024	Office equipment repair	062	Food
025	Membership in professional	063	Equipment
	organizations	**070**	**Food service**
030	**Administration**		
		071	Payroll
031	Payroll	072	Purchase of vehicles
032	Textbooks	073	Lease of vehicles
033	Library	074	Maintenance of vehicles
034	Teaching supplies	075	Fuel and lubricants
035	Educational grants/loans	076	Insurance
036	In-service training	**080**	**Transportation**
037	Membership in professional		
	organizations	081	Employee insurance
038	Health service	082	Student insurance
040	**Instruction**	083	Property/liability insurance
		084	Taxes/licenses
041	Payroll	085	Employee expense
042	Athletics	**090**	**Fixed charges**
043	Extension ministries		
044	Fine arts	091	Site improvements
045	Yearbook	092	Remodeling of facilities
046	Other student activities	093	Equipment (other than office,
050	**Extracurricular activities**		M & O, and transportation)
		100	**Capital outlay**

110 Debt Service

120 Depreciation (accrual system)

150 Total Income

A simple form of numbering for this chart of accounts starts with 001 and runs through 015 for income, and begins with 016 and runs through 150 for expenses. It is a good idea to leave several numbers unassigned at the end of each category when the accounting program is initially set up so that if it becomes necessary to add account numbers, it will not be necessary to renumber the other items in the chart of accounts. This procedure will be especially helpful as a history of financial information is developed over a period of years. If the school has existed for a period of time but has not had a budget, you can develop one by using the financial history provided by previous financial statements.

Regular Budget

One of the best sources of information to prepare the initial budget for a new school will be administrators from other Christian schools of a size similar to the one you are starting. Most Christian school personnel will be willing to help those beginning a new school because, almost without exception, they are indebted to others who helped them begin their ministries.

Preparing a budget for an existing school is time consuming, but it is not complicated. The school simply reviews past financial data and adjusts these data to accommodate anticipated changes. As much as 80 percent of the budget is usually designated for personnel expenses. These expenses are not difficult to project accurately. The remaining budget categories may be slightly more difficult, but certainly not impossible. Later in this chapter, step-by-step guidelines will be given to help in planning a school's budget.

Establishing a budget is more difficult for a new school. The first step in actual budget planning for the new school is the most difficult: accurately estimating the number of students who will enroll per grade level. Next, set up the budget by specific categories that would include a breakdown of both expenses and projected income. These categories are then combined into a chart of accounts.

Whether budgeting for a new or an existing school, an administrator should first estimate the expense of operating your school. Do not attempt to project anticipated income and then make the expenses fit the income. It may be necessary to adjust anticipated expenses in line with anticipated income at some point in the budget process, but that is not how to start.

Remember—the budget expresses the educational plan in dollars and cents. This should be based on the best estimate of what personnel, the instructional program, extracurricular activities, physical facilities and equipment, ancillary services, and capital improvements will cost.

The purpose of budgeting is not to save money but to allocate it properly so that the institution's objectives may be realized. Too many people confuse budgeting with money-saving activities. We have a responsibility to provide the best Christian educational program as economically as possible. This is not the same, however, as coming up with a budget reflecting the smallest possible expenditures for the year.

The following steps for setting up a budget are a good guide for all schools. Specific guidelines are presented for establishing an expense budget and for setting up an income budget.

Expense Budget

1. Determine the total enrollment and the enrollment for each grade level to be offered.

2. Determine the number of personnel that will be required to meet the needs of these students (administrative staff, instructional staff, clerical staff, maintenance and operation personnel, custodial staff, and ancillary staff).

3. Estimate the cost of the salary and benefit program for the various types of personnel to be employed.

4. Calculate the employer's share of taxes on his employees (FICA, unemployment, and workers' compensation fund or insurance).

5. Estimate the expenses to be incurred in the other categories of the budget, on an item-by-item basis.

6. Increase the expense-budget total (exclusive of salaries and fringe benefits) by 10 to 15 percent to cover errors, unforeseen expenditures, and cost increases.

Income Budget

1. Decide what portion of the budget is going to be borne by those receiving the benefit and what portion will be borne by others.

2. Decide how the expense to be borne by those receiving the benefit will be divided among them (level tuition, discounted tuition—if discounts are to be given, on what basis and in what amounts they are to be given, whether the total expenses of the school will be borne by all students alike or whether some effort will be made to distribute charges to those who actually benefit from them).

3. Decide how the money to be raised outside the parent constituency is to be raised (gifts, church supplements, endowments, grants, etc.).

Once the amount needed to be raised by tuition is determined, it is fairly simple to establish the tuition levels required to generate the desired income. Figures 8.3 and 8.4 give two mathematical formulas for calculating tuition. One illustrates discounted tuition based on a percentage of the base tuition; the other illustrates discounted tuition on a flat dollar amount reduction from the base tuition.

Figure 8.5 is a sample budget for a typical church-school of seven hundred students offering kindergarten through grade twelve. Be careful, however, not to take this or any other numerical data from a model budget as the basis for an actual school budget. The numbers are only for illustration. No two schools are exactly alike; therefore, no two school budgets will be exactly alike. It is impossible to prepare a sound budget for a school without being thoroughly familiar with the school's activities and operational history. Whether your school is smaller or larger, the basic principles of budgeting do not change.

FIGURE 8.3

MATHEMATICAL FORMULAS FOR CALCULATING DIFFERENT LEVELS OF TUITION

Many schools have different levels of tuition for families with more than one child enrolled in the school or for different grade levels within the school. The differences are usually reflected in percentages or in flat dollar amounts. Once you have determined the total amount of income you need to develop, the formulas below will enable you to establish quickly the appropriate tuition.

Percentage Basis: $N_1t + N_2 (\%t) + N_3 (\%t) = B$	**Example:**
B = Budget	B = \$2,500,000
N_1 = Number of students at the first level of tuition	N_1 = 760 students
N_2 = Number of students at the second level of tuition	N_2 = 325 students
N_3 = Number of students at the third level of tuition	N_3 = 115 students
t = Base tuition	
% = Percentage of base tuition desired	

The levels of tuition desired are 100% for the first level, 90% for the second level, and 70% for the third level.

$760t + 325(90\%t) + 115(70\%t) = 2{,}500{,}000$
$760t + (325 \times .90)t + (115 \times .70)t = 2{,}500{,}000$
$760t + 292.5t + 80.5t = 2{,}500{,}000$
$(760 + 292.5 + 80.5)t = 2{,}500{,}000$
$1133t = 2{,}500{,}000$
$t = 2{,}206.531$
$t = 2{,}206.531 \times 760 =$ $1{,}676{,}963.56$
$90\%t = 1{,}990 \times 325 =$ $645{,}410.35$
$70\%t = 1{,}545 \times 115$ $177{,}625.78$
$\overline{\phantom{2{,}499{,}999.69}}$
$2{,}499{,}999.69$

The above calculations have given us tuition levels that develop total income within 31¢ of the desired budget income. Some adjustment of these figures is desirable to make them easier to work with throughout the year. The annual tuition could be divided by the number of months in the payment year and rounded to the nearest dollar evenly divisible by that number. If your school is on a 10-payment plan, the tuition could be rounded to even numbers as follows:

t = 2,210 x 760 =	1,679,600	
90%t = 1,990 x 325 =	646,750	
70%t = 1,545 x 115 =	177,615	
	2,504,025	

FIGURE 8.4

MATHEMATICAL FORMULAS FOR CALCULATING DIFFERENT LEVELS OF TUITION

Different Levels of Tuition (fixed dollar basis)

Fixed Amount Basis: $N_1 t + N_2 (t - \$_1) + N_3(t - \$_2) = B$	**Example:**
B = Budget	B = 2,500,000
N_1 = Number of students at first level of tuition	N_1 = 760 students
N_2 = Number of students at second level of tuition	N_2 = 325 students
N_3 = Number of students at third level of tuition	N_3 = 115 students
t = Base tuition	
$ = Amount of reduction from base	

The levels of tuition desired are base tuition for the first level of student, base minus $100 for the second level of student, and base minus $200 for third level of student.

$$760t + 325(t - \$100) + 115(t - \$200) = 2{,}500{,}000$$

$$760t + (325t - 32{,}500) + (115t - 23{,}000) = 2{,}500{,}000$$

$$(760 + 325 + 115)t - (32{,}500 + 23{,}000) = 2{,}500{,}000$$

$$1{,}200t - \$55{,}500 = 2{,}500{,}000$$

$$1{,}200t = 2{,}555{,}500$$

$$t = 2{,}129.58$$

$$t - \$100 = 2{,}029.58$$

$$t - \$200 = 1{,}929.58$$

$t = 2{,}129.58 \times 760 =$	1,618,480.80
$t - \$100 = 2{,}029.58 \times 325 =$	659,613.50
$t - \$200 = 1{,}929.58 \times 115 =$	221,901.70
	2,499,996.00

$t = 2{,}130 \times 760 =$	1,618,800
$t - \$100 = 2{,}030$	659,750
$t - \$200 = 1{,}930$	221,950
	2,500,500

As in the previous example, rounding may be expedient to obtain levels of tuition that are easier to work with.

Cash-Flow Budget

As important as the regular budget is, a cash-flow budget may be more important. Many schools have confidently started a fiscal year with a carefully balanced budget only to find that they are short of cash three or four months into the year. Their error was not in miscalculating their income and expenses but rather in failing to consider the timing of these factors.

Few organizations have income and expenses evenly distributed throughout the year. Unless the school makes the right decisions, its income will run consistently behind its expenses much of the year. A school usually has heavier expenses at the beginning of the year; these expenses level off as the year progresses. A private school's income can be fairly even if it is collected as billed. If its collection procedures are poor, it will be in serious trouble no later than November 1 of the school year.

Figure 8.6 provides a sample cash-flow budget showing how the income and expenses might be distributed over the course of a typical school year. By utilizing the data from Figure 8.5, this figure will help you see the importance of having some fees come due early in the year. The surplus of funds it generates will help balance the difference between regular income and expenses. Money collected for registration fees and supply fees at the beginning of the year help build up this surplus. The first monthly installment for tuition should be due at least thirty days before the first regular payroll. This approach is based on the assumption that no more than 5 percent of the tuition and fees billed will remain unpaid at the end of any month and that all other income will follow the pattern of previous years. Figure 8.7 provides a detailed explanation of some of the assumptions on which the cash-flow budget is calculated and an explanation of the various components of the budget.

Budget Revisions

Once the budget has been prepared and properly approved, it is not to be set aside and viewed as the Law of the Medes and the Persians. The budget is to be a guide and should be referred to continuously throughout the school year. There are at least two specific times when the budget should be reevaluated—at the end of the current school year and at the beginning of the next school year. By the end of May, most schools have a reasonably accurate picture of what their enrollment for the coming year will be. Since Christian schools are tuition driven, changes in enrollment, whether up or down, are very important in the budget process.

FIGURE 8.5

SAMPLE ANNUAL SCHOOL BUDGET

Income

001	Tuition	$1,450,000
002	Unearned tuition and other fees	$0
003	Food service	$62,500
004	Interest	$2,500
005	Sale of promotional material	$125,000
006	Loan proceeds	$54,250
007	Sale of school assets	$0
008	Gifts and pledges	$50,000
009	Athletic activities	$9,000
010	Fine arts activities	$5,000
011	Yearbook	$13,750
012	Other student activities	$0
015	Total income	$1,772,000

Expenses

030	Administration	$375,500
040	Instruction	$512,500
050	Extracurricular activities	$50,000
060	Maintenance and operation	$62,500
070	Food service	$62,500
080	Transportation	$162,500
090	Fixed charges	$162,500
100	Capital outlay	$65,000
110	Debt service	$160,000
120	Depreciation	$157,500
150	Total expenses	$1,770,500

The budget must be flexible, however, because of the many variables in school administration that are unique to individual schools. No fixed formula can be given for making budget adjustments. Some general guidelines may be helpful. Increases in enrollment are the easiest to deal with from the standpoint of the budget. If sufficiently more students are enrolled, then the school will need to hire additional staff, purchase more textbooks and supplies, obtain more furniture, and in extreme cases consider finding additional classroom space by renting another facility or using a temporary building. Generally tuition and fees from the additional students will pay for the additional expenses.

Reductions in enrollment are not as easy to handle but are more important considerations than increases because you may find yourself unable to fund the commitments made in your budget. Unless judicious reductions are made in a timely manner, you will face a shortfall of revenue that will put you in the position of having to borrow money or leave bills unpaid.

Reductions in enrollment must be evaluated carefully. Is the reduction a general one in which your losses are spread evenly across the grade levels, making it difficult, if not impossible, to reduce costs by reducing your staff? If this is true, consider reductions in other areas such as capital improvements that can be reduced in scope or delayed indefinitely. If the reduction is isolated within a grade where multiple sections are offered, consider eliminating a section of a grade, even if it means having more students in a class than you actually want to have. If the school does not have multiple sections but enrollment changes are in two classes such as fifth and sixth grade, it may be necessary to combine these classes with one teacher to reduce expenses. A teacher contract should always make it possible for either party to cancel the contract with thirty days notice and with the school providing thirty days salary in lieu of notice. No school administrator would want to exercise this option, but it would be more honorable to notify a teacher at the beginning of the year that circumstances beyond his control made this necessary than to proceed through the year and then not be able to pay the salary earned when due.

FIGURE 8.6

SAMPLE CASH-FLOW BUDGET

Income

	July	Aug.	Sept.	Oct.	Nov.	Dec.
001	$62,000	$222,500	$115,000	$115,000	$115,000	$115,000
002						
003				$7,000	$7,000	$7,000
004						
005					$125,000	
006			$54,250			
007						
008						
009				$1,000	$1,000	$1,000
010						$2,500
011						
012						
015	$62,000	$222,500	$169,250	$123,000	$248,000	$125,500
	$188,180	$410,680	$579,930	$702,930	$950,930	$1,076,430

Expenses

	July	Aug.	Sept.	Oct.	Nov.	Dec.
030	$50,000	$74,000	$38,500	$38,500	$38,500	$38,500
040	$2,500	$12,500	$57,500	$57,500	$37,700	$37,700
050	$0	$1,250	$4,875	$4,875	$4,875	$4,875
060	$5,000	$5,000	$5,000	$5,000	$5,000	$5,000
070	$0	$1,000	$6,500	$6,500	$6,500	$6,500
080	$5,000	$12,500	$14,500	$14,500	$14,500	$14,500
090	$12,500	$12,500	$12,500	$12,500	$12,500	$12,500
100	$5,000	$25,000	$12,500	$12,500	$0	$0
110	$13,333	$13,333	$13,333	$13,333	$13,333	$13,333
150	$93,333	$157,083	$165,208	$165,208	$132,908	$132,908
	$93,333	$250,416	$415,624	$580,832	$713,740	$846,648

Income

	Jan.	Feb.	Mar.	Apr.	May	June
001	$115,000	$115,000	$115,000	$115,000	$115,000	$130,000
002			$25,000	$12,500	$12,500	$12,500
003	$7,000	$7,000	$7,000	$7,000	$7,000	$6,500
004						$2,500
005						
006						
007						
008	$37,500					$12,500
009	$1,000	$1,000	$1,000	$1,000	$1,000	$1,000
010					$2,500	
011				$13,750		
012						
015	**$160,500**	**$123,000**	**$148,000**	**$149,250**	**$138,000**	**$165,000**
	$1,236,930	$1,359,930	$1,507,930	$1,657,180	$1,795,180	$1,960,180

Expenses

	Jan.	Feb.	Mar.	Apr.	May	June
030	$38,500	$38,500	$38,500	$38,500	$38,500	$38,500
040	$37,700	$37,700	$37,700	$37,700	$37,700	$37,700
050	$4,875	$4,875	$4,875	$19,875	$4,875	$4,875
060	$5,000	$5,000	$5,000	$5,000	$5,000	$7,500
070	$6,500	$6,500	$6,500	$6,500	$6,500	$3,000
080	$14,500	$14,500	$14,500	$14,500	$14,500	$14,500
090	$12,500	$12,500	$12,500	$12,500	$12,500	$12,500
100	$0	$0	$0	$0	$0	$20,000
110	$13,333	$13,333	$13,333	$13,333	$13,333	$13,333
150	**$132,908**	**$132,908**	**$132,908**	**$147,908**	**$132,908**	**$151,908**
	$979,556	$1,112,464	$1,245,372	$1,393,280	$1,526,188	$1,678,096

FIGURE 8.7

ASSUMPTIONS SUPPORTING THE CASH-FLOW BUDGET

1. A cash balance of $125,680 will be brought forward from the previous year. This includes a cash surplus from the previous year and prepaid tuition and fees received during the previous fiscal year.

2. Income is budgeted on a monthly basis on the assumption that at least 95 percent of the tuition and fees billed will be collected by the end of the month.

3. Income in each instance is projected conservatively. When there is a question about the timing of the receipts, always calculate receiving them in the next month.

4. Prepaid tuition and fees are projected to be collected during the months of March through June. This money collected during the current year is next year's income and should be reserved for next year's expenditures.

5. Loan income of $54,250 is projected for a bank loan for new equipment.

6. Gift income is projected on the basis of past experience when about 75 percent is received during December, and the remainder is received sporadically throughout the year. Therefore, 75 percent is budgeted for December, and the remaining 25 percent is projected for June.

7. Income from athletic activities begins in early September, but since it cannot be counted on for September expenses, it is projected over nine months beginning in October.

8. Yearbook income is budgeted for April. This amount will be collected from student fees for the yearbook that will actually be billed on March 1. Since we do not know how rapidly this income will come in, it is budgeted to be received in April when the yearbooks are distributed to the students who have paid for them.

9. One of the largest categories of expense is administration. June and July have been overestimated to be certain that adequate funds are on hand.

10. With the exception of July, when little activity is taking place, the expenses for transportation are spread evenly throughout the year.

11. M & O expenses are fairly evenly distributed over the year. Additional money was budgeted for June when summer maintenance projects begin.

12. Capital expenditures budgeted for July through October and for June represent special projects. These projects can be modified if the enrollment projected does not materialize.

13. The amounts budgeted for debt service represent regular payments on bank loans.

14. The cash-flow budget reflects a significant surplus at the end of the year. Much of this money will be set aside to fund depreciation so that when major capital expenditures are incurred, they do not have to be funded out of one year's budget. Also, it is not necessary to borrow all the money required for the year.

Every school should also recalculate its budget during the first month of school. It is important to know whether the enrollment projections were actually realized. It is also important to reconsider any factors that may have changed since the original budget was calculated. We cannot overemphasize reworking and adjusting any factors in the budget that need correction. At this point in the budget process, reductions in expenditures should be limited to discretionary funds when possible. Such adjustments are much easier to do in September than in November or December when many of the discretionary funds have already been spent.

A recommended timetable for budget preparation is given in Figure 8.8.

A formula for predicting student enrollment is presented in Figure 8.9. Specific examples are also provided.

FIGURE 8.8

BUDGET TIMETABLE

November

Carefully review previous year's financial statement and compare with the current year to identify any significant changes (enrollment, faculty/staff, capital outlays, and so on).

Calculate the average salary of all professional staff members.

Calculate the average salary of all nonprofessional staff members that are full-time.

Calculate the average hourly wage and the average number of hours worked by part-time staff members.

Project enrollment for the next year.

Estimate personnel needs for the next year.

Convert all nonsalary/wage expenses to a per pupil expenditure (except for those items such as capital outlays) and other items of a noncontinuing nature by dividing this total by the average number of students enrolled during the year. These expenses should be considered by group where the number of students participating can be isolated, as in the transportation program.

Calculate the cost of educational resources and capital improvements planned for next year. Seek input from all those in leadership concerning their needs for the year.

Project the increased cost of providing needed resources by comparing inflation rates and plans for expansion of the ministry and capital outlays.

Increase all nonpersonnel-related expenses 10 to 15 percent to cover errors, omissions, and unanticipated cost increases.

December

Review budget data and establish tuition and fees to generate the income needed to finance the educational program for the year.

Compile a tentative budget detailing income and expenses for the coming year.

Present the budget to the school board or church group responsible for the oversight of the school.

January

Print materials for reenrollment and new student recruitment.

February

Launch reenrollment campaign.

March

Launch new student enrollment campaign.

June

Reevaluate the budget, taking into consideration actual salaries of personnel employed for the coming school year and anticipated enrollment.

September

Reevaluate the budget on the basis of actual staff employed and the enrollment. Readjust anticipated expenditures as needed to balance the budget.

FIGURE 8.9

PREDICTING STUDENT ENROLLMENT

Planning future school programs, budgeting, and determining staff needs all require some knowledge of future enrollment. Of course, there is no known way to determine future enrollment with certainty; however, if a basic history of enrollment is available for five or more years, it is possible to make estimates that are statistically significant. These estimates are calculated with the assumption that certain given factors that interacted to influence enrollment during the past decade will continue to interact in the same manner.

The forecast method suggested below is based on linear correlation (commonly called the "least squares" methods) of two lines of regression. The formula frequently used is the following:

$Y_p = a + bX$ where Y_p = predicted enrollment; X = deviation from the base year from which the prediction is being made; $a + b$ = constants to be derived as follows:

$$a = \frac{\Sigma Y}{N} \qquad b = \frac{\Sigma XY}{\Sigma X^2}$$

In using this formula, always have an odd number of years. A minimum of five years is suggested; however, three may be used. Always use the greatest number of years possible. The median (middle) year becomes the base.

In the following example, SY = school year; X = deviation from the base year; Y = enrollment for the school year; XY = product of the deviation and enrollment; X^2 = square of the deviation; and N = number of years for which data are used.

SY	X	Y	XY	X^2
1984/85	-5	249	-1,245	25
1985/86	-4	313	1,252	16
1986/87	-3	359	-1,077	9
1987/88	-2	391	-782	4
1988/89	-1	425	-425	1
1989/90	0	461	0	0
1990/91	1	475	475	1
1991/92	2	492	984	4
1992/93	3	512	1,536	9
1993/94	4	561	2,244	16
1994/95	5	585	2,925	25
		$\Sigma Y = 4{,}823$	$\Sigma XY = 3{,}383$	$\Sigma X^2 = 110$

$$\Sigma Y = 1{,}823 \qquad \Sigma XY = 3{,}383$$

$$a = \frac{4823}{11} = 438.45 \qquad\qquad b = \frac{3383}{110} = 30.75$$

The enrollment for the school year 1995/96 can be calculated in the following way:

$$Y_p = a + bX = 438.45 + 30.75(6) = 622.95$$

Any year can be calculated by substituting the deviation from the base year for X. We could calculate the enrollment for the 1996/97 school year by substituting the number 7 for X.

Advantages of the "least squares" method of enrollment projection are these:

1. It makes use of data readily available and does not require extensive record keeping.

2. It is a proven mathematical process for prediction based solely on past enrollment.

3. The accuracy of the prediction can be measured mathematically.

Disadvantages of this method are these:

1. It is completely dependent on an adequate and accurate amount of historical data to establish trends.

2. The system is more appropriate to populations large enough to exhibit a steady trend.

3. The system cannot accommodate any extraneous factors (such as socioeconomic change) that will alter enrollments. If such factors are foreseen, the derived projections must be modified by subjective judgment.

4. Although valuable as indicators, projections far into the future are of doubtful reliability, since exponential changes (rising birth rates, city growth, etc.) cannot be included until they are reflected in the historical data.

Forecast of Teacher Needs

To use enrollment predictions to forecast the number of teachers required in the future, the following formula may be helpful:

$$T = \frac{E}{P} = \text{where T = teachers; E = enrollment; P = pupil/teacher ratio}$$
desired.

CHAPTER 9

THE ADMINISTRATION OF CHURCH-SCHOOL FUNDS

He becometh poor that dealeth with a slack hand: but the hand of the diligent maketh rich.

Proverbs 10:4

The proper management of church-school funds is extremely important to the testimony of the ministry and all those directly involved with its financial resources. The key to avoiding difficulty is placing the right people in positions of responsibility and establishing a system of accountability that will insure the integrity of the ministry.

Most churches have a single budget for all the ministries of the church. This is appropriate since the funds for the ministry must be brought together in one common financial statement at least at the end of the year. Typically, the ministry will have several checking accounts that simplify the overall financial management of the church. Monies contributed by the congregation are placed in a general fund and then dispensed to each individual ministry. The schools' funds are, for the most part, from a different source and are usually maintained in a separate account. Although computers allow churches today to manage money for various ministries from one account, separate accounts will prevent many problems.

LEADERSHIP

The leadership of the church is important in developing and maintaining healthy, supportive attitudes. We cannot expect all members of a large congregation to be equally interested in every ministry. The pastor, the church staff, and the lay leadership can do much to prevent the development of petty jealousies over the availability of funds and their use. Good communication is essential. Regular communication that is understood will help the congregation, the school constituency, and the leadership of the church and school to maintain an appreciation for the contributions of each ministry.

The church business manager is the best channel for this communication. He can draw together information from all organizations within the church and report what expenses are being incurred and how revenues are being used. His supervision of all the church revenues will protect lay leaders from a tendency to be protective of information about their separate ministries. (See Appendix D for a representative job description of a financial administrator for a church.)

In churches without a business manager, it is more difficult to keep a proper perspective. In such situations good communication is even more important and financial policies must be well-defined and understood.

POLICIES

Financial policies must detail how all church monies received are to be used. They must also establish the following: (1) who in the organization is responsible for the distribution of monies, (2) which individuals have the authority to financially obligate the church, and (3) what are the overall limits of each individual's authority. The budget process, which is discussed in detail in another chapter, is one of the most efficient ways to implement these policies.

Policy Controls

Clearly defined authority is one of the most important fiscal controls. All duties should be specifically assigned to an individual or group to insure that the organization runs efficiently. An organizational chart and a policy manual should identify the authority and the responsibility of each position. Groups of people, such as the school board, charged with specific responsibilities, should clearly understand how to carry out their duties and report their activities.

Schools also need policies for the appointing, electing, and/or employing of individuals. The qualifications for the persons holding positions should be carefully specified and followed meticulously. If the instructions have become obsolete, impractical, or unworkable, they should be amended through appropriate means. If they are simply ignored or routinely set aside, organizational anarchy results.

Supervisory Controls

Most schools, whether church-related or independent, have some type of board or committee to oversee them. This group must not simply rubber-stamp what is proposed but must offer genuine supervisory direction. The school board or committee that functions in accordance with its responsibilities is a valuable component of the school.

The school board should approve the budget and regularly review the contracts and the financial reports. This review should be in addition to, not in lieu of, the periodic outside annual audit. The board must not rely solely on reports submitted by the administrator, business manager, or bookkeeper for financial information.

Cash is a resource and must receive proper attention if it is to be used to its full advantage. Whenever possible, surplus cash (all cash not immediately needed) should be placed in an interest-bearing account. Idle money is wasted money. Many schools waste thousands of dollars in unearned interest each year. Banking laws have been greatly liberalized, and many opportunities to earn interest on excess cash are available. Additionally, there is a great deal of competition in the banking industry, and banks now have more incentive to help us be good stewards of God's money. As an administrator, you should be certain that these accounts are both safe and liquid. You need to be able to transfer cash immediately. For example, on the day your payroll is released, you would need to transfer money from the interest-bearing account to your regular checking account. Larger schools may be able to negotiate sweep accounts with their bank to lend surplus cash overnight. Consult your local banker about investment opportunities available to you. Check out your options carefully. Do not assume your banker will volunteer to give you the best deal available.

Internal Borrowing

Internal borrowing can cause considerable difficulty. Invariably there will be times when one part of the organization has surplus funds and another has a critical need. If internal borrowing is to be permitted, however, this procedure must have specific guidelines. Either a fund transfer should be distinctly a gift, or it should be clearly a loan. If it is a loan, the terms of repayment should be understood when the loan is made. If internal borrowing is used, consider having such transfers supervised by a neutral group within the church (the deacons, the trustees, or the finance committee). Approval should always require the permission of those not directly involved with the gift or the loan.

Internal Controls

Christian organizations usually employ higher caliber people than do other employers. Even so, it is important to establish certain financial controls that assure both accuracy and honesty in handling funds. A generally accepted principle is that several unrelated persons should be responsible for overseeing the school's assets. Spiritually, the basic objective is to avoid even the appearance of evil (1 Thess. 5:22). Legally, a school has a responsibility for insuring that no individual personally profits from his association with the ministry beyond reasonable compensation for work actually done. This concern is frequently more important in Christian work than the secular business world because of the tendency to have family members heavily involved in our ministries. Proper financial controls not only assure that ethical practices will be observed but they also give confidence to the casual observer who may have reason to question how the organization's resources are managed.

There are three primary purposes for having internal controls:

1. To safeguard the assets of the organization

2. To provide a means to verify the reliability and accuracy of financial statements

3. To insure compliance with financial policies

The capacity to insure the second item is particularly important. Inaccurate reports tend to cause people to lose confidence in future reports and in the people responsible for them. Reliable information is needed to make sound decisions. Reliable information is also needed to evaluate the efficiency of the organization and to permit comparison.

The following suggestions will help an organization avoid the most common pitfalls:

1. Do not permit personnel to handle incompatible duties. Duties should be separated; for example, the same person should not handle both records and assets.

2. Have a well-defined organizational chart, update it as often as necessary, and follow it.

3. Hire qualified personnel, or properly train those you employ.

4. Have a well-written financial policy manual, update it as often as necessary, and insist that the procedures be followed.

5. Audit all policies to insure that procedures are being followed.

6. Be certain audit policies establish an environment that inhibits prohibited activities.

7. Cross-train personnel and rotate duties.

8. Pay bills from invoices rather than monthly statements. Mark invoices paid to avoid duplicate payments.

In a small school these controls could easily be managed by assigning independent responsibilities to the school bookkeeper, another clerical employee, the administrator of the school, and the treasurer of the school board. In this illustration the bookkeeper could handle all the routine financial matters, i.e., receipting, taking deposits to the bank, and writing checks to pay the school's bills. Whenever, possible, cash and checks should be counted and prepared for deposit by a clerical employee other than the bookkeeper. The principal could approve bills for payment, periodically review the records of the receipts and expenses from the general ledgers, and be the individual assigned to open and examine the bank statements when they arrive in the mail. He could compare the deposits shown in the receipt book with the deposits listed in the bank statement. The treasurer could balance the bank statement and review the statements of accounts every quarter. Figure 9.1 describes more so-phisticated internal controls needed by larger schools. An additional re-source in this area is *The Church Guide to Internal Controls* (Vargo, 1995). This book contains a list of fifty internal control practices designed for churches, many of which are applicable to Christian schools.

Finally, when establishing fiscal controls, ask the following questions: "If this control did not exist, could an individual be tempted to dishon-esty? Is there a greater possibility of error? Could the government or the general public question the integrity of the entire organization?"

FIGURE 9.1

CASH CONTROLS FOR CHRISTIAN SCHOOLS

1. Have a written, current financial policies manual.

2. Audit all personnel involved in financial activities to insure that writ-ten policies are being followed.

3. Have an internal audit program that verifies all financial transactions periodically.

4. Have an external audit of all financial activities annually.

5. Use prenumbered receipts for all income. Deposits should indicate the receipt numbers. All numbers should be accounted for. Depos-its should be noted in the receipt book and referenced to the bank statement when it is reconciled.

6. Whenever possible, two people should count all cash. They should prepare it for deposit and present the deposit to the bookkeeper intact. The bookkeeper should not handle cash receipts.

7. Someone other than the bookkeeper should open and prepare for deposit all receipts received by mail.

8. All checks should be restrictively endorsed and deposited daily with other receipts. No part of the cash receipts should be used to pay expenses.

9. All disbursements should be made by check, and supporting docu-mentation should be kept whenever possible.

10. A specific individual(s) should be assigned to approve payment of accounts payable.

11. Someone other than the bookkeeper should sign the checks and ap-prove them for release.

12. Someone other than the bookkeeper should receive and reconcile the bank statements.

13. Someone other than the bookkeeper should authorize the writing off of any unpaid tuition.

14. Excess cash should be kept in a separate interest-bearing account.

15. Specific instructions should be written for transferring money from one account to another.

16. All persons regularly handling cash and signing checks should be bonded.

17. Student activity funds should be kept in a separate account. Deposits to the account should be prepared, given to the bookkeeper, and deposited. All expenditures should be approved in writing by the principal and the person responsible for the activity.

Financial Reporting

No entity within the organization, particularly the school, should operate as if it were independent of the church. At least quarterly (in larger schools it should occur monthly) all financial activity should be compiled and a comprehensive report prepared showing all the financial activity of the organization. As we mentioned earlier, a business manager is a distinct asset in this regard. But even churches without a business manager should make provision for such reports. Financial reports will be discussed in detail in chapter 10.

It is especially tempting for the school to operate as if it were financially independent. There are at least two reasons for this tendency. First, because of the large number of salaried personnel, the school budget can easily exceed the size of the general church budget. Second, since the school has an external source of funds, its leadership is sometimes reluctant to submit to church authority. However, if the school is permitted to operate as if it were financially independent, this attitude will invariably carry over into other areas.

The school must be given the authority and liberty to raise necessary funds to operate, but those who make the school's financial decisions are accountable to the church leaders who have established the overall financial policies. This accountability is only fair, for the church is held legally and morally responsible for any school debts or contractual agreements.

To say that the school is responsible to the church is not to imply that it must answer directly to the entire congregation for its financial activities. It is unwise to allow the church body to become directly involved in the school's budget process. This procedure is too detailed and complicated to debate in an open-church conference, where even sincere people with the intention of being of help do not have the information necessary to make informed decisions. The church certainly must have a voice in the budget process, but its voice should be through people elected, appointed, or employed as its representatives. The budget should be presented and carefully explained to the congregation, but specific items in the budget should not be open to line-item veto. The congregation should not be able to increase appropriations nor add items to the budget. If the congregation as a whole has major concerns about the budget, those concerns should be expressed to those responsible for the preparation of the budget, and they should review the budget and bring it back to the congregation again at a later time.

All churches should provide for regular audits. It is common for churches to authorize the finance committee to conduct internal audits periodically. Such a provision should certainly include all school funds. This review should include some predetermined points of reference. A simple review of reports prepared by others without verifying any of the data is not adequate.

Purchasing Controls

The budget is the first step in controlling expenditures. The next step is to give selected persons the authority to do the purchasing. This helps to insure that each decision is given adequate consideration. Schools usually delegate this authority to the administrator, business manager, and/ or the board treasurer.

Once the responsibility for purchasing has been delegated, it is wise to establish a specific limit for spending. Any purchase exceeding this limit should be approved by the board. It is also customary to require the board's approval for any contractual negotiations. The school's attorney should then review contracts.

Competitive bidding can often save money, particularly for schools in large cities. Major purchases such as vehicles, large quantities of furniture, insurance, and equipment should always be put out for bid. Bidders should be required to give specifications and cost. You should fix a maximum bid and state in advance how many bids you must have. Exceptions to these policies must be approved by the board. Schools located in small communities where limited options for purchases and services are available may not be able to implement these suggestions fully.

Schools with large budgets often find it helpful to have a purchase-order system. Advance approval should always be required for purchases made by employees for which they expect to be reimbursed. While this system may be a nuisance for small schools, it is an important control for larger organizations.

Auditing

There is no substitute for a thorough periodic audit of a school's operations and finances. All church funds should also be periodically audited by an outside agency. This audit should include all school funds as well. If the school is a ministry of the church, the church's financial statement is not complete unless it includes a full accounting for all financial activity.

Such an audit is more credible if conducted by a CPA. Many Christian schools consider professional audits too costly. However, the cost is relative to the size of an organization and the complexity of its operations and can be reduced if the organization has sought professional advice from the beginning. Every Christian school should have professional, legal, and accounting counsel throughout its years of operation.

Not all "audits" are alike. There are three basic services provided by CPAs: a compilation, a review, and an audit. When an accountant does a compilation for your organization, he takes your data and arranges it in an orderly fashion so that it can be presented in a standard format. The accountant does not verify any of the data you provide in a compilation. He may call to your attention things that do not appear correct, but a compilation does not require him to do so.

A review provides more helpful information. When an accountant does a review, he examines the information your organization has prepared to see if it appears to be in order for the test of being "reasonable." Once again, there is no verification of the data you provide to him.

The audit is more rigorous and is, therefore, more useful, both to those within and outside your organization. In an audit the accountant performs certain tests to verify the data provided and uses statistical analysis to make recommendations as to the fiscal soundness of your organization. The accountant will call to your attention any inconsistencies between the manner in which you have operated and current government regulations. He may also make certain recommendations based on his overall observations. An audit is characterized by the issuing of an opinion by the CPA. The opinion is the official message to the reader as to the financial status of the organization.

Government Regulations

The IRS has the authority to audit any nonprofit organization, including a church, to determine whether the organization is operating according to government regulations. The IRS checks to see that the basic character of the organization is what it says it is. While this is very offensive to some groups, the courts have upheld the authority of the IRS.

A school that accepts any government assistance—whether at the federal, state, or local level—must recognize the authority of that body to audit its activities for the protection of the public. For example, in some states, church bond programs must have the approval and supervision of the government.

Each organization must develop internal procedures that insure that its activities are being adequately monitored. It must also be willing to use outside assistance and to conform to necessary external regulations if it is to maintain its testimony.

CHAPTER 10

THE ACCOUNTING PROCESS

Not slothful in business; fervent in spirit; serving the Lord.
Romans 12:11

Let all things be done decently and in order.
1 Corinthians 14:40

This chapter will be a simple discussion of cash, accrual, and fund accounting. It will not make accountants or bookkeepers of pastors, administrators, or board members, but it will show the accounting responsibilities of those who supervise a school's fiscal affairs and help them understand the records and reports they are expected to keep.

PERSONNEL CONSIDERATIONS

Those who have the primary responsibility for overseeing the school's finances will be held accountable for the success or failure of the school. They must realize that competent personnel are needed to establish and to maintain business records in order to plan for the future, to give account to its constituents, and to meet the requirements of government agencies.

Certified Public Accountants

Every new school should establish accounting records under the supervision of a CPA who knows the operation and reporting requirements of nonprofit organizations. Not all CPAs keep up with these requirements. Find an accountant who specializes in this field or is willing to become informed.

Do not make the selection of the CPA on price alone. While you have a responsibility to use the Lord's money wisely, a good CPA, by his suggestions alone, will save you more than he charges you. There may be a good CPA in your church or school constituency who will help the school without charge or for less than his regular fee. Administrators should, however, consider the disadvantages of accepting free service.

When a CPA's schedule forces him to choose between you and a paying client, it does not take much imagination to know who is more likely to get the attention.

Bookkeepers

Hire a competent bookkeeper. Since maintaining records is much easier than establishing them, you especially need a good bookkeeper when you are first starting. Be willing to pay a reasonable salary and provide sufficient time for the individual to do his work. Small schools will usually find that this person will have time to help with other clerical functions.

ACCOUNTING METHODS

Whether a school is for profit or is nonprofit determines the accounting system it will use. Several other important distinctions are made on that basis as well (Gross Jr., McCarthy Jr., and Larkin, 2000). Other differences include the treatment of fixed assets; transfer and appropriations; and contributions, pledges, and noncash contributions. These differences are important for nonprofit organizations and must be understood by all who are involved in the supervision of the school's financial affairs. Nearly all for-profit organizations should be on an accrual basis and would not need to consider the above distinctions.

The main difference between cash and accrual accounting is the manner in which income and expenses are recorded. Historically churches have used the cash basis of accounting. Private schools have generally used the accrual method. Christian schools, however, have tended to follow the pattern of churches. The American Institute of Certified Public Accountants (AICPA) recommends the accrual accounting basis for both churches and schools. An explanation of the basic advantages and disadvantages of each method will help you decide which system is best for your institution.

Cash Accounting

An organization on a cash basis does not need to report the cost of operating, but it should do the following:

1. Record cash when received

2. Record expenses when paid

3. Report a summary of cash inflow and cash outflow

Since cash accounting is simple to use, it is appealing. A small organization can actually use checkbook stubs that are completed properly instead of a general ledger. Financial statements can be made up directly from the checkbook stubs. Many Christian organizations start out small using this accounting method and find it difficult to change to the more complicated accrual method after they have grown.

It is easy for an organization to unintentionally misrepresent its financial condition or to feel falsely secure when using the cash system of accounting. Remember, the purpose of accounting is to enable you, and anyone else in your organization that needs the information, to know exactly what the financial standing is at all times.

Accrual Accounting

An organization on an accrual basis will do the following:

1. Record income when earned, whether the cash is received or not

2. Record expenses when incurred for goods received or services rendered, whether cash is spent or not

3. Report totals and net revenues earned and expenses incurred

4. Report the cost of operating

Use accrual accounting if the cash method makes it difficult or impossible to reflect accurately the financial condition of the school. One legitimate question when considering a change in accounting methods is this: Will the changes in the way we operate justify the time and the expense of this method? If the answer is negative, there is no basis for making a change.

One reason nonprofit organizations do not operate on an accrual basis is that they are not comfortable recording income before it is received. This apprehension is more justified for a church with only gift income than it is for a school where parents have obligated themselves by contract to pay tuition at the time of enrollment.

There are, however, several advantages for a small or medium-sized Christian school to operate on an accrual basis. Cash accounting does not always give a true picture of the condition of the organization. For example, fees for reenrollment are collected in the spring but are actually income for the following year. Schools on a cash basis record this income as it is received, artificially inflating the income for the current year. The year-end financial statements are then distorted. On the other hand, tuition income earned during the current year but not collected until the following year would be recorded as next year's income. In both instances, the true financial condition of the organization would be unintentionally distorted.

As mentioned in an earlier chapter, depreciation is an important expense for any organization; cash accounting fails to provide for depreciation. Many Christian leaders believe that only profit-making organizations need to consider depreciation. They assume that when the assets are worn out, obsolete, or otherwise unserviceable, they will simply replace them. This idea may work well with computers, but when the gymnasium needs to be replaced, it is quite another matter. Such an approach jeopardizes fiscal stability.

It is easy to see a supply of paper diminish, but it is harder to see the depreciation of buildings and equipment. The fact is that buildings are "consumed" much the same way as other items, and eventually they need to be replaced. Depreciation makes it possible to recognize this legitimate business expense.

Some people are confused about the way depreciation is handled. Many believe cash is actually being reserved in a sinking fund for replacement. This, of course, is not normally true. Depreciation is usually recognized by a reduction in the asset account. This process is illustrated in Figure 10.3 in the sample balance sheet. It is possible to have a special account to set aside funds equal to the annual depreciation expense. The amount set aside will probably not totally fund depreciation because of inflation. But it will be a beginning. (The AICPA has recently stated that most nonprofit organizations should depreciate assets.)

Unfortunately, most private elementary and secondary schools have not been following depreciation accounting techniques in the past. . . . One of the reasons many private schools have run into financial difficulties is that boards of trustees have not been fully aware of the true cost of their schools, and accordingly have set their tuition fees too low. Depreciation is a cost, albeit not a cash cost, and should be reported as an expense if financial statements are to accurately reflect the actual cost of operating a school. (Gross Jr., McCarthy, and Larkin, 2000)

Modified Cash Accounting

There is an alternative to accrual accounting that may be worth consideration for some organizations—the modified cash basis. The basic principles of cash accounting are used; however, additional information is provided. This additional information prevents the reviewer from making erroneous conclusions.

By adhering to the following steps, you can change from strict cash accounting to the modified cash basis and thus minimize distortion of your financial condition.

Steps for Income

1. List by category all income received that is not earned the current year (prepaid tuition, enrollment fees, delinquent fees from the previous year, etc.).

2. List and age all accounts receivable (unpaid tuition and fees, 30 days, 60 days, 90 days, etc.).

3. Identify any unearned income received (loans, bond sales, etc.).

4. Identify any income received through reduction of assets (sale of property or equipment).

Steps for Expenses

1. List all accounts payable by age (30 days, 60 days, 90 days, etc.).

2. List all other obligations (loans, including amounts outstanding, with dates due; all other loan term obligations; leases with terms, amounts owed; etc.).

These additional notes will permit those familiar with accounting to make a rough approximation of their actual financial condition minus the cost of operation. Some modification of the cash basis is incorporated in the detailed accounting of income recommended in Figure 10.1.

Fund Accounting

One other method of accounting should be considered, and that is fund accounting, which is unique to nonprofit organizations. This method causes problems for those unfamiliar with reading financial reports based on the system. Fund accounting uses separate accounts for funds restricted for special purposes. Fund accounting is recommended for colleges and universities and is used in modified forms by many churches and schools. Any church or school that maintains separate funds for missions, building construction or remodeling, or scholarships is already involved in a modified form of fund accounting.

Fund accounting is not difficult. But a person who is not well acquainted with this method should consult a CPA before deciding to use it and should get help in establishing the accounts. The transfer of money from one fund to another can be complicated to record accurately and understandably. To receive an unqualified audit report, an organization using fund accounting must be on an accrual basis. This provision alone may cause some organizations to reconsider this method. If an organization receives substantial gift income designated for several different purposes, fund accounting offers definite advantages. Otherwise, it probably has little to offer you.

Your choice of an accounting method is an important one. If you can function effectively with a simple accounting system, by all means use the cash method. If your organization is complex, the accrual method is better for you. Few church-related Christian day schools are likely to need the complexities offered by fund accounting, although some independent schools might. Some modifications of basic cash or accrual may provide the additional details that you need.

For a church with a Christian school, the entire organization should be on the same accounting method, even when separate accounting systems are maintained. If the school is part of the church, the financial activities of the school must eventually be incorporated with all other fiscal activities of the church for a consolidated statement. Combining data will obviously be simplified if both use the same accounting methods.

Examples of financial statements illustrating both the cash and accrual methods are presented at the end of this chapter as Figures 10.1, 10.2, and 10.3.

PREPARING FINANCIAL STATEMENTS

Though it need not be detailed, some accounting information is necessary to understand school finance. Large schools should have a CPA to prepare financial statements and conduct regular audits. For smaller or new schools without such an arrangement, this information is necessary. Those with CPAs will be able to judge better what services they need.

The method of accounting, cash or accrual, will determine the type of financial statement that should be prepared, what content will be included, how it will be described, and what name is given to the statement.

An excellent discussion of financial reporting for churches, much of which applies equally to Christian schools, may be found in *The Church Guide to Financial Reporting* (Vargo, 1995).

Cash-Basis Financial Statements

The organizations that use cash accounting do so because it is simple. The financial statements for this method are not as thorough in areas that some consider to be essential. Figure 10.1 shows a financial statement based on the sample chart of accounts presented in Figure 8.1. The full chart of accounts should not normally be made available to anyone outside the organization.

For a financial statement to be meaningful to the reader, it should contain both the beginning and ending balances and the comparison of actual income and expenses with those projected in the budget. Some statements also compare the current-year figures with those of the previous year; some use this comparison instead of the budget comparisons.

The modified cash method makes cash accounting statements more useful. This method is more flexible because it includes information not usually required in strict cash accounting. For example, in Figure 10.1 all information below the line *Cash Balance, June 30, 1995* is additional information. The items listed there are self-explanatory.

FIGURE 10.1

STATEMENT OF CASH RECEIPTS, DISBURSEMENTS, AND CASH BALANCE

Receipts	Actual	Budget
Tuition and Other Fees	$569,128	$566,800
Food Service	$24,543	$20,000
Investment Income	$947	
Sale of Promotional Material	$44,323	
Loan Proceeds	$21,700	$21,700
Sale of School Property	$2,804	
Gifts	$16,837	$20,000
Athletic Activities	$5,531	$5,000
Yearbook	$5,721	$5,500
Other Student Activities	$3,558	
Total	$695,092	$639,000
Disbursements		
Administration	$329,316	$330,000
Instruction	$46,278	$45,000
Transportation	$66,879	$65,000

Maintenance and Operation	$24,715	$25,000
Extracurricular Activities	$21,632	$20,000
Fixed Charges	$66,701	$65,000
Capital Outlay	$24,438	$25,000
Debt Service	$63,397	$64,000
Total	$643,356	$639,000

Excess Cash Receipts over Distributions	$51,736
Cash Balance, July 1, 1994	$19,471
Cash Balance, June 30, 1995	$71,207

Cash Balance Summary

	$6,388
Money Market Account Balance	$64,819
Accounts Receivable	$14,845
Loans Payable	
Short-term	$63,397
Long-term	$126,792
All Other Accounts Payable	$39,346

Accrual-Basis Financial Statements

Figure 10.2 illustrates the accrual method of accounting for the same organization as in 10.1. In addition to a statement of income, expenses, and changes in fund balances, this method provides a balance sheet like the one in Figure 10.3.

There are two distinguishing factors in the figures:

1. Fund balances (Figure 10.2) replace cash balances (Figure 10.1). Fund balances include ready cash and the organization's assets less depreciation.

2. Depreciation is included as an expense. Income should be increased to fund this additional expense.

FIGURE 10.2

STATEMENT OF INCOME, EXPENSES, AND CHANGE IN FUND BALANCES

Income	Actual	Budget
Tuition and Other Fees	$590,628	$580,000
Food Service	$24,543	$25,000
Interest	$957	$1,000
Sale of Promotional Material	$44,323	$50,000
Loan Proceeds	$21,700	$21,700
Sale of School Property	$2,804	
Gifts and Pledges	$21,837	$20,000
Athletic Activities	$5,531	$5,000
Yearbook	$5,721	$5,500
Other Student Activities	$3,558	
Total Income	$721,602	$708,200
Expenses		
Administration	$329,316	$336,200
Instruction	$48,778	$45,000
Transportation	$68,379	$65,000
Maintenance and Operation	$27,715	$25,000
Extracurricular Activities	$21,632	$20,000
Fixed Charges	$66,701	$65,000
Capital Outlay	$56,784	$25,000
Debt Service	$63,397	$64,000
Depreciation	$62,257	$63,000
Total Expenses	$744,959	$708,200
Excess of Income over Expenses	($23,367)	
Fund Balance, Beginning of Year, July 1, 1994	$1,073,070	
Fund Balance, End of Year, June 30, 1995	$1,049,703	

FIGURE 10.3

BALANCE SHEET

Current Assets

Cash	$6,388
Money Market Account	$64,819
Accounts Receivable	$14,845
Total Current Assets	$86,052

Fixed Assets, at Cost

Land (43 acres)	$162,965
Buildings	$850,000
Furniture/Equipment	$97,000
School Buses	$216,000
Athletic Facilities/Equipment	$23,500
Total Fixed Assets	$1,349,465
Less Accumulated Depreciation	$311,285
Net Fixed Assets	$1,038,180
Total Assets	$1,124,232

Liabilities and Fund Balance

Current Liabilities

Accounts Payable	$39,346
Prepaid Tuition	$46,750
Total Current Liabilities	$86,096
Deferred Salary Payable	$11,800

Fund Balance

Accumulated Excess of Income over Expenses	($23,367)
Total Fund Balance	$1,049,703
Total Liabilities and Fund	$1,124,232

You must weigh the value of additional information against the additional time, personnel, and expense required for the accrual method. However, a CPA cannot give an unqualified statement according to accepted accounting principles unless you are using the accrual method. Seek the advice of a competent CPA before making your decision.

CHAPTER 11

SALARIES AND FRINGE BENEFITS

For the labourer is worthy of his hire.

Luke 10:7

Do ye not know that they which minister about holy things live of the things of the temple? and they which wait at the altar are partakers with the altar? Even so hath the Lord ordained that they which preach the gospel should live of the gospel.

1 Corinthians 9:13–14

I t is important that those making provisions for the financial security of the Christian school also make provisions for the financial security of its employees. People, not things, make organizations effective. If the Christian school is successful, it will be largely due to the quality of the personnel employed. Many Christian organizations take advantage of their employees and attempt to offer low-cost Christian education at their expense. This philosophy is morally and ethically wrong, and there is no better time than at the beginning of the school to make plans to avoid this error. Many established Christian schools that have not developed fair and equitable salary and employee-benefit programs cannot understand why they have a high rate of employee turnover (Jer. 22:13; Col. 4:1; James 5:4). Inadequate salaries and benefit programs are consistently mentioned as the leading cause of faculty turnover.

The quality of a school's professional staff is significantly related to student achievement. The quality of education provided by our Christian schools has been questioned. Many schools are doing an excellent job, but some have serious deficiencies. One problem is that the high rate of turnover in personnel makes developing a quality faculty difficult.

An informal study of Christian school teachers indicated that over 75 percent of them are mobile. They have had relatively short terms of service at the schools where they taught.

Christian school administrators generally agree that low salaries and minimal fringe benefits are directly related to the turnover of married teachers and single teachers about to be married. As teachers assume greater family responsibilities, they often find their salaries inadequate and seek higher-paying positions elsewhere, generally outside the field of Christian education. Christian teachers also find that low salaries make it difficult for them to do advanced study in their fields. Therefore, Christian teachers who stay in the profession are unable to develop their expertise. See Appendix E for a sample Compensation and Employee Benefits Philosophy statement.

What do these facts mean to the Christian community? Possibly the major portion of the financial burden of Christian schools is being placed on the wrong people. We have been influenced by the world to allow others to assume our responsibilities. Some even aggressively seek to transfer their responsibility to others. Christian schoolteachers, by re- duced salaries and benefits, are in many cases paying 25 to 50 percent of the real cost of providing Christian education. Is being robbed of their rightful wages a just reward for dedication? If the Bible gives parents the primary responsibility to educate their children, on what authority do parents transfer the financing of this responsibility to others? The an- swer, of course, is that there is no biblical basis for this action.

A major reason for inadequate salaries for Christian-school teachers is the unbiblical priorities of some of the leadership of our churches and independent schools and of the families sending their children to the schools. The prophet Jeremiah warned that those who used the wages of workers to build their own houses would be in danger of judgment (Jer. 22:13–17). It is wrong for churches and schools to oppress teachers in order to build big buildings and impress their brethren with the ac- cumulation of things (Deut. 24:14–15). The apostle Paul warned that the one who failed to provide for his own family was "worse than an infidel" (1 Tim. 5:8).

The purpose of our discussion is not to stir up dissatisfaction or unrest among Christian workers. The Word of God clearly teaches us that we are to be content with what we have and trust God rather than man for the provision of our needs (Luke. 3:14; Phil. 4:10–14; 1 Tim. 6:8–10). This principle, however, does not relieve those in authority from their responsibility to treat their employees fairly. Nor does it excuse those who choose to take advantage of the charity of others rather than to fulfill their own responsibility. This section is addressed to those who make the financial policies governing the administration of our Christian schools.

Christian schools are at a crucial point in their development. People are the most important asset God has given us. If we are to retain those people whom God has called into Christian education, we must be willing to pay them salaries sufficient to meet their personal and family responsibilities. Christian schoolteachers have the same needs for transportation, housing, food, and Christian education for their children as do other believers. If we expect them to maintain the testimony God expects of them, we who use their services must be willing to permit them to receive their just reward (Mal. 3:5–6; 1 Cor. 9:9–14; Col. 4:1).

The administration should make sufficient provision for full-time employees to live on the income earned at school so that it will not be necessary for them to be under the burden of personal financial pressures (Mal. 3:5). Employees who are forced to hold a second job to meet their personal needs will not perform as effectively as those able to concentrate exclusively on their service to the school.

Personnel-related expenses are a major portion of the school's budget. Sixty to 80 percent of the budget will be allocated to this area. For the well-established Christian school, the figures will probably be between 70 and 75 percent. A new school with heavy expenses for remodeling, building, or equipment acquisition may find the percentage of the budget allocated to salaries and other personnel-related expenses lower for the first few years, but in time it should assume its normal place, if personnel needs are being addressed in a reasonable manner. The percentage of the budget allocated to personnel expense will indicate the quality of personnel you are seeking and the relative value you place on them.

Our nation has never demonstrated that it placed a high value on its teachers. Compared with other professions and other types of work requiring similar training, those in education are considerably underpaid.

Private schoolteachers have always been paid less than their public school counterparts. Salaries of Christian school workers would compare even less favorably with those in private industry. The data in Figure 11.1 shows how Christian schoolteachers' starting salaries compare with those in public education.

FIGURE 11.1

A COMPARISON OF PUBLIC/CHRISTIAN SCHOOLTEACHERS' STARTING SALARIES 1994 TO 2005

Year	CST	Purchasing Power	PST	Purchasing Power	Difference	Cost of living
1974/75	$5,050		$8,230		$3,180	147.70
1984/85	$8,600	$10,637	$15,400	$17,335	$6,800	311.10
1994/95	$12,911	$15,454	$23,915	$25,185	$11,004	452.00
1995/96	$13,285	$15,608	$24,285	$25,437	$11,000	456.5
1996/97	$13,800	$16,069	$25,012	$26,188	$11,182	469.98
1997/98	$15,320	$16,438	$25,735	$26,788	$10,415	480.76
1998/99	$15,079	$16,701	$26,639	$27,217	$11,560	488.45
1999/00	$15,642	$17,069	$27,989	$27,818	$12,347	499.24
2000/01	$16,412	$17,643	$28,986	$28,753	$12,574	516.02
2001/02	$17,124	$18,135	$30,719	$29,554	$13,595	530.4
2002/03	$17,748	$18,422	$31,351	$30,023	$13,603	538.8
2003/04	$17,983	$18,843	$31,704	$30,708	$13,721	551.1
2004/05	$18,475	$19,345	$31,753	$31,527	$13,278	565.8

1. The average Christian school's beginning salary is based upon the salary survey conducted each year among Christian school administrators attending the annual BJU Christian School Recruitment Conference.

2. The average public school's beginning salaries were obtained from the American Federation of Teachers from 1994 to date.

3. The Cost of Living Index was established by the U.S. Department of Labor Statistics with a base of 100 in 1967.

4. The figures in the third and fifth columns from the left represent the amount that would have been required to equal the purchasing power of the starting salary in the base year of 1994/95.

5. Differences in annual increments for Christian schoolteachers and public schoolteachers expand the differences in their annual salaries rapidly for experienced teachers. The average annual salary for public schoolteachers in 2004/05 was $31,753 (the most recent year for which data are available). The average annual Christian school salary in 2004/05 was $18,475.

6. Christian schoolteachers' salaries also compare unfavorably with levels of personal support required of fundamentalist mission boards for home missionaries. These boards require at least $3,000 monthly ($36,000/year) support apart from work funds.

INCREASING TEACHER SALARIES

Let's assume you have been convinced that Christian schoolteachers' salaries need to be raised. How do you go about doing it? Most Christian schools are dependent primarily on tuition to finance their schools. Raising tuition is the logical step for most schools desiring to raise teacher salaries. Realistically, tuition increases will normally be required to appreciably increase available revenue.

Suppose your school decides it should raise all teacher salaries $2,000 a year. If your school has 600 students and a pupil/teacher ratio of 20 to 1, your school employs 30 teachers. A $2,000 raise for your teachers will increase your budget $60,000. In a school of 600 students, that amounts to $100 per student or $10 more per month over the ten-month school term. Few parents would balk at paying $10 per month more for tuition if they knew that their child's teacher would receive an additional

$2,000 per year as a result. Smaller schools with reasonable pupil/teacher ratios can raise salaries just as easily.

Don't overlook your current budget as a source of additional revenue. A review of the school budget may show several thousand dollars not associated with a priority as high as teachers' salaries. By reviewing your budget, you can increase teachers' salaries. Some of the items you delete from the budget can be restored by making them special projects. People are more willing to give for some specific item than to make a general contribution to the overall budget.

You may also want to consider entirely new sources of revenue. Since the school is in most cases a ministry of the church, perhaps the church should consider a regular investment in the school ministry. A church with thirty teachers in its school could give each of its teachers a $1,000 increase in pay by including a $30,000 permanent supplement for the school in its annual budget. For example, one church actually gives $500 a month to the school through its missions program. Five hundred dollars monthly amounts to $6,000 a year, which divided equally among 30 teachers, could be an annual salary supplement of $200 each.

Another local church with a Christian school has what it calls a Teacher Salary Supplement Fund. The congregation is encouraged to give to this fund for the specific purpose of supplementing teachers' salaries. Teachers know about the fund but are not guaranteed any specific amount from it. This church reports gifts for the fund have averaged about 8 percent of the teachers' monthly salaries, with a low of 5 percent and a high of 20 percent. The money can be distributed among the teachers on a month-by-month basis, or it can be given to them as a year-end bonus to help them through the summer months when they may be without income.

A church-school might also ask other local churches whose members use its school to place the school ministry in their budgets on a regular basis to supplement teachers' salaries. Tactfully done, many churches could be encouraged to provide supplements based on the number of children enrolled from their church. The administration should explain that it wants to keep Christian education affordable while meeting its biblical responsibilities to its faculty/staff. Churches could be told that unless there is some additional source of revenue, significant increases in tuition and fees will be required. That could make Christian education unaffordable for some of their membership. It would be far less expensive for the church to help the school where its members' children are being educated now than for it to start its own school.

ESTABLISHING A SALARY/WAGE SCALE FOR YOUR SCHOOL

The Scripture clearly teaches that an employer is responsible to provide a living wage, as we discussed previously in this chapter. Since most pastors and Christian school administrators discourage their faculty from holding part-time jobs during the school year, it is obvious that they must be given adequate compensation to meet their needs.

Christian educators must determine appropriate salaries and wages for their personnel based on the actual cost of living expenses for the community in which the school is located. The salary must be high enough to provide adequate food, clothing, shelter, transportation, medical care, and other personal needs for the employee and his or her family. The salary must also allow for savings for future needs. Failure to provide adequately for these needs forces the employee to look for more profitable employment or condemns him to the life of a pauper. Such failure also subjects the employer to God's condemnation.

The administrator and/or the school board should regularly evaluate the cost of housing, utilities, and food in the community to insure that compensation programs remain at adequate levels. There is no reason that Christian school employee compensation should be kept unreasonably low. It would be helpful to compare from time to time the school employees' salaries with the salaries of the school's constituents.

Figure 11.2 suggests the percentages of an individual's income that should be budgeted for personal needs. Though these figures may need to be adjusted to take into account situations unique to your area, they will provide a point of reference to help you determine the level of income needed to live in your community.

FIGURE 11.2

PERSONAL BUDGET GUIDELINES

Expenses	% of Net Income	Portion of Net Income
Housing	30%	$350
Food	15%	$174
Transportation	15%	$174
Utilities	8%	$93
Clothing	7%	$81
Insurance	5%	$58
Medical Care	5%	$58
Personal Care	5%	$58
Debt and Investments	10%	$116
Total		$1162

The above salary figures are based on an annual salary of $20,000 payable monthly over a 12-month period. All calculations are based on a single teacher claiming himself as a dependent, resulting in deductions of $143.25 for federal withholding, $127.50 for Social Security taxes, $66.58 for South Carolina income tax, and a tithe of $166.67 on the gross monthly salary, leaving a disposable income of $1,162.67 each month.

TEACHER SALARIES

There are several ways for schools to approach teachers' salaries. The simplest and perhaps the most frequently used method is a straight salary. The teacher is contracted to work for a fixed dollar sum for a specified period of time, usually nine to ten months. He is sometimes given the option of spreading the salary over a twelve-month period. Other options, however, enable the school to do more for the teacher with the same number of dollars.

Since most Christian schools are nonprofit organizations, certain tax advantages are available both to the schools and to their employees. Many of these advantages are not available in the normal secular employer-employee relationship. In some situations, for example, it is possible for an employer to provide housing and utilities for employees in lieu of a portion of their salaries. Under certain circumstances the housing and utilities are nontaxable income to the employee and obviously then are more valuable to him in that form. In such a situation the employer, with no additional expenditure of funds, is providing the employee with benefits that would require a substantially higher salary under other conditions. It is also possible under certain circumstances to provide meals for the employee on a tax-sheltered basis. Since these opportunities are available only under special circumstances, and since the rules governing these circumstances are constantly changing, a school should have a CPA investigate carefully the provisions applicable to tax-exempt organizations.

Even when employer-provided housing, utilities, and meals must be taxable, it is frequently more cost-effective for the church or school to provide these for the employee than for him to secure them on his own. The institution has a limited amount of funds available for compensating its employees. If the school can own the housing and provide it to its employees cheaper than the employee can rent housing on his own, the school can use the savings to pay higher salaries than would otherwise be possible. While this may not be an attractive alternative to married staff planning to invest a number of years in your ministry, typically schools have substantial numbers of single staff who would be looking for apartments to rent. Housing available close to the school, in a safe environment, at a cost less than the market rate would always be attractive to some staff members. Schools that have a full-scale cafeteria can provide noon meals for teachers for less than they can provide them for themselves. If the teachers are required to eat in the cafeteria for the convenience of their employer, the value of the meals is not taxable.

It is traditional to base a teacher's salary on his level of education and years of experience. Most schools find this is a fair way of arriving at an acceptable salary. Figure 11.3 illustrates the most common approach to teacher salary schedules. The salaries shown in the illustration are consistent with those currently being paid by many Christian schools. Church staff salaries have been factored as a guide to churches desiring to insure equity in their compensation program.

FIGURE 11.3

TEACHER/CHURCH STAFF SALARY
LEVELS BASED ON POSITIONS

Position	Monthly Basis	Salary
Kindergarten Teacher (p.t.)	10 Months	$11,300
Kindergarten Teacher (f.t.)	10 Months	$20,000
Elementary Teacher	10 Months	$20,000
Secondary Teacher	10 Months	$20,000
Guidance Counselor	11 Months	$23,100
Elementary Principal	11 Months	$27,500
Secondary Principal	11 Months	$28,600
Administrator	12 Months	$34,800
Business Manager	12 Months	$32,400
Assistant Pastor	12 Months	$32,400
Associate Pastor	12 Months	$33,600
Senior Pastor	12 Months	$36,000

The salaries are based on an individual with entry-level skills and experience for his position. He could be provided additional compensation for advanced degrees, extra duties, and experience in addition to the base salary noted. For those who qualify, a portion of the salary may be designated as housing allowance.

The salaries in Figure 11.3 for the administrative and pastoral staff positions are based on the rationale noted below:

Guidance counselor—regular teacher's salary for the number of months employed plus a 5 percent supplement for administrative responsibilities.

Elementary principal—regular teacher's salary for the number of months worked plus a 25 percent supplement for administrative responsibilities.

Secondary principal—regular teacher's salary for the number of months worked plus a 30 percent supplement for administrative responsibilities.

Administrator—regular teacher's salary for the number of months worked plus a 45 percent supplement for administrative responsibilities.

Business manager—regular teacher's salary for the number of months worked plus a 35 percent supplement for administrative responsibilities.

Assistant pastor—regular teacher's salary for the number of months worked plus a 35 percent supplement for pastoral staff duties.

Associate pastor—regular teacher's salary for the number of months worked plus a 40 percent supplement for pastoral staff duties.

Pastor—regular teacher's salary for the number of months worked plus a 50 percent supplement for pastoral duties.

It is important that church staff salaries, including school staff salaries, be equitable on some common basis.

Compensation is intended to provide to those who minister an income that is sufficient to meet their needs. In most organizations there are differing levels of compensation taking into consideration the relative value of the contribution of employees fulfilling certain responsibilities. There are a number of rationales that could be used for determining salary differentials. It is not so important what base is used so long as the base is common to all church staff members. It would have been just as easy to build this model starting with the salary of the pastor and reducing the salaries for all those whose work is considered to be of less value than his. A few schools negotiate with each employee on an individual basis. Under this system the employee that is the best bargainer may earn the most, and the one who is the poorest negotiator may end up with the least. Thus, there is potential for serious morale problems. It is generally considered best to establish some sort of salary program and apply it equitably to all or to have classification of employees and treat all alike within a classification.

ADMINISTRATOR SALARIES

Administrative personnel are usually employed on a different financial basis from classroom teachers. The administrator is typically paid more than anyone he supervises. Other members of the administrative staff (guidance counselor, elementary principal, secondary principal, and business manager) are typically paid a salary somewhere between that of a classroom teacher and that of the administrator. It is a common practice to pay them more than any person they supervise, regardless of the years of experience or level of education, in recognition of the fact that their work can require their attention at any time, seven days a week. One approach is to establish the beginning salary of the chief administrator at a level 25 to 45 percent above the monthly salary of the highest paid person he supervises. The monthly figure must be used, since a teacher's salary is based on nine month's work and an administrator normally is employed on a twelve-month basis.

COMPENSATION FOR EXTRA DUTIES, ADVANCED STUDY, AND EXPERIENCE

It is customary for a number of school responsibilities to be carried by professional staff members with other primary responsibilities. Their compensation is based on their primary responsibilities. Playground, parking lot, and study hall duties are routine in teaching, and no one should expect additional compensation for them. However, when a teacher assumes the responsibility for supervising the yearbook, managing the cheerleading squad, or coaching an interscholastic sport, either additional compensation or some relief from that teacher's normal duties is appropriate. In most schools additional compensation is provided. This is typically provided by means of a salary supplement based on a percentage of the regular salary or a flat dollar amount. This approach is illustrated in Figure 11.4.

Entry-level teachers in professional education are expected to have a baccalaureate degree. The professional teacher cannot consider himself fully prepared academically unless he has completed his education through the master's degree level. Consequently, in education it is customary to provide financial incentives for the completion of graduate degrees. Typically they are paid annually in the form of supplements to the base salary in the form of a percentage or flat dollar amount. This is illustrated in Figure 11.4.

FIGURE 11.4

COMPENSATION FOR EXTRA DUTY
AND ADVANCED STUDY

Extra Duties	Compensation
Cheerleading Sponsor	$1,600
Varsity Coach (per sport)	$1,400
Jr. Varsity Coach (per sport)	$1,000
Yearbook Advisor	$1,400
Master's Degree	$1,000
Specialist in Education Degree	$1,000
Doctorate	$1,400

Note: For those who prefer to use percentages, the preceding figures can be converted into percentages by dividing them by the school's base salary.

Experience is also rewarded with additional compensation. Unless there is a common basis for recognizing experience, salaries that started out well balanced on the basis of the individual's responsibility in the organization will quickly get out of balance. Supplements for experience (Figure 11.5) can also be based on a percentage of the base salary or fixed dollar amounts.

FIGURE 11.5

COMPENSATION FOR EXPERIENCE

Experience	Compensation
Christian education	$700
Secular education	$300
Experience after employment (per year for 10 years)	$700

NONPROFESSIONAL STAFF

Every school will employ a number of nonprofessional employees—secretaries, custodial help, bus drivers (if there is a transportation program), and perhaps even a mechanic. Compensation for these positions will have to be calculated in line with whatever program is adopted for the teachers. Most of these employees will be paid on an hourly rate. Those who are given a salary should receive compensation comparable to those on an hourly rate. In most cases the lesser-skilled employees are paid at a level beginning with the minimum wage or a slightly higher hourly rate. The secretary, the bookkeeper, and the mechanic are usually the highest paid nonprofessional employees. All of these suggestions are general guides, of course, and each school will have to consider its own situation and make policies appropriate to it.

SPECIAL PROBLEMS

Church-schools present special problems in establishing salary programs. Some friction is almost inevitable in those situations where no logical explanation exists for substantial differences in salaries paid to workers performing similar work. Since many churches make matters of finance, including salaries, topics of discussion in church conferences, this knowledge is available to anyone interested. In view of these problems, the administration would do well to follow a compensation policy that bases all salaries within the church ministry on the base salary for the pastor.

Figure 11.6 illustrates how such an index can be used to relate all staff members' compensation to a common base. The idea behind this proposal is that the pastor, as the chief executive officer of the organization, should have a higher base salary than any other employee in the organization. The index proposed shows all salaries as a percentage of the pastor's salary, based on a subjectively chosen system of relative value. The specific values assigned in this model may not be appropriate for your church, but they can serve as a guide to help you develop a similar salary program to meet your specific needs. The duties assigned to individuals in different situations could warrant revisions in both relative position and percentage of the base salary. Some positions would be relatively equal in value and should be shown as such. The relative importance of each position in the model as it relates to other positions is based upon certain assumptions concerning the job description provided for each one. Since your organization might be very different, it is not appropriate to impose a model such as this on your personnel. It is intended to serve only as an illustration of how it could be done.

FIGURE 11.6

SALARY INDEX BASED ON PASTOR'S BASE SALARY

%	Position	Monthly	Annual
1.00	Pastor	$3,000*	$36,000*
.89	School Administrator	$2,225*	$26,700*
.87	Associate Pastor	$2,610*	$31,320*
.83	Business Manager	$2,490*	$29,880*
.82	Assistant Pastor	$2,460*	$29,520*
.82	High School Principal	$2,460*	$29,520*
.80	Elem. School Principal	$2,400*	$28,800*
.76	Guidance Counselor	$2,280**	$27,360**
.76	Classroom Teacher	$2,280**	$27,360**
.74	Music/Youth Pastor	$2,220*	$26,640*
.74	Maint./Trans. Supervisor	$2,220*	$26,640*
.60	Secretary	$1,800***	$21,600***
.58	Bookkeeper/Treasurer	$1,740***	$20,880***
.52	Custodian	$1,560***	$18,720***
.52	Receptionist	$1,560***	$18,720***
.50	Clerical Office	$1,500***	$18,000***
.50	Kitchen	$1,500***	$18,000***

*Actual monthly salary, actual annual salary, since this person works twelve months a year

**Actual monthly salary, annualized salary for comparison purposes, since this person works only a portion of the year

***Actual monthly salary if this person works 40 hours/week, annual salary if this person works full-time all year, annualized salary for comparison if this person works less than 52 weeks a year.

If an existing organization wants to adopt the salary index model, some adjustments will need to be made to deal with inequities that exist in the current salary structure. Obviously, it would be unreasonable to reduce the salaries of employees who are already above the level appropriate for them on the new index. Depending on how great the difference is, the salaries of these people could be frozen until such time as they earn an increase on the basis of the new index, or they could receive token increases in salary until they earn an increase on the new scale.

Once you have developed the overall salary program you should review it carefully to see that it is internally consistent. Whatever standard is adopted for compensation of employees, it must be fair and equitable if it is to honor the Lord and promote harmony among the employees.

IMPLEMENTING SALARY ADJUSTMENTS

It is not unusual to find inconsistencies in a salary program. In one church-school, for example, the church secretary received a $9,000 salary for a twenty-five-hour workweek, while the school secretary received $7,500 for a forty-hour workweek. Such is the fuel Satan seeks to create internal strife. How can you make reasonable adjustments if you decide the salary program you are using now contains inequities? You may want to adopt an organization-wide salary program such as is illustrated in Figure 11.6.

Eliminating inequities in a salary program is never easy. The inequities you see will not necessarily be the inequities the employees see. Once you have determined that a change is necessary, you should develop the new program and implement it the next fiscal year.

Have a meeting with all employees to explain the new program. Tell them that any employee that is currently earning more than the new salary scale permits will not receive a reduction in salary, but he will not receive an increase until justified by the new program. This approach will soften the impact for those adversely affected. Some of these people will undoubtedly leave the organization if they face a lengthy period without a salary adjustment. You will have taken a moderate approach to resolving a serious problem and reasonable people will appreciate it.

BENEFITS

Fringe benefits offer advantages for employer and employee alike. Because fringe benefits are not usually subject to any taxes, they provide compensation that exceeds the dollar amount spent by the employer. The tax saving is perhaps the most obvious advantage, but not necessarily the most important in establishing a good benefit program.

Federal regulations prohibit discrimination among employees except on the basis of strict guidelines. An employer may, for example, discriminate by class of employee. He may give all administrators more group life insurance than is provided for clerical workers. He may give more group life insurance to teachers than to clerical workers but less than to administrators. The employer must clearly define the classifications and be able to justify the classification given to each employee.

Benefit programs are valuable only when they provide something of perceived worth to the employee. There is little general benefit in providing family hospitalization at the school's expense when only two of thirty-three employees have families. Likewise, there will be little value in free tuition for faculty and staff children if few of the faculty and staff have children. Some employers in the business world set up fringe benefit programs on a cafeteria basis. The employer decides how much money per employee he can afford to spend. He then lists the benefits he is willing to provide and their costs. The employee selects the ones most meaningful to him. This idea could also work for Christian schools. Consult with your CPA if you decide to pursue this angle. It must be structured very carefully to stay within the law.

Fringe benefits for Christian school personnel commonly include the following items:

1. Paid sick leave

2. Paid holidays

3. Paid vacation

4. Paid personal days

5. Paid professional days

6. Paid time off for military training

7. Paid time-off for jury duty

8. Tuition grants and/or faculty loans for advanced education

9. Paid insurance (hospitalization, major medical, disability, or life insurance)

10. Free tuition or reduced tuition and fees for children of faculty and staff members

11. Expense-paid trips to professional meetings

Few, if any, Christian schools could afford all of these. A few of the more common are discussed in the following paragraphs.

Sick Leave, Holidays, and Vacations

Most school personnel are paid for nine months' work over approximately ten months' time, roughly August 15 to June 15. Teachers' vacations are limited to the time students have off. Teachers normally have time off for Labor Day, Thanksgiving, Christmas, spring break, and in some areas Memorial Day as holidays. They are not paid holidays, however, since the teacher is usually contracted for a 180-day school year rather than a specific period of time.

Sick days are an important benefit for all school employees. Since a Christian school employee's salary is generally low, he cannot afford to lose pay when sick. Most Christian schools offer some paid sick leave beginning with the first year of employment. Most give five days the first year and may give additional days for increased years of service. Some schools permit employees to accumulate unused sick leave from one year to another to protect them in the event of an extended illness or surgery.

Tuition Grants/Faculty Education Loans

It is generally recognized as beneficial to the school for teachers and other professional employees to obtain advanced degrees. To encourage employees to continue their education, many schools offer tuition grants (i.e., gifts) to employees to help pay for advanced work. Other schools prefer to offer loans that may be forgiven by future service. Typical plans forgive 10 percent of a loan for each year of service after the loan is granted. Grants and loans usually are restricted to faculty who are returning the following year. A minimum number of years may be required before the employee becomes eligible.

Tuition Assistance for Employees' Children

Most Christian schools require their employees to enroll their children in the school if the school is equipped to meet their needs. Since attendance is required, the schools feel responsible to help the faculty with the expenses. Tuition aid varies from granting full tuition and fees to discounting from 25 percent and up. This fringe benefit will attract married faculty members to your school and will help your school retain competent faculty.

Expense-Paid Trips

Every state with a sizable Christian school population offers some in-service training for the teachers, usually in the form of a statewide convention. In states without such meetings, the teachers can sometimes travel to a regional meeting. These sessions provide opportunities for personal development and for encouragement for teachers, administrators, pastors, and board members. All schools should provide time and money for their professional staff to attend these meetings periodically.

Special Benefits

Sometimes administrators of church-schools may be entitled to housing allowances and reimbursement for utilities without being subject to taxes. Consult a good religious-worker's tax guide or your CPA to see whether your administrative personnel might be eligible.

A valuable benefit to both the school and the employees would be free medical examinations for full-time staff members. The frequency of these examinations would depend on the age of the employee. By offering this benefit to all employees, it is possible to get a group discount. Medical problems requiring attention could be detected early and corrected, helping both employee and employer.

CHAPTER 12

PERSONNEL ADMINISTRATION

> For as the body is one, and hath many members, and all the
> members of that one body, being many, are one body: so also
> is Christ. For by one Spirit are we all baptized into one body,
> whether we be Jews or Gentiles, whether we be bond or free;
> and have been all made to drink into one Spirit. . . . But now
> hath God set the members every one of them in the body, as it
> hath pleased him.
>
> **1 Corinthians 12:12–13, 18**

The function of personnel administration is to achieve the goals of the
institution through people. The selection, orientation, supervision,
training, and meeting of the needs of these people are all critical components of the personnel administration function. All these functions
will be dealt with in subsequent chapters. This chapter will focus on the
personnel records and government regulations relating to employees.

RECORDS

Good records are just good business. One rarely regrets having documents, but many have been known to mourn their absence. Most organizations keep the items discussed below in individual employee's
personnel files. There are good reasons for keeping some of this information in other places as a matter of convenience. Our discussion assumes
they will be kept in one place. The important consideration is that they
be kept in a place where they are readily available when required.

Personnel Records

Personnel records must be kept current. They should also be kept where
their confidentiality and security may be assured. These records are typically maintained in the school administrator's, business manager's, or
bookkeeper's office.

If properly maintained, these records will provide historical documentation that may be needed in the future. By law they must show that the organization has complied with all current government regulations. These records must also satisfy outside auditors. As a minimum, personnel records should contain the following:

1. A copy of the employment application

2. Official transcripts of all pertinent academic work

3. Letters of recommendation

4. Notes of telephone recommendations

5. Copies of all pertinent certification and licensing documents

6. A copy of the I-9 form

7. Health documents

8. Test score data

9. Employment contracts or letters of employment

10. Payroll records

11. Tax records

12. Evaluation reports

13. Letters of resignation

Applications

Personnel files should be maintained on all employees, and they must be retained for at least three years, if not permanently, after the employment is terminated. The personnel file should start with a copy of the application for employment and any related correspondence. If your school does not presently have an employment application, you should develop one. Even applicants you have known for a long time should complete an application before being employed. An example of a good employment application may be found in Appendix F. If there is no application, you should keep the applicant's written résumé.

Copies of the application may, at times, serve as protection because they provide a written summary record of important information considered for the employment decision. For example, if you hired a young woman to serve as a kindergarten teacher, you assumed that she had a degree in elementary education. When you later learned that she attended school but did not graduate, you might want to discontinue her employment. If, however, she stated that she never said she had a degree, you would be in an awkward circumstance. Even if you knew that the young woman was lying, without evidence, you might be forced to keep her, at least until the end of the year.

Transcripts

The personnel file should contain a copy of an official transcript from every school the applicant has attended that is pertinent to his employment. A transcript should be accepted as official only if sent directly to you by the issuing institution and if it bears its official seal. Watch for evidence of falsified or altered credentials. Such instances of fraud have become an increasingly serious problem in recent years. Nonprofessional positions that do not require postsecondary education need not follow this guideline. However, even a high school transcript might reveal information about the person that would make you reluctant to employ him in any capacity. On the other hand, it might reveal some expertise that may prove helpful

Letters of Recommendation

The personnel folder should contain copies of all recommendation letters or notes of telephone recommendations. Full names, addresses, telephone numbers, and names of organizations should be kept in case you need them again. Do not accept letters of reference from relatives. They are not normally of any value in making an employment decision.

Certification and Licensing

Copies of teacher certification should also be reviewed carefully. In most cases you cannot have originals of these documents sent directly to you; however, the employee should have an original in his possession. Ask the applicant to bring the original to you so that you can have a copy made for your files. Be wary of accepting photocopies. The original could have been altered and the alteration concealed by photocopying.

If a license (as in the case of a bus driver) or a certificate of health (as in the case of a kitchen worker) is required, a copy of the original document should be kept in the personnel folder. An employer must verify that all legal requirements are satisfied.

I-9 Form

The Immigration Reform and Control Act of 1986 requires all employers to collect I-9 forms from all new employees. This form was developed by the Immigration and Naturalization Service to verify the eligibility of applicants for employment in the United States. If your school has never secured these forms from employees, it would be wise to obtain them from all employees that were employed after November 6, 1986. They must be maintained in the employee's personnel file and be available for inspection at any time.

New Hire Reporting

Within twenty days of employment, employers must report all new hires to their state. The purpose of this reporting is to allow states to check new hires against a centralized database that helps the government to track deadbeat parents. The government also uses this information to look for misuse in worker's compensation and unemployment compensation programs. The employer should contact the appropriate entity within his state to identify the appropriate reporting protocol.

Health Records

Some states require verification of immunization or the results of other medical tests. Any such data should be maintained in the personnel file.

Test Scores

Any test scores that you review before employing someone should be sent directly to you by the testing agency or, in the case of Graduate Record Exam or Praxis scores, from the applicant's institution of higher education. Some scores may be sent to you as part of an official transcript.

Contracts

The personnel folder should also contain a copy of the contract or of the letter describing the conditions of employment. The conditions of employment should be specific. Many schools have a written contract for all professional employees as well as letters describing the conditions of employment. The employer's expectations should be clearly detailed. A common mistake made by a number of Christian schools is to use contracts designed for teachers for other professional positions where there are significant differences in the expectations the organization has for these employees. Since there are relatively few people employed as administrators, guidance counselors, and so on, it may be better to have letters of employment for those positions if you do not want to design an entirely different contract.

Payroll Records

A record of the employee's salary and employment history should also be included in the personnel folder. Figure 12.1 gives a simple example. It should record not only the beginning salary but also the amounts and dates of any changes. You may find it convenient to include a note of explanation or the minutes of the meeting at which the salary change was approved. A change in job assignment or description should also be recorded along with the dates and authorization for these changes.

Smaller schools often record all payroll transactions in the personnel folder for each employee. Larger schools usually have payroll records completely separate from other personal data. In either case, the record should include as a minimum the following information:

1. Employee's full legal name
2. Date of birth (month, day, and year)
3. Social security number
4. Total salary and/or wages paid
5. The date payments were made
6. The amount and type of withholdings made

FIGURE 12.1

EMPLOYMENT AND SALARY HISTORY

Legal Name of Employee   Date of Birth

Social Security Number   Date of Employment

Date Began   Job Description   Beginning Wages or
                                                   Salary

Record all future changes in job descriptions and wages or salaries below.

Date Began   Job Description   New Wages or Salary

Date Began   Job Description   New Wages or Salary

Date Began   Job Description   New Wages or Salary

Date Began   Job Description   New Wages or Salary

Date Began   Job Description   New Wages or Salary

Date Began   Job Description   New Wages or Salary

Conditions of job termination:
                                                   Date of Termination
_____ Resigned in good standing, would
      reemploy

_____ Resigned, would not reemploy

_____ Dismissed, would not reemploy

Signature   Administrator/Pastor/Board Members

Tax Records

All employers required to withhold taxes on salaries and wages must have an employer's identification number. If your church or school does not have an identification number, you should secure a Form SS-4 from the local IRS office and make application for one. Copies of all payroll records forwarded to various government agencies must be maintained in the employee's personnel file.

The IRS requires that each employer document (Form W-4) either the number of dependents claimed for withholding purposes or the reason that there are no dependents considered. The employer must advise the IRS if the withholding exemptions that are claimed appear to be unreasonable. The IRS provides a special form for this purpose. Every school needs a copy of *Circular E Employer's Tax Guide*, an IRS publication designed to help employers meet such obligations.

With few exceptions, employers are required to withhold federal income taxes and Social Security taxes (FICA). States with income taxes likewise require taxes to be withheld from salaries and wages. Some local communities have small income tax levies that must be deducted from all paid salaries and wages. In addition, many employers are liable for federal unemployment taxes (FUTA). For example, this tax is one that the employer must pay on the first $7,000 of an employee's income in South Carolina. Each state sets its own maximum and its own rate.

The size of your payroll determines how often you are required to deposit payroll taxes. Instructions are given in *Circular E*. Once you have an employer's identification number, the IRS will send you forms quarterly for reporting your deposits. Deposits may be mailed to the IRS or made at any commercial bank.

A quarterly and annual report of all salaries paid and all taxes withheld must be made to the IRS, to most states, and to some local governments. The specific details of these reporting requirements are too detailed for this book. They are given in *Circular E* and other documents available from the local IRS office, your state revenue department, and local tax-collection offices.

Because of rising tax rates, employers and employees have both explored means of sheltering income from taxation. Most employees of the Christian school will find that tax shelters will not work for them; they cannot afford to put money toward anything but current expenses. Therefore, personal benefits in lieu of salary have become popular. These benefits will be discussed in the next chapter along with other employee compensations.

Evaluations

You should also keep some written record of the employee's performance. This is especially important if the employee's performance has not been satisfactory and you are considering discharging him or not renewing a contract. Each organization should have a formal program of evaluation for all employees. The program should specify who is responsible for the evaluation, what is to be the basis of the evaluation, how often it is to be done, and how and to whom the results are to be reported. All performance evaluations and subsequent recommendations should be reviewed with the employee. The employee should sign the form indicating that he has received a copy of the form and understands the performance appraisal. A signed copy of the evaluation should be kept in the personnel folder. A copy of any recommendations given on the basis of the employee's performance at the school should also be kept in the folder.

Letters of Resignation

When an employee terminates his employment, his letter of resignation or a copy of his letter of dismissal and related correspondence or reports should be placed in the file.

GOVERNMENT REGULATIONS

Government regulations affecting all types of employers have increased dramatically in recent years. The remainder of this chapter will identify and discuss some of the more important ones for schools. The reader is reminded that this is not an attempt to list all of them that are in effect at the time this book is written, and the reader is further reminded of the constantly changing employment environment. Administrators must recognize that they need to make every effort to keep abreast of these ever changing conditions. A website located at www.churchlawtoday.com is an excellent source of current information in this area.

Employment Law

A basic premise of law is that ignorance of it is no excuse. It is imperative that Christian organizations make a serious attempt to understand the laws and regulations that govern them. This is important for the sake of their testimony as well as for their financial security. Employment decisions are influenced by employment contracts, laws and regulations, and court decisions, and employers must be knowledgeable of them.

Many Christian leaders are of the impression that if their ministry is part of a church, then they can hire and fire anyone for any reason or for no reason. While that was true some years ago, it is not true today. The changes that limit our freedoms in these areas have not all been bad. Some of these changes have guaranteed to employees rights that, in all fairness, they should have had all along. Other changes have placed unreasonable and expensive requirements on our ministries.

Civil Rights Concerns

Many Christian leaders mistakenly believe that churches and other religious organizations are not subject to Title VII of the Civil Rights Act of 1964. Title VII regulates discrimination by employers on the basis of race, color, religion, sex, or national origin. It protects applicants for employment as well as employees. Title VII exempts churches from discrimination on the basis of religion; however, if they are engaged in interstate commerce and employ fifteen or more employees, they are subject to the remainder of the regulation. Churches could easily be considered to be engaging in interstate commerce as a result of national and international missions activities. It would be wise for employers to follow the requirements of Title VII, even when not legally bound to do so, unless there is a convictional basis not to do so.

Independent schools and church-schools that are separately incorporated would not be exempt from Title VII, except for the area of religion if they are religious schools. Even though such groups may not be legally bound to abide by the regulation, that does not keep them from being challenged and having to face the costs of defending their position by someone who believes they are covered by the ruling. Churches that claim the exemption on the basis of religion must be able to prove they are a distinctly religious organization entitled to the exemption. Those organizations subject to Title VII are prohibited from "failing or refusing to hire or to discharge any individual or otherwise discriminate against any individual with respect to his compensation, terms, conditions, or privileges of employment."

During the 1990s the Equal Employment Opportunity Commission (EEOC) filed suit on behalf of an applicant for a teaching position at a private school in Hawaii who was denied a position because she was not a Protestant. The school had been founded by a member of the Hawaiian royalty who specified that the school would remain distinctly Protestant and hire only Protestant faculty. The EEOC successfully challenged the school for alleged discrimination by demonstrating in court that the school had ceased to be distinctly Protestant in its practices and no longer was entitled to the religious exemption (*Kamehameha Schools v. EEOC*, U.S. Supreme Court, 1993).

Sexual Harassment

Sexual harassment is a major problem in the secular workplace and is a greater problem in Christian work than is generally believed. Certainly no Christian should treat another person, whether of the opposite or same sex, in a manner that would be defined as sexual harassment. Yet, we know the problem exists; all of us could name numerous people in Christian work who have been exposed for sexual impropriety. Most of the time that we hear about this problem, it involves two consenting individuals who entered into a sinful relationship. It stands to reason that, as prevalent as this problem is, there is a strong probability that there are numerous instances of unwanted and unappreciated approaches being made to staff members within our organizations. We should be concerned about this behavior because it is wrong. It is offensive to our Lord and damaging to the testimony of our organization. It also subjects us to legal jeopardy.

EEOC guidelines place heavy responsibility on employers for sexual harassment in the workplace, especially if an administrator is involved. Employers have been held accountable even when sexual harassment has been specifically identified as prohibited behavior. It is imperative that employers take reasonable action to make it known to all employees that sexual harassment is prohibited. In defining sexual harassment, EEOC guidelines say that

> unwelcome advances, requests for sexual favors, or other verbal or physical conduct of a sexual nature constitute sexual harassment when (1) submission to such conduct is made either explicitly or implicitly a term or condition of an individual's employment, (2) submission to or rejection of such conduct by an individual is used as the basis for employment decisions affecting such individuals, or (3) such conduct has the purpose or effect of unreasonably interfering with an individual's work performance or creating an intimidating, hostile or offensive environment.

Schools should have written policies defining sexual harassment with an explanation of how sexual harassment should be reported and should make clear that incidents of sexual harassment will result in very serious consequences.

Age Discrimination

Age discrimination in the workplace is prohibited by all employers who are engaged in interstate commerce and have twenty or more employees. The Age Discrimination in Employment Act (ADEA) prohibits discrimination against employees aged forty and above. The determination as to whether a church was engaged in interstate commerce would have to be made by a court. We observed earlier that it would be easy for a church to be considered involved in interstate commerce. It would appear safest to consider the church subject to the law if it has twenty or more employees.

Employees are protected under this act beginning at age forty, but there is no upper limit. Mandatory retirement is not permitted under the ADEA except in very limited ways. If you want to have a mandatory retirement age, consult your attorney to avoid being in violation of the ADEA.

Disabling Conditions

The Americans with Disabilities Act of 1990 has been noted as the most important civil rights legislation since the Civil Rights Act of 1964. The law covers discrimination in employment, public services, public accommodations and services operated by private entities, telecommunications relay services, and miscellaneous provisions. With regard to employment, the law prohibits discrimination against an individual who, except for his disability, would be considered qualified for the position. Once again, a qualifying provision includes employers that are involved in interstate commerce, a provision not yet defined by the courts. Churches and schools are probably included.

Churches and other religious organizations are given some latitude in their employment decisions. They are permitted to select another candidate who may not be more qualified than a disabled person but who is of the religious faith sought for employment in the organization. They are also free to require that employees adhere to the religious tenets of their organization.

As currently written the ADA does not place the following individuals in the protected category:

> homosexuals, bisexuals, transvestites, transsexuals, pedophiles, exhibitionists, voyeurists, persons with gender identity or sexual behavior disorders, kleptomaniacs, pyromaniacs, individuals currently using illegal drugs and current alcoholics who cannot perform job duties or whose employment threatens the property or safety of others.

The law requires that an employer make "reasonable accommodation" for an otherwise qualified individual so long as it does not constitute an "undue hardship" on the employer. Neither "reasonable accommodation" nor "undue hardship" is well defined, and the definition will ultimately be resolved by the courts.

In 1995, Campbell University, a Southern Baptist school in North Carolina, was the first institution to have this legislation applied to AIDS. They lost a wrongful dismissal case involving a faculty member dismissed because he had AIDS. They were required to give the former faculty member his job and a substantial financial settlement.

Wage and Hour Concerns

Compensation of employees is covered by the Fair Labor Standards Act. The language of the act clearly covers churches that operate nursery, elementary, or secondary schools, and the operation of independent schools. Of particular interest to churches and schools is the requirement that they pay minimum hourly wages to all employees and that age restrictions for the employment of minors be observed.

The current minimum wage is $5.85/hr. (This wage will increase to $6.55/hr effective July 24, 2008, and then $7.25/hr effective July 24, 2009.) Employees must be paid time and a half for all hours worked over forty in one week. It is important to note that it is a violation of the law for an employee to volunteer to work more than forty hours on tasks that are normally considered part of his job. In other words, you cannot avoid payment of overtime by having an employee volunteer his time. He can volunteer to do things without pay that are not normally his responsibility. There is a special exemption for religious camps, conference centers, and institutions of higher education that permits them to pay less than the minimum wage under very specific conditions.

Employees cannot be given a salary to avoid paying them the minimum wage. To qualify the position for exemption from regular wage and hour provisions, the individual must be considered to be an executive, administrative, or professional employee. Very specific criteria must be satisfied to be able to place people in these categories. Generally, to be considered an executive employee, the individual must be used in a managerial capacity, regularly supervise two or more employees, be involved in the hiring and firing of employees, exercise discretionary authority, and receive a salary of $455 or more a week.

To be considered an administrative employee, the individual must primarily be involved in nonmanual work that is managerial or general business operations in nature or the performance of general administrative work in a school's academic area and make a salary of $455 or more, or at least equal to the entry level salary of teachers.

To be considered a professional employee the individual must have a special area of knowledge acquired through a long course of instruction or that is original and creative in a recognized artistic field based on imagination, invention, or talent or that involves teaching, which requires the exercise of judgment and discretion, and receives a salary of $170 or more a week. The Department of Labor does not recognize all those who are called teachers as actually being teachers. This is especially important in the areas of nursery schools and kindergarten, where "teachers" are employed who do not have the normal professional preparation expected of teachers. A provision that applies to all three areas of exempt employees is that not more than 20 percent of their time can be spent in activities not enumerated above.

The law requires equal pay for equal work without regard to gender or marital status. This effectively rules out so-called head-of-household plans that have provided additional compensation for those who are married and have family responsibilities. Two separate district courts have ruled against church-schools with such programs as being discriminatory. While technically these decisions are only legally binding in the geographic regions covered by those district courts, from a practical perspective it seems as if the handwriting is on the wall as to the future direction of similar decisions.

The law permits anyone eighteen years or older to do any kind of work without regard to the hazards commensurate with the job. Children sixteen and seventeen years of age may be employed in nonhazardous work. Hazardous work for example would include roofing or driving a motor vehicle. Those fourteen and fifteen years of age have considerable restrictions on the type of work they may do. Not only may they not be involved in hazardous work, they also have significant restrictions regarding the amount of time they are permitted to work. Younger children may work in family businesses (so long as it is not manufacturing) and deliver newspapers or work in radio, television, or the movies. Additional information regarding child labor laws can be obtained from the Department of Labor's website (www.dol.gov).

The law also requires employers to keep accurate records so that compliance with the law can be verified.

Affirmative Action

Churches are not subject to affirmative action, but schools that operate as tax-exempt entities are prohibited from practicing discrimination on the basis of race, color, and national and ethnic origin in all phases of their ministry, including employment, even when the schools are operated as integral ministries of a local church.

Medical Leave

The Family and Medical Leave Act of 1993 has substantially changed the rules that govern the provision of medical leave. The law provides no exemption for churches or religious organizations. It applies to all employers with fifty or more employees. As a result, most churches with schools will be subject to this act. To be eligible for the provisions of the act, an employee must have been employed for at least twelve months and must have worked at least 1,250 hours during the previous twelve months.

Employees that are eligible for the benefits provided by the act are entitled to twelve weeks of unpaid leave during any twelve month period for one of the following reasons: to provide care for a child under the age of eighteen born to the employee, to provide for a child under eighteen placed in the home for adoption or foster care, to provide care for a child, spouse, or parent with a serious health condition, or because the employee himself has a serious health condition preventing him from performing his normal duties.

AIDS

Any Christian that would not demonstrate empathy and compassion for a person with the HIV virus or AIDS would be most unusual. If as an employer you are covered by the Americans with Disabilities Act discussed earlier in this chapter, you are prohibited from discriminating against a person because he has AIDS, because he has a family member with AIDS, or because he associates with someone who has AIDS.

Since AIDS is transmitted through the exchange of body fluids, there should be minimal risk involved in an employee/employer relationship. That is not to say there is no risk or that other employees, church members, students, and parent constituents will not be concerned about it. Information about this disease is constantly coming to our attention. Each organization should develop an AIDS policy. Free information is available from the Communicable Disease Center in Atlanta, Georgia.

Employee Disciplinary Action

Discipline is always an unpleasant subject, particularly as it pertains to adults. Most Christian organizations tend to develop a family atmosphere that makes unpleasant personnel problems even more difficult to handle. It is important to have a carefully worded written policy manual that delineates in considerable detail the expectations you have as an employer for your employees. The manual should carefully detail the process of reporting infractions and some idea should be given as to the consequences of certain behaviors.

It is important that your approach to discipline be as positive as the circumstances permit. Obviously, some situations will be so serious that upon verifying that they actually happened you have no option but to terminate the employee. Most situations will come to your attention well in advance of that stage, and if you handle them correctly they can be resolved with a minimum of inconvenience and embarrassment to all concerned.

It is necessary to determine the facts in the situation. Things will not always turn out the way it appears they will initially. Guard against making a decision before all the facts are available. It is always best to be certain of the guilt of the party before taking action (Deut. 19:15). We believe it is better to allow a person to get away with something you are confident he has done than to risk taking action against someone who turns out to be innocent (Prov. 18:17).

In most infractions of regulations, it is appropriate to give a warning about the unacceptability of certain behavior with a reminder that subsequent problems may result in more serious action. This warning would normally be verbal in nature but would be documented in writing for the record. A subsequent breach of rules should result in a stern written reprimand. The next step would normally be probation followed by termination. Depending on the seriousness of the offense, step three might be bypassed and termination be effected on the third occasion.

Frequently employees subject to disciplinary action will request the opportunity to resign. In most cases it is probably best to allow them that option. Disciplinary action should always be undertaken with the attitude that the employee will want to change his behavior appropriately. If there is no indication that this is true, it may be wise to attempt to bring the employment relationship to a conclusion rather than pursuing disciplinary action.

The material discussed in the second portion of this chapter is constantly changing as new laws are passed, new regulations are written, and new court decisions are handed down. There has been no intent to provide an exhaustive study of the issues raised here. There are differences of professional opinion on some of these issues, and some situations are too complex to be treated in a book of this nature. Our purpose has been to call attention to problems and to provide general guidance to the handling of personnel matters. As has been mentioned in other places in this book, it is important to maintain a relationship with an attorney and a certified public accountant who regularly deal with nonprofit organizations to discuss issues of specific concern to your church and school.

CHAPTER 13

INSURANCE

But if any provide not for his own, and specially for those of his own house, he hath denied the faith, and is worse than an infidel.

1 Timothy 5:8

It is common practice for us to protect ourselves, our employees, those we serve, our property, and our businesses through insurance. Since we do not know if or when we will suffer loss, we willingly pay a minimal fee (in the form of a premium and sometimes a deductible) in order to avoid the risk of having to pay for unforeseen damages. The insurance company assumes the risk and spells out the conditions of that agreement in a contract usually referred to as a policy. The goal of the company is to place its customer in essentially the same position after a loss that he was in prior to the loss. Since an insurance company realizes that not all of its customers will suffer loss, the underlying principle of operation is to spread the risk over as broad a population as possible

There are, however, exceptions to this basic principle. Life insurance and fidelity insurance are two notable examples. In offering life insurance a company realizes that all its policyholders will eventually die. However, not all of these people will keep their insurance in force until they die. Those who do not keep their insurance in force will not receive death benefits, but the premiums they paid can be used for those who do keep their policies in force. The company also knows that many policyholders are in good health and that the insurance company has several years to invest the premiums paid in order to raise additional money to cover liabilities.

Fidelity insurance is another exception. Companies that market fidelity insurance plan to recover substantial portions of the money they pay out for employee dishonesty; such funds are recovered through reimbursements from those whose dishonesty they cover.

For our purposes, we will divide insurance into two very general categories: protection for the church-school and protection for its employees.

CHURCH-SCHOOL PROTECTION

There are three categories of risk that church-schools need to be concerned about:

1. Legal liability

2. Property damage from natural disasters, accidents, and vandalism

3. Property loss due to employee dishonesty

Legal Liability

Essentially, liability insurance is designed to protect an institution from financial loss that could result from negligence or an accident for which it may be found legally liable. Premises liability, automobile liability (required in most states), and professional liability are three general types of liability insurance. Because some hazards overlap one another, it is a good idea to have all liability coverage provided by the same company to avoid disputes over which company is responsible for the claim.

Premises liability is not required but should be obtained by all church-schools. A $100,000 limit is recommended for property damage liability for automobile coverage. A seemingly minor incident can turn into a financial disaster. For example, premises liability could occur as a result of a student's injury on a piece of playground equipment that was in need of repair, a parent's injury resulting from a fall in an unlighted area of the property, or a student's injury because of an accident in a science lab where unsafe conditions are alleged. In each of these instances, the school may be found innocent of any legal liability; however, it could still incur substantial expense to defend itself. Premises liability insurance would pay for the cost of defense, and if the school were found to be legally liable, the insurance company would reimburse the school for the damages assessed, subject to the limits of the policy. In many instances, insurance companies settle claims out-of-court without regard to legal liability in order to reduce settlements or avoid adverse publicity.

There are three general sections in the standard liability policy: bodily injury, property damage liability, and medical payments coverage.

Bodily injury liability covers personal injury resulting from accidents for which the policyholder is found legally liable. The limits of liability are normally expressed in dollar amounts on a per person/per accident basis. For example, a policy may provide $100,000 per person with an aggregate limit of $300,000 per accident. This means that up to $100,000 could be paid to one individual and a total of $300,000 could be paid as a result of one accident. Some policies state limits of liability as single limits. For example, a policy may have a limit of $300,000 per accident. This means that regardless of the number of people involved, no more than an aggregate of $300,000 would be paid in one accident. The latter method provides more protection to the insured and should be chosen if the option is available.

Property damage liability is designed to cover the cost of damage to property for which the institution may be found legally liable. For example, suppose a parent attending a sports event at your school falls to the ground when a bleacher gives way. As a result of the fall, an expensive camera is broken and his suit is irreparably damaged. Property damage liability will pay for the loss. Property damage limits are usually reported in single limits in increments of $5,000.

Medical payments coverage is included as a part of most liability policies in an effort to reduce the size of claims. Remember that a liability policy pays only when the policyholder is legally liable for damages. Not all issues are clear-cut. Since most people simply want to be reimbursed for their actual losses, medical payments coverage has been added to make it possible for damages to be paid without regard to legal liability. Medical payments limits are usually expressed as per person and are issued in $1,000 increments.

Schools should consider substantial limits of liability to be certain they are adequately protected. Limits of $1,000,000 are recommended as a minimum for both premises and automobile liability. A property damage limit of $50,000 is probably adequate for premises liability. Medical payments with a limit of $25,000 should be considered the minimum for premises and automobile coverage.

Damage to Property

A church-school of any size will have a substantial investment in facilities and equipment. Assets should be insured for full replacement value. When full replacement coverage is purchased, most companies offer automatic coverage adjustments on an annual basis that adjust for inflation. The most common disasters are fires, storms, earthquakes, explosions, water damage, vandalism, and accidents. Accurate estimates of original cost and/or replacement costs are important in selecting limits of coverage. Failure to insure for full value will normally result in considerable loss in the event of property damage. Accurate inventories of special equipment and building contents are very important in the event of a major loss. Companies require some substantiation of your claim.

Basic property insurance policies are written to cover these and other hazards. Institutions with substantial amounts of glass, or with special equipment such as a pipe organ, should consider insuring some property for specific amounts rather than relying on blanket coverage. Coverage should be based on full replacement cost.

Physical damage to vehicles is covered by an automobile policy. Coverage is generally intended to protect against loss from collision, fire, theft, and vandalism; premiums are based on the value of the unit at the time the policy is written and are adjusted annually on the basis of current value. Deductibles should be considered. By accepting a deductible, you agree to insure against losses up to the amount of the deductible. Deductibles for collision normally range from $500 to $1,000. For other physical damage, deductibles normally range from $100 to $500. Deductibles can result in substantial premium savings. Choose as high a deductible as you can afford. It is not normally considered worthwhile to purchase collision insurance for a vehicle with a value of less than $2,000 to $3,000.

Student Accident Insurance

Student accident insurance is similar to medical payments coverage. It is intended to provide coverage for injuries resulting from normal school activities. Coverage is afforded without regard to legal liability and is frequently in addition to other coverage that may apply to the loss. Some student accident policies are often written as excess over other existing coverage and therefore offer greatly reduced premiums. Such policies pay only after all other coverage has been exhausted.

Student accident insurance will normally cover all intramural and interscholastic athletic activities (except football and soccer, which may be covered for an additional premium). Coverage is generally in force for one hour before through one hour after school or after the end of the school activities for the day. Most companies offer twenty-four-hour coverage for an additional premium. Try to obtain a policy that provides coverage for 100 percent of the charges for treatment of covered incidents.

Coverage is normally sold on an individual student basis. Many companies make it possible for a school to purchase a blanket policy covering all students enrolled. This is a good option. It avoids the possibility of a clerical error in failing to process coverage for a child who requested it, leaving the school responsible for any loss in the event of an uncovered accident.

Loss of Property Due to Employee Dishonesty

As unpleasant as it may be to consider, the possibility of loss as the result of employee dishonesty must be faced. Many believe that because Christian organizations employ only Christians, they do not need to consider this hazard. This approach is unrealistic. In fact, the attitude of complete trustworthiness and no accountability is the very condition that tends to lead to employee dishonesty. Most employees do not set out to be dishonest. Rather, they are tempted by what they see as an opportunity. Anytime there is the appearance of no accountability or low levels of accountability, the likelihood of employee dishonesty increases.

Employee dishonesty normally takes one of three forms: embezzlement, theft, or forgery. Fidelity bonds are a form of insurance designed to protect employers from all three risks. When a loss is discovered, the fidelity bond will provide for reimbursement to the employer, subject to the limit of the bond. The insurer will assume responsibility for reporting the crime to the authorities and instituting action to recover the loss. This coverage is relatively inexpensive and provides an important measure of security. The presence of a fidelity bond also serves as a warning to employees that the employer has a concern about employee dishonesty and has taken steps to protect the interests of the school.

Establish the limit of the fidelity bond at a minimum of 25 percent of the annual budget. All persons responsible for funds should be covered.

EMPLOYEE PROTECTION

Employee protection can be divided into two categories: (1) that which is required by law and (2) that which is provided voluntarily as an employee benefit.

Insurance Required by Law

Three forms of insurance are generally required by law (although there is some variation in these requirements from state to state and from one category of employer to another): unemployment insurance, social security, and worker's compensation.

Unemployment insurance, where required, is intended to protect workers by guaranteeing income for a specified period of time under specified conditions. It is a federal program administered by the Department of Labor of the respective states. The program is funded by payroll taxes assessed against the employer. A major problem with this program is that it gives to the state a measure of control over the employment decisions of institutions. Numerous court cases have challenged this program, but at present it is still a requirement for some religious employers.

Social security is a federal program originally designed to provide retirement benefits. Since its inception in the 1930s, however, disability coverage, survivors' benefits, and health care have been added. Most categories of employees are now required to participate in the program. It is financed by a tax on the employer and the employee that is based on the employee's earnings.

Worker's compensation is required by law of most employers in most states. It is intended to protect employees and their families by providing for disability income and death benefits in the event of work-related accidents and illness. In some states, worker's compensation is administered through a state fund; in others it is handled through private insurance companies. Your insurance agent will be able to advise you concerning your responsibilities in this area.

Group Health Insurance

It has become increasingly popular for employers to provide several forms of group insurance to their employees on a voluntary basis as a fringe benefit. This is a good practice and provides at least three special benefits we need to consider:

1. The value of the insurance is usually tax-free.

2. The coverage available through a group is usually less expensive than if the same coverage were purchased through individual policies.

3. Insurance provided as part of a group policy is generally broader in coverage than that which can be purchased individually.

Group insurance is commonly offered as part of an employee benefit package. Several types of insurance may be included in the plan:

1. Hospitalization

2. Surgical

3. Regular medical

4. Major medical

5. Dental

6. Optical

7. Catastrophic (cancer, intensive care, etc.)

8. Life

9. Disability income

10. Professional liability

To purchase group insurance, the employer must pay some portion of the premium. This is not true group insurance. Some forms of coverage included in such a plan include disability income, cancer insurance, and optical and dental coverage.

A benefit often afforded by group insurance is that every employee is eligible for coverage without regard to his insurability or to the insurability of his dependents. Some policies, however, exclude coverage of pre-existing conditions. Since this is a popular way for companies to reduce their liability, administrators should inquire about this feature and avoid companies that will not remove this limitation. Otherwise, employees who file claims related to previously diagnosed conditions may have their claims denied.

Health insurance programs usually provide for regular medical expenses, hospitalization, surgical procedures, and major medical expenses. These benefits are usually based on the room rate selected in the basic hospitalization policy. It is recommended that the policy cover 100 percent of the semiprivate room rate in your area. A stop-loss clause of $2,500 to $5,000 is also recommended. The stop-loss clause limits the out-of-pocket expenses for covered charges that an employee must pay in one policy year. After the stop-loss provision is satisfied, major medical insurance covers the balance of covered expenses subject to the limit of the major medical program. This is an important feature for persons on a limited income.

One popular feature of group health insurance is that it provides employees with the opportunity of obtaining coverage for the entire family at attractive rates. In most cases employers encourage workers to cover the entire family, although they must often do so at their own expense.

Several forms of health insurance are not routinely provided as part of a standard group medical insurance program because of their relatively high cost. These include dental, optical, and catastrophic coverage. The benefits provided under dental and optical coverage are obvious; catastrophic coverage, which is compensation for expenses of an extended illness, is an area with which some may not be acquainted.

All health insurance is limited to certain conditions. Specified amounts are paid under the policy in accordance with the plan selected by an employer. Rarely will a small employer (one with less than 100 employees) be able to afford coverage that approaches 100 percent benefits for all types of illness. Illnesses such as cancer can often linger for years, and the cost of repetitive confinement and expensive testing, treatment, and drugs will frequently exceed the benefits afforded under a good policy. Supplemental insurance can be purchased to serve as excess coverage after regular benefits have been exhausted or to supplement the cost of treatment covered under the basic plan. When this insurance is purchased, it is usually arranged by the employer but paid in full by the participating employees.

Term Life Insurance

It has become a common practice to include a limited amount of life insurance for employees as part of the basic group insurance package. Term life insurance, unlike whole life coverage frequently purchased by individuals, does not normally accumulate dividends or cash value. That means the policyholder cannot borrow against its cash value or cash in a policy after a period of time because it has no accumulating value as an asset: it is pure protection against the death of the insured. It is, therefore, very inexpensive.

Term life insurance is a valuable benefit, particularly to new employees just joining the work force. With so many other items needed for setting up housekeeping on his own for the first time, a single person may not think about life insurance. A limited amount of term coverage gives him the assurance that should he have an unanticipated early death, he will not inconvenience others by failing to provide for his final expenses.

Term coverage is perhaps even more valuable to the just-married head of household who is facing many financial pressures. The knowledge that a minimal amount of life insurance has been provided as part of the employment package can be reassuring.

Like other forms of group insurance, group life insurance has the feature of accommodating all employees without requiring them to provide evidence of insurability. If an employee has some physical condition that would otherwise make him uninsurable or would cause him to be rated as substandard, the group life insurance program is especially helpful to him. Additionally, an employee has the option of converting his group life insurance coverage to permanent life coverage if he applies within thirty-one days of leaving his employer. This provision would also be of interest to someone with special health needs.

Professional Liability

Our society has become "lawsuit crazy" and, unfortunately, Christians have not been exempt from this trend. Christian educators (pastors, board members, and other school employees) may be subject to an individual suit because of acts of negligence related to their responsibilities as employees or board members. Standard personal liability policies do not usually provide coverage for professional activities. Church-schools should consider providing insurance for employees and board members since any liability incurred by these persons would, in most cases, result from their efforts to carry out their ministries.

Consider, for example, the teacher whose student loses his eyesight in an accident while the teacher is momentarily out of the classroom, or the coach who, by sending an injured player back into a game, unknowingly causes the injury to be compounded, or the bus driver who spanks a rider—contrary to school rules—and is charged with child abuse because of bruises attributed to the spanking incident. Even if the employee is later proved innocent of such charges, he could incur considerable expense defending himself.

Professional liability insurance would pay the cost of his defense and any damages awarded, subject to the limits of the policy.

The cost of such coverage is relatively low. A limit of $1,000,000 of coverage is recommended.

DEVELOPING AN ADEQUATE INSURANCE PROGRAM

In recent years companies have tended to combine various forms of coverage into package or multiple perils policies. There are significant advantages to purchasing insurance this way. Chances of gaps in coverage are reduced. Typically coverage afforded is broader than if purchased in individual policies: there may be the opportunity to include coverage that would not otherwise be available, and there is generally a substantial savings in premiums.

It would be possible to purchase most of the insurance we have mentioned by simply calling one large company in your community. However, that might not be in the best interest of the school. Although basic insurance coverage differs little from one company to another, there are considerable differences in minor coverage that may prove important to you. And frequently there are substantial differences in premiums charged for the same coverage. Perhaps even more important, some companies have developed better reputations than others for service provided to their clients.

Insurance companies are regulated by state governments and must justify all their rates to the state insurance commissioner. They also have an interest in remaining competitive by keeping their rates as low as possible. These rates, however, are based on the experience they have for paying the claims of their own policyholders; consequently, rates can vary greatly between otherwise competitive companies. It pays to check rates and coverage with several different companies before making a decision.

It is possible to conserve time in comparing rates by contacting one or two large, reputable brokers who represent several different companies. By giving them an opportunity to bid on all your business—or at least a substantial portion of it—you will be giving them an incentive to present to you the most competitive proposal possible. Furthermore, by dealing with just one or two agents you minimize the confusion involved with filing claims when a loss does occur. Frequently incidents are related to more than one type of insurance coverage, resulting in attempts by one company to pass the loss on to another. When you are dealing with a broker who has all of your business, struggles between companies become his problems, not yours.

There is an additional advantage to dealing with large brokers. Occasionally companies will make substantial increases in premiums due to the excessive losses in your geographic area or with your type of risk. A good agent will anticipate your desire to consider other insurers and will begin shopping for you well in advance of renewal time so that you will not be forced to make a decision with few options.

When choosing an agent, you should consider not only his general reputation in the community but also his professional credentials. A mark of excellence in life insurance is the CLU designation, which stands for Chartered Life Underwriter. In the casualty and property lines, a mark of professionalism is the CPCU designation. CPCU stands for Chartered Property and Casualty Underwriter. These titles are given to agents after extensive, rigorous training in their respective fields. An agent with this recognition is generally one whose judgment and advice can be trusted.

A good program of insurance is important to the school. Start off right by talking with a reputable agent and having your insurance needs analyzed by a professional. You cannot afford to be underinsured.

CHAPTER 14

ANCILLARY SERVICES

Now he that planteth and he that watereth are one: and every man shall receive his own reward according to his own labour.

1 Corinthians 3:8

And whatsoever ye do, do it heartily, as to the Lord, and not unto men.

Colossians 3:23

Three areas of service that are commonly part of a Christian school are referred to as ancillary services. That is, they are often associated with the school ministries but are not directly related or essential to the provision of a quality Christian education. As such, it is important that the need for the services is present before serious attempts are made to offer them. The cost of providing these services is quite large, and many parents are not willing to pay what they cost. Consequently, the school must determine both that the services are desired and that they can be provided at a cost the parents are willing to pay for them.

TRANSPORTATION

The school bus is as much a part of the tradition of education in twentieth-century America as is the classroom teacher. For years few educators would have considered operating a school of any size without at least one school bus. That was, of course, in the days when gasoline cost thirty-five to forty cents per gallon. With schools now paying substantially more for gasoline, the costs for transportation are now 300 to 400 percent above the cost of a few years ago. Consequently, few schools offer bus service to and from school.

The Cost

The tremendous additional cost for transportation, along with the general escalation of tuition and other fees, is placing some parents under serious financial strain. Since schools cannot offer services for less than their cost, they have been forced to reevaluate those services offered. As with any other service, a Christian school should ask concerning its transportation, "Is this a necessary component of our total program of educational objectives?" While just a few years ago some schools bused 75 to 80 percent of their students to school, many of these same schools have totally eliminated their bus service. An increasing number of schools are determining that a transportation program for them is an unnecessary burden.

Obviously, children must have a way to get to and from school. In facing this problem, one has to consider the alternatives. In the days of neighborhood schools, children could walk to school. Unfortunately, Christian education is not normally popular enough for the school to have a student body composed of students who live within walking distance of the school. Many will travel a number of miles each way. Consequently, cost becomes a major factor for parents, regardless of the method of transportation chosen. The most common methods are for parents to bring their own children or to use carpools, public transportation, or school-supplied buses. Public transportation, obviously the cheapest means, is rarely an option for parents of Christian school children. For many parents, a carpool may be a good choice. All things considered, parents living a modest distance from the school can probably transport their children to and from school in cooperation with others for less than the school would have to charge for bus transportation. Parents who need transportation will usually find that the convenience of bus service is well worth any additional cost. From the perspective of the parent, bus service is a good deal.

What is a bargain for parents is not as good a situation for the school, however. Aside from the actual expense of operating a bus program, the school is assuming a responsibility that will absorb a major portion of administrative time. Many schools, in calculating the cost of providing bus service, fail to take into consideration the administrative costs. Transportation costs have fluctuated so rapidly in recent years that many schools have been unable to anticipate them adequately. The options for covering the cost of transportation are rather limited. Most schools attempt to determine the cost of transportation as accurately as they can and charge a fee designed to cover it.

Though there may be no approach that is right for every school, charging fees that approximate the projected cost of providing the service is the best approach for most. There is some justification for charging a portion of the cost against the general budget to cover the expense incurred by other student activities. However, this cost is proportionately small compared with the total cost of the transportation program. Fundraising is a questionable solution because parents soon tire of being plagued by various projects to cover the cost of regular and continuing expenses.

Generally when we think of transportation, we are referring to transporting children to and from school. Schools with a comprehensive curriculum that includes field trips and those with a secondary-level program with interscholastic athletics and aggressive programs of fine arts will find they need at least one large bus to transport students for these activities. An activities bus cannot normally be counted on for a regular transportation route since extracurricular activities often overlap the times the bus would be needed for transporting these students. A few schools have very active travel programs for their students, and they find it helpful to have a large diesel bus, such as a used Greyhound vehicle, for long trips. A great deal of caution must be exercised when getting into the used vehicle market.

Choosing the Vehicles

After deciding to provide bus service, the school needs to decide what kind of vehicles to use. The answer to that question will depend on several other factors—the type of service to be provided, the number of students to be transported, the size of the geographic area in which these students are located, the ages and physical size of the students, and the money the school is prepared to invest initially.

The first question that must be answered is the type of service to be offered. The easiest and cheapest bus service to offer is based on selected pickup points within the general area in which your students live. If a

sixty-six-passenger bus can be filled by stopping at four selected loca
tions, your school will have the ultimate in simplified bus service. Unfortunately, it is rarely that easy. One of the main reasons parents need
transportation for their children is that they are unable to provide it
themselves. Either there is only one car in the family or, more frequently,
both the father and mother are working and are unavailable to take the
children to a pickup point.

Door-to-door transportation is the most convenient service for parents, but it is the most expensive for schools to provide. Most Christian
schools that provide bus service offer a combination of door-to-door service and pickup points. A school using pickup points will usually find
buses of thirty-four- to sixty-six-passenger capacity the most economical.
Vans, long a component of most private school fleets, are no longer legal
for use as school buses.

When the school is small or is picking up students in a relatively
small geographic area, larger buses have definite advantages. The problem that must be anticipated, however, is how long it will take to pick up
all the students and take them to the school. Any bus route taking more
than one hour, unless unusually great distances are involved, is too long.
Occasionally a group of parents from a distant community will choose
to send their children to a school, making longer routes necessary. This
exception cannot be avoided. Regular routes, however, must be kept to
manageable lengths to avoid unnecessarily long rides that adversely affect the children's Christian school experience.

There are, of course, some financial considerations that will affect the
choice of a school bus. If it were possible to set aside all considerations
but cost, the best choice would be the largest bus possible. One bus hauling sixty children is more cost effective than four buses hauling fifteen
each. There is one driver to pay in the former situation, four in the other;
one set of tires for the large bus, four for the smaller buses; one engine to
maintain in the large bus, four in the other situation. Although providing a driver and maintaining the larger bus costs more than the smaller
one, it does not cost four times as much.

Another consideration is whether to obtain new or used vehicles. A used bus is attractive in initial price, but its maintenance cost is an unknown. A new bus will cost more, but the school is virtually assured of several years of very low maintenance expense. The largest source of used school buses is the public school system. Most public schools keep the buses seven or more years. Unfortunately, that means that such a bus will already have given its most productive service, and the years to follow are going to require extensive maintenance. If late-model buses can be found, they generally represent a good buy, if the price differential between them and comparable new vehicles is wide enough. Schools must also watch for used buses coming from northern areas where salt is used on the highways; many of these buses will have bodies in very poor condition. Another factor affecting the decision to buy a new or used vehicle is whether the employees will do the maintenance or whether all your work will need to be sent to a local mechanic. If you are prepared to do your own work, used buses will be a more attractive option than if you have to hire all the maintenance work that is done.

Financing

Whether to lease or purchase a bus is also an important consideration. If a school is in a position to pay cash for a bus, an outright purchase is undoubtedly cheaper. However, if a school must finance a purchase, leasing may be a viable option. Certain tax advantages make leasing attractive for taxable organizations. Leasing offers certain cash-flow advantages that are worthy of consideration.

Schools with limited cash will often find that leasing enables them to have buses at considerably less cost on a fiscal year basis due to the fact that they can be leased with little or no down payment and the monthly lease payment will be substantially less than the monthly note on a vehicle that is being financed conventionally. Research indicates that if the vehicles were compared on the assumption that a purchase would be financed 100 percent over a five-year period, the cost of leasing the same unit for thirty-six months and then financing the purchase for twenty-four months would be similar.

Fueling

Fuel economy is an important consideration in selecting both the size of the bus and the type of transmission. Sixty-six-passenger units operate at three to six miles per gallon when used for stop-and-go bus routes. Though gas mileage varies considerably with the kind of terrain, the average load on the bus, and the driver, schools have found that a vehicle with a standard transmission can offer twice the gas mileage of one with an automatic transmission.

Refueling vehicles is the most common maintenance procedure. Schools with large fleets of buses (ten or more) may want to consider the advantages of purchasing fuel on a bulk basis. It is possible to obtain a used 1,000- to 2,000-gallon tank and pump for installation on the premises. Sometimes the bulk dealer will supply and maintain the pump at no charge. This will enable the school to purchase gasoline at dealer cost if the volume is great enough.

It is not always feasible for a school to service its own fuel needs. The purchase and installation of a bulk tank, depending upon its condition and size, can cost several thousand dollars. It will take some time to experience a savings of that amount. In addition, the school will have to provide not only someone to refuel the buses but also a suitable location for a refueling operation. In most communities the location of the tank and the pump will have to be approved by the fire marshal.

Maintenance

The cost of maintenance for a developing fleet of vehicles is difficult to project. It will depend largely on the condition of the vehicles, the care they are given by students and drivers, and the preventive maintenance practices followed. Many Christian school consultants recommend that the school have its own garage and mechanics. However, only the largest schools could justify the expense necessary to provide the building, equipment, and personnel to do their own maintenance. It may be better to arrange for the school's vehicles to receive priority attention at a garage that specializes in commercial work. The important thing is to get a garage that has the capacity, equipment, and personnel to handle the wide range of needs encountered in operating a fleet of school buses and one that can assure the school's vehicles will receive prompt attention. Avoid depending on volunteer labor. Only the smallest fleet of buses can be serviced by volunteers over an extended period of time.

Vehicle maintenance is important to the school's testimony as well as for the safety and utility of the vehicles. Well-maintained, clean buses may not bring extra attention to a school, but if the vehicles are frequently seen standing along the road awaiting a tow truck, the school's image will not be improved. Lettering and paint on the vehicles should be well maintained. Many Christian schools find that their buses are among their best sources of advertising.

It is also wise never to scrimp on safety-related repairs. Routine maintenance should include replacing worn windshield wipers and burned-out bulbs; keeping tires properly inflated, balanced, and aligned; and replacing tires as needed.

Drivers

Bus drivers are an important part of the transportation program. Good drivers can be valuable assets in a public relations program; a bad driver can destroy the efforts of an army of public relations experts. A bus driver is much more than the operator of the vehicle. He spends time with students in an atmosphere that affords the opportunity to enhance or destroy effectiveness of the entire school program. Bus drivers must be born again, sold on Christian education in general and their school in particular, and good with children. Their attitude toward the school and its program, is as important as their ability to drive a school bus.

All states require a commercial driver's license (CDL) for bus drivers of vehicles capable of carrying more than fifteen passengers, including the driver. A check with the local driver's license testing office can give details. It would also be wise to require that each applicant for a driver's position provide a statement of satisfactory physical condition from their physician. The Christian school should seek the most capable, responsible drivers available. It should provide training to be certain they understand the operation of the bus and school policies. The insurance company may have a free safety program to assist in the training of drivers as well. It is imperative that they understand how to react in an emergency.

Mothers generally make good drivers. Usually they need to help pay their children's school bill, they have their own children on the bus, and they have a vital interest in the school. This involvement gives them a concern not likely to be present in others. Occasionally a school that cannot find mothers for specific bus routes will consider teachers, church members, or relatives of school families without school-age children.

Bus Regulations

A transportation program requires supervision that normal school policy does not usually cover. An entirely new set of rules is required to handle this area. The driver must be in a position to enforce discipline; yet he cannot devote so much time to administering discipline that his ability as a safe driver is impaired. Many schools have systems of monitors, using older students to supervise children during the time the bus is enroute to and from school. Bus rules should be included in the student-parent handbook. Infractions of bus rules should be treated like infractions of any other school rule. Students who do not respond readily to correction should not be permitted to ride on the bus.

FOOD SERVICE

There is a considerable difference in the breadth of food services provided by Christian schools. Few Christian schools offer full-scale hot-lunch programs, largely for economic reasons. Any school that contemplates offering a hot-lunch program should enter into the venture with a full understanding of the problems involved. However, any Christian school willing to allocate funds for the facility and personnel can offer hot meals for students and faculty. Some schools that have such programs have broadened their market to include other categories of customers; at least one school even operates a cafeteria open to the general public.

Cost

The major problem Christian schools face in providing hot lunches to students is making meals available that suit the appetite without exceeding the budget. This is no minor problem. Since Christian schools are usually not eligible for or desirous of surplus government foods, they are, for all practical purposes, operating a commercial eating establishment. Though they do not desire a profit as such, neither can they afford to operate at a loss. Since it is nearly impossible for a small school to purchase food products cheaply enough or operate efficiently enough to serve a satisfactory lunch at a moderate cost, most do not attempt to do so.

The following figures may give the reader a point of reference: Bob Jones Elementary students obtain a hot lunch with a beverage for $3.00/day. Bob Jones Academy students may purchase a meal in the university dining common for $5.25. This is essentially an all-you-care-to-eat meal with beverage. A local church-related school offers a regular hot meal with beverage for $4.00/day. These prices are beyond the means of many families and children often bring a lunch from home and purchase a beverage at school.

Regulations

Aside from the cost of food, there are other factors that must be considered, even when options for full-scale hot-lunch programs are preferred. First, local health departments have very strict requirements involving the storage, preparation, and cleanliness necessary to serve meals where a charge is being made. Some schools have chosen to ignore the existence of these rules and have suffered bitter consequences as a result. Whether food is to be served as lunches or as refreshments at school-related activities, basic health rules and regulations must be taken into consideration. A school cafeteria is subject to essentially the same rules as any other institution serving food to the general public.

One of the options considered by many schools is prepared food products that are ready for cooking but are sealed so that the hands of the preparers do not actually touch the food. These are available from several suppliers, in the form of sandwiches and regular meals. Because the food is purchased, prepared, and served without handling, most standards involving its preparation are the responsibility of the vendor. The school can heat the food in an oven when necessary and serve it to the students in its original container. No expensive equipment is required. In fact, suppliers of the food often make freezers and ovens available at no additional charge. It is a practical way to provide a hot meal with a minimal investment on the part of the school. Unit costs of the food items are not cheap, however. But they usually are cheaper than preparing a hot meal from scratch.

Sandwiches can be supplemented with other packaged items, such as potato chips, pretzels, corn chips, peanut butter crackers, and so forth. An attractive variety of health-food items is also available, although these tend to be more expensive.

By adding milk and other beverages to its supply of food items, the school can very quickly round out its food program. Most local dairies will agree to supply milk daily, or at least several times a week. Many dairies will also provide a cooler free of charge if the school's volume is adequate to justify this expense.

Facilities

If the school is large enough and other considerations seem to indicate that a full-scale hot-lunch program is desirable, the administrators can plan a more aggressive program. First, the health department and the fire department should inspect the facilities. The school also needs to determine whether the physical facilities are suitable, or whether extensive renovation is required to make them suitable. If a new facility is anticipated, the architect can plan for a cafeteria from the beginning. Cost will not be so critical with new construction. New equipment is not especially desirable unless someone is giving it to the school. Excellent used equipment that will meet the school's needs is available from restaurant equipment suppliers. By comparison with a commercial restaurant, the demands of school cafeterias are light. Used equipment can save thousands of dollars. The school should check with dealers in used restaurant equipment before making a purchase.

It is also advisable to visit several schools operating successful (and unsuccessful) cafeterias and to talk with their people to find out how these programs differ. Unless a school can overcome the problems of those with unsuccessful programs, it should not consider entering into such a venture.

Employees

Schools usually employ lunch workers on an hourly basis. Depending on the volume, one adult and one or two student workers may be adequate to handle the program if prepared foods are served. Some schools, particularly those with limited food service, have been successful in operating their programs with volunteers. It is worth considering. However, the disadvantage is that the employee/employer relationship is lost when the worker is not paid.

The most important question to answer in providing certain ancillary services is "Do we really need this service to conduct our Christian school ministry effectively?" The assumption that every school must have a hot-lunch program is false. For years schoolchildren took lunches, including beverages, to school. With the various containers that are available to keep beverages, soups, and similar items, a student can bring a wide variety of food items to school for his own personal consumption without the school being involved in any way. A lunch program is a convenient service and should be recognized as such.

When determining how to spend scarce resources, administrators must keep needs and wants in proper perspective. Neither a transportation program nor food-service program is a necessity.

BOOKSTORE

Increasingly, churches and schools are making bookstores part of their ministries. Particularly when schools sell students their textbooks there is good reason to consider making a bookstore a part of the ministry. In addition to textbooks, there are many school-related resources and supplies that could be marketed to students. While it would be difficult to compete with large retailers, the convenience factor would make a church/school bookstore attractive to parents. Once the bookstore exists, it could be the means by which Sunday school materials and other study materials are made available to the church and school constituency.

CHAPTER 15

PHYSICAL FACILITIES AND EQUIPMENT

Then the chief of the fathers and princes of the tribes of Israel, and the captains of thousands and of hundreds, with the rulers of the king's work, offered willingly, and gave for the service of the house of God of gold five thousand talents and ten thousand drams, and of silver ten thousand talents, and of brass eighteen thousand talents, and one hundred thousand talents of iron.

1 Chronicles 29:6–7

For which of you, intending to build a tower, sitteth not down first, and counteth the cost, whether he have sufficient to finish it? Lest haply, after he hath laid the foundation, and is not able to finish it, all that behold it begin to mock him, saying, This man began to build, and was not able to finish.

Luke 14:28–30

M any Christian schools have limited their opportunities because of inadequate provision for physical facilities. Others, who took time to study and evaluate alternatives, have exemplary physical plants. Whether renovating existing buildings or anticipating new ones, pastors, school boards, and administrators need to give thorough consideration to planning, financing, materials, utility, furnishings, and maintenance.

PLANNING

Improper planning has probably contributed to more mistakes in the provision of physical facilities than has any other factor. Pastors, school administrators, school board members, and building committees will be better prepared for their responsibilities in providing physical facilities if they will take the time to study such passages of Scripture as Genesis 6–7 (construction of the ark), Exodus 25–27 (construction of the tabernacle), 2 Samuel 7 and 1 Chronicles 17 (construction of the temple), Ezra (rebuilding of the temple), and Nehemiah (rebuilding of the wall). In these passages are valuable principles dealing with leadership, courage, form and function, materials, government regulations, finances, and timing that could provide needed direction for Christian educators today. The Bible does not always have specific answers to specific questions, but it has something even more valuable: basic principles that give needed guidance. The wise builder will learn to look for such principles.

Every school contemplating construction of new facilities or extensive remodeling should have a committee selected by the appropriate body in the organization and charged with the responsibility of overseeing the project. Those selected should be spiritual, genuinely interested in the activity, and knowledgeable about construction. Since building programs are often sources of division in Christian organizations (although they should not be), a definite means of communicating progress, limiting authority, and obtaining necessary approvals should be established from the very beginning. A building project is one of the best opportunities for God's people to see Him provide for material needs.

Because planning is essential to the construction of useful facilities, building committees should not hesitate to take advantage of the professional services of architects, engineers, and contractors experienced in the construction of facilities similar to what they need. The committee must also consider government regulations that may affect the type of construction, location of facilities, and type of material to be used.

No construction project should be started without a plan that has been carefully developed to show the end as well as the beginning. The plan should be approved by all appropriate parties before the first shovelful of earth is turned.

Space

The first consideration is adequate space. Churches that add schools to their ministries after being in one location for a number of years frequently face problems on this point. The Council of Educational Facility Planners, International, recommends the following minimum area for schools:

1. Elementary schools—10 acres plus one acre for each 100 pupils

2. Junior high schools—20 acres plus one acre for each 100 pupils

3. Senior high schools—30 acres plus one acre for each 100 pupils

These figures should be used as a general guide. A Christian school offering K5 through grade 12 with a total enrollment of six hundred would be well situated with twenty to thirty acres of land. This is assuming, of course, that all of the acreage is usable.

Classroom size will be determined largely by the pupil/teacher ratio desired. Twenty to twenty-five square feet per student is generally required by local building codes. Classrooms should be designed to hold at least thirty students. Consequently, each classroom should be 600 to 750 square feet. Avoid odd-shaped rooms that are hard to use. Classrooms should be essentially square or nearly square to have the most efficient instructional space. Other dimensions, such as the width of hallways, stairways, and entrances and exits, will also be specified by building codes. Space for special classrooms, offices, and storage, which will depend on individual situations, can be worked out with the architect or builder. It is important to provide adequate space, properly located within the building, for custodial supplies and equipment.

Several aspects of the physical plant used for instruction deserve special attention: the science laboratory, the computer laboratory, the home economics room, and the library. Special mention is made of them because they are frequently left out of initial construction plans or are provided for in an inadequate manner.

No secondary school curriculum is complete without provision for lab sciences like earth science, biology, chemistry, and physics. It is difficult, if not impossible, to give students adequate exposure to these subjects without facilities that will permit them to participate in practical experiments. In a small school, a science lab can be placed in a regular-sized classroom, but it must have at least the following special equipment: countertops for student work, sinks with running water, and natural gas outlets. In addition, the room used as a science lab should be equipped with an exhaust fan, a fire extinguisher, an eye wash, and an emergency shower. Larger schools need to plan to provide space for science labs that accommodate the normal pupil/teacher ratio in addition to the special equipment needed. It is also imperative that adequate storage space be provided for laboratory equipment and materials. The space must be capable of being secured. Schools should check with local fire marshals for additional requirements on the local level.

The modern Christian school needs a computer laboratory. Once considered a frill, a computer laboratory today is an essential for any school. Many Christian schools attempt to provide access to computers by having one in most classrooms. This is helpful and should not be discontinued even when the school has a computer lab; however, computers in the classroom will not substitute for a laboratory where instruction and appropriate experiences can be provided to an entire class of students.

More and more schools are attempting to offer home economics classes. A special classroom is needed to provide appropriate experiences for cooking and sewing. The provision of a classroom and the required supporting equipment is often viewed as excessive for the small number of students served since home economics is an elective course typically taken only by students in the general academic track. However, a good home economics program is an asset to any school and should be provided if there is sufficient interest and if the resources are available.

Every Christian school needs a library. In an existing school a regular classroom space can easily be converted to a library. In a new school, a room the size of a regular classroom will generally be suitable for an elementary school library, but the secondary school library should be at least twice that size. Whenever possible, the elementary and secondary school libraries should be separate.

Some schools have successfully combined secondary libraries with study hall and lunchroom facilities. While this arrangement is not ideal, it can be satisfactory if the use of the facility is carefully scheduled.

A school library should have at least ten books per student, with a minimum of five thousand per school. In addition to basic reference books, the school should provide supplementary reading materials for classes offered in the school and books and periodicals for pleasure reading.

Library collections should also contain Bible commentaries, biographies of exemplary Christian leaders, as well as conservative Christian periodicals. Teachers can often recommend books useful to the classes. Planning should anticipate adequate shelf space for the library, allowing for storage, and still providing room for students to study. The school library should be a pleasant place with an atmosphere conducive to study.

Government Regulations

Besides space considerations, churches adding schools to their ministries are finding that more stringent fire, safety, and health regulations are being imposed upon them. Some have taken the position that since the school is part of the church, the school regulations do not apply to them. Generally the courts have not agreed with this position. Churches with schools are unwise to resist reasonable standards simply on the basis that the rules do not apply to a church. We need to recognize that the operation of a Christian day school is more hazardous than the ministry of a church and should accept the additional cost as part of the expense of having a school.

FINANCING

We are living in very uncertain days. Our economic environment is fraught with uncertainty. Many churches and schools that have over-extended themselves financially have failed, and the testimony of the Lord has suffered in the community. Those responsible for expansion of physical facilities cannot be too careful about financial obligations.

Because of the uncertainty of the future, many Christian organizations refuse to borrow money for the expansion of facilities. It is interesting to note that there is no example in Scripture of borrowing money to finance construction. While there is no prohibition of borrowing, the absence of an example at least suggests that it is not the preferable method.

Examples we have in Scripture indicate that God's people were called on to give money and/or materials to be used in the project (Exod. 35:4–5, 21), without the improper pressure too often used today. Many modern practices for raising funds are highly questionable. It was the willing donor whose gift was desired. There is also a biblical precedent for asking for outside assistance (Neh. 2:7–8). However, any method considered must be carefully examined in the light of Scripture.

A church or school that elects to finance a building project has a number of options. The amount borrowed should be kept to a minimum, of course. The arrangements for repayment must be realistic in terms of the organization's current ability to pay. No financing should be based on future growth or on the maximum current ability to repay. While a number of "rule-of-thumb" principles have been suggested to determine the ability of a church or school to repay a loan, the best policy is simply to determine the amount the group can comfortably pay based on its current income and obligations. To exceed this limit is to presume upon God.

Existing economic conditions will dictate to some extent the appropriate means of raising funds. Churches and schools have used traditional financing through banks, bond programs, donations, and life insurance programs, to name just a few. Each has its own advantages and disadvantages. Without question, the safest and cheapest method of financing construction is to build with cash on hand.

MATERIALS

Artists and architects usually follow the principle that form follows function. This concept has a direct bearing on the selection of building materials that perform economically and efficiently and are also aesthetically pleasing.

The choice of building materials is limited most often by cost, and occasionally by availability. Usually people unfamiliar with construction are most influenced in the choice of materials by the initial cost. However, this shortsighted approach frequently results in more expense even in the short run. The choice of materials should be governed by several factors—relative cost, availability, durability, comparative costs of maintenance, and the practice in the community. As stewards of the finances entrusted to them, members of the school boards must construct facilities that will meet the need at the minimum cost, which is not necessarily the same as the minimum initial cost. The initial cost of an item may be less until compared with its useful life and maintenance cost.

For example, several years ago it was common to install hard-surface flooring in classrooms. Various types of tile were in common use because they initially cost far less than carpet. However, over a ten-year period, the cost of the maintenance resulted in more expense for a hard-surface floor than the initial cost of carpet and its maintenance over the same period of time. As an additional consideration, many view carpet as far more desirable acoustically and aesthetically. Therefore, even though it has a higher initial cost, carpet is often a better choice.

Building committees should seek advice in the selection of materials: not only the opinion of sales personnel (who have a commission resting on the choice) but also the advice of expert, impartial consultants.

Another major factor influencing the choice of materials should be the impact of the building on the testimony of the Lord. Quality of materials is an indirect reflection of the institution's attitude toward the Lord. This perspective, of course, must be balanced by practical considerations. However, the finished building should demonstrate that the Christians involved place a higher value on the Lord's work than on their own material means. Therefore, the materials selected should reflect a higher level of quality than might be selected for their own homes.

On the other hand, money should not be spent foolishly on materials just for appearance's sake. There is no need for a school located in Georgia, for example, to purchase marble from Italy when marble is available within the state. A school located hundreds of miles from the nearest brick foundry could well consider another material more readily and economically available in its locality. Practical consideration should be a part of any material selection.

UTILITY

Planners sometimes get so engrossed in a project that they forget the purpose of a facility; for example, when choosing items for a gymnasium, they might choose furnishings that are actually more appropriate for a church auditorium. Sometimes problems arise because the building committee does not consult those who will use the building. One church even omitted the school administrator from the building committee when a building was being constructed for the primary use of its school. Such action is extremely shortsighted and will certainly lead to difficulty.

FIGURE 15.1

GYMNASIUM DESIGNED FOR 1,500 SPECTATORS
COURT SIZE MEETS HIGH SCHOOL STANDARDS

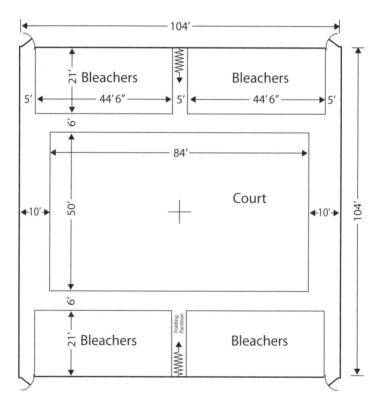

The seating area includes folding bleachers; capacity calculation allows 16 inches per person. If seating for 750 would be adequate, the overall building width could be reduced by 21 feet, reducing the total area of the building by 2,184 square feet.

Figures 15.1 and 15.2 provide guidelines that can be helpful in planning for school athletic activities.

All groups that will use a building should either be represented on the building committee or be consulted on a regular basis. Consider the frustration of the athletic department when a locker room with showers was built with a perfectly level floor and, with the exception of the actual shower stalls, had no floor drains installed. No one considered the fact that the teams would be entering the room covered with mud and that the entire room would have to be washed down. Even though drains were later installed, there was no way to give the floor slope; consequently, when the floor was washed down, water ran freely out the door into the carpeted hallway and always had to be pushed to the drains with a squeegee—a most unsatisfactory situation that could have been avoided without additional expenditure.

Locker facilities that will be used by athletes playing outside should be located at the end of the building or have an exterior entrance leading directly into the room. This will prevent athletes from tracking dirt through the school in order to reach the locker facility.

Planners must also consider the nature of certain activities when locating rooms for them. For example, the band room should not be located next to the library, the church/school offices, or the lower elementary grades. Students should have all their activities in the same section of the building. Older children should not have to use the same restroom facilities as younger children, and faculty should not have to use the same restroom facilities as students. Planners can avoid most potential problems by involving in the design and furnishings of the facilities those people who will use them.

FURNISHINGS AND EQUIPMENT

In selecting furnishings and equipment, considerations of functions are of primary importance. Church-schools must consider school functions as well as church functions. The Sunday ministry must not be sacrificed or hindered for the sake of the Monday through Friday ministry. However, thorough advance planning and design will insure that the needs of all are adequately provided for and that the church-school facility is better equipped than either a church or school acting alone could afford to be.

FIGURE 15.2

MINIMUM AREA REQUIRED FOR
COMMON ATHLETIC ACTIVITIES*

Activity	Grades 1–6	Grades 7–9	Grades 9–12	Overall Area Size w/ Buffer Zone
Basketball	40 x 60	50 x 84	50 x 84	7,200 sq. ft.
Volleyball	25 x 50	25 x 50	30 x 60	2,800 sq. ft.
Badminton			20 x 44	1,800 sq. ft.
Table Tennis			20 x 44	1,800 sq. ft.
Tennis		36 x 78	36 x 78	6,500 sq. ft.
Shuffleboard			6 x 52	640 sq. ft.
Tetherball	10 (circle)	12 (circle)	12 (circle)	400 sq. ft.
Croquet	38 x 60	38 x 60	38 x 60	2,200 sq. ft.
Baseball	210 x 210	300 x 300	300 x 300	160,000 sq. ft.
Archery		50 x 300	50 x 300	20,000 sq. ft.
Softball	150 x 150	200 x 200	275 x 275	75,000 sq. ft.
Football (12-man)			160 x 360	80,000 sq. ft.
Football (6-man)			120 x 300	54,000 sq. ft.
Football (touch)		120 x 300	160 x 360	80,000 sq. ft.
Soccer				
(men, mm.)			165 x 300	65,000 sq. ft.
(men, max.)			240 x 360	105,000 sq. ft.
(women)			120 x 240	40,000 sq. ft.

*All dimensions are in feet.

PHYSICAL FACILITIES AND EQUIPMENT

A wide variety of furniture and equipment designed for school use also lends itself to use by the Sunday school and church youth group. The Council of Educational Facility Planners, International, suggests that the following criteria be taken into consideration in furniture and equipment selections (the order is not significant): (1) appearance, (2) flexibility, (3) safety, (4) durability, (5) maintenance, (6) comfort, (7) building codes, (8) guarantees, (9) costs, (10) services of the manufacturer and/or distributor.

Many schools have found surplus equipment available for sale from local public schools. When it is available in good condition and at reasonable cost, such equipment may be a good buy. Used furniture and equipment are worthwhile investments when the overall physical condition and appearance warrant their purchase. Schools do not want to give the impression, however, that their building committees raided a second-hand furniture store for equipment.

Figure 15.3 presents helpful information for choosing chalkboards and tackboards for the classroom.

FIGURE 15.3

RECOMMENDED MINIMUM REQUIREMENTS FOR CHALKBOARD AND TACKBOARD*

Space to Be Served	Chalkboard Length	Tackboard Length
Kindergarten/elementary classrooms	16	16
English, social studies, language classrooms	16	16
Mathematics classrooms (one section ruled)	24	12
Science classrooms	24	16
Science labs (if different from classrooms)	8	8
Business education classrooms	16	16
Music classrooms (one section ruled)	12	12
Arts and crafts	12	24

Space to Be Served	Chalkboard Length	Tackboard Length
Industrial arts	12	12
Offices (each)		6
Health	8	8
Physical education		
gymnasium		8
classroom	8	8
locker room	8	8
Library		8
Professional library/teachers' workroom (each)		8
Cafeteria		8
Kitchen		4
Home economics	8	8
Main entrance area/lobby		8
Halls		8 every 100
One or two areas frequented by custodial help and bus drivers		4

*All dimensions are in feet.

Figures 15.4 and 15.5 provide information useful when selecting and locating equipment and furniture.

FIGURE 15.4

WORKING HEIGHTS FOR FURNITURE AND EQUIPMENT*

Item	Kindergarten	(1–3)	(4–6)
Cabinet, display (top)	54	56	66
Cabinet display (bottom)	26	29	34
Cabinet, pupil use (top)	50	56	65
Chairs and bench	10–11	10–13	12–16

Item	Kindergarten	(1–3)	(4–6)
Chalkboard (bottom)	22	24	29
Counter, cafeteria	27	31	36
Counter, classroom work (standing)	24	24	30
Counter, general office	27	31	36
Desk and table, classroom	18	20	23
Doorknob	27	31	36
Drinking fountain	24	27	32
Hook, coat	36	41	48
Lavatory and sink	23	26	29
Light switch	27	35	40
Mirror, lower edge	35	38	43
Panic hardware	27	31	36
Pencil sharpener	27	31	36
Rail, hand	21	24	29
Shelf, storage	41	46	54
Soap dispenser	27	31	36
Stool, work	19	21	26
Table, work	26	29	34
Table and bench work (standing)	26	29	34
Tackboard (bottom)	22	24	29
Telephone, wall mounted	35	37	43
Toilet stall, top of partition	44	52	61
Towel dispenser	27	31	36
Urinal (bottom)		3–15	3–17
Wainscoting	54	54	54
Water closet (seat)	10½	11½	13½
Window ledge	29	30	34

*All dimensions are in inches.

FIGURE 15.5

WORKING HEIGHTS FOR FURNITURE AND EQUIPMENT*

Item	Grades 7–9	Grades 10–12
Cabinet, display (top)	74	77
Cabinet, display (bottom)	38	39
Cabinet, student use (top)	74	79
Chair and bench	13–17	14–18
Chalkboard (bottom)	32	34
Counter, cafeteria	40	42
Counter, classroom work (standing)	34	36
Counter, general office	40	42
Desk and table, classroom	23–28	24–29
Desk, typing	29	29
Doorknob	40	42
Drinking fountain	36	40
Hook, coat	54	55
Lavatory and sink	33	35
Light switch	46	50
Mirror, lower edge	48	52
Panic hardware	40	42
Pencil sharpener	40	42
Rail, hand	32	33
Shelf, storage	60	62
Soap dispenser	40	42
Stool, work	28	29
Table, work	38	39
Table and bench, work (standing)	38	39
Tackboard (bottom)	32	34
Telephone, wall mounted	48	52
Toilet stall, top of partition	67	69
Towel dispenser	40	42
Urinal (bottom)	4–18	4–19
Wainscoting	60	60

Item	Grades 7–9	Grades 10–12
Water closet (seat)	14½	15
Window ledge	38	41

*All dimensions are in inches.

MAINTENANCE

The custodial function of maintenance is an area in which schools often try to save money, especially during the early years of the building's use. This shortcut, however, not only affects the school's testimony but also contributes directly to the cost of maintenance in future years. Actually the custodial function should be viewed as basic maintenance. Equipment and buildings that are properly cleaned and serviced will look better and will usually last longer.

The number of custodial personnel and the amount of time they must spend keeping facilities in order will vary greatly with the size, the furnishings, and the geographic area in which the facilities are located. Figure 15.6 gives some helpful guidelines. State departments of education frequently develop handbooks for custodians of local school districts and often make these available to others without charge.

All buildings and equipment should be inspected regularly for malfunctioning and signs of wear. Every school should have a system of referral that will call needed repairs to the attention of the appropriate person. Repairs may legitimately be delayed until convenient if the delay does not result in a safety hazard or threaten future use of the building or equipment. All other repairs should be handled without delay.

The exterior of the building also requires care. Maintenance personnel should keep it clean, repair broken items, and repaint as necessary. As an additional part of the school's testimony, grounds personnel should mow the lawn, weed the flowers, trim the shrubbery, and correct erosion problems.

Christian school facilities should be show places for God's glory. They should reflect and enhance the overall quality of the institution.

Thorough planning and consistent upkeep are the keys to maintaining quality facilities.

FIGURE 15.6

TIME REQUIREMENTS FOR COMMON
CUSTODIAL DUTIES*

Duty	Frequency	Time Required
Classrooms (30 x 30 area)		
Trash pickup	Daily	1/room
Dusting	Daily	5/room
Sweeping (hard surface)	Daily	12/room
Vacuuming (carpet)	Alternate days	15/room
Checking for wear	As needed	5/room
Checking chalk tray	As needed	5/room
Damp mopping	As needed	20/room
Wet mop and rinse	As needed	30/room
Machine scrubbing	As needed	30/room
Machine polishing	As needed	15/room
Wet vacuum pickup	As needed	15/room
Restrooms	Daily	30/room
Toilet bowl and seat		
Urinals		
Wash sink and counter		
Mopping and disinfecting floors		
Stairways	Daily	
Hard surface		10/flight
Carpeted		15/flight
Hallways	Daily	
Hard surface (damp mop/ sweep)		1–2/100 sq. ft.
Carpet (vacuum)		1/100 sq. ft.
Drinking fountains	Daily	1/each

Duty	Frequency	Time Required
Auditorium	Weekly	2/200 sq. ft.
Gymnasium floor	Daily	5/1,000 sq. ft.
Cleaning glass	As needed	1/10 sq. ft.
Machine scrubbing traffic areas	As needed	
Light soil areas		9/100 sq. ft.
Medium soil areas		10/100 sq. ft.
Heavy soil areas		11/100 sq. ft.

*All times are given in minutes. Times given are for accomplishing the task under normal conditions. Unusual weather conditions or other extremities must be considered individually. Preparation time is not included.

CHAPTER 16

PUBLICITY

A faithful witness will not lie: but a false witness will utter lies.

Proverbs 14:5

Withal praying also for us, that God would open unto us a door of utterance, to speak the mystery of Christ, for which I am also in bonds: that I may make it manifest, as I ought to speak.

Colossians 4:3–4

Just as a manufacturing company boosts its sales by promoting its product, so the Christian school that promotes its program will enhance its ministry. A school that is giving students a quality Christian education should make people aware of the service the school can provide them. Promotion is a perpetual task, designed to accomplish Christ-honoring goals.

GOALS OF PROMOTION

One of the main goals of promotion is to help the Christian school enroll more students, not necessarily for the purpose of bringing more money into the school but with the goal of conforming more lives to the image of Christ. The Christian school should be designed to enroll students from homes where parents desire a truly Christian education for their children, not just an escape from the public schools. Therefore, the Christian school should seek the right type of students.

Another goal of promotion is to reach families in the community with the gospel. The promotion of your school will generate many contacts with whom Christian workers from the school or church may eventually share the plan of salvation. Some of the best soulwinning contacts are people who inquire about the possibility of enrolling their children in a Christian school; many parents have found Christ as their Savior during a visit initiated through such an inquiry.

Another important reason for the promotion of the Christian school is the development of a good reputation in the community.

Jesus said that we are the light of the world (Matt. 5:13–14). The Christian school can show to the community the quality job it is doing in teaching young people "not only how to make a living, but also how to live." It can develop the reputation of having a quality program that builds spiritual character and academic excellence in the life of each student. Promoting your school is important not only for informing those who might be interested in the school to satisfy the needs of their family but also for informing those in the community who may hear of your school and of its quality academic and spiritual program. Of course, it would be unethical to promote this outstanding program unless the school genuinely practices it.

The ultimate goal of the Christian school must be to bring honor and glory to the Lord Jesus Christ (1 Cor. 10:31). Christian education cannot take place without God's working in the lives of young people; "for it is God which worketh in you both to will and to do of his good pleasure" (Phil. 2:13). Therefore, any credit for achievements in the lives of the students belongs to God alone. Promotion should not take place just so that people will see the Christian school or the Christlike students but so that they will ultimately see Christ Himself (Col. 1:18). Promotion must be designed to reveal Christ to the people in your community through your ministry.

METHODS OF PROMOTION

The best way to promote the Christian school is by direct conversation. Money cannot buy any better advertising than that which you will receive when families that have been satisfied with your school have the opportunity to share with others how your school has met their needs. Satisfied customers are always the best advertisement. Conversely, unhappy parents can be your worst enemies. Always try to mend fences with unhappy parents before you part ways. Even when the issue that divides you is one on which you have no room to compromise, let them know you respect their views and demonstrate an interest in seeing that they find a means of providing the education they want for their children.

Parents should be encouraged to talk with their friends and relatives about the quality education their children are receiving at the Christian school. People who are investigating the school can be directed to satisfied parents to get more information. Schools should also strive to develop in the students a love for other students who might be considering attending. Happy students go a long way toward promoting the school. Some schools have successfully used financial incentives to get parents of students currently enrolled to recommend the school to others. They have offered cash credits for those families who recommended the school to a new family with prospective students.

A second promotional tool is the appearance of the school itself. It automatically reflects—positively or negatively—on the ministry. Hundreds of people pass the school every day, developing an impression by what they see. The Christian school that has sloppy grounds and buildings is telling the public that it has no concern for excellence. The school that has attractive landscaping and well-kept grounds, on the other hand, is showing people that it desires quality in all areas. An attractive sign placed on the front of the grounds near the road is an efficient and important means of promotion. Schools that provide bus service should consider their buses as advertising tools. A well-maintained bus that is driven by a courteous driver will gain the attention of those who might be interested in your school. Also, have your school name and telephone number placed in a prominent place on the exterior of the bus.

Of course, school programs are excellent promotion as well. Parents are always happy to show off their children. Programs that provide opportunities for the children provide a satisfying experience for the students and their parents and you can gain considerable benefit by encouraging parents to invite others to come. An open house once or twice a year gives parents an opportunity to bring their friends and neighbors to see your school for themselves. Identifying a week as Christian school week and extending a special invitation for people to visit the school can also be a very productive approach. With teachers in their classrooms and work creatively displayed, all who attend can see not only the outstanding work that students are doing but also the godly personnel of the school. Also effective are special speakers brought into the school or church to promote the importance of Christian education and to motivate people to enroll their children. Furthermore, school plays and musical programs give opportunities to show the variety of activities that students can be involved in at the Christian school. Graduation exercises demonstrate to the community the type of students being developed at the school.

Special programs at different churches also help promote the school. Since the Christian school is designed primarily for Christians, other Bible-believing churches provide natural places from which to draw students. A video presentation of the school ministry, a biblical message on Christian education preached by your school administrator, and testimonies and/or special music provided by the students or faculty can make prospective students and their parents enthusiastic about Christian education.

The advertising media of the local community should also be used for promotion. Newspaper advertisements, designed to inform the public about what Christian education is and why it is important, can include pertinent information about the school—the address, phone number, and grades available. A statement of nondiscrimination on all printed advertisements is required by law.

FIGURE 16.1

STATEMENT OF NONDISCRIMINATION
RECOMMENDED BY THE IRS

The _____ School admits students of any race, color, national and ethnic origin to all the rights, privileges, programs, and activities generally accorded or made available to students at the school. It does not discriminate on the basis of race, color, national and ethnic origin in administration of its educational policies, scholarship and loan programs, and athletic and other school administered programs (Department of the Treasury, Publication 557, 2005, 23).

The Christian school administrator who gets to know the various editors of a newspaper can work with them in designing articles that the newspaper would like to print. This personal contact will many times get articles printed that may otherwise be ignored.

Though radio and television are expensive ways to promote, they are also effective in reaching large numbers of people quickly. Short advertising spots repeated frequently are better than just a few longer advertisements. Again, the advertisement may consist of human-interest stories or coverage of newsworthy events. The Christian school should contact the television and radio stations when it plans special events or gives special awards. Even though radio and television stations are very particular about the material they use, a Christian school's persistence can pay off in a considerable amount of free advertising. All radio and television stations are required to provide free public-service announcements. The school may also be able to sponsor a program on a local Christian station.

Other possible advertising media are billboards, marquees at malls, and the yellow pages of the telephone book. If the school is independent, then the ad should be placed under the section "Schools—Private." If the Christian school is a ministry of the local church, the church and school should be listed in the yellow pages under both "Churches" and "Schools—Private."

Another effective promotional method is to have an exhibit at the local county fair with displays showing pictures of school classrooms, student work, and extracurricular activities. Student leaders from the school can hand out information about the school and can record contacts. If the fair allows, some of the school's musical groups may perform hourly programs in order to draw people to the exhibit. The fair is not only a good place to promote the school but it also affords an excellent opportunity to witness. Similar public awareness can be developed by participation in parades and other public events where individual and group participation is invited.

The school's alumni (and their parents) are another source of excellent public relations. A satisfied customer will tell coworkers, neighbors, and other relatives of the satisfactory experience that they had at your institution. The administrator should encourage "word-of-mouth" advertising amongst the various stakeholders of the school. Alumni should be encouraged to keep in touch with the school through various school activities (e.g., alumni associations, class reunions, homecoming events) and other communications. It is especially gratifying when alumni choose to send their children to your school because of the positive experience they had there as a student.

One of the best methods of promotion is to use quality printed materials. An attractive letterhead that gives the name of the school, the address, the telephone number, and the people in charge presents an image of quality to all who receive school correspondence. Never forget that your printed materials may be the only opportunity you have to impress a person with the quality of the education offered by your institution.

One of the most frequently used promotional materials is the school brochure, given to every person interested in the school. This brochure, updated annually to present the school's purpose, program, personnel, and procedure for enrollment, will generate more interest if it includes action photographs taken at the school. Also, if it is designed so that one of the folded sides is a self-mailer with the school's return address already printed on it, the brochure could easily be mailed to every household in a certain ZIP-code area or community.

One very simple and economical promotional tool is the flyer, an 8½ x 11-inch sheet of paper with a printed design in contrasting colors. The flyer can promote the entire school ministry or a single special program or event. Flyers can be handed out, mailed, or placed in businesses throughout the community.

Colorful posters can also be printed and put up on bulletin boards, in windows of businesses, and in shopping malls. These should be designed so that the name of the school is large enough to be seen from a distance.

The school yearbook is not only a good keepsake for students but also a good means of promotion. For this reason, every school should put together a well-organized annual using a company that professionally produces such a document. It is extremely important that this book be of excellent quality since by its very nature it is thought to be portraying exactly what the school is like. The yearbook needs to be proofed carefully before being sent for final printing. It would be better to have no annual at all than one of poor quality.

A school newsletter can serve not only as an effective means of communicating information to your constituency but also as a promotional tool. A monthly newsletter can be sent to each member of the church, to the pastor of every church that has children from their church enrolled in the school, real estate agencies that work in the neighborhood, and selected local elected officials, in addition to those who have children in the school. Consider publishing a special issue or two each year that focuses on your enrollment campaign and discusses all of the programs offered by your school.

Money for promotion is more wisely spent on a few high quality materials than on many sloppy ones. If the artistic expertise is not available among the school's personnel, it would be wise to hire professional help in developing the promotional material. It is better to pay to have the job done well than to have it done free but poorly. With the advent of desktop publishing, those with quality computer equipment can develop very attractive printed materials in-house at a modest cost.

FOLLOW-UP

If the promotional program is operated properly, many people will be motivated to seek more information about the school. The follow-up on these contacts is extremely important. First, the people who handle telephone calls should always be warm, friendly, and pleasant and must be well informed about the educational philosophy and program of the Christian school. It is important for them to recognize when inquiries are beyond their personal knowledge; they should quickly acknowledge it and promise to get the information to the inquirer promptly. They must be sure to get all pertinent information (name, address, phone number, number of children, grade levels, and so forth) from each inquirer who calls. After a phone contact is made, representatives of the school should be prepared to follow up on the inquiry with written materials or a visit to the interested parents. Those who visit must be not only thoroughly familiar with the school but also confident soulwinners.

Seize every opportunity to develop a mailing list of people genuinely interested in Christian education. Use the mailing list as a means of sending them copies of your school newsletter, brochures, and other promotional material from time to time.

The best way to acquaint people with the Christian school is to have them visit the school while it is in session. Trained personnel can give interested parents a tour of the facilities and acquaint them with the school's philosophy and program. It is worth much to parents to observe classes in session (especially the grades their children would attend) and to have their questions answered. It is ideal for the administrator of the school to spend time with visiting parents, but if he or she is not available, other people with pleasant personalities may be chosen for the task. Often the secretary makes a good tour guide. People who are treated kindly and courteously by the school personnel automatically form a favorable impression of Christian education.

CHAPTER 17

SELECTING AND RECRUITING PERSONNEL

> Wherefore, brethren, look ye out among you seven men of honest report, full of the Holy Ghost and wisdom, whom we may appoint over this business.
>
> **Acts 6:3**
>
> And the things that thou hast heard of me among many witnesses, the same commit thou to faithful men, who shall be able to teach others also.
>
> **2 Timothy 2:2**

A chain is only as strong as its weakest link and an organization is only as good as the personnel who carry out its functions. Selecting personnel for the Christian school deserves more attention than it usually receives, for no position is insignificant, and no employee chosen to fill that position can be taken for granted.

To simplify consideration, all employees of the Christian school can be categorized as either professional or nonprofessional, the distinction being primarily the amount of education required to perform the job. All teaching, counseling, and administrative personnel are considered professional staff; all secretarial, clerical, bookkeeping, maintenance, custodial, kitchen, and transportation personnel are considered nonprofessional.

Before hiring the first person, the school administrator or the school board needs to develop written standards of employment. Since policies are effective only to the degree that they can provide meaningful assistance in the decision-making process, they should be sufficiently detailed to provide specific direction but not so restrictive as to require constant exceptions. They should also reflect the demands of the individual institution and the availability of personnel in the area. For positions requiring only one employee, formal written standards may not be necessary. Specific standards for word processing skills, however, will simplify the hiring of clerical workers. Figure 17.1 represents a suggested statement of employment policy. The standards in this policy may be higher than those the reader is accustomed to finding; however, the standards suggested here are the minimum that should generally be accepted.

Frequently Christian school administrators find themselves with loyal employees who lack the specific skills necessary to do the work assigned. Because of their loyalty, it is difficult to terminate them. Since most Christian schools are not large enough to absorb inefficient employees, the school finds itself with the problem of having to terminate a loyal employee who never should have been employed. It is far better to evaluate the person's capabilities before he is placed on the payroll.

STANDARDS FOR HIRING

Spiritual Standards

The most important criterion for Christian school employees is spiritual fruit. Every employee must be born again and must be able to give a coherent testimony of his salvation experience. All professional employees must be able to give evidence in writing and in a personal interview that they have Bible-based assurance of personal salvation. Giving a clear, concise testimony is obviously more important for a teacher than for a custodian, but unless each can give convincing evidence of his faith in Christ, he should not be employed. The longer the person has been saved, the more evidence he should demonstrate supporting his conversion experience.

It is also important to evaluate other areas that reflect on the spirituality of the applicant. Such matters as church membership, personal involvement in the church's visitation program, attendance at church meetings, and financial support of the work indicate spiritual concern. These activities are usually very important to church-related schools and should be to other Christian schools as well. To avoid future misunderstandings, the employee should understand what other criteria, such as loyalty and support of school policies, may later be used in evaluating his performance.

FIGURE 17.1

CHURCH/SCHOOL EMPLOYMENT POLICY

Part I, All Employees

1. Must be born again.

2. Must be an active member of the sponsoring church or a church of like faith and practice.

3. Must agree without reservation to the doctrinal statement of the church and standards of conduct for students and employees.

Part II, All Nonprofessional Employees

1. Must have a high school diploma or the equivalent.

2. Must demonstrate, through experience or testing, the ability to perform the duties required.

3. Must meet all legal requirements for the position.

Part III, All Professional Employees

1. Must agree to abide by the policies contained in the faculty manual.

2. Must agree to fulfill other reasonable requirements that normally relate to this position, which include, but are not limited to, such activities as performing clerical functions, supervising study halls, and assisting in the supervision of extracurricular activities outside the normal school day.

3. Kindergarten teachers: must hold a bachelor's degree in early childhood education or elementary education.

4. Elementary or secondary teacher: must hold a bachelor's degree in early childhood education, elementary education, or secondary education (depending on teaching assignment).

5. Counselor: must hold a bachelor's degree in some area of education and a master's degree in counseling or personnel services, or be willing to work toward that degree.

6. Administrative positions: must hold a bachelor's degree in some area of education and a master's degree in educational leadership, or be willing to work toward that degree.

7. Preference will be given to those who have attended Christian colleges.

Part IV, Counselors and Administrative Employees

1. Must have a minimum of three years of classroom teaching experience.

2. Preference will be given to those with prior teaching or administrative experience in Christian schools.

Beyond these qualifications, it is especially important for each employee to have a servant's heart (Matt. 20:27) so that he is willing to give of himself rather than being concerned about what he will be getting for himself. It is easier to train a teacher to be more effective in the classroom than to help cultivate a servant's heart.

Every employee in the school is in a position to influence the overall testimony of the school for good or bad. Christian schools cannot let down their spiritual standards to meet a "need." For example, they cannot become so desperate to hire a football coach or a science teacher that they take just anyone, regardless of spiritual weaknesses. It is better that an academic area suffer temporarily than that the spiritual objectives of the institution be compromised. A Christian school is as much a ministry unto the Lord as a church is; school board members and administrators must trust Christ to meet their needs and not rely upon their own resources.

Academic Standards

Generally speaking, as a minimum requirement for nonprofessional positions, every employee of the school should be a high school graduate with an ability to communicate clearly. Since the school is in the business of providing education, the image projected by all employees reflects to some extent the quality of the education offered by the school. While any parent should recognize that bus drivers are not teachers, a bus driver unable to communicate with reasonable effectiveness may reflect adversely on the quality of education offered by the school.

All professional staff members must hold college degrees. For some positions, graduate degrees will be advisable, if not required. Administrators of different schools may disagree over the type of degree required for a particular position, but there should be no disagreement over the fact that a degree is required. Christian schools claiming to offer an education that is academically comparable to that offered by other private and public schools cannot depart from traditionally accepted standards of professional competence and preparation and expect to maintain the respect of the community.

There are specific, generally accepted academic expectations of the faculty for every level of formal education. Each teacher should certainly have a higher level of education than that of the students he instructs. To be considered professionally prepared, those who teach in elementary and secondary schools should hold as a minimum a bachelor's degree.

There is some difference of opinion among those in Christian education about what kind of college is best suited to prepare teachers and what degree programs are most appropriate. Some, for example, believe that all teachers should be Bible majors and should have attended a Bible school. Most others, on the other hand, believe that the best preparation is to be an education major at a Christian liberal arts college.

The Bible college has as its primary purpose the training of young people for positions of full-time Christian service; consequently, the curriculum places a great emphasis on the study of the Bible. Since it is customary for such schools to require every student to take thirty or more semester hours of Bible, every student at the school is a Bible major. In the liberal arts college there is no less concern for the preparation of students for Christian service; yet its curriculum provides a more broadly based education. It is generally the philosophy of such a school that a more well-rounded student is a more effective servant. Most Christian liberal arts colleges with the objective of training teachers for the Christian school have a department of education whose program of study includes not only Bible courses and content courses in the student's area of study but also professional education courses. The capstone experience of a quality teacher education program should be student teaching. Such instruction helps him to understand the depraved nature of his future students and how they learn and to examine the most effective teaching techniques known.

A number of Christian school administrators, having ranked prospective teachers on the basis of the school they attended and the program they pursued, ordered their preferences in the following manner:

1. A graduate of a Christian college who majored in education

2. A graduate of a Christian college who holds a degree in some area other than education but a major or minor in the field needed for the teaching responsibility

3. A graduate of a Bible college with a minor in the teaching field needed

4. A graduate of a secular school

This ranking of applicants is based only on their academic preparation. Other factors are equally important.

Many administrators also compare the biblical standards of their schools with those of colleges or Bible colleges training teachers; that is, fundamentalist Christian day schools usually hire graduates from fundamentalist Christian colleges.

In addition, schools should be certain that all teachers are qualified to teach the subject matter involved, that they have mastered the subject, and that they will offer an understanding of the course content sufficient to lead students into a knowledge of the material (Ps. 78:2–4; Luke 6:39–40). Although this is a particularly important requirement at the senior high level, there is no level of education at which the content to be taught in the school is so elementary that the professional preparation of the teacher can be ignored. Administrators also need to be careful not to burden teachers with more preparations than they can reasonably be expected to handle. Though some doubling up is to be expected, a high school teacher with a degree in science and a minor in English can probably teach four or five courses in those fields. To assign him to teach math, Bible, history, or business classes as well will no doubt dilute his effectiveness.

Government Regulations

All employees should meet legitimate government regulations. For example, bus drivers should be taught all necessary safety regulations and should meet all special license requirements. Kitchen personnel must meet local health standards. Deliberate attempts to skirt these matters will eventually cause serious difficulties, often resulting in great embarrassment to the school.

Most states do not have certificate or licensure requirements for Christian school teachers. As a general rule there is nothing gained by requiring a teacher to be state certified. However, teachers who are eligible for state certification or licensure should be encouraged to maintain it. On the other hand, requiring certification by a state or national Christian school organization could add credibility to your faculty in the eyes of your constituency.

THE HIRING PROCESS

The Application

A large, well-established Christian school will find that it often has more applicants than positions available and that screening applicants can be a time-consuming task. A well-designed, carefully worded application can help the administrator reduce the number of applicants that he actually needs to interview. The application should not be longer than necessary, but it should require enough information to enable an experienced person to determine whether the applicant has the basic employment prerequisites to justify a personal interview. (See Appendix F for a sample application.)

Requesting applicants to provide a resume can often prove helpful. Some applicants will volunteer information in a resume that you could not otherwise legally obtain. When this information is provided voluntarily, you are free to use it.

The Interview

The personal interview is an indispensable part of the employment process; it aids the interviewer and also gives an opportunity for the applicant to tour the facilities and meet other employees. Because it is easy to talk with a prospect for an hour or so and still not get answers to some relevant questions, establishing interview guidelines will insure that the interview covers all pertinent areas.

Most administrators who interview on a regular basis find it helpful to develop an interview guide, like that shown in Figure 17.2, to help keep them on the right track.

If the interview is to be productive, the interviewer must allow ample time; a minimum of thirty minutes, and preferably an hour. It is equally important that the place be reasonably quiet and free from interruption.

The first step is to make the applicant feel at ease as early in the interview as possible. While providing appropriate feedback and responses, the interviewer should not appear to pass judgment on the feelings and beliefs the applicant expresses. Rather, the interviewer should allow him to open up and reveal his true thoughts about any issue relative to his employment. It is best not to ask questions in a way that reveals the answer sought. For example, an interviewer should not say, "You do believe in corporal punishment, don't you?" Instead he might ask, "What do you think about using corporal punishment in a Christian school?"

A successful interviewer appears genuinely interested in the applicant and what he has to say; he avoids taking extensive notes but instead looks directly at him as he speaks. The interviewer often repeats some of what the applicant has said to let him know he has been understood correctly, and he asks the applicant questions to be sure that he perceives his view accurately.

FIGURE 17.2

EMPLOYMENT INTERVIEW FORMAT

The interview should be brought to a conclusion whenever the interviewer feels he has enough information to make the employment decision or believes it will be important to have the input of another interviewer.

1. Start the interview with small talk, making the applicant feel as comfortable as possible. "How was your trip?" "Did you have any trouble locating the school?"

2. Some interviewers like to start the interview by giving the applicant an overview of the philosophy and history of the school.

3. "Tell me something about yourself." (This allows the applicant to begin wherever he is comfortable; follow-up questions can be used to fill in any areas of interest to the interviewer.)

4. Ask the individual to provide some information about his salvation experience and follow up with questions about his church membership and areas of Christian service.

5. Question the applicant about his experience in soulwinning. Has he ever led a person to Christ?

6. "Do you believe the Lord has given you the gift of teaching? What evidence do you have of that?"

7. "Have you read the doctrinal statement of the church? Can you subscribe to it without reservation?" (If the applicant has not had the opportunity to read the statement of faith prior to the interview, it is important that a copy be provided for him and that he provide an affirmative answer to the questions before his employment is finalized.)

8. "Are there any areas of Bible doctrine that are very important to you that are not discussed in the statement of faith?"

9. "What is your view of the modern charismatic movement?"

10. "What strategies do you use to maintain classroom control?"

11. "What strategies do you use to discipline students?"

12. "Do you see any conflict between the various theories of evolution and the Genesis account of creation?"

13. "What do you believe about the nature of man? What, if any, impact does this have on the educational process?"

14. "Do you believe the Bible requires parents to provide a Christian education for their children?"

Whenever possible, it is helpful to have at least one additional person—perhaps the pastor or assistant principal—interview the prospect a few days later. If the first interviewer follows a format such as that suggested in Figure 17.2, the second interviewer need not be as thorough, simply getting a general impression or following up on any points the first interviewer has doubts about or fails to cover adequately. If it is not possible for more than one person to interview the prospect, a second person may sit in on the original interview, though this is not as desirable since it may tend to make the applicant nervous.

Employment processes vary widely, and some schools require the teacher to come before the entire board before being hired. However, in the interest of protecting the time of all concerned, schools might reconsider this requirement. Unless the board actually enters into the interviewing procedure, there is no need for them to be involved in employment decisions. Their input should be felt in the development of the employment policy. All applicants for positions in a church-school should meet the pastor and have the opportunity to spend some time with him. It is important that the pastor is comfortable with the school employees and that the employees in the school are comfortable with the pastor. The pastor might give an overview of the church and of his expectations of the teachers. An applicant who will not make a reasonable effort to visit the church for at least a Sunday morning service should not be employed in a church-school. Since a major source of friction in church-schools is a misunderstanding between the congregation and the employees of the school, a wise administrator will eliminate many of these problems by employing teachers who are supportive of the overall work of the church.

Recruitment

In seeking personnel to fill vacancies in the Christian school, it is almost as important to avoid provoking an interest in those who would not qualify for the position as it is to locate those who would meet the qualifications. Unintentionally soliciting unqualified people creates two problems. First, if an interviewer is not sufficiently thorough or if an applicant does not answer questions honestly, it is possible to fail to discover parts of the applicant's background that would disqualify him spiritually. Administrators occasionally become careless, assuming that those applying for a position in a Christian school already understand and agree with the spiritual standards. Second, a person judged to be unqualified because of spiritual standards may become belligerent and attempt to take legal action against the school on the basis of discrimination. While the chances of his success in such an action are rather remote at this time, the legal expense and public attention created would not be helpful to the school's ministry.

Because of these and similar problems, it is generally unwise to advertise for personnel by means of media that reach all segments of the population. Advertising vacancies in the local newspaper, for example, is often not a good source of prospects for a position in a Christian school.

On the other hand, one of the best ways to obtain applicants for positions is through the school constituency. Parents, their friends, and church members are all excellent sources of contacts, as are friends and relatives of present faculty members.

Although it is possible to find people from local contacts to fill some of the vacancies on the professional staff, it is usually necessary to reach out further. The most productive sources of professional employees for the Christian school are Christian colleges with departments of education. The colleges usually have a formal placement program or an office of placement services where administrators can advertise their vacancies to current students and recent graduates. A few colleges have special recruitment conferences to which Christian school representatives are invited to meet prospective teachers.

School administrators will often find it advantageous to develop a personal relationship with the education department head and several members of the education faculty from Christian colleges by inviting them to visit the school or to speak to the faculty or parents. Administrators should encourage these college personnel to develop a personal interest in the school, since a placement adviser is more likely to recommend schools he is personally familiar with.

National, regional, and state Christian school organizations offer assistance to both schools and prospective employees by publishing lists of vacancies and personnel seeking positions. These services, usually free, have been responsible for getting many schools and prospective teachers together.

Another means of contacting prospects is through Christian publications. Many of these have inexpensive classified listings in which prospective employers and employees can make their needs and availability known.

One of the greatest assets to recruiting can be the overall image the school has in the Christian community. A school that develops a reputation for being efficiently run, having good standards, and treating its employees fairly will in time have more applicants than vacancies. However, a school with a reputation for having a shoddy operation, a weak academic performance, a low set of standards, and a high annual turnover of faculty probably could not be helped by a Madison Avenue public relations firm.

Above all, an administrator should pray about his need, asking the Lord to send just the right person who will be able to do the job that must be done and will also become an asset to the overall testimony of the school.

Making the Decision

After gathering information on prospective candidates and interviewing those who appear to be the best qualified, the administrator or school board must come to a decision. This process is conducted in a variety of ways in Christian schools. Each school will need to consider the options and develop a system that is efficient and satisfactory to the board.

Much of what is done in Christian education is a carryover from public education. In public education the school board traditionally approved all contracts, except in the larger systems where this function was sometimes delegated to the human resources department. This practice is now changing; policy decisions are being centralized, but the actual decision to employ or reject a specific applicant is increasingly being left to the administrator who will supervise the teacher. Christian schools would do well to adopt this practice.

Few men who serve on Christian school boards are as qualified as the school administrator to make employment decisions. Requiring that applicants be interviewed or contracts be approved by the school board results in the employment process becoming unnecessarily cumbersome. If the board has employed a competent administrator, it should permit him to function in that capacity.

The choice among a number of qualified applicants can be made somewhat easier by adopting a rating scale to evaluate their qualifications objectively. Although the administrator need not tie himself finally to the outcome of the evaluation, it helps to separate the prospect's qualifications from his personality. Figure 17.3 shows one way of evaluating applicants for professional positions. In the final analysis, the administrator must trust the Lord to reveal the right person for the job.

FIGURE 17.3

RATING SCALE FOR SELECTING PROFESSIONAL EMPLOYEES FOR CHRISTIAN SCHOOLS

Rate the applicant on each of the following categories immediately following the personal interview. Each person involved in interviewing the applicant should do an evaluation.

Applicant

	U	S	A
1. Personal appearance			
2. Poise			
3. Clarity of expression			
4. Educational background (major or minor)			
5. Educational background (school attended)			
6. Overall grade point average			
7. Grade point average in major			
8. Grade in directed teaching			
9. Teaching experience (Do not consider a negative if none.)			
10. Christian testimony			

*U = Unsatisfactory   S = Satisfactory   A = Above Average

A person who scores unsatisfactory in any area should not be employed. Look for people who are above average in as many areas as possible. Spiritual excellence is an absolute prerequisite.

Evaluated by: _____   Date: _____

Once the administrator makes his decision, he should notify all parties being considered. The applicant selected should receive a warm personal letter with a contract and a definite deadline before which he is expected to accept or reject the position. Ten days is usually sufficient. Those who were unsuccessful in obtaining the position should be informed that the position has been filled. It is not ethical to offer false hope. If an administrator does not consider a person fit for the position, he should not suggest that the applicant contact him later. However, if an applicant is qualified and the administrator might consider him for another position, he should keep the door open. In either event, the administrator should be friendly and help the prospect look upon the school as favorably as possible.

Some school administrators are notoriously slow in making employment decisions. This is unfair to those who have applied for positions and need employment to provide for their families. It is also unprofitable for the school because the applicant may pursue another position, thinking he will not be employed. God will provide for the needs of the school, and God will provide avenues of service to those He has called into His service. However, that does not excuse school administrators from acting responsibly in making employment decisions in a timely manner. Any applicant who is no longer under serious consideration for a position should be informed of this decision. Dealing properly with applicants is time consuming, but it is part of the overall responsibility of the school administrator.

The Contract

The professional employee contract is another item Christian schools have adopted from public education. It has both good and bad points. The good side is that a well-written contract carefully details the employment agreement between the school and the employee, theoretically guaranteeing to each those matters of relative importance. The bad side of contracts is that they tend to cause people to think that each year they have to determine God's place for them afresh. This decision-making process sometimes results in a period of turmoil for the entire school as everyone focuses on who is and who is not returning the following year. It can also tempt an employer to institute an abnormally long-term contract, which in turn can cause attitude problems among employees. Overall, the good points of the annual contract process outweigh the bad.

Since every school is in some points unique, it naturally follows that its contract should be unique. Those who simply copy what everyone else is doing can find themselves in difficulty if they do not think through the consequences of contractual obligations. Reviewing the contracts of others is not a bad idea, but once a school has decided what elements to include in its contract, the school attorney should formulate for the consideration of the board a contract that represents the expectations and commitments of the school and its employees. There is no substitute for the expertise of a professional attorney at this point. (Appendix G contains examples of sample contracts.)

God has chosen to accomplish His work on earth through men. He even sent His own Son in the form of a man to be our salvation. As we choose men to do His work, we must continually be aware of their importance.

CHAPTER 18

SUPERVISION AND STAFF DEVELOPMENT

And Moses did look upon all the work, and, behold, they had done it as the Lord had commanded, even so had they done it: and Moses blessed them.

Exodus 39:43

Ye shall do no unrighteousness in judgment: thou shalt not respect the person of the poor, nor honour the person of the mighty: but in righteousness shalt thou judge thy neighbour.

Leviticus 19:15

A reproof entereth more into a wise man than an hundred stripes into a fool.

Proverbs 17:10

If the right kind of personnel are employed, rarely will a Christian school need to terminate an individual's employment because of unsatisfactory service. However, it is similarly rare that an employee has already developed his potential to the degree that a good staff development program cannot sharpen those skills.

Staff development is directed toward the correction of perceived weakness in the staff. Supervision, on the other hand, measures the effectiveness of the staff and provides direction to the staff development program. Schools need to do a better job of developing the talents of those individuals whose hearts God has touched for His service. Too often we have more lofty ideals than God has about the inherent quality of the persons we want to work for us (1 Cor. 1:25–31). Supervision and staff development can be effective instruments in helping people become what God wants them to be.

STAFF SUPERVISION

Responsibility

An administrator has a definite biblical responsibility for selection and supervision of his personnel. Classroom instruction is one of the most important activities of the Christian school, and, unfortunately, in many schools, it is the most neglected. Obviously, the teacher is the key figure in the instructional process. In Matthew 18:6 God seems to place special emphasis on the training and education of the young. James 3:1 reminds Christians of special responsibilities assumed by those who teach. Therefore, it is clear that those involved in Christian education have a calling that is certainly close to the heart of God.

A school administrator needs to give special attention to the scriptural teaching concerning personal accountability. "So then every one of us shall give account of himself to God" (Rom. 14:12). Spiritual leaders have responsibility not only for themselves but also for those they supervise. Hebrews 13:17 reminds servants to obey their authorities, "for they watch for your souls, as they that must give account, that they may do it with joy, and not with grief."

Since most Christian schools today are church-schools, pastors also have some responsibility for supervision. In Acts 20:28 pastors are specifically reminded of their responsibility in this area. "Take heed therefore unto yourselves, and to all the flock, over the which the Holy Ghost hath made you overseers." Few pastors have the time or training to personally supervise instruction. However, if the Christian school is a church ministry, it is ultimately the pastor's responsibility to see that instruction is supervised and that it is done properly, "as unto the Lord." This responsibility will normally be satisfied through his supervision of the administrator, who will have more direct responsibility for staff supervision and development.

If supervision is to be effective, it must have the support of the pastor, who has a vision of the importance of the ministry of Christian education and is willing to pay the price of personal preparation for his part in it. This responsibility will require at least a cursory understanding of academic affairs and accepted standards of professional competence.

Aside from pastors, there are also others involved in the Christian school ministry (especially the independent school) who are accountable for the activities of others. Because pastors and administrators are accountable for the instructional process, they must evaluate those who participate in it. Since the ultimate aim of Christian education is to help conform young people to the image of Christ, anything or anyone that interferes with this objective represents a serious problem. Although all the activities of the school require supervision, this chapter deals primarily with the portion involving the teacher.

Purpose

Few people really like supervision. Some have difficulty evaluating themselves objectively; yet unless workers examine themselves (1 Cor. 11:28) and allow others to observe them critically, they are not likely to perform as well as they should. Others associate supervision with termination of employment. Though supervision occasionally will result in such action, administrators who have been careful in selecting their personnel should rarely have to terminate an employee.

The primary purpose of instructional supervision is to improve the quality of instruction. When employees know this and believe that the administration believes in them, they will usually cooperate. Supervision involves classroom observation, and these visits are of great importance. However, supervision is a continuous process that involves observing the teacher in any activity that is even remotely related to his teaching. A teacher teaches what he is; therefore, in Christian education the school is as interested in what the teacher does on his "days off" as in how he conducts his classes. Supervision in the classroom tends to be a rather formal process, whereas observation of activities away from the school tends to be rather informal. Both, however, are important. Support for supervision must come from the top of the organization. In a church-school, the pastor, the board, and the administrator must believe in supervision if it is to be effective.

Teacher Evaluation

The supervision of instruction in small Christian schools is most often the direct responsibility of the administrator. In larger schools there will frequently be others on the administrative staff that can be used to assist him. The administrator should be personally involved to some extent, even if he has a large enough staff to be able to delegate most of this work. Teachers should know that he at least reviews the evaluations. This can be verified by having a place on the evaluation instrument that requires his signature.

A written copy of the completed evaluation should be reviewed with the teacher, signed by both parties, and then a copy placed in the teacher's personnel file.

FIGURE 18.1

TEACHER OBSERVATION EVALUATION CRITERIA

Personal Characteristics

Dress and Grooming Habits—Does the teacher practice neatness, cleanliness, and moderation in his clothing styles and grooming?

Rapport with Staff—Does the teacher have a good relationship with other staff members? Does he help unify the staff behind the school?

Rapport with Students—Do students have confidence in the teacher? Are they willing to confide in him? Do they feel comfortable in his presence?

Rapport with Parents—Do parents have confidence in the teacher? Do they feel he has a genuine interest in them and their children? Will they confide in him?

Professional Characteristics

Continuing Education—Does the teacher attend at least one educational conference annually and read professional journals in his field?

Promptness in Completing Assignments—Does the teacher respond quickly to requests for information or reports (unless providentially hindered)?

Punctuality—Does the teacher arrive at work and at scheduled meetings on time (unless providentially hindered)? Is he generally on time for regularly scheduled church services (church-schools only)?

Classroom Performance

Housekeeping—Is the classroom neat except when class activities justify otherwise?

Bulletin Boards—Are bulletin boards suitable for the grade levels and subjects taught in the classroom? Are they maintained and changed in accordance with school policy?

Physical Arrangement—Is the furniture provided by the school arranged in such a manner as to encourage appropriate classroom activity?

Contribution to Student Interest—Is classroom instruction conducted in a manner that will reasonably insure student incentive to participate in his learning experience?

Quality of Voice—Does the teacher's voice stimulate interest and attention? Are there any unpleasant or distracting vocal qualities?

Lesson Plans—Is there evidence of definite direction and planning for a logical progression through the course? Would someone filling in for the teacher know what to do?

Content—Is that which is taught related to the course, accurate, and presented at a level appropriate for the students?

Audiovisual Materials—Is the technique used appropriate for the content of the lesson and the age and ability of the students? Is it well done?

Teaching Techniques—Does the teacher utilize a variety of teaching techniques in presenting material to stimulate student interest and clarify content?

Classroom Management—Is the classroom orderly? Are students respectful of the teacher, classroom, instructional materials, one another, and the subject?

Discipline—Are disorderly students dealt with appropriately? Are disciplinary actions consistent with school policy? Are the actions taken appropriate for the infraction and age level of students? Is there evidence of consistency? Is discipline dispensed in a manner that conveys love and a desire for a corrective response?

Spiritual Characteristics

Regular Church Attendance—Is the teacher present at all regularly scheduled services? (Allow for reasonable absence for vacation, providential hindrance, etc.)

Involvement in Church Activities—Does he actively participate in (not just attend) any church activities (e.g., choir, teaching Sunday school, visitation)?

Interest in Spiritual Welfare of Students—Does the teacher ever make a special effort to contact parents or faculty members concerning the spiritual problems of students? Does he ever request prayer for the needs of students or demonstrate interest in any other overt manner?

Additional Responsibilities—Does the teacher volunteer to assist in the school ministry in areas not specifically required by his job?

Since supervision of instruction should be objective, it is necessary to have some kind of plan for observations. For example, the administrator (or his designated representative) may observe all first-year teachers three times their first year; all teachers new to the school, but having prior teaching experience should be observed twice—once the first quarter and once the third quarter; and all other teachers once each year, during the second or third quarter. The observer should immediately complete an observation evaluation to be reviewed by the administrator.

The information in Figures 18.1 and 18.2 helps draw objective conclusions about what has been observed, though some clarification of the criteria may be necessary. Each school will have to determine what level of performance it considers satisfactory. When teachers are experiencing difficulty, more frequent observation and feedback are appropriate.

When the evaluation has been completed, the person completing it can score it by assigning a numerical value to each item: Excellent—5, Above Average—4, Satisfactory—3, Needs Improvement—2, and Unsatisfactory—1. A rating of Excellent should be reserved for performance that is truly outstanding. A rating of Unsatisfactory should indicate a very serious deficiency.

A second method of teacher evaluation that schools may want to consider is evaluation by parents. Educators, especially Christian educators, are sometimes reluctant to give the impression that parents have major input into administrative decisions of the school. Though most schools consider parents' comments with regard to teachers, they do so on an informal, unprofessional basis that tends to encourage primarily negative comments. If parents' comments are to be considered, it would be best to structure the system of feedback to insure an honest, accurate response from a large segment of the parent constituency.

FIGURE 18.2

TEACHER OBSERVATION EVALUATION

This form is to be completed annually for each professional staff member. For first year teachers, it is to be done three times: the first week of the second, third, and fourth quarters. For all others it must be done once during the second quarter, prior to the contract offer for the next year.

Teacher _____   Date of Evaluation

Grade Level/Subjects _____

	U	N	S	A	E*
Personal Characteristics					
Dress and grooming habits	___	___	___	___	___
Rapport with staff	___	___	___	___	___
Rapport with students	___	___	___	___	___
Rapport with parents	___	___	___	___	___
Professional Characteristics					
Continuing education	___	___	___	___	___
Promptness in completing assignments	___	___	___	___	___
Punctuality	___	___	___	___	___
Classroom Performance					
Housekeeping	___	___	___	___	___
Bulletin boards	___	___	___	___	___
Physical arrangement	___	___	___	___	___
Contribution to student interest	___	___	___	___	___
Quality of voice	___	___	___	___	___
Lesson plans	___	___	___	___	___

	U	N	S	A	E*
Content	___	___	___	___	___
Audiovisual materials	___	___	___	___	___
Teaching techniques	___	___	___	___	___
Classroom management	___	___	___	___	___
Discipline	___	___	___	___	___

Spiritual Characteristics

Regular church attendance	___	___	___	___	___
Involvement in church activities	___	___	___	___	___
Interest in spiritual welfare of students	___	___	___	___	___
Additional responsibilities	___	___	___	___	___

U = Unsatisfactory   N = Needs Improvement   S = Satisfactory   A = Above Average
E = Excellent

Evaluated by: _____

Seeking parental views is worthwhile. The parent evaluation form in Figure 18.3 is designed to elicit meaningful parental responses. The form could be used to poll all parents or a representative sampling. The responses, coupled with the school's evaluation, should give a good broad-based evaluation for the teacher's encouragement and improvement. Some school leaders do not like to give the parents an opportunity for formal criticism.

FIGURE 18.3

TEACHER EVALUATION BY PARENTS

The school is interested in an ongoing evaluation of its entire program, including its instructional staff. Our faculty members are evaluated at least annually by the administration. We would like to know the perceptions of the faculty held by parents. Your evaluations will help us in the overall evaluation process. Please complete an evaluation for each teacher who has your child for one or more subjects. For students in K4–grade 6, indicate the grade; for students in grades 7–12, indicate the subject. Answer the questions as honestly as you can. Please note that there is a place to indicate that you are unable to evaluate an item. Your cooperation is appreciated.

Teacher _____

Grade Level/Subject(s) _____

Place an *X* in the appropriate column.	**N**	**U**	**S**	**A***
1. How do you evaluate the teacher's knowledge of the subject(s)?	____	____	____	____
2. Is the material presented in a manner that the average student can grasp?	____	____	____	____
3. Is the grading system fair?	____	____	____	____
4. Does your child feel that the teacher has a personal interest in him/her?	____	____	____	____
5. Are the homework assignments reasonable?	____	____	____	____
6. Is the teacher interested in the spiritual welfare of the children in the class?	____	____	____	____
7. Do you feel free to talk with the teacher about your child's progress?	____	____	____	____
8. Compared with other teachers in this school, how would you rate this teacher?	____	____	____	____
9. If you had another child to come through this grade or subject, would you choose this teacher? Yes _____ No _____	____	____	____	____

N = Not Able to Evaluate   U = Unsatisfactory   S = Satisfactory   A = Above Average

However, it is important to realize that these parents are our customers, and they have an opinion of the teacher. The opinion may not be accurate, and it may not agree with ours; however, it is important to them, and it should be important to us.

One additional form of evaluation can be very effective: self-evaluation as presented in Figure 18.4. More important than anything that is actually written down is the mental exercise teachers go through as they consider themselves in light of the expectations of others. This can be a very productive exercise for the experienced as well as the novice teacher. Both strengths and weaknesses that may not have been identified by others but are known to the teacher can become an important aspect of encouragement and self-improvement. Figure 18.4 offers suggestions concerning factors that should be included in a good self-evaluation.

Although most board members would not want to participate in the formal evaluation of classroom teachers, it is a good idea to encourage board members to visit the school and to informally observe classes. For many, it will be the first visit to a classroom in many years and will serve to freshen their insight into the ministry of the school.

The administrator should see and sign every evaluation. If he has doubts about the validity of the evaluation, he should conduct one himself within a reasonable period of time. The administrator or someone he delegates should discuss each evaluation with the teacher involved in a frank, honest, kind, and thorough conversation. He should emphasize the positive first, but not to the exclusion of the negative. It is not necessary that the teacher agree with the evaluation, but it is imperative that he understand it. Any negative comments should be accompanied by specific suggestions for improvement. The teacher must be assured that the administrator wants to help him become satisfactory in any area in which he is currently unsatisfactory.

After an appropriate period of time, the administrator should re-evaluate the teacher's problem areas. First-year teachers, whether new in teaching or new to the school, should not be given a contract for the following year if their second evaluation results in an overall unsatisfactory rating. At the administrator's discretion, the teacher may be told that a contract could be offered if, on the third evaluation, the rating comes up to a satisfactory level overall.

Though it is never easy to terminate a teacher, it is easier after his first year than at any other time. Poor teachers will often press an administrator for another chance. At that point the administrator must decide whether he is running a school to train weak teachers or to educate children. The two objectives are not compatible.

FIGURE 18.4

TEACHER SELF-EVALUATION

Name _____

Academic year _____

Grade level/courses taught this year_____

Number of years' experience teaching public schools (K–12) _____

Christian (K–12)_____ Number of years on faculty _____

Total experience in education _____

List the types of professional activities in which you have regularly participated this academic year.

List the titles of in-service programs and workshops you have attended and/or conducted during this academic year.

What local church activities have you been engaged in during the past year?

List the professional organizations to which you currently belong.

List the education books you have read during this academic year and the professional education journals you read regularly.

What courses have you taken during the last five years that will better prepare you for your present or future teaching responsibilities?

What changes have you made this year to revitalize and update the courses you have previously taught?

Have you made a conscious effort this year to identify students in your classes that need special attention in order to be successful in meeting your course requirements? What strategies did you utilize to help them?

Do you make a conscious effort to utilize a variety of strategies in teaching your classes? What are some of the strategies you are currently utilizing?

What media have you used in your teaching this year?

Have you recently evaluated the library resources available to support the courses you teach? Are they adequate?

Teacher _____   Date _____

The purpose of supervision is not to give teachers poor grades or to pump up their egos; its purpose is to improve instruction. If a school goes to the trouble and inconvenience of in-class supervision of instruction and evaluations and then does nothing with the results, it is wasting its time. The administrator should schedule a conference with the teacher to review the results of the supervision of instruction program. In schools with a more highly structured administration, it would be a good idea for the elementary principal or the secondary principal to do the reviews. This underscores their responsibility for the employee and makes it easier for them to make suggestions for change.

Administrator Evaluation

Administrators also need evaluation. It is in the administrator's own best interest that a specific means of appraising his work be agreed upon, if not before he assumes his duties, at least shortly thereafter. More than one administrator has thought things were going well only to be suddenly confronted with such strong dissatisfaction with his performance that he was forced to resign.

In the typical Christian school, the administrator is held ultimately accountable for everything that happens. The school board or pastor looks to the administrator to provide the professional and spiritual direction needed for the school's success. This expectation is quite reasonable. It is not reasonable, however, to fail to give the administrator sufficient direction for him to understand just what the board's concept of successful operation is.

Figure 18.5 provides suggestions to be used in the evaluation of an administrator.

The pastor and/or the school board should give the administrator a clear picture of their expectations, which should be constantly reevaluated and communicated to the administrator on at least an annual basis. Too many board members and pastors pass on their feelings about the job the administrator is doing in a very casual and informal way. Often the administrator does not recognize such remarks as being intended to convey their feelings about his leadership. Meanwhile the pastor and board members may feel they have fulfilled their responsibility of informing him of their feelings about his work.

FIGURE 18.5

ADMINISTRATOR EVALUATION

This form is to be completed for each administrator at least annually. First-year administrators and those receiving an unsatisfactory evaluation in more than one area should be evaluated twice annually. Any unsatisfactory areas should be fully explained with specific suggestions for improvement.

Administrator _____   Date of Evaluation _____

	U	N	S	A	E*
Personal Characteristics					
Dress and grooming habits	____	____	____	____	____
Rapport with staff	____	____	____	____	____
Rapport with students	____	____	____	____	____
Rapport with parents	____	____	____	____	____
Professional Characteristics					
Continuing education	____	____	____	____	____
Response to board/pastor leadership	____	____	____	____	____
Leadership qualities and performance	____	____	____	____	____
Professional image	____	____	____	____	____

	U	N	S	A	E*
Administrative Performance					
Spiritual climate of the school	___	___	___	___	___
Curriculum development	___	___	___	___	___
Personnel selection	___	___	___	___	___
Personnel supervision and development	___	___	___	___	___
Academic achievement	___	___	___	___	___
Administration of discipline	___	___	___	___	___
Financial management	___	___	___	___	___
Administration of transportation services	___	___	___	___	___
Administration of food services	___	___	___	___	___
Management of plant and grounds	___	___	___	___	___
Spiritual Characteristics	___	___	___	___	___
Regular church attendance	___	___	___	___	___
Leadership	___	___	___	___	___
Interest in spiritual welfare of students	___	___	___	___	___
Expansion of school's spiritual ministry					
Testimony of family	___	___	___	___	___

U = Unsatisfactory N = Needs Improvement S = Satisfactory A = Above Average
E = Excellent

Pastor _____ School Board Chairman _____

The pastor and board have a responsibility to do a formal evaluation of the work of the administrator. This evaluation should be in line with the job description he has been given (Figure 4.5). The administrator should receive his annual review of his work within that basic framework. Figure 18.5 is an evaluation form designed to assist the pastor and the school board in evaluating their administrator. When the evaluation has been completed, the person completing it can score it by assigning a numerical value to each item: Excellent—5, Above Average—4, Satisfactory—3, Needs Improvement—2, and Unsatisfactory—1. A rating of Excellent should be reserved for performance that is truly outstanding. A rating of Unsatisfactory should indicate a very serious deficiency. Though this form is general, it is intended to relate to those expectations the administrator has already been informed of. It is unethical to hold the administrator accountable for specific expectations that have never been communicated to him.

As in the case of teachers, the purpose of the administrator's evaluation is to help him become more effective. Those who conduct his evaluation must keep this goal in view. Once he has been evaluated, the results should be reviewed with him as soon as possible, preferably in a board meeting with the full board receiving the benefit of the evaluation.

Since each school will need to evaluate its administrator in view of its unique situation and expectations, each will need to define the various areas included in the evaluation. Every school using an evaluation system like the one described here should develop its own definitions and give them to the administrator when he is employed, making certain he understands that the definitions will provide the basis for reviewing his performance on the job.

The results of supervision should generally lead to positive changes. People who are doing a good job should be encouraged by receiving this information from their supervisors. Those whose work is in need of some improvement should be advised of the areas of concern and should be provided with help to remediate any deficiencies. Much of the time this will mean providing specific direction on an individual basis. On other occasions it will mean that a general approach is needed to correct a deficiency that is more widespread. In each instance, a plan of action should be formulated that will identify the action required and the individuals who are responsible. Once the remedial action has been taken, there should be a reevaluation to see whether the problem has been resolved.

STAFF DEVELOPMENT

Exposure

Although personal development and staff development are usually viewed as separate programs, a good staff program will emphasize individual development as well. However effective a program of staff development may be on an individual basis, it is limited by the willingness of the staff to assimilate and apply personally the things that are taught. Those administrators responsible for staff development should seek to encourage staff members to have a personal program of development consisting largely of a schedule of personal reading and reflection. Professional staff members in particular should be encouraged to have a disciplined reading program. Good professional journals should be provided in a section of the school library or the faculty lounge. The emphasis should be on quality and not quantity, since the reflection is often as important as the reading. Also, since most professional journals are written by the unsaved, the Christian must exercise great care in balancing professional reading with time in the Bible to insure that worldly views do not displace God's views. Teachers should also be encouraged to exchange and weigh ideas with people who share their interests and responsibilities.

In addition, the school should have a formal program of staff development. Much of the content of this program will center on activities away from the school. Though some fail to recognize the value of state and regional Christian-school conventions, these meetings represent some of the best sources of professional help at a reasonable cost. These conventions usually offer fifty to seventy-five topics dealing with issues important to Christian education. They are particularly useful in helping pastors and others who are not specially trained in Christian education to develop an overall appreciation of the uniqueness of this field. Staff members should be given sufficient time and financial assistance to attend.

Staff Sessions

Most schools spend three or four days at the beginning of each school year with a preplanning session. Administrators should consider expanding the time to one or two weeks and encouraging curriculum development and lesson planning. A longer time will also provide opportunities to refresh old staff and acquaint new staff with school policies.

Though one or two weeks of preplanning may seem like a long time, it gives an opportunity to present information to the staff in a relaxed manner with time for reflection—time for personnel to get acquainted with one another as well as with the school program. After this time the staff will be prepared mentally, spiritually, and physically for a good school year.

The preplanning sessions should be scheduled to mingle instruction with time for classroom preparation. If all the instruction is given first, teachers become bored and fretful about getting their rooms ready for the students. Planning a varied schedule keeps the day more interesting and gives the teachers confidence that they will have ample time to prepare.

In addition, several times during the year a school should have in-service meetings to provide instruction in areas where the administrator has observed needs. These meetings can be conducted by the administration, the pastor, a number of teachers, or an outside speaker with professional expertise in a given area. The administrator and pastor should give most of the instructions, not only to identify them as knowledgeable educators but also to assure the teachers of their personal interest. However, they obviously should not attempt to deal with subjects with which they are not familiar.

Every school year should end with a post-planning session, including praise for jobs well done, identification of areas that need improvement, and encouragement to use the summer for relaxation and preparation. Encouragement and praise are especially important at this time, since the feeling of relief that another year is over is also accompanied by a letdown, a time of depression. Since teachers need to know that their efforts were worthwhile, this is the time to recognize both general and special individual achievement.

The faculty meeting is also an important part of the school's staff development program. It consists of a combined period of prayer, orientation, instruction, and fellowship, all of which are vital to a healthy Christian organization. For most schools, such a brief meeting can be held daily. Occasionally, special meetings will be needed to communicate with the faculty and staff about urgent matters. Properly handled, faculty/staff meetings can keep the faculty and staff in a family relationship, helpful and interested in one another, and vitally concerned about the needs of the organization.

Continuing Education

All professional staff should be encouraged to continue their formal education at least through the master's degree. Faculty that are not eligible for graduate study or are not interested in pursuing a graduate degree should be encouraged to take undergraduate course work in their field periodically to keep fresh. The administrator should counsel with each member of the professional staff, becoming familiar with the education and experience of each and making specific recommendations for a continuing education program. The administrator should provide a good example in this area as well. Whenever possible, staff members should be encouraged to continue their education in a fundamentalist Christian college.

The school should develop a good program of financial aid that will encourage teachers to take additional work, help them pay for the education, and reward them for its successful completion. To use wisely the money available, it is important to identify faculty members who will be of the most value to the school over the long run. You would not normally encourage faculty who will be with you only a year or two to pursue graduate studies at your expense.

Orientation of Faculty and Staff

The purpose of the school should be delineated in the faculty handbook. (See Appendix H.) The rules and regulations designed to help the staff accomplish this purpose should be included. Though this information can be given to teachers during in-service meetings, even the most conscientious will not be able to retain it all. It must be written down in a concise manner that will provide an easy-to-use source book for future reference. All school policies and any routines that are important for the teacher to follow should be written down, along with the method in which they are to be carried out. All employee benefits and responsibilities should be discussed. In the manual the teacher should be able to find answers to any questions about his responsibility and relationship to the school. An administrator can use the faculty handbooks of other schools to provide a structure for his. The school can then revise it each year, since it will never cease to need revision if it deals with all important issues. No handbook can meet the needs of another school completely, although it can provide good ideas. Be careful not to copy other schools' handbooks.

Though much of this chapter deals with the professional staff, the nonprofessional employees should not be ignored. Where possible and appropriate, they should be included in general sessions and social activities. They should be made to feel a part of the group and kept up-to-date with the school's activities. Special meetings just for them should be called from time to time as needs arise.

CHAPTER 19

CURRICULUM

> Get wisdom, get understanding: forget it not; neither decline
> from the words of my mouth. Forsake her not, and she shall
> preserve thee: love her, and she shall keep thee. Wisdom is the
> principal thing; therefore get wisdom: and with all thy getting
> get understanding.
>
> **Proverbs 4:5–7**
>
> Study to shew thyself approved unto God, a workman that
> needeth not to be ashamed, rightly dividing the word of truth.
>
> **2 Timothy 2:15**

O f all the terms in educational vocabulary perhaps *curriculum* is the most nebulous. For some, it means simply a listing of the courses that are taught at each grade level. Others would add to that a list of textbooks, instructional materials, and detailed instructional objectives with determinants for their evaluation. Others would say that curriculum includes the total educational experience resulting from the student's enrollment in school.

For the purpose of this book it is simplest to define *curriculum* as the planned program of educational experiences offered by the school. With this limited definition, the topic falls into two separate categories: academic and extracurricular activities. Academic activities include all of the course work and related activities consciously directed toward the development of the cognitive, affective, and psychomotor domains of the student. Extracurricular activities, to be covered in chapter 20, include all social activities, fine arts programs, and intramural and interscholastic athletic programs.

DESIGNING A CURRICULUM

No prescribed curriculum is universally accepted by public and private schools at either the elementary or secondary level. However, some basic guidelincs can serve as reference points in evaluating the curriculum of an existing school or developing one for a new school.

One source of these guidelines is the Department of Education of the state in which the school is located. While most states' laws do not give the Department of Education the authority to regulate the private school curriculum, Christian schools would be wise to consider the standards of the public schools in developing their curriculum. Some Christian schools that boast they are better than the public schools have academic programs that are anemic by comparison. When public school curriculum standards do not conflict with biblical principles, Christian schools should consider them as general guidelines.

Most Christian schools are organized under the old concept of elementary (K–8) and secondary (9–12), or elementary (K–6), junior high (7–9), and high school (10–12) grade levels. In public education the most common approach now is early childhood (K–4), middle school (5–8), and high school (9–12). Most colleges and universities with teacher education programs have modified their teacher education majors to conform to this organizational format. In the meantime while other colleges and universities are phasing in the reorganization plan, elementary teachers are presently placed in K4–grade 8, secondary education teachers may be used in grades 7–12, and middle school-teachers may be used in grades 5–8. Eventually the change in teacher training will have an impact on the curriculum of Christian schools as administrators have to take into consideration the changing preparation of teacher applicants.

Schools that take the early childhood, middle school, and secondary level approach will normally have their middle-school-teachers assigned on a course content basis rather than the traditional self-contained classroom concept of the conventional elementary school. Middle-school-teachers typically have the equivalent of two majors in subject matter content. Actually, most Christian school administrators will like the opportunities provided by this approach once they become familiar with it. Since the content in the middle school years is becoming more challenging academically, departmentalization along content lines will enable the school to provide better instruction in all areas so long as appropriate personnel are employed.

The curriculum of an elementary school offering kindergarten through grade six includes courses in each of the following subjects:

Five-year Kindergarten:

- Bible
- Mathematics
- Music
- Reading

Grades One–Six:

- Art
- Bible
- English
- Foreign Language
- Handwriting
- Mathematics
- Music
- Physical Education
- Reading
- Science
- Social Studies
- Spelling

Naturally, the treatment of the content varies from simple to more complex as the student moves upward from kindergarten through the sixth grade. Since the student is receiving the foundation for his further education in a broad range of subjects, this facet of education is very important. Serious voids at this level can greatly impair future learning.

Elementary students do not necessarily receive letter grades for all subjects in the curriculum. Phonics may never be graded as a separate subject but may be assessed as part of a reading grade. For art, music, and physical education, a report card may simply indicate individual achievement in general terms (excels, is satisfactory, needs improvement) rather than letter grades.

At the elementary level, most Christian schools offer basic music and art instruction on a group basis, usually one or two periods a week. Additional instruction in these areas could be made available on an individual lesson basis for an extra charge.

Instruction at the junior and senior high school levels focuses on basic instruction in Bible, English, mathematics, science, and social studies. Although a few schools offer some electives at the seventh- and eighth-grade levels, most do not offer electives aside from music, art, physical education, and foreign language until at least ninth grade. Electives become a more vital part of a student's program in the tenth, eleventh, and twelfth grades.

The curriculum in grades seven through twelve in a Christian school with a college preparatory emphasis typically includes courses in each of the following subjects:

Grade Seven:
- Bible
- English
- Life Science
- Mathematics
- Music
- Physical Education
- World History

Grade Eight:
- Bible
- Earth Science
- English
- Mathematics
- Music
- Physical Education
- United States History

Grade Nine:
- Algebra I
- Bible
- English
- Health and Physical Education
- Physical Science
- World Geography or World History

Grade Ten:
- Bible
- Biology
- English
- Geometry
- Health and Physical Education

Grade Eleven:
- Algebra II
- Bible
- Chemistry
- English
- United States History

Grade Twelve:
- Advanced Mathematics
- American Government/ Economics
- Bible
- English
- Physics

Senior High Electives:

- Art
- Band
- Choir
- Clothing
- Computer Applications
- Computer Graphics
- Computer Science
- Consumer Mathematics
- Debate
- Drama
- Driver Education
- Family Living
- Foods
- French I, II
- German I, II
- Journalism
- Keyboarding
- Orchestra
- Reading
- Spanish I, II
- Speech: Introduction
- Speech: Performing Arts
- Speech: Public Speaking
- Study Skills
- Wood Shop
- Word Processing

Many small Christian schools find it difficult to hire teachers to cover all the elective courses needed for a college preparatory program. New technology is offering exciting options for them.

High school graduation requirements vary somewhat from state to state, but the example for the state of South Carolina shown in Figure 19.1 is typical of what is required.

FIGURE 19.1

SOUTH CAROLINA HIGH SCHOOL GRADUATION REQUIREMENTS

English/Language Arts	4 units
Mathematics	4 units
Science	3 units
U.S. History and Constitution	1 unit
Economics	0.5 units
U.S. Government	0.5 units
Other Social Studies	1 unit
Physical Education or Junior ROTC	1 unit

Computer Science (Incl. keyboarding)*	1 unit
Foreign Language or Career and Technology Education**	1 unit
Electives	7 units

* The student must demonstrate computer literacy before graduation.

** For a student in a College Prep program to meet the state high school diploma requirements, one unit must be earned in a foreign language (most four-year colleges/universities require at least two years of the same foreign language); for a student in a Tech Prep Program, one unit must be earned in a Tech Prep Program, one unit must be earned in Career and Technology Education.

REQUIREMENTS FOR HIGH SCHOOL GRADUATION

Simply offering a program of study is not sufficient to insure that students will avail themselves of the opportunities afforded. Christian schools should also consider the standards of the public school system of their state and district in establishing graduation requirements. Although Christian school academic standards should never be lower than public school standards, it is not necessarily important that they be higher.

Graduation standards need to be flexible enough that transfer students meet them, yet they must be stringent enough to insure that every student receiving a diploma has received an adequate education. Because the integrity of the institution is at stake, the administration must not make exceptions to graduation requirements without valid reason. Missionary children educated partially outside the United States, however, may be among those who do need some special consideration.

The answer to this problem is for the local Christian school to offer sufficient breadth in its curriculum to meet the needs of students enrolled there. There is little academic justification for encouraging students who have not yet satisfied high school graduation requirements to begin a college-level education.

Christian high school graduation requirements vary considerably from one geographic region to another, depending primarily on the future vocational and educational objectives of the student body. Figure

19.2 illustrates the graduation requirements of Bob Jones Academy, an academically competitive college preparatory Christian high school.

FIGURE 19.2

BOB JONES ACADEMY
GRADUATION REQUIREMENTS

English	4 units
United States History	1 unit
Government/Economics	1 unit
World History or Geography	1 unit
Algebra 1	1 unit
Geometry	1 unit
Mathematics elective	1 unit
Science (including one biological and one physical)	3 units

College-bound students are encouraged to take two units of foreign language.

Bible must be taken every semester.

A minimum of one unit of health/physical education must be taken; a maximum of two units of credit will count toward graduation requirements.

A minimum of 22 units of credit must be earned.

Course titles should reflect the content taught, and course descriptions should be available to the parents, particularly at the high school level. Schools should refrain from attempts to "spiritualize" courses by giving them distinctive titles such as "Christian psychology" or "Christian history." Since it is assumed that all courses taught in the Christian school will reflect the school's Christian philosophy, it is not necessary to distinguish them further by changing the course title. In fact, this practice occasionally contributes to problems for students transferring to other schools, which may question whether the content of the course is what they require.

There is a trend to permit high school students to enroll in college prior to completion of a high school diploma, especially in high schools where curriculum offering is rather limited. In such an instance, a student is sometimes permitted to take one or two courses per semester at a local college for later inclusion in a college-level program. Sometimes the high school gives the student credit toward high school graduation for these courses. This practice presents several problems for the student. First, many colleges will refuse to award credit for a college-level course completed prior to completion of a high school diploma. It is not proper for a student to receive credit for the same course twice—i.e., as college credit and as high school credit. The greater danger, however, is that by permitting the Christian student to enroll in a local college, which normally is a secular private or public institution, the school has contributed to introducing him to a system of education that is diametrically opposed to a Christian philosophy of education (Prov. 19:27). As a result of this experience, the student may be less likely to leave home and travel several hundred miles to continue his education in a Christian college or university.

GRADE PROMOTION

Every school needs a well-defined promotion policy based upon objective criteria. Advancement from one grade level to another and the awarding of diplomas should be in recognition of satisfactory completion of predetermined educational objectives. Secular educators are often reluctant to hold children back when they fail to meet specific criteria for promotion—if, in fact, such criteria exist. However, prompting a child who is not mentally, physically, or socially mature enough to handle his schoolwork adequately is a disservice to him. Elementary school children who fail to master the requisite skills for success in the next grade level should be held back as early as possible to help them shore up weak skills and gain the confidence necessary to complete school successfully.

Promotion policies vary from school to school. A common policy for grades one through six is to require a student with two Fs, an F, and two or more Ds, or in some cases more than four Ds to repeat the grade. Some schools have an even more stringent policy for grades one through three, requiring a student to repeat the grade if he receives an F in either reading or math or a D in both subjects. Though such a policy at first seems overly strict, it really is a valuable approach, since reading and math are fundamental to a child's success in school. Success in schoolwork is dependent as much on maturation and readiness as it is related to the child's level of intellectual functioning. Spending extra time in an early grade gaining basic skills should never be regarded as a stigma; many children bloom spontaneously with an extra year's maturity.

At the junior and senior high levels, repeating an entire grade becomes less profitable and is only rarely appropriate. Some schools, whose curriculum is sufficiently flexible to do so, permit the student to repeat only those classes he has failed. Sometimes it is possible to make up deficiencies through a summer-school program or independent study or with the help of a tutor who is acceptable to the school.

At the senior high level, the student is required to repeat only required courses while having the option of repeating or replacing elective courses in which he has received failing grades. Grades, promotion, and diplomas should primarily be awarded on the basis of performance. Rewarding failure encourages others to perform at levels beneath their ability. Occasionally a small school may legitimately socially promote a youngster who has not satisfied its normal requirements for promotion if its program does not have the flexibility to meet the child's needs at the grade level or if the child has made as much progress as he is able and the school does not have special education services.

Social promotion never cures anything, and sooner or later the student will probably face an insurmountable obstacle again; the school will then have to make a decision about retaining the student in the school.

It is generally not a good idea to have a child enrolled in a grade that is more than two years older chronologically than normal for that grade level.

WRITING THE CURRICULUM

The beginning Christian school will not be likely to have a more comprehensive curriculum than that already discussed. The developing Christian school, however, needs to refine its curriculum by writing a course description for every course taught at every grade level. Initially, this could be simply a paragraph or two written by the teacher, but gradually it should include not only the description of the course but also instructional objectives.

In many Christian schools the textbook provides the major direction for determining the course content and the emphasis. This approach places the school in an extremely dangerous position. Many textbooks used by Christian schools are not completely trustworthy in content and philosophical direction. Even those textbooks that are trustworthy will insure adequate coverage of the content only when used in conjunction with other texts with which they are intended to be used. Since many Christian schoolteachers are inexperienced, neither they nor the textbook can be relied upon solely for the direction of the school curriculum. These weaknesses highlight the importance of using the very best textbooks available.

The fact that curriculum writing is hard work no doubt accounts for the fact that little of it is done in Christian schools. It is essential, however, unless the school's academic program is to be left to chance.

Curriculum writing is of necessity a cooperative effort. Since it is unlikely that any one person in a school is knowledgeable enough to write the curriculum for even one discipline, the administrator should take the lead in designing a well-balanced curriculum and should enlist the aid of well-prepared, experienced teachers in completing the details. Although teachers can do a portion of this writing as they plan and evaluate their lessons during the year, the major writing should be done before or after the school year at in-service sessions.

Once the curriculum is prepared and approved, it needs to be reviewed by the entire professional staff. All teachers should receive a copy of the portion that relates to their teaching areas, review it annually, and revise it as necessary.

IMPLEMENTING THE CURRICULUM

As important as a well-planned curriculum is to a quality education, an administrator must realize that it is only a plan. The key to successfully implementing it rests with the individual teachers. For example, although the curriculum may call for composition instruction in every grade, students may not receive it from teachers who do not enjoy the subject or who feel ill prepared to teach it.

It is helpful for teachers to submit their lesson plans for the following week each Friday. With these, the administrator can assess fairly accurately the pacing and balance in each classroom, as well as plan for substitute teachers should they be required.

In addition, an administrator may schedule a monthly fifteen minute conference with each teacher to check problems in curriculum. He may also appoint department heads in the secondary grades or lead teachers in the elementary schools to be responsible for small groups of teachers. These teachers should consult with their groups regularly and report any irresolvable curriculum problems to the principal.

A well-planned curriculum, founded on biblical principles and using Christian materials, is at the heart of successful Christian education.

CHAPEL

Chapel is a vital facet of the Christian school curriculum. The administrator should give it a permanent place in the schedule to avoid giving the impression that it is just something extra and to prevent it from being cancelled because of recurrent conflicts. Though every Christian school should have chapel, not every good Christian school will have the same chapel schedule or program format.

The number of students enrolled in a school, and the grade levels offered, will have a great deal to do with the length and frequency of the chapel program. Ideally, chapel programs should be divided so that young people of about the same age attend together. Kindergarten through third grade, fourth through sixth grades, seventh through ninth grades, and tenth through twelfth grades make good groups to work with.

A few schools have chapel for all grades every day. A more common routine, however, is for elementary students to have weekly chapel programs. Junior and senior high school students usually have weekly or daily chapel, depending on the structure of the school's Bible program. Schools that have full-length Bible classes on a daily basis usually have chapel weekly. Those that have Bible two or three times a week are more likely to have chapel daily.

The length of the chapel period also varies from school to school. Those schools that have chapel daily tend to have shorter chapel periods than schools that have it weekly. The most important aspect of chapel planning is not whether chapel is held daily or weekly, for thirty minutes or an hour, or whether students are grouped ideally by ages. The important factor is that chapel have a place of primary importance in the curriculum and that this emphasis be effectively communicated to students, parents, faculty, and staff.

The Bible should have a preeminent place in the school (2 Tim. 3:15–17). Nowhere in the curriculum should the Bible be more in evidence than in the chapel program. God's Word promises that the souls of men will be saved through preaching (1 Cor. 1:21), so preaching should have a primary place in the chapel programs for all ages of students. Though it is appropriate occasionally to use gospel magic or puppets to illustrate the Scriptures, schools must be careful not to allow "unique" presentations of the gospel to supplant old-fashioned preaching of the Word.

CHAPTER 20

EXTRACURRICULAR ACTIVITIES

And Jesus increased in wisdom and stature, and in favour with
God and man.

Luke 2:52

Whether therefore ye eat, or drink, or whatsoever ye do, do all
to the glory of God.

1 Corinthians 10:31

But refuse profane and old wives' fables, and exercise thyself
rather unto godliness. For bodily exercise profiteth little: but
godliness is profitable unto all things, having promise of the life
that now is and of that which is to come.

1 Timothy 4:7–8

Opportunities for participation in extracurricular activities vary
greatly from Christian school to Christian school depending upon
the school's development stage, philosophy, and grades offered. Unfortunately, many Christian schools devote their greatest attention and funds
to interscholastic sports, giving the impression that the sports program.
is more important than any other facet of the extracurricular program.
However, the key to a successful extracurricular program is balance. Extracurricular activities should not compete with or supplant the academic
program nor can they make up for it; rather they enrich it.

PLANNING THE EXTRACURRICULAR PROGRAM

A good extracurricular program in a Christian school does not just happen. Few Christian schools have good, well-balanced extracurricular
programs. It is especially challenging for a church-school to develop a
program that will not compete with the youth program of the church.
(See chapter 25.) However, pastors, deacons, school boards, and administrators who plan carefully can help assure a beneficial extracurricular
program.

First, the school must determine what activities are appropriate and will complement the philosophy and objectives of the church and school. Any activity that conflicts with the purpose of the Christian school must be excluded. Furthermore, activities must be carefully selected to provide a balanced school program without competing with the overall program of the sponsoring church or, to some degree at least, with programs of other fundamentalist churches sending students to the school. However, schools should plan some activities that might be viewed as specifically spiritual, such as soulwinning, jail ministries, and children's clubs, often slighted in favor of other school activities. A cooperative spirit will be the key to developing a successful church-school extracurricular program. In a church-school of any size, it will be impossible to avoid some conflicts, but as long as all the leaders are willing to work together, there should be no serious problems.

Most extracurricular activities in the Christian school will fall under the following three categories: athletics, extension ministries, and fine arts. Even though most of the students will have ample opportunities for spiritual outlets in their local churches, it is important to have some spiritual outreaches within the organized activities of the school. Unless these outreaches are included, students who are not from good churches will not have appropriate opportunities to develop in these areas, and there is also the danger of giving students the idea that outreach activities are not necessary in a well-balanced Christian life.

Once the scope of activities is determined, the school administrator, in conjunction with the pastor and school board, should be responsible for developing the program. If a school participates in interscholastic athletics, its calendar will often be less flexible because the games are scheduled by an outside athletic association. The school administrator, however, should be prepared to be flexible in other areas where he does have control of the schedule.

Administrators need to develop specific written guidelines for participation in extracurricular activities. Some activities, such as a camera club, could be open to all students; however, the yearbook staff, cheerleaders, and persons selected for athletic teams represent the school in unique ways that present special problems. To avoid conflicts and misunderstandings, and to provide direction, administrators and sponsors should make some basic decisions about purpose and scope before other faculty and students become involved.

Types of Programs

Athletics

Even in Christian schools the sports program represents the larger portion of the extracurricular activity program. Boys' activities often include tackle football, flag football, soccer, basketball, baseball, track and field, wrestling, golf, and tennis. The girls' activities include volleyball, basketball, softball, soccer, field hockey, track and field, and tennis. Because competitive sports encourage vast emotional swings that most youngsters are not mature enough to handle, elementary schools should avoid them unless they can be assured of stringent guidelines that protect the youngsters from excessive pressure.

One of the problems the Christian school encounters in developing a good interscholastic program is finding suitable teams to play without compromising basic philosophical concerns about becoming unequally yoked with unbelievers or unnecessarily exposing young people to unwholesome behavior or immoral influences. A number of schools avoid this situation by playing only Christian schools. Many have even been successful in forming Christian school athletic associations. Although this practice helps, schools are still plagued with friction from differences in dress standards and acceptable conduct. Unfortunately, a number of Christian schools are located in areas where there are few other Christian schools. To have an interscholastic athletic program, they would need to participate with public and secular private schools, and such participation would perhaps seriously compromise their standards and objectives in the process.

One solution to this problem is an aggressive intramural program. Schools large enough to field at least three teams in a given sport may find this approach acceptable. A well-managed intramural program can provide for participation of a higher percentage of the student body than an inter-scholastic program would allow. It can also develop healthy competition through careful assignment of the students to the various teams. In addition, the financial savings in transportation alone would be considerable.

Another problem encountered in conducting athletic programs is balancing opportunities for boys and girls. Since boys are usually more aggressive, there is a tendency to do more to insure the success of their program. Girls need not have a sport to balance every sport offered for boys, since there frequently are not enough girls interested in athletics to field the teams; however, when boys have opportunities for competitive sports, girls should also. When a school can afford only one team, it may go ahead with just the boys' team. However, by adding a second boys' team before offering a girls' team, a school indicates that it does not have balanced priorities.

A final problem with Christian school athletic programs is that they require careful monitoring. Before the first game is played, the board must develop an overall philosophy and supportive policies and must insure that the administration, athletic director, and coaching staff implement these. The administrator should maintain close contact with his coaching staff and regularly observe practice sessions and games. Though the administrator would not interfere in the actual coaching of a sport any more than he would interfere with the instruction in a classroom, administrators still need to keep their hands on these programs as a precautionary measure. Some coaches may interpret policies in ways that enhance their team's competitive advantage while undermining the overall objectives of the Christian education program. The competitive nature of sports is such that it is very easy for coaches and players to lose sight of the overall purpose of Christian education and the fact that athletics is only a part of the program, not an end in itself.

A positive benefit of any Christian school athletic program should be the development of healthy attitudes toward competition and of winning and losing in life. Unfortunately, these attitudes frequently do not develop. Competition can sometimes bring out the worst in one's character unless careful guidance is provided to direct these emotions appropriately. Everyone wants to win; no one wants to lose. Such an attitude is not wrong. However, whenever an activity is structured in such a way that two individuals or groups are pitted against one another in a contest that is designed to have but one victor, there will be a winner and a loser. Few contests end in ties, and those that do typically leave the participants with a less than satisfactory feeling.

The nature of sports is such that the manner in which activities are structured results in more losers than winners. It is imperative that we as Christians learn how to lose gracefully, and when God permits us to win, to do so gracefully, as well.

It is also imperative for Christians to learn to compete vigorously without losing their testimony. Athletic competition provides ample opportunity for young people to learn the importance of doing one's best, of making every effort to win, but doing so within the established rules of the game, and respecting the authority of the officials charged with the interpretation of the rules as they serve as judge and jury in the heat of the moment. This approach clearly makes the following unacceptable: cheating, hoping you will not get caught, deliberately breaking a rule even when you are willing to accept a penalty to gain some unfair advantage. In many Christian schools, student athletes have to contend with not only their own emotions but also the bad examples of the faculty and staff, administrators, pastors, and their parents.

The success of any athletic program is inseparably tied to the people given the responsibility for their day-to-day administration. Hiring the person to be the coach of your team is every bit as important as the teacher you hire for any course taught in the school. A good teacher is not necessarily a good coach. It is disappointing to see how spiritually mature an individual can appear to be in most areas while being an absolute infant in his understanding of the spiritual aspects of competitive sports.

Extension Ministries

Organized extension ministries should be as natural a part of the Christian school as the soccer team or basketball team; however, they seldom are. This clearly sends the wrong message to students and their parents. Extension ministries are essential for the normal development of the spiritual leadership of our young people. Young people need the experience of defining the needs of a group they perceive is in need of ministry, of developing a plan to meet specific needs, of organizing a group for ministry, of identifying people among their peers who have the requisite skills to insure that the needs are met, and the opportunity for personal spiritual growth afforded by actual participation in the ministry.

There are abundant ministry opportunities in every community. These outreaches can include ministries to the elderly that involve reading the Bible to them, preparing a meal, doing yard work, visiting with them, and seeking to meet spiritual needs that come to their attention. There are outreach opportunities for children in the community. They can read to preschool children of working mothers, they can assist in daycare facilities, they can be teacher's aids, and they can minister in children's homes or juvenile facilities. They can reach out to churches that send children to the school and offer to perform services for them such as yard work, general cleaning, and assisting with various ministry outreaches.

Short-term missions trips offer wonderful opportunities for service and personal growth as well. Such a mission trip can be an individual project where one student offers to go help a missionary for a summer, or it can include a group of young people making themselves available for missionary service. It can take place in a foreign country or right here in the United States. Not only will the missionary directly benefit from their efforts but also the young people will have the opportunity of a unique challenge for Christian service.

Staff leadership is crucial. The people given the opportunity of supervising ministry activities must be genuinely spiritual individuals whose personal testimony already is characterized by involvement in various ministries. The degree of success of extension ministries is almost always directly related to the quality of the leadership behind the program.

Fine Arts

No Christian school program is complete without appropriate opportunities for the development of student talent in art, speech, and music. Christian schools are doing acceptable jobs overall in music in the regular curriculum but less well in the extracurricular areas. Few schools do much in the way of developing the students' interests in art. Both are important, and as the extracurricular program develops, ample provision must be made for them.

It is as important for schools to have bands and orchestras as it is for them to have football and basketball teams. In fact, it could easily be demonstrated that there is much more long-term utility in the skills developed participating in a band or orchestra than on a football or basketball team. But both are important.

A school band and orchestra can enhance the overall spirit of the school and can contribute significantly to the atmosphere we desire to have in our school programs. The development of the artistic talents of our students is not quite as easy, but there are good opportunities for their development as well. Perhaps the most obvious are in support of the school newspaper and yearbook. Artistic students can be used to promote numerous activities in the school.

Training and experience in speech, which may include dramatic production, is invaluable for all Christian young people. It may whet their appetite for future service in the local church.

Once again, the leadership and support of an appropriate staff member is essential.

Yearbook

Another important extracurricular activity, particularly for schools with senior high programs, is the yearbook. It not only provides meaningful experiences for the students who work on the staff but it also can be an excellent promotional tool for the school itself. Participating on the yearbook staff provides unique opportunities for some students to develop leadership abilities and special interests in facets of their school program to which they had not been exposed previously. Though it involves a proportionately small number of students, it is a significant part of the school's extracurricular program. In most schools, serving on the yearbook staff is one of the opportunities good students cherish most.

Administrators and sponsors should carefully select the yearbook staff, choosing those who are above average academically, who have demonstrated leadership qualities in other school-related experiences, and who are recognized by the faculty and students as spiritual young people. Next, they need to implement careful guidelines to insure that nothing will get into the yearbook that will adversely affect the school's testimony or bring reproach on the name of Christ. They should require all copy and photographs to be reviewed by at least one faculty member who has been thoroughly instructed concerning school policy. The wise administrator will find time to review much of the material personally.

Clubs

Some schools have a number of clubs that meet on special days. Usually these clubs focus on hobbies or special interests, such as coin or stamp collecting, photography, history, or foreign languages. Sponsors of these clubs should have a genuine interest in the activity; they should not be assigned merely to fill a gap in the program. It would be better not to offer an opportunity for a club than to have a club with an uninterested sponsor. These clubs are most effective when they meet during the regular school day.

Socials

Another important area of extracurricular activity is social functions, such as parties and banquets. The administrator should clearly distinguish between official and unofficial activities. Official activities must be conducted in accordance with the school's well-established policies, with procedures for approving and scheduling included in the faculty manual and the student handbook. The school should publicize its policies so that parents can distinguish between official and unofficial activities. Since parents often rely more heavily than they should on the judgment of the school to determine the suitability of social activities, administrators must be careful to screen activities so as not to offend the consciences of the parents or supporting institutions and also to insure that students are properly chaperoned. It is also a good idea to limit the number of activities for each grade or group, especially to avoid competition with youth programs of the sponsoring church or supporting groups.

Schools would be wise to minimize activities for which students feel compelled to date. Since many parents prefer that their children not date or at least not date singly until at least after high school, schools should be careful to structure their activities so as not to offend these parents.

Trips

Although not usually considered a part of the curriculum, school trips could be included in our definition of extracurricular activities. Some Christian schools have done rather exciting things—grade level or graduation trips to Christian camps, colonial Williamsburg, and the nation's capital; tours of such historical areas as New England, prominent American cities, and even Europe. These trips, remembered for a lifetime, represent unique educational and spiritual challenges; they are expensive, however, and the financial limitations of the parents and students are a major factor in considering such activities. Some schools add a certain amount to the monthly tuition to defray costs; other schools have bake sales, car washes, and other fundraisers to help raise necessary money.

Awards

Most organized extracurricular activities are structured in such a way that exemplary individuals come to our attention. It is natural to want to recognize them in some way. Most schools have an annual awards program that provides an opportunity for recognition of students who have excelled in various activities. In a Christian school, the quality of the student's testimony should never be lost in the consideration of criteria that will identify students worthy of special recognition. It is inconsistent with our purpose of having a school if the student athlete of the year is about to be placed on probation for excessive demerits or is otherwise seriously deficient in Christian character. The development of Christlike character should overshadow all other goals in our institutions. If we reward behavior that is inconsistent with our goals, we are defeating ourselves.

Do not be tempted to give too many awards. Some awards programs at Christian schools have given virtually every student recognition for something. This cheapens the whole concept of reward. Only exemplary performance should receive special recognition.

The unique, the thrilling, the glamorous is always easier to sell and even to finance than the basic educational program. Extracurricular activities, however, must be kept in their proper place. There is no room for tackle football or trips to the Holy Land when teachers' salaries or textbook bills are still unpaid. The activities play an integral part in any school program and should not be just tacked on. The merits of each activity should be carefully considered. If it does not complement the school's overall philosophy, then it should not be added, and administrators should be careful not to yield to pressure.

CHAPTER 21

SELECTION AND RECRUITMENT OF PUPILS

For whom he did foreknow, he also did predestinate to be conformed to the image of his Son, that he might be the firstborn among many brethren.

Romans 8:29

And thou shalt teach them diligently unto thy children, and shalt talk of them when thou sittest in thine house, and when thou walkest by the way, and when thou liest down, and when thou risest up.

Deuteronomy 6:7

Teaching them to observe all things whatsoever I have commanded you: and, lo, I am with you alway, even unto the end of the world. Amen.

Matthew 28:20

For the educator who believes that every Christian young person needs a Christian education, it is difficult to think in terms of limiting enrollment. It is usually not practical, however, to consider developing a school that will open its doors even to all students from Christian homes. Because of differences in mental ability, social behavior, spiritual maturity, and vocational interests, no one school is likely to be able to minister effectively to all young people. (See chapter 27.)

Few Christian schools are large enough to offer programs sufficiently diverse to meet the academic needs of all students. Differences in behavioral patterns are such that students on either extreme do not profit from being in the same school environment. Most Christian schools are designed to address the needs of those whose behavior is acceptable in conservative Christian circles and whose mental abilities are above the twenty-fifth percentile. Most Christian high school curricula are tailored to prepare students for college; they have few courses for those who will leave high school and go directly into the world of work. This choice of curriculum is borne out by the fact that a large majority of Christian high school graduates go on to college. Admissions standards must be designed to limit enrollment to those students for whom the school program was designed.

Increasingly, Christian educators are showing concern for students with mental, physical, and learning disabilities. As parents of exceptional children seek Christian education for their children, it is likely that more schools will make programs available to them. At the present, the cost of providing education for exceptional children and the lack of personnel trained to meet their unique needs have made it difficult for schools to address this problem. Christian schools should endeavor to make Christian education available to as broad a spectrum of students as possible.

LIMITATIONS ON ADMISSION
Academic Standards

Assuming that the school will be emphasizing instruction for the student within a specific range of ability, the school must establish a means of measuring the ability of those who apply for admission. (See Figure 21.1.) Group standardized tests of mental ability and academic achievement tests, the most commonly used examinations in Christian schools, are quite reliable as predictors of future school success.

All new students should be screened for ability and achievement. Most of the nationally standardized group measures of general ability and academic achievement can serve the purpose. If the school is using such tests regularly throughout the school, it makes good sense to use the same test for admissions purposes. Some of the more commonly used achievement tests are the California Achievement Test, the Iowa Tests of Basic Skills, the Metropolitan Achievement Tests, and the Stanford Achievement Tests. Probably the most commonly used group intelligence test is the Otis-Lennon School Ability Test. The Slosson Intelligence Test for Children and Adults, which is given individually, may be administered and scored in a brief period of time.

FIGURE 21.1

SUGGESTED AGE AND ACADEMIC
CRITERIA FOR ADMISSIONS

1. A student must be five years old by September 1 (or by the date pre-scribed by state law) to be eligible to enroll in five-year kindergarten.

2. A student must be six years old by September 1 (or by the date pre-scribed by law) to be eligible to enroll in first grade.

3. A student will be admitted to grades two through eight on the basis of successful completion of the previous grade and satisfactory scores on the admissions examinations.

   a. A student scoring at his grade level or above on a recognized achievement test will be admitted to the next consecutive grade level for which he has applied.

   b. A student who does not score more than one year below his grade level on a recognized achievement test and has an in-telligence quotient in the average range (approximately the twenty-seventh percentile or above) might be admitted on a probationary status to the grade level for which he has applied; however, it is best to keep the number of students in this category to a minimum in each grade level.

   c. A student who scores more than one year below his grade level on a recognized achievement test but has an ability score on a recognized mental maturity test that places him in the average range (approximately the twenty-seventh percentile or above) will be admitted one grade level below that for which he has applied.

   d. No student will be accepted if his grade placement is more than two years below the normal grade placement for a student of his chronological age. Unless the school offers classes in special edu-cation with qualified teachers or special tutorial arrangements, it should not take students of below-average mental ability.

4. A student applying for grades nine through twelve will be accepted only if he has completed the academic requirements for the previous grade level and has an ability score on a mental maturity test that places him in the average range (approximately the twenty-seventh percentile or above). Generally speaking, the higher the grade level, the more certain the administration must be that the applicant can graduate by meeting the requirements of the school.

A third useful measure of academic progress is the grades earned in school subjects already completed. They are less reliable as predictors on their own because of the diversity of academic standards from school to school and from teacher to teacher. However, if considered along with standardized test scores, they can provide a better picture of the student's potential than can the grades or test scores alone.

The academic record of the student should always be carefully compared with his mental ability and achievement test scores to see whether they are consistent. Any inconsistencies should be carefully explored. Sound educational judgments by the administration will be necessary when variations exist between test results and performance as evidenced by records from schools the applicant has previously attended.

Conduct Standards

While it may be legitimate to operate a school for students who have been in serious trouble (unwed mothers, severe discipline problems, students who have been on drugs, and so forth), most Christian schools are not organized for this purpose. A school that attempts to enroll a substantial number of students who have a record of behavioral problems, especially in the immediate past, is courting trouble. Most difficulties with behavioral problems are encountered with students seeking admission at the seventh-grade level and above.

For elementary students it is usually adequate to review the student's conduct record and to see whether there has been an expulsion or suspension in his past. Students who have unsatisfactory conduct records or have been suspended or expelled should be considered carefully and accepted on disciplinary probation, if at all.

Students transferring at the seventh-grade level and above need to be interviewed very carefully, and their parents should be interviewed as well. Overt behavioral problems with drugs, alcohol, and tobacco represent obvious difficulties. Students who have habitually used them recently should not be considered for admission. Unless the student has recently been saved and has stopped his offensive habits, it is wise to require that he be free of them for one year before considering his admission.

Junior and senior high school students who are under suspension or expulsion from another school at the time of application generally should not be accepted. An exception should be considered only when there is overwhelming evidence that the behavior that resulted in the disciplinary action is not typical of that student or that the student has repented. In that event the decision should be made by a committee to avoid the influence of unwarranted sympathy shown by one person. Christian school personnel, despite their image, are usually tenderhearted people. They can sometimes be easily swayed by emotional situations and may make concessions that jeopardize the welfare of the other students enrolled in the school. Unless the school is organized to handle students who have behavioral problems, by accepting them, the administration will place the other students in jeopardy of temptations that their parents have enrolled them in the school to avoid.

Other questions that need to be raised involve conflicts with legal authorities. Has the student ever been arrested? Was he ever convicted? Has he ever been incarcerated? Is he on parole?

Just as important as problems of overt behavior are the student attitudes that conflict with the school on matters involving acceptable activities. Does the student listen to rock music or attend rock concerts? Does he dance? Does he attend movies at commercial movie theaters?

Student dating habits can also present problems for Christian schools. Students who have been permitted to participate in heavy petting, whose dating practices have not been restrained at all, will find it difficult, for example, to adjust to a school whose policy forbids hand holding. These matters need to be explored and fully discussed in advance of acceptance. Christian educators generally agree that unwed mothers present problems that most Christian schools are not able to cope with. A young girl or young man who has been sexually intimate is not likely to fit into the typical Christian school program. They should usually be referred to schools especially designed for problem young people.

Spiritual Standards

Though standards of conduct have spiritual overtones, the Christian school must have spiritual standards that go beyond those discussed in the previous section. The overall program of the Christian school operates within the framework of a well-defined biblical philosophy or doctrinal position. In the case of the independent school, it will be defined in the school's statement of faith and statement of purpose. The church-school will function within its traditional doctrinal position. Parents considering the institution must understand its position and the implications it will have on the educational process.

It is the school's responsibility to clearly communicate its philosophy to parents and students alike. It can do this through promotional materials and especially through the personal interview conducted as part of the admissions process. The person conducting the interview should observe the parents and students to discern clues that enable him to clarify points that appear confusing or need special emphasis. It is far better to come to a cordial understanding with a parent that the school and the student are not a good match for one another than to have to expel the student for violation of some school policy six weeks later.

There is a place in the Christian school, however, for some young people who do not come from Christian homes. Many times, because of the effective work of a Sunday school program or some other evangelistic ministry of the church, young people have trusted Jesus Christ as their Savior even though their parents are unsaved. God commands other Christians to teach the convert all things. This teaching process can be accomplished in the Christian school; however, if the parents do not sympathize with the school's spiritual aims, the student will likely suffer pressure that may undermine any of the spiritual benefits the school can provide him. For the ultimate good of the young Christian, then, it may be best to defer enrollment until the parents can wholeheartedly support the aims of the school. Sometimes these parents can be won to the Lord in the preadmission proceedings.

On the other hand, some churches have established Christian schools as evangelistic arms of their local churches, accepting any young person who agrees to abide by the schools' standards, whether he wants a Christian education or not. With this evangelistic philosophy of admissions, the school may have more unsaved than saved students enrolled, hindering its effectiveness with unsaved and saved students alike. Attempts to provide a Christian education to unsaved students are doomed to failure; "without a regenerated, willing student, Christian education cannot carry out its purpose" (Horton, 1992, 5). In addition, this philosophy ignores the important principle that "a little leaven leaveneth the whole lump" (1 Cor. 5:6). The influence of unregenerate young people, particularly in the secondary grades, can cause evil to spread throughout the entire school and frequently has, as many schools that have operated under an evangelistic philosophy in the past can testify. Because the purpose of Christian education is not to evangelize the lost but rather to educate saved young people to be Christlike, this type of admissions policy unfairly penalizes parents who choose for their children a Christian school that will shelter them from evil influences and encourage Christian growth.

There are circumstances under which a school may be properly organized for evangelistic purposes. For example, there are some Christian schools in foreign countries that have been organized as extensions of other missionary activities, and these have been very successful. These schools capitalize on the strong values that parents in their cultures place on education, and they use the schools as a means of having a captive pool of students to evangelize. Even these schools, however, usually recognize that as the students enter the junior and senior high school level, the evangelistic pressure of their programs will significantly reduce their enrollment and generally these schools have proportionately smaller high school enrollments than they have at the elementary level.

The area that creates perhaps the greatest number of problems is differences in doctrinal beliefs between the student or his parents and the school. Many parents equate "Christian education" with general "religious education." Many find out too late that fundamentalist Christianity and their concept of religion have little in common. The school can save itself much grief if it will make a point to emphasize contrasts between the school's doctrinal position and that of the family. These differences do not need to serve as a barrier to the enrollment of the student, but the parent should be aware of the potential conflict before enrolling his child.

An area of predictable conflict with unsaved students and those from homes where parents make no profession of faith in Christ is the straightforward preaching of the gospel. Parents must understand that it will be the school's goal to see each student come to a saving knowledge of Jesus Christ. For this reason some schools insist that all students come from homes where at least one parent is already saved. Explaining the school's position is a good opportunity to witness to lost parents. Parents who are unwilling to have their children exposed to this kind of teaching should be advised to consider another school. Accepting students from families associated with cults such as the Jehovah's Witnesses, the Mormons, Eastern religions, witchcraft, and other religions not based on Scripture is not compatible with the purpose of the Christian school; it will destroy the child caught in the cross pressure between home and school.

Curriculum

Although some schools claim to be able to meet the educational needs of nearly all students, they rarely can. Administrators typically find they must define the curriculum limits and adapt the school's admissions procedures to insure that parents are not misled concerning the academic offerings available.

Most Christian schools are designed for the average and better than average student, with the assumption that the student intends to pursue his education through at least four years of college. This is not done with the intent of having an academically elitist school but simply reflects the pool of students available to the school. The curriculum is usually geared to prepare students for enrollment in a Christian college. Although this curriculum also provides a well-rounded education for the student intending to enter a career immediately upon graduation from high school, it does not provide many course options for the student desiring to develop vocational skills in high school. Usually only a limited number of vocational courses are offered. Perhaps one home economics course is available, but rarely more. Few Christian schools offer courses in drafting, shop, or automobile mechanics. The reason is not that the school is not interested in such programs or does not feel that they are worthwhile. Christian schools do not normally have sufficient enrollment of students interested in these courses to offer them. Parents who are seeking this kind of program for their children will not be happy with a school that does not include it in the curriculum.

Some schools have had rather painful experiences in the area of vocational education. After receiving some inquiries, they proceeded to implement a program of vocational education, only to realize too late that the cost of such a program is considerably higher than that for a college preparatory program. It is better practice for schools to offer programs that are genuinely needed and affordable. Christian schools must sell what they can provide, not always what the customer wants.

The current emphasis on career and technical education may have an impact on the expectations of parents enrolling children in Christian schools. Career and technical education has eliminated the general track and the vocational track in education. It offers applied academic courses preparing students for future study in business, engineering technology, applied science, industrial technology, health, agriculture, or other appropriate technological fields of study. Students in these fields are normally planning to attend two-year colleges upon graduation from high school. The high schools and colleges frequently work out articulation programs to facilitate the transition from one institution to another. Of course, no school typically offers courses in all these areas. Course offerings are determined by the interest level of the students enrolled in these schools.

PROCESS OF ADMISSION

Every school should have enrollment applications and questionnaires. Carefully designed admissions forms will provide a considerable amount of information about the prospective student and his family. Schools have several types of applications for new students: inclusive applications for all grades as well as individual forms for kindergarten, elementary, and junior or senior high school. The applications are usually designed to be completed by the parent and to provide basic information about the family, the child's previous school experience, and the reason for sending the child to a Christian school. Sometimes there is also a statement pledging family support to the school and its policies. See Appendix I for a sample application. The student questionnaire, where used, is designed to indicate the student's attitudes about Christian education in general, his views about worldly practices, and his interest in attending the school. See Figure 21.2 for an example.

All applications should require a fee. Not only is this fee an important part of the financial plan of the school but, from the standpoint of admissions, it plays another significant role: the fee will limit applicants to those seriously contemplating enrollment. A school cannot afford to close classes on the assumption that they are full, only to find that 10 percent of those applying were only thinking about it.

Every application should be carefully screened. If it is immediately apparent, based on the school's admissions criteria, that the student cannot be given favorable enrollment consideration, the application should be declined and the family notified without further delay. Where such decisions can be made by review of the application, it is customary to return the application fee.

FIGURE 21.2

STUDENT QUESTIONNAIRE, GRADES 7–12

1. Name
2. Grade applied for
3. Attach copy of most recent report card
4. Ever fail a grade in school? What grade?
5. Ever suspended or expelled from school? When? Why?
6. Ever arrested or incarcerated?
7. Ever fail a grade in school? What grade?
8. Ever habitually use tobacco in any form or alcoholic beverages? Last date of use?

9. Ever habitually use illegal narcotics? Last date of use?

10. Ever experiment with tobacco, alcoholic beverages, illegal drugs or abuse prescription or over-the-counter medications? Which? When? Last date of use?

11. Ever dance, listen to rock music, or attend commercial movie theaters?

12. Do you want to attend this school?

_____   _____
Signature of student   Date

All other applicants should be notified of the fact that their application is under consideration. Those whose applications are for grades that are full should be advised of the school's policy concerning admissions testing and should be sent a copy of the testing schedule.

Interviews

After administering the tests, the school should arrange an interview for any student coming from a new family—that is, one that has not previously had children in the school. The personal interview must be conducted by someone who is thoroughly familiar with the school program—in most schools it is the administrator, but sometimes a vice principal or the school's guidance counselor.

An interview is most effective if it follows a prescribed pattern, as in Figure 21.3. A minimum of twenty to thirty minutes should be allowed for each interview, with at least one parent and the prospective student present. The interviewer should be familiar with the application and test results prior to the interview. As the interviewer gains some experience, he will learn of the areas that need to be pursued in greater detail. Depending on school policy, the interviewer may advise the parents of the decision at the time of the interview or by a letter at a later time. There is an advantage to advising all families of the admission decision by letter. Since some families will react unfavorably to negative decisions, advising them of your decision by mail can sometimes help you avoid some unpleasant responses.

FIGURE 21.3

STUDENT/PARENT INTERVIEW

1. Be certain the application is completed. Every question must be answered, and the application must be signed.

2. Discuss: Check off each item as it is discussed with parents.

   _____ Purpose of interview

   _____ History of school

   _____ Christian emphasis

   _____ Plan of salvation for parents who do not appear to be born again

   _____ Aims of the school

   _____ Curriculum information

   _____ Discipline policies and procedures

   _____ Student handbook

   _____ Tardiness and absence

   _____ Dress and grooming standards

   _____ Student's attitude (mainly for students above grade 4)

   _____ Parents' cooperation

3. Review items to be turned in at office: supply fee, certification of immunization, and changes of address and telephone numbers.

4. Remind parents that reservations are not held until all fees due have been paid.

5. Ask whether the parents have any questions.

Rejections

Rejections should be handled carefully. It is best to avoid making judgmental statements concerning the student's behavior, his test results, or whatever other criterion has resulted in his rejection. This policy makes it easier for parents to accept the decision, and they are less likely to be critical of the school. The administrator is interested, of course, in what they think of his school, since they will be in a position to influence others who may be considering enrolling children there. Figure 21.4 contains sample letters of rejection.

FIGURE 21.4

LETTERS OF REJECTION

Dear Parent:

The application submitted for your son John has been carefully reviewed by our admissions committee. As you probably realize, we receive more applications for admission than we can accept; consequently, every applicant's credentials must be reviewed carefully. We consider both the impact the school may be able to have in shaping the student appropriately for the future and the impact his presence will make on the student body of the school. Because of your son's previous discipline problems, we do not believe he is an appropriate candidate for admission to the school at this time. We would be willing to reconsider an application for admission next year.

Thank you for your interest in our school.

* * *

Dear Parent:

The application submitted for your son John has been carefully reviewed by our admissions committee. As you probably realize, we receive more applications for admission than we can accept; consequently, every applicant's credentials must be reviewed carefully. The curriculum has been developed to meet the needs of students who generally apply for admission to the school and, to be fair to all students, it is necessary to limit enrollment to those students for whom our curriculum has been designed. John's admission test scores were below the minimum scores required for acceptance. These minimum scores are consistent with test scores earned by students currently enrolled. We believe it is inappropriate for us to accept students who are not likely to be successful in the academic environment of the school or whose academic needs cannot be satisfied with our program. We regret that we are unable to approve John's application for admission.

Thank you for your interest in our school.

* * *

Dear Parent:

The application submitted for your son John has been carefully reviewed by our admissions committee. As you probably realize, we receive more applications for admission than we can accept; consequently, every applicant's credentials must be reviewed carefully. The curriculum has been developed to meet the needs of students who generally apply for admission to the school and, to be fair to all students, it is necessary to limit enrollment to those students for whom our curriculum has been designed. John's entrance examination scores do not meet the minimum standards established for the grade level for which John has applied. It does appear that John could be successful here if given the opportunity to make up academic deficiencies. We would be willing, therefore, to accept John for enrollment in the next lower grade level. Please call the school office for an appointment to discuss this matter.

* * *

Dear Parent:

The application submitted for your son John has been carefully reviewed by our admissions committee. As you probably realize, we receive more applications for admission than we can accept; consequently, every applicant's credentials must be reviewed carefully. As you are aware, our school is a ministry of our church. Thus, the doctrinal teaching in all our Bible classes and the preaching in chapel is consistent with the historical position of our church. We note that your family is of another faith. Recognizing the considerable differences in our beliefs, we do not think it is in our mutual best interest for John to be enrolled in this school, and we encourage you to consider sending him to a school whose views more closely represent those of your family.

Thank you for your interest in our school.

Waiting List

As a school becomes well established and develops a good reputation in the community, it is likely that it will begin to get more applications for students than it can accept. This is a healthy situation and will enable the school to develop a quality group of students. At this point the administration should develop a waiting list.

When grades become full and a waiting list of reasonable length has been developed, the administrator should be honest with parents and advise them that enrollment in the school for that year is unlikely. If other schools that he can recommend exist in the community, he might want to suggest that the parents consider one of them. Although they obviously prefer the school of their first choice, parents will appreciate the administrator's genuine interest in the needs of their children. After all, it is better that they be enrolled in another good Christian school than remain in one that is secular and humanistic.

When students are placed on a waiting list, the list should be limited to a reasonable number, probably no more than five for any grade level. Testing and interviews should be completed so that if an opening occurs, the child can be placed without further delay.

In addition, those responsible for the admissions policy must keep up-to-date concerning government regulations about admissions. At present the IRS has very special guidelines that must be considered by all tax-exempt, nonprofit schools. Criteria governing admissions policy extend to advertising, statements of policy, record keeping, and other details. This information is contained in Internal Revenue Service Publication 557, "Tax Exempt Status for Your Organization." It is available online or free from any IRS office.

CHAPTER 22

STANDARDS OF CONDUCT

> Whether therefore ye eat, or drink, or whatsoever ye do, do all to the glory of God.
>
> **1 Corinthians 10:31**

> For we are his workmanship, created in Christ Jesus unto good works, which God hath before ordained that we should walk in them.
>
> **Ephesians 2:10**

> For ye were sometimes darkness, but now are ye light in the Lord: walk as children of light.
>
> **Ephesians 5:8**

S tandards of conduct in the Christian school fall into two basic categories. First, in keeping with the Christian school's educational objective, most of the rules promote the development of Christlikeness in the student. Ephesians 4:22–24 admonishes the Christian to "put off concerning the former conversation the old man, which is corrupt according to the deceitful lusts; and be renewed in the spirit of your mind; and . . . put on the new man, which after God is created in righteousness and true holiness." In a parallel passage (Col. 3:10), Paul tells Christians to "put on the new man, which is renewed in knowledge after the image of him that created him." God does not want the Christian young person to walk "as other Gentiles walk" (Eph. 4:17). The Christian should think differently and act differently from the unsaved young person. Since the pattern for the student in the Christian school is not other students but the image of the Lord Jesus Christ, the student's behavior should be directed at all times toward pleasing God and glorifying the name of Jesus Christ our Savior (2 Thess. 1:11–12). Thus the Christian school encourages its young people to "do all to the glory of God" (1 Cor. 10:31).

In addition, many of the regulations in the Christian school are necessary for the efficient operation of a school organization. Paul states clearly in 1 Corinthians 14:40 that Christian organizations should "let all things be done decently and in order." For a number of students in a Christian school to use the same facilities at the same time, certain rules must be established. For example, students should be in class on time; they should not loiter in the hall; they should park their bicycles or cars in specified spaces.

Similarly, the Scriptures make clear the importance of standards in certain areas such as dress and grooming; however, the Scriptures do not provide specific criteria on how these standards are to be applied. The lack of specificity provides room for cultural differences and differences in taste and style that change from time to time. Nevertheless, some specific guidelines are required to provide consistency and to insure movement in the right direction. Consequently, when defining standards of grooming and dress, administrators of Christian schools should acknowledge that these standards are based on principles of Scripture rather than on specific instructions from Scripture.

DISCOURAGING UNCHRISTIAN BEHAVIOR

In Ephesians 4 Paul encourages Christians to put off certain undesirable types of behavior and to replace them with godly types of behavior. He specifically names five sins, which must be controlled especially in the Christian school.

Lying

In verse 25 Paul says, "Wherefore putting away lying, speak every man truth with his neighbour." A lie is a statement contrary to fact, spoken with the intent to deceive. For example, it is not a lie when a student, thinking it so, tells the principal that a classmate is in the gymnasium, when in fact the classmate's parents have taken him to the doctor. On the other hand, if the same student told the principal misinformation in order to protect a classmate who had skipped class, he intended to deceive and therefore lied. Many students may attempt to lie to help themselves or other students. Even though lying may seem to eliminate some immediate, unwanted consequences, the students need to learn that lying will ultimately destroy them.

Anger

In verse 26 Paul admonishes Christians to be "angry, and sin not." Anger may be good or bad. God Himself became angry (e.g., Num. 25:4; Deut. 9:8, 20; Jer. 4:8), as did Jesus, the Son of God (John 2:15–16). However, anger for the wrong reasons is sin (James 1:20). Since the Christian school trains students to be in control of their emotions, fighting and other exhibitions of uncontrolled anger cannot be tolerated. Especially on the athletic fields, students (and coaches) must strive for complete control of their behavior.

Stealing

In verse 28 Christians are told not to steal. A person steals when he takes something that does not belong to him. In the Christian school this might be taking a book, a candy bar, a watch, or even another student's answers (cheating). In direct contrast to the secular world's emphasis on dishonesty, the Christian young person should be encouraged to work for everything he gets.

Corrupt Communication

In verse 29 Paul admonishes Christians to "let no corrupt communication proceed out of your mouth." Christian students must be encouraged to edify one another with their words rather than tear down one another. Improper speaking, vulgarity, profanity, and other sins of the tongue have no place in the Christian school.

Bad Attitude

Paul concludes the "put off" and "put on" section in Ephesians 4 by warning against several sins of attitude and "evil speaking." Students must be expected to maintain a good attitude at all times. Insubordination, deliberate disobedience, negative attitudes, destructive talk, criticism, and griping cannot be tolerated in the Christian school. Students and faculty alike should be "kind one to another, tenderhearted, forgiving one another, even as God for Christ's sake hath forgiven [them]" (Eph. 4:32).

ENCOURAGING CHRISTLIKE BEHAVIOR

Besides these, other areas of Christlike conduct should be incorporated into a Christian school's standards of conduct.

Respecting People and Property (Heb. 13:17; 1 Pet. 2:17)

The students in a Christian school must have a proper respect for teachers, staff, and other students. They should address their teachers with proper respect and should "obey them that have the rule over" them. Children are commanded to honor their father and mother (Eph. 6:4), and since the teachers stand in the place of the parents in the Christian school, they also deserve proper honor. Bus drivers, janitors, lunchroom workers, secretaries, and all other staff members at the Christian school should be treated with utmost respect. A student should treat fellow students with the courtesy and kindness with which he would like to be treated (Matt. 7:12).

If students are to have the proper respect for other people, they must also have a proper respect for the property of others, including the school building, the teacher's materials, and other students' belongings. Defacing school property or personal belongings cannot be tolerated in the Christian school.

One rule that helps keep students from unintentionally harming the school facility is to prohibit gum-chewing or candy-eating in the school building. Sticky candy and chewing gum are two of the messiest items to try to clean off a floor. Once candy or gum is embedded in a carpet or on furniture, it is almost impossible to totally restore the property. By eliminating the use of gum or candy in the school, the administrator will be able to keep the Christian school plant neat and clean for a longer time. Of course, there should be no such rule if it will not or cannot be enforced.

Caring for the Temple of God (1 Cor. 6:19)

In order to encourage the Christian student to take care of his body, the "temple of the Holy Ghost," the Christian school should not allow him to use tobacco, alcohol, or other drugs either at school or at home.

Students should be encouraged to exercise their bodies regularly and to avoid other harmful practices such as overeating and inadequate rest.

Giving No Offense (1 Cor. 8:13; 2 Cor. 6:3)

The principles found in the Word of God clearly instruct the believer to refrain from activities that place him in a setting that is not pleasing to the Lord and that may have a harmful influence on weaker Christians. Students should be instructed from the Word of God to avoid activities that are forbidden in the Scriptures or that violate biblical principles. For this reason students should not be allowed to participate in gambling, dancing, movie attendance, or other worldly activities that do not bring glory to the Lord Jesus Christ. In obeying this rule, the students should be concerned not only about their own personal testimonies but also about the testimony of the Christian school in the community and its influence on others.

Fleeing Fornication (1 Cor. 6:18; 1 Thess. 4:3)

The Bible commands Christians to flee fornication and abstain from every type of immorality. For this reason a Christian school would be wise to follow a "hands-off" policy (no physical contact between boys and girls) at all times, including bus trips, athletic events, field trips, and other activities the school might sponsor. In addition, because student engagements imply a degree of intimacy that these students are not emotionally ready to handle, it is best not to permit such engagements either officially or unofficially. Most Christian school administrators also discourage students from going steady or exchanging rings as tokens of friendship. Since students should always be expected to act as ladies and gentlemen in their relationships to one another, displays of physical affection are out of order. Because the Bible admonishes Christians to avoid "all appearance of evil" (1 Thess. 5:22), couples should never be allowed to seek isolated areas of the campus to be alone.

On the other hand, the Christian church and school are in excellent positions to provide wholesome opportunities for their young people to socialize. Since one of their aims for the future is to build strong Christian homes, young people can benefit from the opportunity for wholesome interaction with other young men and women within the environment of a good church or school. Christian young people need opportunities to meet and evaluate those of the opposite sex. Chaperoned church and school activities can provide excellent times of fellowship and social, as well as spiritual, growth.

Appreciating Good Music (Eph. 5:19)

Students should be taught to listen to spiritual songs that make melody in the heart. Rock music and other music that appeals solely to the flesh undermine that scriptural principle. Since there is much confusion in the Christian world today about what is and is not acceptable music, the Christian school should establish plain standards that it can enforce consistently. Too strict a music standard, one that errs in the direction of being especially careful of the school's testimony, is better than one that is not strict enough. The school should help the students recognize that a song with Christian words is not necessarily Christian, since the type of music involved is as important as the words. Students, then, should be taught what good music is and should be encouraged to listen to music that uplifts rather than tears down.

Attending Church (Heb. 10:25)

The church is an important institution that should be involved in the education of every young person. Many Christian schools expect all their students to attend church regularly so that the students learn the value of participating in a fundamentalist church and serving in it whenever possible. Some schools check weekly to determine how active the students are in local church activities. A Christian school may want to require students to attend a minimum number of church services per week in order to remain enrolled in the school. This type of policy will help discourage parents from enrolling their children for just a private education.

Dressing Appropriately (Deut. 22:5; 1 Sam. 16:7)

The Christian school has an important testimony to maintain in the community. One way the community judges the school is by the appearance of its students and faculty. Even though God looks at the inward man, the world looks at the outward man. Because of a Christian's testimony and the clear biblical teaching of the differences between the sexes, it is absolutely imperative that everyone associated with the Christian school be above reproach in the matter of outward appearance.

The school dress standards should be enforced at all school activities unless the student's parents are notified differently in advance of the activity. Students who wear improper dress should be counseled privately on biblical principles that are being applied to formulate the dress standards. School authorities should have the final word on whether dress meets school standards.

Since fads and clothing styles change almost yearly, the school administrator should reserve the right to make rulings on any new fads and changes in style that may occur. Parents themselves should also be encouraged to observe the school dress standards when attending school functions, such as ball games and programs.

A major principle underlying all standards of dress is modesty. This obviously applies to common decency, but it also involves calling undue attention to oneself. Bizarre dress that makes a person a spectacle is as inappropriate for Christian dress as clothing that calls inappropriate attention to the body.

Making Right Friendships (1 Cor. 5:9; 15:33; 2 Cor. 6:14)

Students should be encouraged to make good friends with Christians who have a positive influence on them. For example, a young person who has a problem with his temper should not seek friends who also lack self-control. He should seek friends with a cool and calm spirit so that they will help him control his temper. Because the friends a young person makes are extremely important to his spiritual growth, the Christian schools should help students make the right kinds of friends by discouraging those who are bad for each other from being together, by warning those who have a bad influence that they will not be retained without significant improvement, and by counseling those who need help in establishing sound relationships.

Over the years many Christian school administrators have recognized the wisdom of emphasizing group activities rather than individual dating occasions. Group activities provide appropriate opportunities for young people to get to know one another and learn how to behave with one another while minimizing the development of close personal relationships that can become difficult to handle if started too young.

PROMOTING SUCCESS IN CHRISTLIKENESS

Teaching proper behavior is a large part of the school's concern. In addition, it is important that a school seek creative ways to encourage and reward exemplary Christian behavior. Regulations in themselves are not sufficient motivation.

Academics

An administrator should encourage his teachers to seek out the reflections of God in the subject matter they teach and to find practical applications for them. For example, students in a family living course studying the aged could spend time entertaining or visiting in a nursing home. An English class (or government class) can write letters to their congressman on issues affecting the home, church, or school.

Role Models

Besides their daily contact with godly school personnel, students will benefit from other contacts with exemplary Christian models. Missionaries serving as chapel speakers, men and women from the supporting churches speaking about ways they apply their Christianity to their jobs, and a library well stocked with Christian biographies—all these provide students with positive examples to emulate.

School plays and programs, though not always necessarily "religious," should be morally instructive and indeed present excellent opportunities for encouraging patriotism, culture, and school spirit. Other extracurricular activities as well should be scrutinized for the character training available through them.

Rewards

Frequently chapel announcements or bulletin-board notices recognizing exemplary behavior or accomplishments not only reward those who demonstrate Christlike qualities but also encourage others to follow their example. Rewards at the end of the school year for such qualities as citizenship, dependability, and enthusiasm also help promote these as desirable qualities.

PROMOTING EFFICIENT OPERATION OF THE CHRISTIAN SCHOOL

Institutional rules governing behavior and procedures will vary from school to school, depending on the size of the school and the number of facilities available for student use. However, some basic procedures can be implemented to help eliminate potential problems. Rules required for efficient operation will also be governed to some extent by how grade levels are separated at your school. The following suggestions are given in the interest of order and efficiency, assuming that clear distinctions between these grade levels can be made at your school.

Elementary School

Although elementary children need opportunities to share ideas and suggestions, students should raise their hands in the classroom to request permission to speak or to leave their seats. Teachers can most efficiently take their classes to lunch, restrooms, the library, and physical education class by lining the children up in a straight line and moving quickly and quietly through the hallways. Loud talking and horseplay should never be tolerated.

To avoid having several classes using restrooms at the same time, use should be limited to assigned times unless there is an emergency. During the restroom period, children should care for their needs and then line up quietly in the hallway to await the return to class.

When using the playground, children should obey the supervisors at all times. The administrator should set specific boundaries for the actual playground area and establish rules for the use of the equipment.

No roughhousing or fighting should ever be allowed on the playground. When the whistle is sounded (indicating the end of recess), the students should line up quickly and quietly by individual class and await the return to the classroom.

Many Christian schools have established a no-talking policy during the elementary lunch time, not to keep students from enjoying one another but to make lunch time more efficient. There is no question that disallowing student talking at lunch time encourages them to eat their lunches faster. However, it may also cause unwanted rumors in the community about the severity of your school practices. If talking is closely monitored in the classroom and when students are moving about the building, it would be wise to structure the lunch period to permit them to talk with one another. Students should be encouraged to talk in a low, conversational tone. Shouting should never be allowed. The privilege can be taken away periodically if necessary to maintain appropriate control.

Elementary students need a great deal of external control from the teacher in order to behave themselves properly. As the students mature, however, teachers should find that they can eliminate some of the procedural rules by encouraging students to be self-controlled rather than teacher-controlled. However, some controls should always be maintained; for example, students should always have to ask permission to talk, to move about the room, or to leave the room.

Junior and Senior High School

Junior and senior high school students, presumably more self-controlled than elementary school students, should be able to behave in an orderly fashion with much less structure. However, they should generally raise their hands before speaking in class or asking for permission to leave their seats to move about the classroom or to leave the classroom. When in the hallways and restrooms, they should not be involved in horseplay or loud, boisterous talking. If their behavior becomes unacceptable, some of the restrictions placed on elementary children may have to be applied again to the older ones. Such restrictions, however, should be only temporary, since the teacher should be striving to teach students self-control.

Each secondary teacher should establish and post his own set of classroom rules that students are to obey—subject, of course, to the overall rules of the school. There may also be a need for some institutional rules regulating the use of the lunchroom, library, gymnasium facilities, and so forth. The goal in secondary education should be to develop orderly, self-controlled students without applying excessive external control.

Bus Rules

Any student riding a school bus should comply promptly and cheerfully with the requests of the driver. Students should be required to be seated on the bus when it is moving and to have their seat belts securely fastened. They should never throw waste paper on the floor, deface the bus in any way, or place their hands or any other part of their body outside the bus. It is also wise to forbid them to eat, drink, or chew gum on the school bus. School officials should be careful not to allow students to depart the bus at a stop other than their own without written approval from their parents and the school office. Of course, all the behavioral rules of the Christian school apply to the students while they ride the bus. Since bus drivers are not professional school employees, they should not be permitted to exercise any form of physical discipline with students.

COMMUNICATING THE RULES

Because it is extremely important that students and parents understand the standards of conduct for the Christian school, a student-parent handbook should be published to state all the rules and other necessary information. Parents should be required to sign a statement that they understand and will enforce the rules of the school. This can be included as part of the application for enrollment or reenrollment in the school. Parent-teacher meetings can also be used to announce particular areas of concern during the school year. Students should be continually reminded of the rules during chapel services and through school announcements because successful discipline relies on frequent repetition and constant enforcement.

Students need not only to know the rules but also to understand the reasons for the rules. They should distinguish between those developed to help the students become Christlike and those made for the efficient operation of the school so that they can adopt the former into their behavior away from school as well. Students may not always agree with a rule, but the administration should always be able to give a reason for the rules and should encourage those who do not understand the standards of the school to talk with the administration in order to determine the underlying purpose for the rule in question. If the administration does not have a good reason for a rule, they should either find a reason or change the rule.

CHAPTER 23

DISCIPLINE

Withhold not correction from the child: for if thou beatest him
with the rod, he shall not die.

Proverbs 23:13

For whom the Lord loveth he chasteneth, and scourgeth every
son whom he receiveth. Now no chastening for the present
seemeth to be joyous, but grievous: nevertheless afterward it
yieldeth the peaceable fruit of righteousness unto them which
are exercised thereby.

Hebrews 12:6, 11

D iscipline is the process of changing a student's wrong behavior
into the right behavior. A teacher should never be satisfied with
merely stopping wrong behavior; he should desire to teach the student
to do what is right. Scripture tells us that punishment ("chastening")
is used to develop right living ("righteousness"). We call this process
discipline.

The proper motivation for discipline is love (Prov. 3:12; Heb. 12:6).
An effective administrator does not discipline a student out of anger
or for the sake of convenience but always with a loving desire to help
the student to do what is right. Without this genuine love for students,
teachers and administrators cannot expect discipline to be effective.
Though few students desire discipline, they greatly need it in order to
become Christlike.

ELEMENTS OF EFFECTIVE DISCIPLINE

Communication

The first step toward making discipline effective is making sure the
students understand the school's regulations. The school handbook,
chapel programs, parent-teacher fellowships, and individual conferences are all effective tools for doing this. If a student is to obey the
rules, he must know what they are and understand the reasons behind

them. Students should appreciate the fact that they are not merely obeying the school when they follow rules; they are obeying God and His principles.

Comprehensive Enforcement

The school administrator alone cannot enforce the school regulations. Teachers, parents, and students alike need to share the responsibility. Some teachers feel that their responsibility to the school begins and ends with the academics of the classroom. They are reluctant to enforce rules or question students about suspicious behavior. Since character training is the most important part of a student's education, however, teachers need to be admonished that enforcing regulations is an integral part of their responsibilities.

One common student complaint is that some Christian schools have a double standard, requiring students to comply with certain restrictions while faculty are allowed to flout them. Teachers should be apprised of student dress regulations, music guidelines, and so forth, and they should also agree to abide by them both as a matter of upholding the authority of the school and from a desire to be good role models for their students.

Students often feel a conflicting loyalty between their relationship with their peers and their responsibilities to uphold school rules and foster Christian character. Elementary students in particular need to distinguish between tattling (telling on a student for something insignificant to get him into trouble) and reporting an infraction so that the student can be helped and any damage repaired.

Some Christian schools encourage students to face their peers who have broken school rules, telling them to report the infraction on their own so that the observer will not have to report it. The purpose is certainly not to foster a Gestapo-like atmosphere in the school (a common charge but an unlikely outcome) but rather to teach students that it is everyone's responsibility to maintain the quality of the school's atmosphere and to foster godliness in one another.

School rules cannot be enforced without the support of parents. It is important to maintain a good relationship with parents. Whenever serious differences of opinion over school rules develop, it is a good indication that perhaps the child should not be a student in the school. The school rules are intended to reinforce parental concerns. When this is not true, an important facet of the school's relationship with the family is missing.

Control

No matter how accomplished the administrator, how biblical the rules, or how well behaved the students, the key to consistent discipline is the teacher. The teacher must be in control of the classroom at all times. He should have standard operating procedures and enforce them consistently. Poor lesson preparation that leads to gaps in instruction or boredom in the students frequently leads to discipline problems. The teacher who "goofs off" with the students will often not be taken seriously when he attempts to discipline one of the students. An administrator who has a teacher complain of frequent discipline problems may want to observe the class to see whether the problem can be remedied by a change in the teacher's practices. Figures 23.1 and 23.2 give some of the areas in which teachers can help prevent and correct discipline problems.

The physical environment will help or hinder the control of the students. For example, classrooms that are not heated or lighted properly will encourage misbehavior. On the other hand, carpet on the floors helps eliminate much unnecessary noise.

Consistency is the key to good discipline. If students learn early in the year that rules will be enforced without exception, they will be more likely to follow them. However, if students get away with wrong behavior, they will probably continue to misbehave, assuming that the rules will not always be enforced. It would be better not to have a rule than to have one that is inconsistently enforced. Christian schools that do not demand strict obedience to all the regulations are teaching students that laws are made to be broken. Young people ought to be learning that disobedience brings serious consequences.

TYPES OF CORRECTION

Teacher's Displeasure

For the teacher who has won the respect and love of students, a show of displeasure for wrong behavior will often correct the problem. The teacher may show his displeasure through a facial expression (e.g., a frown), through vocal expression, or both.

Most students desire to please their teacher; his disappointment is often sufficient punishment to bring about the desired behavior.

FIGURE 23.1

PRACTICAL TIPS ON PREVENTIVE DISCIPLINE

The effective teacher—

1. Learns the names of his pupils quickly.

2. Calls upon those pupils whose attention is wavering. This practice discourages daydreaming, interest in neighbors, and so forth.

3. Does not turn his back to the class and does not remain stationary.

4. Studies carefully the seating of the students. Certain students have a bad effect upon each other and form potentially explosive combinations.

5. Begins each class promptly and enthusiastically.

6. Is businesslike. Class time is for work, not play. However, businesslike classes should not be boring.

7. Is prepared with an interesting program of worthwhile material for each hour.

8. Watches his voice. It should be pleasing, but not soothing; varied, never a monotone.

9. Remembers that a sense of humor and a smile are very important tools in teaching.

10. Uses special occasions to show the students that he is vitally interested in them. He should go to their games and call or send cards when students are sick.

Elimination of Privileges

Students who misbehave may lose the opportunity to do things they enjoy. The most common loss of privilege used for discipline in the elementary school is keeping students in from part of their recess. Students should rarely, if ever, miss an entire recess. If one does, he should run around the school yard for a few minutes to get rid of stored energy. Otherwise, keeping a student in from recess can do more harm than good. On the secondary level, students can lose extracurricular privileges (e.g., opportunities to play upcoming ball games and be in performances). For severe infractions a student may be removed from an office or prohibited from participating on a team.

Teachers should also give privileges to those students who exhibit good behavior. Special jobs, enrichment activities, and even little gifts could be given to those students who are consistently obedient. Just as the Lord will reward teachers for their faithfulness, so teachers should reward students for their obedience.

FIGURE 23.2

PRACTICAL TIPS ON CORRECTIVE DISCIPLINE

The effective teacher—

1. Stops the little thing, nipping disciplinary problems in the bud.
2. Uses indirect warnings, then specific rebuke, to correct misbehavior.
3. Never humiliates a student in front of others, correcting students in private whenever possible.
4. Does not use sarcasm, scorn, or ridicule.
5. Does not make threats he cannot enforce and never uses the threat of withdrawing love or affection.
6. Is consistent in his discipline. He has no favorites.
7. Teaches that disobedience is primarily against God.
8. Allows the student to express his view of the problem. He helps him to evaluate his wrong behavior biblically.
9. Always administers discipline with a heart of love, never in anger, since the goal of corrective discipline is to right the wrong behavior so that fellowship with God can be restored.

10. Always tries to handle his own problems but calls for assistance when necessary.

Trips to the Principal's Office

Teachers who have a continual problem with a given student may exercise the right to send him to the principal's office for correction. Especially for the elementary student, the experience alone may be punishment enough. The principal must give stern warnings so that the children do not enjoy the experience.

This is not to say, however, that there should not be times that a child's experience in the principal's office is pleasant. To be an effective principal, one must call students in not only for disciplinary measures but also in response to good behavior and outstanding accomplishment. The student body should realize that the principal is there to punish evil and reward good.

Though a trip to the principal's office can be very effective in solving a discipline problem, it generally should be a choice of last resort. Whenever the teacher has to go to the principal for help, there is an important sense in which the battle has been lost. In the future the student may play a game to see how bad he can be without being sent to the principal.

Corporal Punishment

Spanking is an effective means for correcting wrong behavior and is clearly recognized in Scripture as an appropriate tool to correct improper behavior (Prov. 13:24; 22:15; 23:13–14; 29:15). It is important to note, however, that all references to spanking children in the Bible have to do with parental actions. The authority schools have to use corporal punishment comes from the parents of the students. If the authority of parents to spank their own children is being seriously questioned, it is certain that the authority of the school will be subject to question.

A number of states forbid the use of corporal punishment in public schools, and many public school districts in other states have prohibited it on a district level. Advocates for strict legislation to prevent child abuse are increasingly looking at corporal punishment, even when administered by parents, as child abuse. At least one state now considers abusive any physical discipline that results in a mark that can still be detected 24 hours later.

The U.S. Supreme Court has not yet opposed the "reasonable" spanking of a child in school. The court (*Ingraham v. Wright*) in 1977 ruled that corporal punishment was not cruel and unusual as the plaintiff had argued and that it was not necessary to have a hearing before corporal punishment was administered. In spite of the absence of any court case opposing the use of corporal punishment in schools, caution should be exercised. Any Christian school located in a state or local school district that prohibits corporal punishment would be well advised to seriously consider not using corporal punishment.

If a school decides to utilize corporal punishment, it must proceed with caution. Before a child is admitted to the school, his parents should sign a written statement giving the school the authority to discipline students by spanking. In any event, the parent should be notified when corporal punishment is used, and the administrator would be wise to have another witness present. It is important to remember, however, that if bruises are left on the child as a result of corporal punishment, there is a strong possibility that the courts would consider the punishment excessive and therefore constitute child abuse. Some schools require the parent to administer the spanking himself in the school office. Those that use this approach hope to avoid legal liability for corporal punishment; however, if this is done and the parents have legal problems as a result of administering it, it is likely the school will also have problems if they required the parents to do it.

Because of the uncertain legal climate in our society, many no longer recommend that schools use corporal punishment. This approach, of course, means that some children who could otherwise be served by the school will not be able to be enrolled. It is better to miss the opportunity of ministering to a few children than to risk your entire ministry over this issue.

Suspension

The Christian school may want to establish a policy of suspension for certain major offenses. Usually suspensions are for one, two, or three days. "In-house" suspension is sometimes better than allowing the student to stay at home; however, it places an additional burden on the school to supervise the student while he is under discipline. Such a policy could require him to be at school doing various maintenance jobs or other work. He could also be placed in a special room with extra projects or reports to do. However, consistent use of essays, math problems, or Bible memorization as punishment will discourage students from enjoying those areas and thus may be self-defeating for an educational institution. Suspension is a severe disciplinary measure and should be reserved for serious disciplinary, problems.

Expulsion

When a student's behavior is such that it affects the attitudes and behavior of other young people, the "leaven" must be purged. Such a student should be expelled for an entire school year, and the expulsion should be entered on the student's permanent record. He should be allowed back after his period of expulsion only after a thorough interview and the assurance that he has a repentant spirit and has maintained a good testimony.

Certain severe first-time offenses warrant immediate expulsion: stealing, cheating on a midterm or final examination, sexual immorality, drinking, and the use of illegal drugs. The Christian school should never tolerate these behavioral problems. If this type of problem student is not expelled, his influence will affect and possibly ruin the lives of many other students. In cases involving smaller offenses, usually a student is expelled only after a well-established pattern of unacceptable behavior.

Some schools expel students for the remainder of the school year. This policy brings about obvious problems. The expulsion of a student during the first quarter of the year brings about a far more serious punishment than expulsion that occurs during the fourth quarter. If adjustments are made to take into consideration the difference in timing, it is still difficult to make certain that the adjustments result in fair treatment for all. Consequently, most Christian schools expel students for an entire calendar year. Some would ask that the student be readmitted only at the beginning of an academic period such as the beginning of a grading period.

ADMINISTERING DISCIPLINE

There is a proper way to discipline a young person so that he is "exercised thereby" rather than just punished. First, the administrator or teacher should make sure that the student knows why he is being punished. A student cannot correct his behavior if he does not know what he did wrong and what he should have done. The disciplinarian should explain the offense carefully to the student.

Second, the student must realize that his wrong behavior is a sin against God, seeing scripturally how his offense violated God's law. Thus the disciplinarian needs to understand Scripture thoroughly and be able to communicate God's truth to the student, teaching the young person that there is always a price to be paid for sin and that wrong behavior brings suffering (Rom. 2:8–9; 6:23).

Third, the student should confess his sin to God. Forgiveness comes freely to the Christian student who will tell God about his sin and be sorry for his wrongdoing (1 John 1:9). In order to confess properly, the student must have a genuinely repentant heart and a desire not to repeat the offense.

Fourth, the student should be punished swiftly and definitely, but fairly. The punishment a student receives should produce a desire to avoid repeating the offense. This does not mean, for example, that discipline must be severe. The key is that the discipline is appropriate for the offense and the age level of the child. The removal of privileges should grieve the student, but losing the privileges should not be excessive. Work assigned should be demanding, but not unreasonable. In considering the severity of the consequences, however, the school is not responsible for the fact that the offense occurred or was discovered just before a championship ball game, the senior trip, or the school commencement activities.

Consequently, the timing of the offense or its discovery should not enter into the nature of the discipline administered.

Fifth, the student and the disciplinarian should pray together, asking the Lord to help him to do the right thing in the future. The student needs to know that it is not possible for him to correct his wrong behavior without the power of God (Phil. 2:13).

Sixth, the student should leave the disciplinary session with confidence that he can change his behavior in the future, and he should be ready to apologize to the appropriate person(s) and provide restitution if necessary. Without this last step, the discipline may be a failure. The disciplinarian should let the student know that he does not expect to have to discipline him again for the same offense. He should tell the student that he will be praying for him, and then he should pray for him. As he has the opportunity in future weeks, he should also praise the student for proper behavior. This exhortation may be just the right medicine to effect some positive behavioral changes in the student.

SYSTEMS OF DISCIPLINE

In the elementary school the teacher should be in charge of the classroom discipline, using the school principal only when there is a problem that the teacher is unable to control. In the junior high and high school, however, the school should have a system for consistently recording and reporting the students' disciplinary problems. There are several systems that Christian schools have used successfully.

Demerit System

The demerit system, which works best on the junior and senior high levels, assigns a specific number of demerits to each offense. Each time a student violates a rule, the number of demerits assigned to that offense is recorded on his disciplinary record. If the student accumulates a specific number of demerits, he is assigned various penalties and/or specific disciplinary action.

The school handbook or disciplinary letter need not contain a list of all offenses and their demerit values. However, if a school so desires, some of the more severe offenses and a range of demerit values may be included. To avoid legal action, the school should specify in writing the behavior that may result in expulsion.

In many schools students receive demerits from their teachers when they violate a rule. They are informed at the time of offense what the demerits are for. The teacher then turns in a demerit slip to the school at the end of the day so that it can be recorded. The school should keep a record of each student's demerits and take appropriate action when the student reaches a specific level.

Another possible method is to have a disciplinary committee, rather than the teachers, give the demerits. This committee could be made up of faculty and student representatives. When a student violates a rule or is charged with an offense, the offense is reported by a faculty member or an administrator. After the offense is reported, the student is required to appear before a committee, which then determines guilt and assigns the appropriate number of demerits. By setting distance between the faculty member and the assigning of demerits, this system provides a check and balance and creates a greater confidence that the discipline process is fair.

Whether the school administrator, teacher, or discipline committee determines the number of demerits a student receives, they must remember that the purpose of the demerit system is to provide a record of the student's disciplinary problems. Though the demerit system should not be the only discipline for behavioral problems, it can add weight and force to any disciplinary action.

Detention System

The detention system requires students who violate rules to remain in a detention hall after school. The advantage to this system is that parents are immediately informed of any behavioral problems and are required to make arrangements to leave the child after school. Thus the system forces parents to become involved in the discipline problems of their children. The disadvantage is that it requires extra supervision from school personnel. Detentions that are not strictly proctored can turn into fun times that lose their effectiveness as punishment.

The detention hall is usually set up two times a week (e.g., Tuesday and Thursday), and parents are informed at least one day ahead of the assigned detention period. Parents sign the detention form and return a copy to the school office. The length of the detention period may vary; however, it should be at least forty-five minutes. Students should stay in the detention hall and work on special assignments or work projects.

The administration should take other disciplinary action with students who continually go to the detention hall. Many minor infractions in the school may not in themselves warrant a detention period. However, an accumulation of these small offenses should be reason enough for a student to spend a period in detention. A set number of minor infractions (for example, three to five) should be established so that the teachers will be consistent in giving detentions.

Conduct Grade

The school may give grades as part of a demerit and/or detention system, or the conduct grades may be used as a system in themselves. Under this system, which works best at the elementary level, each teacher gives his students a conduct grade. (Number grades are preferable for conduct; letter grades should be reserved for academic subjects.) Each student's average grade (the mean of the grades from all his teachers) appears on his report card so that the parents are aware of their child's general behavior. In averaging the conduct grades, the administrator should take note of any specific problems that show up after the grades are averaged. For example, grades may be weighted to take into account the fact that one teacher may have a student more often than another.

If the school desires to be more specific in grading, some particular areas of behavior could be graded for each student. Students receiving conduct grades below average may be put on disciplinary probation. Two semesters of such probation would prevent a student from reenrolling. Of course, severe disciplinary problems would have to be dealt with accordingly. Conduct grades should always be recorded on the permanent record card and placed in the file of each student. Any major offenses that occur should also be noted on the disciplinary report. The conduct grading system is not as detailed as either the demerit or the detention system, but it does allow schools to communicate to parents how the teachers view the behavior of the child.

DISCIPLINING STUDENTS FOR INCIDENTS OCCURRING AWAY FROM SCHOOL

There is much difference of opinion about whether a Christian school has the right or ability to discipline students for actions that take place away from the school or during the summer months. Christian school leaders should expect parents who have enrolled their child to agree with the overall philosophy and policies that the school implements. For this reason, the Christian school should expect parents to discipline their own child while he is not on the school grounds. However, if the school decides to have certain standards that must be followed year-round, it must make sure that any disciplinary action implemented for a student's conduct away from school is spelled out in writing. Parents and students alike must be aware of the consequences of disobeying school rules while away from the school. Many schools have had parents and students sign statements promising that they will abide by certain rules and standards of life no matter where they may be. This practice is especially helpful in maintaining the right type of students in the junior and senior high school.

In order for the Christian school to develop young people who will stand for Christ, it must be willing to exercise consistent, loving discipline. This discipline should not be limited to the external control exerted upon students by the teacher or administrator, but the students must be taught self-discipline and responsible behavior as well.

The Christian school's disciplinary program must not only stop the wrong behavior of students but also develop in students the desire to exhibit Christlike character. A program that stops wrong behavior but does not teach self-control is a failure.

CHAPTER 24

PUPIL PERSONNEL SERVICES

> Without counsel purposes are disappointed: but in the multitude of counsellors they are established.
>
> **Proverbs 15:22**
>
> Hear counsel, and receive instruction, that thou mayest be wise in thy latter end. There are many devices in a man's heart; nevertheless the counsel of the Lord, that shall stand.
>
> **Proverbs 19:20–21**

Pupil personnel services, a field of education unfamiliar to those not directly involved with the profession, covers eight categories of services commonly offered to students: orientation, counseling, educational and vocational planning, informational services, job placement, follow-up programs, curriculum study, and child study and testing. An additional category, not always connected with pupil personnel services but directly related to those activities, is maintaining and reporting student records. Pupil personnel services is usually associated with junior high and senior high programs, but most of these activities also have application for elementary schools.

Few Christian schools have well-developed programs of pupil personnel services. This is unfortunate because the services falling under this category are directly related to the core mission of every Christian school. Christian school administrators should carefully review the manner in which their school program handles the provision of these services and, when the school is large enough to do so, seriously consider employing one person, usually a guidance counselor, to administer the entire pupil personnel services program.

GUIDANCE COUNSELOR

One of the criticisms leveled against Christian schools is that they lack professionalism. Unfortunately, this charge is too often true. The poor way in which many schools handle pupil personnel services is one illustration of this lack of professionalism. A Christian school should have a guidance counselor as soon as possible. Certainly a school with an enrollment of four or five hundred students can accommodate the financial expense involved in a full-time counselor. By combining duties, it is possible to obtain a counselor's services even earlier.

The guidance counselor should have overall responsibility for all the duties described in this chapter. It is not necessary that he actually perform these tasks, but the people who do them should be responsible to him. The counselor also has a unique opportunity for a ministry within the student body. Particularly if he is not also a classroom teacher, he has the potential of relating to the students in a manner that is not available to any other professional staff member.

What does a school do until it can afford a guidance counselor? It cannot ignore the need for the services; it must find a way to provide them by parceling out the duties to a number of staff members. Though this procedure is inefficient and provides occasion for some things to be omitted, it is better than no attempt at all. Someone must assume the responsibility for overall supervision of the programs. Usually the principal handles most of these duties. A typical division of the eight categories of pupil personnel services among personnel at a church-school not yet large enough for a full-time guidance counselor might be as follows:

1. Pastor/Associate Pastor or Bible Teacher—counseling

2. Administrator—orientation, job placement, informational services, curriculum study

3. High School Principal, Vice Principal/Supervisor—educational and vocational planning, child study and testing program, follow-up program

The potential for the division of duties is limited only by the capability of the personnel at a school. Some of these responsibilities can even be assigned to a classroom teacher, if necessary. Because the long-term testimony of the entire school program is at stake, the decision to provide these services should not be made lightly.

ORIENTATION

An orientation program exists to communicate the purpose of the school. In order for a Christian school to accomplish its purpose, it must have students and parents who are in harmony with its goals. A program of orientation assures the school that parents, and students who are old enough to comprehend it, understand the school's philosophy and the way in which it will be implemented in the school program (see Appendix J).

Orientation is not a single event, but rather a program of activities consisting of at least three elements: a comprehensive student-parent handbook, a student-parent interview, and a meeting of the student body. A meeting with parents of new students, if it can be arranged, is also helpful.

Every school needs a handbook that describes its programs and policies. This serves as a ready reference for students and parents who desire to cooperate with the school but who frequently find it difficult to remember all the details of their relationship with the school. The handbook should be updated annually and made available to those enrolled or seriously considering enrollment. Schools may find it convenient to have the handbook produced to fit into a standard business envelope.

Administrators should interview the parents of every child to be enrolled in the school for the first time. There is no substitute for a face-to-face discussion of the school's policies and programs. Any negative response from parents about the spiritual program of the school should be carefully considered and explored. The children should also be present.

Boarding schools, however, have special problems in the matter of interviewing. Though the interview is still the most desirable procedure, it may not be possible because of distances involved. In such a case the information normally obtained in the interview must be obtained through telephone conversations, letters, applications, and recommendation forms.

In addition, the school should conduct a meeting of the student body. It can be handled in several ways, depending upon the size of the school, the grades offered, and the number of new students involved. In high schools there may be special meetings for new students only; classroom teachers could give the information to younger children. Every student should review school policies annually. Those policies that have presented the most difficulty, of course, are the ones that should receive the greatest amount of emphasis.

COUNSELING

The opportunities for counseling families involved with your Christian school are almost unlimited. Pastors of church-schools who take advantage of these opportunities will have the blessing of helping people and will add many families to their local churches as well.

The most important qualifications for Christian counseling are a close personal relationship with the Lord, a thorough knowledge of the Word of God, and a love for people.

Most counseling sessions will be with the student but it will not always be possible to solve his problem without involving others. Frequently, parents, teachers, friends, and the pastor will need to be included. Keep the group as small as possible, but be willing to expand it as necessary.

Beginning in grade seven, someone from the school should have at least one interview with every student every year to determine his spiritual condition and the role of the school in meeting his needs. A minimum of twenty to thirty minutes should be allowed for this meeting. Students should also be encouraged to seek counseling on their own, and they may be referred for counseling by a teacher or another adult. Besides discussing a specific problem or general attitudes, the interview should include a discussion of the student's personal relationship with the Lord.

A brief record of this interview should be either kept by the counselor or placed in the student's permanent record folder. Some basic principles of counseling are summarized in Figure 24.1.

FIGURE 24.1

PRINCIPLES OF COUNSELING

1. Every problem is a spiritual problem and, therefore, has a biblical solution (1 Cor. 10:13; Heb 4:15).

2. Everyone is responsible for his actions regardless of the circumstances (2 Cor. 5:10; Heb. 9:27).

3. The real counselor is the Holy Spirit. The human counselor, aside from what God has done for him and will do through him, has nothing to offer those in trouble (Isa. 9:6; 11:2; John 14:16–17; Gal. 3:1, 3).

4. All counseling should be based on the Word of God (John 17:8, 14–17).

5. Christian counseling must be directive. God has a will for every person and a solution to every problem. The job of the counselor is to help the troubled person come to genuine peace with God by developing a right relationship with Him and then to assist him in finding God's will for his life (Prov. 2; John 14:26).

6. The counselor must help the student depend directly upon the Holy Spirit to guide him (1 John 2:27).

EDUCATIONAL AND VOCATIONAL PLANNING

Christian schools have a responsibility to provide direction to students in the selection of their future vocation and to help them plan an educational program that will prepare them for that choice. The guidance counselor must remember that his job is to lead the student to make a decision, not to make it for him.

Any planning for the student's vocational choice must emphasize God's will for the student's life and the importance of continuing preparation in a Christian educational institution. The school has a responsibility to help guide the student in the selection of the college that not only will provide the academic training required but also will continue the spiritual training offered by the Christian high school. Students who choose to pursue secular training when Christian education in their field is available should be counseled that such a choice is in conflict with clear-cut biblical instructions (Ps. 1:1; Prov. 19:27; Col. 2:8).

INFORMATIONAL SERVICES

Informational services exist as an outgrowth of educational and vocational planning. Information should stress opportunities for Christian work. Because not all students will be called to full-time Christian work, however, the school should also provide materials on other vocations suitable for separated Christians.

In addition, the school should develop a current file of college catalogs. Begin by asking several Christian colleges, as well as local vocational schools, to send a catalog. From this point on, the school can request catalogs as students express an interest in a particular college or university.

JOB PLACEMENT

Most students graduating from the Christian high school will be continuing their education somewhere else. Those who do not pursue college training may appreciate guidance in seeking out suitable places of employment. Traditionally schools have provided placement assistance through the guidance counselor. The school can provide a great service by helping students find employment situations that do not create conflicts in their efforts to maintain a separated Christian testimony.

FOLLOW-UP PROGRAMS

One of the last projects many Christian schools think of in the area of pupil personnel services is instituting a follow-up program for their graduates. Given the resources and the desire, this program can be a valuable asset to the school's overall ministry.

A follow-up program can be useful in evaluating the long-term impact of the school on the lives of its students. But perhaps of more value is the opportunity to provide help and encouragement to any former student who has begun to flounder spiritually. The student who does not go on to a Christian college is most susceptible to backsliding after a few months. A contact from the school to inquire about his general welfare, his spiritual life, and his work situation would usually be genuinely appreciated.

Curriculum Study

Pupil personnel services has an indirect but important influence on curriculum. The development of the curriculum in the Christian school could be a constantly evolving process. As a school grows, offers more grade levels, gains more students, and consequently offers more courses, the curriculum becomes more complex and requires more careful management. Pupil personnel services is a natural component of the curriculum development team because of the intimate knowledge of students' needs that it provides.

Guidance counselors should constantly review college entrance requirements, comparing them with the curriculum of the school, calling to the attention of the administration any apparent shortcomings, and recommending changes to correct the problems.

Child Study and Testing

Every school should have a comprehensive plan for a school-wide testing program. This program should include general mental ability and achievement testing at the first, fourth, eighth, and eleventh grades as a minimum. If it can afford to do so, the school should have achievement testing at all grade levels every year. All seniors should be required to take either the ACT or SAT to give the school a good indicator of the level of its students' preparation for college. Since the ACT is used by most Christian colleges, it is probably the better choice. This overall testing procedure will assure the school of having some results of standardized testing for every child enrolled.

The results of standardized testing can be very useful to school personnel in predicting student potential for future scholastic success. They also provide information concerning the achievement levels of the student body as a whole, which, compared with mental ability scores, give some indication of whether the students are performing as well as they should. Properly used, the results of standardized testing can also give some indication of teacher effectiveness. Appendix K contains information regarding a suggested testing program.

At the secondary level the guidance counselor may want to consider some tests of vocational interest and/or aptitude. The results of such testing can be useful in guiding students in the exploration of vocational opportunities. Several tests designed for this purpose are available from local government and private employment agencies as well as publishers of test materials.

Results of standardized testing can be helpful in evaluating the school and promoting its program. Since many Christian schools are not accredited, specific indicators of quality education are useful in talking with others about the school's performance. The results of standardized achievement tests are generally acceptable as indicators of relative quality. Schools must be certain to report the results carefully and honestly, not making claims that the testing does not substantiate.

All results of standardized testing for individual students should be made available to parents upon request. Schools should voluntarily report the school-wide results of achievement testing, explaining in layman's terms what test scores mean, so that the parents can understand them. A copy of a form with an explanation of how to interpret the scores is a good way to advise parents of this information. The report could also include, along with the student's scores, the mean for the class and the relationship of these scores to the national average. Results of mental ability tests should be handled carefully. Since this is information you developed as a result of permission granted by the parents, you have an obligation to share this information with them. Such scores should be released only on an individual basis, with the results described in general terms. You should be prepared to meet with parents to provide additional explanation if necessary. Parents should be reminded that educational testing is not an exact science and scores are not to be thought of as exact measurements, like body temperature or blood pressure.

STUDENT RECORDS AND REPORTING

Student records include applications for enrollment and reenrollment, emergency information, academic progress reports, records of extracurricular activities, conduct records, health records, standardized testing results, personal evaluations, and correspondence with the family.

Academic Records

Reporting academic progress to parents is an essential part of the communication process. These reports should be comprehensive yet simple, providing an evaluation of the student's work in a form that the student and the parent alike can readily understand. (See Appendix L for a sample report card.) Most schools divide the school year into either six-week or nine-week grading periods. Some, particularly those using the nine-week grading period, divide further by issuing interim progress reports.

Report cards should provide a grade for each course in which the student is enrolled. Conventional letter grades (A, B, C, D, and F) are the most easily understood methods of grading. Pass/fail grades are not suitable except for such courses as physical education, art, or music, where precise grading is difficult or unnecessary. The advent of outcome-based education has brought innovative means of reporting progress. Unfortunately, these new methods of reporting tend to conceal more than they reveal and, consequently, are generally not very satisfactory substitutes for tried and true marks that communicate. As Christian educators we should not close our minds to things just because they are new, but we should exercise caution to make sure that new things are also better before we adopt them.

Schools using progress reports commonly indicate only whether the student is passing or failing at the midpoint of the grading period. This report gives parents an opportunity to work with the teacher to salvage the quarter or six-week grade before it becomes a matter of permanent record.

One of the most common uses of the school's permanent records is to provide transcripts. A school should never send the original record to another school or give the original record to the parents, even though they will sometimes request it. The school has a legal obligation to maintain a permanent record and cannot do so if it surrenders the record to another person or institution.

All states have compulsory school-attendance laws and require some form of attendance records demonstrating that the student has actually been enrolled and attending school on a regular basis. Attendance record books, available from school supply houses, provide a simple way to comply with this requirement. In some states public school attendance record forms are available for private school use. Attendance records are usually kept by the homeroom teacher or the school office personnel.

The academic record must be maintained on a permanent basis. State law frequently specifies the options a school has if it closes. The most common course of action in such an instance is to request that another school agree to be a depository of the school's permanent records. This approach means that such schools also have to agree to provide transcripts as needed by the former students. The other most frequently used alternative is to turn the records over to the state department of education to service former student requests for transcripts.

Nonacademic Records

All academic information discussed in the preceding paragraphs should be retained in a cumulative record folder. This folder contains a permanent record of the student's activities at the school; additional nonacademic information, to be discussed in this section, may be added at the school's discretion.

Schools are often accused of keeping voluminous records. This accusation is no doubt warranted, but there is a truly amazing amount of information that must be maintained to provide the educational service traditionally associated with a school. At this writing, Bob Jones University has the original academic records of over 70,000 students that have attended the institution since it began in 1927.

Personal and family data are usually obtained through applications for enrollment and are updated annually by means of reenrollment applications. They are frequently supplemented by emergency information cards, printed on 3" x 5" cards for easy reference. These materials provide information enabling the school to act on behalf of the parents in the event of an emergency involving the student. The applications and/or emergency cards often contain a release of liability and permission for the school to act for the benefit of the child on behalf of the parents. However, because the courts have ruled that parents cannot relinquish the right of the child to sue, such releases have limited value.

Many schools have parents sign a general permission for their child to participate in such activities as field trips and athletic contests. These forms call specific attention to the fact that certain activities may be engaged in so that parents who object can make other arrangements. They also save the school the nuisance of sending releases home before each special activity. These forms should be retained in the child's cumulative record folder.

Legislation enacted by all states requires certificates of immunization for all children as part of the enrollment process. Usually parents are required to have them on file by the first day of school but not later than the end of the first month of school. A local health department can supply information for rules in this area since laws vary considerably from state to state.

Though it is not required, schools should have a copy of the student's birth certificate, since they frequently are called upon to verify the student's age.

Schools should also keep all correspondence with parents of children enrolled in the school. Correspondence may be kept in the student's cumulative record folder until he leaves the school, at which time most schools completely eliminate correspondence from the academic file and leave only that information that would be made available to others inquiring about the student. Correspondence and other related material could be maintained in a correspondence file or a general file, depending upon the structure of the individual school.

Another important aspect of the student's record is a disciplinary file. All disciplinary action should be carefully recorded. Teachers should keep records of all incidents involving corporal punishment. As a minimum, this record should contain the date of the incident, a description of the offense, the disciplinary action (include the number of swats), the names of the persons involved (teacher, witnesses, students), and comments concerning any discussion with parents. These reports can be summarized and sent to the school office to become a part of the cumulative record at the end of the school year.

Storage of Records

We have stated previously the importance of maintaining permanent records. It is important to recognize some of the steps that must be taken by an institution to insure that records will be preserved for future use.

In spite of the advances made possible through computer technology, most Christian schools still keep records on paper. Records kept on paper are generally considered usable for fifty years. That time period assumes that they were originally put on good quality paper and were stored in a safe place that protected them from elements such as fire, water, and insects. Good quality storage cabinets that resist fire damage are expensive and many Christian schools fail to secure their records suitably because of the cost of storage facilities. This is a normal cost of doing business, though, and good stewardship requires it.

In addition to having good storage facilities, schools need backup copies of all records that are to be maintained permanently. Most schools can accomplish this by means of electronic storage. Schools typically can scan their records on a regular basis and store them electronically. It is recommended that electronic files be stored on a hard drive located outside the physical school site. Once a student is no longer enrolled in the school, his records are typically filed with inactive students and are secured until needed.

Duplicate documents and the regular records need to be stored separately, or the school risks both copies being destroyed in a disaster.

For a more complete discussion of pupil personnel services, see *Charting the Course* by James W. Deuink (Greenville, SC: BJU Press, 2003).

CHAPTER 25

THE SCHOOL AND ITS CONSTITUENTS

The words of a talebearer are as wounds, and they go down into the innermost parts of the belly. A brother offended is harder to be won than a strong city: and their contentions are like the bars of a castle.

Proverbs 18:8, 19

And if a house be divided against itself, that house cannot stand.

Mark 3:25

Follow peace with all men, and holiness, without which no man shall see the Lord: looking diligently lest any man fail of the grace of God; lest any root of bitterness springing up trouble you, and thereby many be defiled.

Hebrews 12:14–15

Most Christian schools in America are established as ministries of local churches. The remaining Christian schools are independent, controlled by a school board rather than by one church. The problems with church-school relationships are similar in both types of Christian organizations.

PROBLEMS WITH CHURCH-SCHOOL RELATIONSHIPS

Problems of Priorities

The church and the Christian day school both operate most efficiently when they maintain a healthy relationship. Though these two ministries are really one organization, the fact that there is a dual operation in many areas can result in problems.

The Christian day school is a ministry of the local church and not vice versa. This relationship must be understood and respected even though the Christian school may have a larger budget, staff, and constituency than the rest of the church. God ordained the church, not the Christian school.

Problems with Property and Equipment

Ideally, the buildings, grounds, vehicles, and equipment can be used by both the church and the Christian day school. However, conflicts arise when a church group and school group want to use a facility at the same time. Thus, it is very important to set up a schedule for the use of all property and equipment. Staff personnel should be encouraged to sign up at least one month in advance if they need to use any equipment or facilities.

Other problems arise when school classrooms are also used by the Sunday school. Sometimes school children's things are disturbed or even stolen by children on Sunday. The Christian school may have to remove items from the classroom for the weekend and put them in a safe location. However, if a Sunday school teacher has a well-controlled class and keeps a close watch on the young people, there should be no reason for the school classroom to be disturbed. The Sunday school teacher should continually teach his students to respect the property of others (Phil. 2:3–4). Some school classrooms, such as science or computer labs, should not be used for Sunday school because of the temptation their equipment represents for the students. The library probably should be available only to adult classes to control access to books and equipment stored there.

Problems with Programs

In many fundamentalist churches most of the evenings are taken up with some kind of meeting or activity. This makes it difficult to schedule events for the school without some overlap. Many parents are asked to attend a church meeting and a school activity on the same night. A master calendar for church activities, established on a yearly basis, can eliminate most of these conflicts. Major activities for all the ministries of the church should be preplanned and placed on the calendar before the beginning of the school year. This calendar can then be posted in the main church office for all the staff to see. It should be changed only with proper approval. The school calendar should always be planned in conjunction with the pastoral staff.

Another suggestion that has helped many Christian schools maintain a good relationship between the school program and other programs of the church is to designate specific nights of the week for school activities and other nights for church activities. For example, Monday, Tuesday, and Friday nights may be set up for school activities, leaving Wednesday, Thursday, and Saturday nights for other church activities. In order for a member of the church or school staff to schedule any activity on a night not designated for such, he would have to coordinate it with the head of the other ministry.

The athletic program of a Christian school requires more "extra nights" than anything else that takes place in the church ministry. If the entire athletic schedule is established at the beginning of the year and if the games are played on nights designated for school activities, few problems will arise, especially if the athletic program is kept in proper balance with other school activities. A special problem is created when the school is a member of an athletic association and the association schedules its games.

The athletic contests that a Christian school participates in during each season should be kept to a reasonable number. Every year opportunities arise for groups from the Christian school to travel to other areas to participate in contests and tournaments. Without proper planning these groups can spend too much of their school time going to such events. Such activities provide exceptional opportunities; however, the Christian school will have to predetermine how many such trips will be allowed in a given school year, evaluating each contest or tournament, not on how much prestige it brings but on how lasting the impact of the experience will be on the lives of the young people. Each local church will have to determine whether a student can miss other church activities to attend these events and how many school days a student will be allowed to miss in a year for such activities. It is important to remember that these activities are extracurricular and they must not be permitted to interfere with the achievement of the academic and spiritual goals of the school.

Finally, because the first institution ordained of God is the family, church leaders should be careful not to fill up every evening so that there is no time for the family to participate in activities together. The school exists partially to undergird family unity, not to undermine it. Many church organizations have helped solve this problem by planning a specific night of the week on which there are no church or school activities. This night is then designated as "family night."

Large churches with large schools will find it is impossible to avoid some conflicts. Some activities of the church and school are so important as to be essential to the church and school constituency; others are optional. It is important that the church and school leadership and parents properly distinguish between them. The staff needs to consider the needs of the entire organization and recognize that the demands of the total program will make it impossible for anyone to do everything. The leadership of the pastor and school administrator will be critical in ironing out conflicts and approving those that are unavoidable.

Problems with People

Leaders sometimes say, "If it weren't for people, we wouldn't have any problems." Property and programs do not have within themselves the ability to create problems, but the people involved in the church ministry do. Each person tends to consider his own area of responsibility more important than anyone else's; he is likely to push his point of view and his programs whenever possible. As more people become involved in the multiple ministries of the local church, the possibility for problems increases. Personality conflicts and personal ambitions can cause severe difficulty among those who are members of the same organization. It is important that all personnel understand the purpose of the church and its school ministry and that they strive together to accomplish this goal. They must learn that they are colaborers together (1 Cor. 3:9) and that they should bear one another's burdens (Gal. 6:2).

The pastor of the church and the school administrator must have a good working relationship in order for the church and its school to work together harmoniously. The pastor must set the spiritual direction for the school ministry, while the administrator is responsible for the day-to-day operation. The school administrator should keep the pastor informed of major happenings in the school and any problems that may come to the pastor's attention later. On the other hand, the pastor should communicate to the school administrator his desires and direction for the school, but he should not attempt to run it. Many school administrators have left churches because of a lack of freedom to carry out the policies and programs established by the pastor and/or the school board. The pastor must allow his school "expert" to operate with a minimum of interference. However, he should continually check the administrator's work to make sure that the implementation of policy and programs is heading in a biblical direction. The pastor must be the spiritual leader for all ministries of the local church.

Conflicts between the school administrator and the youth pastor may also surface. School administrators and youth pastors are working with many of the same young people, encouraging participation in their respective activities. These conflicts can be kept to a minimum if the administrator and youth pastor communicate their common goals and profitable ideas for accomplishing these goals. Most problems between the youth pastor and the school administrator can be eliminated by the willingness of the two to work hand in hand rather than try to win the young people from one another. The school administrator can attempt to involve the youth pastor in the day-to-day school activities by having him teach Bible classes or give counsel to the male students.

The youth pastor should accept the fact that during the school year the students will be busy with school activities. He should attempt to plan his major activities during the summer months when there will be no school activity in conflict. This is not to say that there should not be any youth activities during the school year; however, the youth pastor should work with the school administrator in determining the number and type of activities that will take place.

Another possible problem between people is the cliques formed in the church by students who are attending the Christian school. Young people who are not involved in the Christian school may feel they are outside the accepted group. These barriers must be broken down. The students in the Christian school should be encouraged to socialize with the church young people who do not attend the Christian school and to encourage some of these young people to desire a Christian school education. Planning intramural athletics and special banquets can help unite those who attend the school with those who do not.

COMMUNICATING WITH PARENTS

The parents of children enrolled in your school are responsible for the education of their children. In order to accomplish this task, they have chosen to delegate part of the job to the Christian school. For this reason it is very important that the school and the parents work together as they attempt to conform the child to the image of the Lord Jesus Christ. It will be impossible to accomplish this goal if the parents and the Christian school are heading in opposite directions.

In modern American society many parents are not as interested in the education of their children as they should be. For the most part, parents have turned this job over to the school and do not desire to be involved. This attitude persists in many Christian schools as well. Often Christian parents will get involved in their children's education only when the school forces them to do so. Of course, this is not the case with all Christian parents; however, far too many parents are not willing to take the responsibility God has given them to educate their children. In either case the school must keep the parents informed of the academic and spiritual progress of their children as well as of any discipline problems that may arise. They should also attempt to acquaint parents with the education their children are obtaining. Since the Christian school is working in place of the parents, the parents must be well aware of what is happening there. Good communication is imperative.

Newsletter

One way to keep parents informed is through the use of printed materials, such as a monthly newsletter informing them of upcoming activities and special announcements. Such a publication can also contain articles that relate to parents' responsibilities in Christian education. A newsletter with such articles printed on one side and announcements on the reverse usually works well. The newsletter is a simple but effective way of keeping parents up-to-date on the activities of the Christian school.

Handbook

Every school should have a student-parent handbook, given to the parents of every child in the Christian school and containing basic information about school policies and procedures (see Appendix J). The handbook can save the school administrator much time trying to explain policies and can eliminate many misunderstandings with parents. The handbook should present to the parents a positive image of the school and concisely explain the school's position on most major issues. Also, the handbook should include a doctrinal statement.

Reports

In the elementary school, students may bring their papers home each week so that parents will be aware of their child's progress. The folder for each student's papers should have a place for parents to sign, stating that they have looked at the papers in the folder before returning it to school. Some teachers also indicate the number of sheets that were sent home in the folder so that parents will be aware if their child tries to keep them from seeing any paper.

Report cards informing parents of their child's educational progress are usually issued every six to nine weeks throughout the school year. The grades given should indicate progress in all the academic areas as well as in areas of Christian character and behavior. Teachers should be encouraged to put a comment on the back of the card to encourage the student and his parents. In these comments the teacher should always compliment the child where appropriate and warn parents of undesirable traits that are developing. Most schools also issue midterm progress reports for all students whose work in one or more subjects is below C level.

Conferences

At the end of the first grading period, many schools set aside a time for the parents of each student to come to talk with the teacher. During this conference the teacher can inform the parents of the child's progress and of areas where improvement is needed. The responsibility for the success or failure of a parent-teacher conference rests primarily with the teacher. The teacher should attempt to build a cooperative relationship with the parents by greeting them in a friendly and relaxed manner. If he is hurried or tense, the parents will sense it. Furthermore, the teacher should encourage the parents to talk and should be willing to listen to what they have to say, since parents can give teachers much insight into the background of their child. If a parent says he is worried about his child's behavior, the teacher should follow through, finding out why he is concerned. The teacher should never assume that he knows why. During the conference the teacher and the parents may find out that they do not view the child in the same way.

If the student has a specific problem in school, the teacher should ask the parents to give the reason they see for the child's behavior. If the parents suggest a plan of action to correct the problem, the teacher should accept it if at all possible. It is better for the parents to try to find the answer than for the teacher to force his own ideas on the child. After all, one of the goals of the parent-teacher conference is to involve the parents in the education of their child. If the parents' plan fails, it is always possible to suggest other procedures that may help get to the root of the difficulty. Of course, if the parents have no suggestions on how to correct the child's difficulty, then the teacher may offer plans of action. He could present these by saying, "What would you think about doing . . . ?" or "We might try . . . and see what happens"; or "This might be a possible solution. . . ." Whether it is the teacher or the parents who think of an acceptable solution, it is helpful if both can agree on steps to improve the student's work and/or behavior.

During the conference the teacher should always have a calm, pleasant spirit. This is never a time for raised voices or arguing. The teacher should not try to push his thinking onto a parent; rather, he should help the parent to see the method of action through a process of discussion and mutual thinking. The conference should be concluded on a constructive and encouraging note. The teacher should encourage the parents to pray with him in regard to the child's needs, and he should let the parents know how glad he is to have the opportunity to work with the child, assuring the parents that he will do all he can to help the student achieve his potential. The teacher should then close the conference in prayer.

Parent conferences are not necessary after each grading period unless the student is having a specific problem and the teacher believes that a conference would be helpful. All parents may be required to come to a conference before the last grading period, since this is the time when parents can be informed of a student's chances of being promoted to the next grade. It is important to warn parents whose children may not pass. Never should a child be retained without his parents' receiving prior warning.

Many times parents will want to have a conference with the teacher during the grading period. They should call the school office to set up an appointment to see the teacher at school and not meet with him on a student matter at church, in a hallway, or on a playground. Often, parents will see a teacher and remember that they would like to talk to him about a student problem. The teacher should always encourage parents to set up a specific time when they can discuss their child's needs or problems privately.

Home Visits

Another excellent way of building good school-parent relationships is for the classroom teacher to visit the home of children in his class. Because of the typical student load carried by most teachers, it is not practical to ask them to visit all their students. Typically an elementary teacher is responsible for twenty to thirty different students. To require the teacher to visit all these students would mean an average of at least one student each week. For junior/senior high schoolteachers, this requirement would be far more serious. They typically have contact with one hundred or more students, and it would be virtually impossible for them to visit in the homes of all their students and meet their other responsibilities. Visits in homes of those with special problems can prove very beneficial. The visit should be designed simply to find out more information about the parents, their background, and the home situation and to acquaint the parents with the child's teacher. This home visit with the parents should always be arranged ahead of time.

Parent-Teacher Meetings

Parent-teacher meetings should be scheduled throughout the school year, allowing all the parents to get together at the school to learn firsthand about the Christian school ministry. Parent-teacher meetings may be scheduled monthly but should be scheduled at least every other month. The attendance of at least one parent from each family should be strongly encouraged. For these meetings the administrator should plan special programs, prepare to give announcements, and make arrangements to open doors so that parents can observe their child's classroom and talk with the teacher. (See Figure 25.1.)

FIGURE 25.1

SUGGESTED PROGRAMS FOR PARENT-TEACHER MEETINGS

1. An orientation meeting for parents, other family members, and their friends at the beginning of each year

2. Outside speakers emphasizing the importance of Christian schools

3. A meeting featuring students giving testimonies about the impact of the school on their lives

4. Thanksgiving, Christmas, and Easter programs

5. Musical programs featuring the school band, chorus, or orchestra

6. Recitals featuring students taking music lessons in the school

7. A program demonstrating the skills learned in various grades

8. A patriotic program
9. Dramatic productions
10. Special speaker on parenting or developing strong Christian families
11. A school-wide banquet
12. An awards program

Parent-teacher meetings will be better attended if students are involved in the programs. Even with a speaker, it is ideal to have one of the classes or musical groups give a presentation to help encourage parents to attend. Parent-teacher meetings can be very valuable in developing good school-parent relationships but must be well planned and worthwhile or they will be poorly attended.

HANDLING PROBLEMS

Whenever an administrator senses that there may be a problem with parents, it is his responsibility to go to these parents to try to work out the difficulty. The school principal should never expect the parents to come to him, even though this would be the right course of action for them to take. He must initiate the contact aimed at solving the problem, perhaps even by going to the parents' home to try to straighten out misunderstandings.

Parents should be encouraged to contact the school if they ever have any questions or concern about their child's behavior or progress. The school administrator should make it plain to parents that they should never discuss school problems with anyone else except the child's teacher or an administrator. Parents who gossip about perceived problems can cause much difficulty for the Christian school. This kind of behavior on the part of the parents not only hurts the children and the Christian school but also is explicitly forbidden in Scripture (Lev. 19:16). If parents have difficulty with the Christian school, it should be brought to the attention of the administrator or teacher. If they are unable to receive satisfactory resolution of their concerns, the parents should feel free to contact the pastor or a member of the school board.

When talking to parents, the administrator should have a meek and quiet spirit, always desiring reconciliation rather than conflict. He should not back down, however, from any of the school rules or policies. Many times parents will threaten to pull their children out of the Christian school unless they get their way. The administrator must call their bluff by letting parents know that if they are not in agreement with the direction of the school, they ought to put their children elsewhere. The administrator should seek to rectify any problem the parents have with the school, but he should never be pressured by the threat of losing students. There may also be times when the parents are right and the school is wrong. In all cases, the administrator must always attempt to do right, no matter what the consequences. Many parents who have attempted to pressure school officials into bending rules by threatening to take their children out of school have later backed down when they found out that this is not threatening to the Christian school.

If a parent comes to a pastor with a school-related problem, the pastor should listen to the parent's concern and then refer the parent to the school administrator. The pastor may later need to get involved in the solution to the problem. However, the first contact with parents must be that of the appropriate school official. Just as a child will try to work both parents against each other, so parents may attempt to work the pastor against the administrator. The pastor and the administrator must maintain good communication and work hand in hand in solving any parental problems.

Problems never go away by themselves. Procrastination is the main problem of many Christian school administrators. Sometimes it seems that it would be easier to let a problem go than to face it.

However, this lack of decisive action will come back to haunt school officials in the future. Problems left uncorrected begin to simmer and then explode later. Successful administrators are willing to confront problems and people even though such meetings may result in unpleasantness. Effective leaders are people of principle.

Parents and school officials must work together if Christian education is to be successful. If the principal becomes aware of parents who are not in agreement with the school's policies and/or procedures, he should talk with those parents to gain their full support. If the parents decide that they cannot support the school, then the administrator must request that they withdraw their children from the school. Parents who pull children in a different direction from the Christian school will cause problems not only for the Christian school administrator but also for the children.

CHAPTER 26

THE SCHOOL AND THE GOVERNMENT

Then Peter and the other apostles answered and said, We ought to obey God rather than men.

Acts 5:29

Let every soul be subject unto the higher powers. For there is no power but of God: the powers that be are ordained of God.

Romans 13:1

Submit yourselves to every ordinance of man for the Lord's sake: whether it be to the king, as supreme; or unto governors, as unto them that are sent by him for the punishment of evildoers, and for the praise of them that do well. For so is the will of God, that with well doing ye may put to silence the ignorance of foolish men: as free, and not using your liberty for a cloke of maliciousness, but as the servants of God. Honour all men. Love the brotherhood. Fear God. Honour the king.

1 Peter 2:13–17

GROWTH OF THE CONFLICT

Christian education as a movement and as part of fundamentalist Christianity is relatively young. For over a century we allowed the state system of education to grow, often with our blessing and encouragement. It became a giant. Private education, of which Christian education represented only a small fraction, became like an ant by comparison.

An awakening among Christians occurred in the 1960s, triggered by a series of Supreme Court rulings beginning with the prayer case (*Engel v. Vitale*, 1962) in New York State. By a 6–1 decision the court said that the recitation of a specially written prayer by public school students amounted to a state-sponsored religious activity and was, therefore, an unconstitutional abridgement of the First Amendment. (Interestingly enough, just one year earlier, in *Torcaso v. Watkins*, the Supreme

Court had recognized secular humanism and other nontheistic creeds as religions.)

In 1963 the Supreme Court ruled on the prayer issue again (*School District of Abington Township v. Schempp*). This time it barred use of the Lord's Prayer and other Scripture passages in opening exercises. Thus, in two decisions in the course of one year, the Supreme Court struck down practices that had been a part of most public school curricula since the beginning of public education. At the time, the court was careful to say that it was not suggesting that religion had no place in school but that its place should be limited to objective studies that were part of a general program of education, not a religious exercise.

In 1967 the Supreme Court of New Jersey prohibited the Gideons' distribution of Bibles in the public schools (*Tudor v. Board of Education of the Borough of Rutherford*). In the years to follow, a number of court decisions dealing with religious issues tended to discourage any religious exercises in the public schools. The result has been to discourage Christian endeavors by born-again educators, and the "salt" that had held back the tide of wickedness over the years was diluted.

During the 1960s there was also an outcry by a segment of the public for freedom from restraint. The hippie movement, the rise of drug abuse, and the renewed use of violence all had devastating effects on the moral character of the nation's public schools. Further unrest was caused by widespread efforts to racially integrate schools with little, if any, regard for the educational impact of these decisions. Christian parents became concerned about the general decline of academic performance generated by the unrest. The lack of biblical morality in the schools also became more and more evident. Christians began to look for alternatives to public education, and the modern Christian school movement was the result.

When several thousand new private schools came into existence in one decade, public educators became concerned. They viewed these new schools as a threat to their financial well-being and their philosophical goals. To make matters worse, the period of greatest growth for Christian schools occurred during the first decrease of the school-age population in a number of years. Public education had a problem. It feverishly sought for a solution. The answer seemed simple: regulate the private schools under the guise of assuring quality of education. Eliminate their uniqueness, and they would die. The move to regulate private schools was on.

Government encroachment is a serious problem to Christian schools. It matters little whether that involvement originates from the federal, state, or local government or whether it occurs in the form of legislation, regulation, or court decree. Much government interference comes as a direct result of the government's insatiable hunger for power—hunger that could destroy Christian schools.

Our day is one that calls for unusual wisdom and insight. Christian leaders are confronted with questions that have not been raised before in our generation. We are treading strange paths. Our response to the problems that lie before us may well determine the quality of religious freedom that our citizens enjoy for years to come. We must not be careless in our response.

Sometimes it is difficult to know where to draw the line. Unfortunately, some serious infighting within our own ranks has occurred because of differences of opinion in these critical areas. We must strive to choose our battles carefully and not exhaust our strength and resources on petty issues that have little long-term significance in our movement. On the other hand, we must be determined to fight any attempt to deprive us of the privileges God intends us to use for His glory.

> And I sought for a man among them, that should make up the hedge, and stand in the gap before me for the land, that I should not destroy it: but I found none. (Ezek. 22:30)

FOUNDATION OF THE RELATIONSHIP

Biblical Foundation

Unfortunately, there is no brief passage of Scripture that gives us simple answers to the problem of government encroachment. One of the things that has made this battle difficult is that good men have differed widely on the proper Christian response. Those who seriously desire God's direction in this matter can begin with a study of the following passages and go on through the Scriptures as the Lord gives direction.

Old Testament

- Exodus 1:8–2:10
- Deuteronomy 6
- 1 Samuel 8
- Ezra 7:25–26

- Psalm 78:1–8
- Proverbs 21:1; 24:1
- Ecclesiastes 8:2–5
- Daniel 1–3, 6

New Testament

- Matthew 17:24–27; 22:15–22
- Romans 12:1–2; 13:1–7
- 2 Corinthians 5:9–11; 6:14–18
- Ephesians 1:20–22; 4:11–15; 6
- Colossians 1:18; 2:8

- 1 Timothy 5:8
- Titus 3:1
- Hebrews 8:1–2
- 1 Peter 2:11–17; 5:1–4

Constitutional Foundation

Pressure from government since 1970 has made Christian leaders more aware of the constitutional limitations on the interference with the practice of religion, particularly the privileged position of the church. The First Amendment to the Constitution begins, "Congress shall make no law respecting an establishment of religion, or prohibiting the free exercise thereof." It has been noted that religious freedom appears in the first of the amendments, and it is the first freedom given there—it is "the firstest [sic] of the First."

Of course, the state has an obligation to limit religious practices that interfere with the rights of others. Human sacrifice, for example, would never be tolerated under the Constitution. The Supreme Court ruled that polygamy was so great a threat to social order, and thus to the stability of the nation, that even sincere practitioners must be restrained (*Reynolds v. United States*, 1878). Regardless of your view of polygamy, this case illustrates the danger of the government's interfering with the practice of one's religion when the practice is not harmful to others. The case was the beginning of the government's view that while an individual has a right to believe what he wants to believe, the government has the right to regulate the practice of those beliefs.

In recent years, however, the federal government has attempted to expand even further its power to restrict religious practice. There is considerable evidence that it will move to prohibit religious groups from discriminating on the basis of sex or sexual preference. Such prohibitions would require these groups to ordain women and homosexuals into the ministry. Thus it is more important than ever that we come to a clear understanding of crucial questions involving the state, the church, and the Christian school.

CONSTITUTIONAL QUESTIONS
Is the Christian School Protected by the First Amendment?

In many cases the government has been reluctant to extend to Christian schools the same First Amendment protection it must give to churches. At least in part this reluctance has been caused by what the government views as a change of tune on the part of the administrators of Christian schools. Until the 1970s it was common practice to organize Christian schools as separate entities even when they were wholly owned and/or controlled by a local church or group of churches. It should be no surprise, then, that the government became suspicious when literally hundreds of churches decided to make their already existing schools integral parts of the local church—many on the basis of "religious conviction." Though the problem may have been caused by our failure to understand the proper role of the school in years past, we must live with the fact that our position in the eyes of the government has been seriously weakened. To the bureaucrats it appears that our "convictions" change as a matter of convenience.

It is also true, however, that our realizing the error of our ways only recently should not require us to forfeit our legitimate constitutional rights. Most educators recognize the inherently religious nature of education. This is even more true of Christian education. The Christian school, whether or not it functions as the arm of a local church, is unquestionably entitled to First Amendment protection as a religious activity. Any regulations that would prohibit recognition of an independent Christian school on the same basis as a church or church-school are discriminatory and should be changed.

What Is the State's Legitimate Interest in Christian Education?

To what degree, then, may the government regulate the Christian school? Once again we face a difficult question, one on which there is little consensus. The following statements represent the diversity of opinion that exists:

> No sane person can deny that the state has a minimal role, even in church affairs. The thrust of the First Amendment is to keep that role at the barest minimum. (Wallis C. Metts)

> We thoroughly agree to the authority of the state to maintain inspection rights; to prevent fraud; and to preserve the public health, public safety, and public morals. (Kent Kelly)

> No one would deny the legitimate interest of the state in these matters [protection against fraud, immorality, and fire and health hazards]. . . . These leaders have nevertheless surrendered the principle of complete separation of church and state by their acceptance of the ideas of compelling interest. (Bob Dalton)

There appears to be general agreement that government has some limited interest in the affairs of the church. However, most fundamentalists agree that the church must not be licensed to do its primary works of spreading the gospel and teaching Bible doctrine. They are not in agreement about such areas as control of church-related daycare and minimum educational standards for Christian schools. The government wants to regulate, license, and control those affairs that it says are "secular," particularly any activity that would be subject to these controls if the activities were not part of a church ministry. The church, on the other hand, says that there is no distinction between the secular and the sacred for the Christian. It is unwilling to look at any of its ministries and agree with the state that any portion of them is secular.

It appears that the government, as guardian of the citizen's right to life, has a role of health, fire, and safety regulations. In this area Christian attorneys have offered three tests of compelling interest.

Is the regulation legitimate to safety?

Though most regulations have come out of concern for genuine problems, the bureaucracy has a tendency to grow. Some rules do not serve legitimate purposes. Others do not fit church situations.

Does it accomplish the end desired?

Sometimes the writers of government regulations have good intentions, but their rules are not realistic. Even if followed to the letter, they would not accomplish the purpose intended. Such regulations are foolish and wasteful.

Is it uniform in its application?

Is every institution in the class expected to comply with the regulations? Or is there a different standard of compliance accepted? If it is uniform, it is fair, even though inconvenient.

What should the administrator do if he finds a law or regulation that does not meet these criteria? Of course, he should first exhaust all legal means of having the laws or regulations removed or changed. Scripturally, he can disobey the law only if (1) there is no legal way to remedy the problem *and* (2) he cannot obey the regulation without violating Scripture. Civil disobedience, though certainly justified in certain cases (Acts 5:28–29), should always be a last resort.

Occasionally the government has attempted to regulate the curriculum of the Christian school. While Christian educators also disagree as to the degree of government responsibility for curriculum, they generally follow one of two lines of thought. On the one hand, educators say that the government has no authority to deal in any regard with what Christians teach. On the other hand, there are those who concede government's responsibility for core curriculum. Those of the latter opinion agree that the government has the right to require that English, history, or mathematics be taught in all schools but not to dictate how they are to be taught, which textbooks are to be used, or who is to be required to teach them. For now, the latter position appears more reasonable.

A few states have attempted to control private schools by requiring that their teachers hold state certification to teach. This is currently the requirement for private school teachers in Iowa, Michigan, and Nebraska. Most Christian school leaders feel this requirement is unreasonable since state certification requirements are designed to prepare teachers for positions in public schools and do not emphasize training in areas important to Christian schools. However, when a Christian school hires a teacher who is eligible for state certification, it is probably a good idea for that teacher to maintain his certification in a current status.

Should a Church or Christian School Accept a Government License or Accreditation?

These are really two very different questions. The matter is somewhat compounded by our choice to combine two different institutions that until recently were distinctly separate organizations. With the exception of daycare ministries, no regular ministry of the church is subject to government licensing requirements. However, when the school is added, it places the entire issue in a somewhat different perspective. The government does not want to recognize a church-related school as a different organization than an independent school. The fact that we see the church-related school as an integral part of that local church ministry has no bearing on how they choose to look at the institution. Consequently, we may need to reexamine our decision to make the church-school a part of the organizational umbrella of the church. We may be better off having the school organized as a separate legal entity owned and controlled by the church. Then when a government licensing or accreditation requirement is presented, we do not have to consider the issue of the government directly regulating our church.

A license has been defined as "a document that reflects the power to dictate whether or not a holder can perform a certain activity." Accreditation by secular agencies carries many of the same connotations as the license. Generally, when we think of accreditation we think of this activity being carried on by private agencies. However, sometimes accreditation is required by state departments of education. It is government accreditation that we are focusing on here. The question becomes immediately apparent. What authority has the power to tell a church or Christian school what is appropriate or how it should operate? Is such an authority the head of the church? If the state can license the church, is it the head of the church? If the church accepts certain controls from the state or the accrediting agency, does it dethrone the Lord? Obviously, each specific situation must be carefully and prayerfully considered in light of its unique characteristics.

The overwhelming majority of Christian schools in the nation today are church-schools. Much of the conflict these schools are experiencing is from long-standing legislation and regulations, made when the concept of a church was much narrower and its activities were much more limited than they are today. Legislation and regulations dealing with schools have tended to be more restrictive than those dealing with churches. A major question Christians need to resolve early is whether their school is properly a ministry of their church. They need to decide if they want the school to function as an integral part of the church organization, or if it would be better for their church-school to have its own legal identity. If the school is to be operated under the direct umbrella of the church ministry, they must decide how they will deal with this matter of legislation and regulation. Given the legal climate we are operating in today, it seems best that the church-school have its own legal identity. This in no way diminishes the character of the school but provides several distinct advantages.

AREAS OF CONFLICT

Of course, legal requirements may originate at the federal, state, or local level. They may take the form of laws, regulations or, as has been common in recent years, court rulings. Regardless of the form, the legal impact is the same. Regulations promulgated recently by the bureaucracy have proved to be the most troublesome.

Federal Government

The IRS—We should be able to assume that the restrictions of the First Amendment apply to any agency created by the legislative bodies of the federal government since its only authority is that given it by legislative decree. Regulatory agencies, however, have come to be a power to be dealt with on their own. At least in the minds of their directors, they have become a law unto themselves. Nowhere is this better illustrated than by the Internal Revenue Service (IRS), which operates, for all practical purposes, by its own "laws." When challenged, its officials are alleged to practice "forum shopping" to find court decisions favorable to their position. If they are unable to find any, they simply fail to appeal a lower court's decision, and thus they avoid unfavorable Supreme Court precedents. At the present time the IRS may represent the greatest threat of government control at the federal level as it monitors the activities of tax-exempt organizations.

The Labor Department—Before 1978, employees of schools below the college level were not required to participate in the federal unemployment program. Most employees were also exempted from participation in state programs. In 1978 Congress deleted the exemption for employees of schools. Secretary of Labor Ray Marshall interpreted this action to include "church-school" employees also, failing to recognize that employees of church-schools cannot be separated from the other church employees. This action started a lengthy controversy.

The Christian school movement reacted violently to Secretary Marshall's insensitive response to their appeals for consideration. Lawsuits were entered all over the country. Christian school personnel could not accept the authority of a bureaucrat to define what is and what is not a proper church ministry. Furthermore, they could not accept a secular agency as a judge over church employment.

In 1981 the Supreme Court ruled in favor of Christian schools, but it did so on the basis that it did not believe Congress intended to include them in the law at that time. The constitutional issue of whether it is appropriate for a secular agency to rule on church employment decisions was not addressed.

The Department of Transportation—The federal government has established safety standards that apply to all school buses manufactured after April 1, 1977. These standards apply to equipment and design in the manufacturing process and to lighting and markings on the exterior of the vehicle. The standards are contained in a number of government publications. The requirements for lighting and exterior markings are contained in Department of Transportation Standard No. 17 (see bibliography).

Manufacturers are prohibited from selling a unit to be used as a school bus if it does not meet federal specifications. An administrator places himself and his school in jeopardy if he purchases a vehicle to be used as a school bus but conceals that fact from a dealer to avoid purchasing a unit with the proper equipment.

State laws generally do not permit a bus to be labeled a "school bus" and to control traffic as it picks up students unless the bus meets all federal regulations for school buses. Among other things, this means the bus must be painted yellow and have all of the required exterior warning devices.

The Department of Education—Most Christian schools have carefully avoided taking government funds with the idea of avoiding government control. Recently, liberals have suggested that aid to the student is aid to the school. The Fourth Circuit Court of Appeals upheld this idea in *Bob Jones University v. Johnson* (1975), and the Supreme Court, by refusing to hear the case, concurred. The *Grove City College v. Bell* (U.S. Supreme Court, 1984) and *Hillsdale College v. Department of Education* (U.S. Supreme Court, 1984) cases resulted in similar conclusions. Consequently, any school whose students receive government aid risks the possibility of being made subject to federal regulation or legislation intended for those who receive direct federal aid. Legislation and regulations on such matters must be observed carefully. It is far easier, and much less expensive, to change them through lobbying than through other legal processes.

Environmental Protection Agency—Since at least 1982 the Environmental Protection Agency (EPA) has been aggressively pursuing a policy intended to free schools of friable asbestos. Friable asbestos (asbestos that has become brittle and is subject to being carried through the atmosphere) is considered by many to be a serious health hazard. Tests have demonstrated that persons exposed to friable asbestos are more likely to become victims of respiratory diseases and cancer of the lungs. The government has given the EPA broad latitude to examine buildings to determine if hazardous materials exist.

Schools are required to have their facilities checked by recognized inspectors to provide assurances that the buildings are safe. Failure to comply with the inspection requirement can result in fines as high as $25,000 per day, even when later investigation verifies that no friable asbestos is present.

Compliance with federal regulations is a serious matter. Schools are encouraged to take all such regulations seriously.

The Congress—Since the word *education* does not even appear in the Constitution of the United States, many are surprised at the degree of involvement of the federal government in education. The United States Congress rarely considers anything that would have a direct impact on the nation's private schools. However, in 1995 the Elementary and Secondary Education Act was revised to provide wording that many believed would have mandated the states to require certified teachers in all private schools and homeschools within their boundaries. This would have been the first attempt ever to regulate private schools and homeschools at the federal level.

When challenged, the author of the amendment insisted that the amendment did not authorize states to require certification of all private school and homeschool teachers, it applied only to public schools. However, he also refused to cooperate in clarifying the wording. Fortunately, other congressmen were able to amend the bill, eliminating this troubling provision. Once again, we were reminded that the price of liberty is eternal vigilance.

The Courts—There are a number of important court decisions that have the potential of impacting Christian schools. The most significant of these decisions will be discussed in the following paragraphs. We have chosen to discuss primarily those decisions that have been settled at the U.S. Supreme Court level since the direction provided by these decisions is as definitive as is available.

In the last several years the direction of our society has been determined to an increasing and alarming degree by court decisions. Although this trend did not begin with the so-called Warren Court, the courts have begun to exert more and more influence on the American way of life by reinterpretation of the Constitution. In this section we will discuss numerous court decisions, focusing primarily on those decided at the Supreme Court level that have had or may have a significant impact on private education in America.

Anti-Private-School Feeling

The anti-private-school sentiment that had developed early in this century is reflected in *Meyer v. Nebraska,* U.S. Supreme Court, 1923 and *Pierce v. Society of Sisters,* U.S. Supreme Court, 1925. Both of these cases involved attempts of the state to insure uniformity in instruction.

Nebraska had a law that prohibited teaching in any language but English in grades one through eight. A parochial school teacher was prosecuted for teaching German to elementary-age children. The lower courts upheld the conviction, and the teacher appealed to the U.S. Supreme Court. Applying the due process provisions of the Fourteenth Amendment, the court ruled in favor of the teacher. It held that an individual right to personal freedom involved not only freedom from bodily restraint but also the right to contract, to engage in any of the common occupations of life, to acquire useful knowledge, to marry, to establish a home and bring up children, and to worship God according to the dictates of one's own conscience. The teacher had a constitutional right to teach German. The court said the statute was arbitrary and without the support of any legitimate state purpose.

The state of Oregon had passed a law requiring all normal children between the ages of eight and sixteen to attend public schools if they had not already completed eighth grade. An injunction against enforcement was sought by a Catholic parochial school and a nonsectarian military academy. Upon appeal, the Supreme Court ruled in favor of the schools on the basis of property rights. The statute, if enforced, would destroy the schools and greatly diminish their property value. The court also called attention to the fundamental right of parents to direct the upbringing and education of children in their control. The court did not treat this case as a First Amendment issue.

Government Aid to Private Schools

Five years later the court was asked to rule on the propriety of providing financial assistance to parents who had children enrolled in private schools (*Cochran v. Louisiana State Board of Education,* U.S. Supreme Court, 1930). Louisiana had passed a statute providing free textbooks regardless of the school the children attended. In Louisiana many children attend Catholic schools. The law was attacked as violating the Fourteenth Amendment by taking property through taxation for nonpublic purposes. The court ruled in favor of the statute, stating that it was the children rather than the schools that were being benefited, and thus was born the "child benefit theory." This case was not a First Amendment issue.

The question of providing transportation to nonpublic school students was settled insofar as federal law and the Constitution were concerned in the case of the New Jersey statute (*Everson v. Board of Education,* U.S. Supreme Court, 1947). The state law "permitted" local boards of education to arrange for transportation of private school students at public expense. A local school board authorized the reimbursement of bus fare money for parochial school students. The law was attacked by a taxpayer in two respects. First, it authorized the state to take by taxation the money of some citizens and bestow it upon others for private purposes in violation of the Fourteenth Amendment. Second, it forced him to contribute to the support of church-schools in violation of the First Amendment.

In a 5–4 decision, the court upheld the constitutionality of the statute. The court said neither the state nor the federal government could aid one religion, aid all religions, or prefer one religion over another;

further, no tax, large or small, could be levied to support any religious activity or institution. However, the First Amendment did not prohibit a state from extending a general benefit to all its citizens without regard to their religious beliefs. The court placed the provision of transportation in the same category as police, fire, and health protection. The statute was viewed as a general benefit aiding all parents equally in getting their children to and from school.

The decision left the issue to each state to decide for itself insofar as conformance to its state constitution is concerned. State supreme courts have subsequently held both ways.

Thirty-eight years later the court ruled 6–3 in favor of a statute requiring local boards of education to lend books to children in grades 7–12 attending nonpublic schools (*New York State Board of Education v. Allen*, U.S. Supreme Court, 1968). The decision was based primarily on the child benefit theory. The court found that the purpose of the statute was to aid in the improvement of the general quality of education, not to enhance religion or aid private schools. No First Amendment issue was raised.

Tax Exemption

The propriety of tax exemption for religious organizations was challenged in a novel case (*Walz v. Tax Commission*, U.S. Supreme Court, 1970). New York City offered the typical tax exemption to nonprofit religious, educational, and charitable organizations that had been extended for years. A local property owner objected to the tax exemptions granted to religious organizations, contending that the exemptions made him an unwilling contributor to these organizations. The U.S. Supreme Court upheld the exemptions, stating that they had not actually taken revenues and given them to these organizations but had simply chosen not to tax their properties. This court decision not only reestablished the concept that tax exemption was not a subsidy but it also established the principle of nonentanglement between government and religion. The court ruled that it was important to avoid entangling government and religion, and if legislation required excessive entanglement of government and religion, the statute could be ruled unconstitutional on that basis alone.

Subsequent Private School Aid Cases

With only one dissent, the court ruled a Pennsylvania "purchase of secular services" statute and a Rhode Island "salary supplement" unconstitutional (*Lemon v. Kurtzman,* U.S. Supreme Court, 1971). Both were held to violate the establishment clause of the First Amendment.

The decision was based primarily on the earlier *Walz* decision that established the judicial principle that there must not be excessive entanglement between government and religion. Any legislation that results in such entanglement would be unconstitutional for that reason alone. To determine whether government entanglement with religion is excessive, it is necessary to examine the character and purpose of the institution to be benefited, the nature of the aid to be provided, and the resulting relationship between the government and the religious authority. The courts said specifically that complete separation was not required.

In the Rhode Island and Pennsylvania cases, the court held that the parochial schools constituted an integral part of the religious mission of the church and involved substantial religious activity and purpose. Determining which expenditures of church-related schools are religious and which are secular creates an intimate and continuing relationship between church and state. The criterion of excessive entanglement has been the basis of invalidating numerous state attempts to aid private religious schools.

In *Public Funds for Public Schools of New Jersey v. Marburger* (U.S. Supreme Court, 1974) the court ruled that reimbursement for purchases of secular textbooks by private school students was not valid because public school students were lent textbooks and because the provision was directed to parents whose children were enrolled in private, primarily religious schools. This special benefit constituted a First Amendment violation.

The U.S. Supreme Court upheld, by a 6–3 decision, the loaning of nonreligious textbooks to parochial school students in Pennsylvania *Meek v. Pittenger,* U.S. Supreme Court, 1975). The books loaned were acceptable for public school use, although they were not necessarily used in local public schools. Also, instructional materials and equipment could not be loaned exclusively to religious schools.

Civil Rights and Education

The *Brown* decision (*Brown v. Board of Education,* U.S. Supreme Court, 1954, 1955) laid the foundation for a whole new outlook on civil rights in education. Ten years later Congress passed civil rights legislation extending the issue by law to nearly every facet of our lives. While race was the initial focal point of the legislation and resultant court activity, discrimination on the basis of sex, religion, and ethnic and national origin was also a part of this law. More recently, discrimination based on sexual preference has come to the forefront.

In 1981 Georgetown University, a Washington, D.C., Roman Catholic institution, was sued for violation of the civil rights of two homosexual students seeking recognition of their organization. Georgetown University refused to provide funds to their student organization because of the homosexual orientation of the organization. The Catholic Church holds that homosexuality is a sin and refused to allow the organization on the campus. The courts held that Georgetown's policy violated the District of Columbia's human rights ordinance prohibiting discrimination on the basis of sexual orientation (*Georgetown University v. Gay Rights Coalition,* District of Columbia Court of Appeals, 1987). The court ruled that the university does not have to grant the student organizations of the university official recognition because that would imply an endorsement of homosexuality, which the university says conflicts with Catholic teachings. However, the court said the university must give gay groups the same access to university facilities that it grants to other student groups. The case was not appealed. Subsequently, many colleges have revised their policies so as to be neutral to gender and sexual preference.

Public Policy Takes Precedence over First Amendment Rights

Two extremely important U.S. Supreme Court decisions were handed down within a two-day period in 1983. Both dealt with tax exemption but have much broader implications. The first decision (*Regan v.*

Taxation with Representation, 1983) involved a nonprofit corporation organized to promote certain interests in regard to federal taxation. The IRS denied the organization's application for exemption because of their lobbying activity. Taxation with Representation sued federal officials claiming they had no authority to prohibit their lobbying activity. On appeal the U.S. Supreme Court ruled that the organization's First and Fifth Amendment rights had not been violated as they had charged. Significantly the court said, "Both tax exemption and tax deductibility are a form of subsidy that is administered by the tax system," completely reversing the rationale used in *Walz*. The court also rejected the "notion that First Amendment rights are somehow not fully realized unless they are subsidized by the state" (see Appendix M for an edited version of the decision).

The rationale of *Regan* was used to rule against Bob Jones University the following day. In *Bob Jones University v. United States* (1983) the court recognized the sincerely held religious views that provided the foundation for the policies contested by the IRS. However, it stated that the government's fundamental, overriding interest in eradicating racial discrimination in education substantially outweighs whatever burden denial of tax benefits places on petitioners' exercise of religious beliefs. Petitioners' asserted interests cannot be accommodated with that compelling governmental interest, and no less restrictive means are available to achieve the governmental interest (see Appendix N for an edited version of the decision).

In two days the U.S. Supreme Court set aside decades of judicial precedent to approve social engineering by the bureaucracy. It removed religious organizations from their previously favored positions to operate under the full protection of the First Amendment and placed them under the shadow of "federal public policy." A drastic turn in direction occurred, almost completely obscured by an issue (elimination of racial discrimination) that had wide public support.

Unemployment Taxes and Religious Schools

The Federal Unemployment Tax Act (FUTA) outlines a federal program of unemployment compensation, administered by the various states under their own legislation. So long as the state statutes meet federal guidelines, employers' are not subject to federal unemployment taxes. FUTA provided for exemptions for employees' "services performed—(l) in the employment of (a) a church or convention of churches, or (b) an organization . . . which is operated, supervised, controlled, or principally supported by a church or a convention or association of churches." No exemption for religious organizations not connected with a church or convention of churches exists. The schools had attempted to raise First Amendment issues as a defense; however, the court, in holding for the church-related school, said, "the language of the legislation and its history support an interpretation distinguishing between church-schools integrated into a church's structure and those separately incorporated" (*St. Martin Evangelical Lutheran Church v. South Dakota,* Federal District Court, 1981). Therefore, the First Amendment issues were not considered.

The state of Oregon did not agree with the Federal District Court decision in *St. Martin*. The Oregon Supreme Court had previously ruled that the distinction between church-affiliated and nonchurch-affiliated organizations, as had been recognized by *St. Martin Evangelical Lutheran Church v. South Dakota,* was not proper because "such a distinction contravenes the equality among pluralistic faiths and kinds of religious organizations embodied in the Oregon constitution guarantees of religious freedom." They ruled (*Coopers & Lybrand v. Archdiocese of Miami,* 1989) that all religious organizations, including churches, were subject to state unemployment taxes on wages and salaries. The Employment Division of the Oregon Department of Human Resources decided it was legally bound, therefore, to tax all religious organizations to remain within the FUTA guidelines. They recognized that while this did place a burden on some religious organizations, not all such burdens are unconstitutional. The state may justify a limitation on religion if it can show that it is essential to accomplish an overriding governmental interest. The court held that few of its responsibilities are more important than guaranteeing the economic security of its citizens. The case was appealed three times, but all appeals were denied. Consequently, except in the state of Oregon, all church-related Christian schools are exempt from participation in FUTA.

Aid to Student, Aid to College

Grove City College decided not to participate in direct institutional aid programs and in federal assistance programs under which it would have had to assess students' eligibility and determine the amount of funds they would receive but enrolled a number of students who received Basic Educational Opportunity Grants (BEOGs) through the Department of Education's Alternate Disbursement System, under which the Secretary of Education calculates awards and makes distributions directly to eligible students. The department concluded that the college was a recipient of federal financial assistance. Because the college refused to sign a statement of compliance with Title IX of the Education Amendments of 1972, which prohibit sex discrimination in any program or activity receiving federal financial assistance, the department initiated administrative proceedings to declare the college and its students ineligible to receive BEOGs.

An administrative law judge ruled in favor of the department and entered an order terminating assistance to the college. The college and four of its students brought suit in the District Court for the Western District of Pennsylvania. This court ruled that student use of BEOGs constituted federal assistance to the college but that the department could not terminate aid due to the college's refusal to execute the assurance of compliance.

The Court of Appeals for the Third Circuit reversed, holding that the department could terminate the students' BEOGs to force the college to execute an assurance of compliance. On review, the U.S. Supreme Court affirmed (*Grove City College v. Bell,* U.S. Supreme Court, 1984). It was held that (1) Title IX applied to the college, even though it accepted no direct assistance, since it did enroll students who received BEOGs, (2) for Title IX enforcement purposes, the education program or activity at the college receiving federal financial assistance was the college's financial aid program, and not the entire college, (3) federal assistance to the college's financial aid could be terminated (but not aid to the remainder of the college) solely because the college had refused to execute an assurance of compliance with Title IX, and (4) the application of Title IX to the college did not infringe the First Amendment rights of the college or its students.

Hillsdale College is a nonsectarian, coeducational college founded in 1844 by a group of abolitionists and Free Will Baptists. One of the ideals held by the founders was that blacks should be able to receive the same kind of education as whites. Because they knew this idea and others they held were not popular views, they recognized they would need to refrain from accepting government funding to insure their academic freedom. Pressure from government, which was antagonistic to their views, did not actually become a problem until the 1970s. The government contended that Hillsdale College had to declare itself to be in compliance with Title IX because it had students attending school on federal loans and scholarships. Hillsdale maintained that Title IX did not apply to it because it had never received federal funds.

In December 1977, relying on Title IX, which prohibits sex discrimination in federally assisted programs and activities, the Department of Health, Education, and Welfare (HEW) instituted an enforcement proceeding against Hillsdale because the institution failed to sign an assurance of compliance with Title IX. This document would have required Hillsdale to attest that it was in compliance with Title IX in all its operations in spite of the fact that Hillsdale had never received federal aid and was not applying to receive it. HEW's position was that Hillsdale's enrollment of students receiving federal educational assistance made the college itself a recipient of federal assistance for purposes of Title IX coverage. Because of their refusal to sign the compliance document, HEW sought an order terminating all federal assistance to students attending Hillsdale. After administrative hearings, HEW found Hillsdale College to be a federal aid recipient subject to institution-wide enforcement in October 1979.

In December 1982, the United States Court of Appeals for the Sixth District entered a decision reversing the agency's decision in part. They found Hillsdale College to be a recipient of federal assistance and subject to Title IX and that federal assistance to Hillsdale's students could be lawfully terminated without any finding of discrimination simply on the basis of its unwillingness to comply with the requirement of signing the statement of compliance. The court ruled in favor of Hillsdale in that the college could not be found in noncompliance in all its programs; only those that were receiving federal assistance would be subject to Title IX enforcement, in this instance its financial aid program. The college appealed, but its appeal was delayed while the *Grove City College* case was being considered by the U.S. Supreme Court.

Upon settlement of the *Grove City* case, in March 1984 the U.S. Supreme Court agreed to hear the *Hillsdale* case (*Hillsdale College v. Department of Education,* U.S. Supreme Court, 1984). Upon review they vacated the decision of the Court of Appeals of the Sixth Circuit and remanded the case back to the Sixth Circuit for review in light of the *Grove City* decision. The Sixth Circuit Court remanded the case to HEW for further administrative review. In June 1985 Hillsdale College notified HEW of its decision to terminate participation in all student educational assistance programs in dispute. Hillsdale no longer enrolls students accepting federal educational assistance.

Subsequent to the *Grove City* and *Hillsdale* cases, the United States Congress passed the Civil Rights Restoration Act in March 1987. This act stated that Title IX, as well as other major civil rights statutes, applied to all phases of the organization, not just to those facets receiving federal assistance. This legislation reversed the program-specific portion of the *Grove City* decision. The legislation did not change the portion of the *Grove City* ruling that stated that aid to students constitutes aid to the institution the students attend.

Employment Discrimination

Kamehameha Schools were founded as Protestant schools through a provision from the will of Bernice Pauahi Bishop, a member of the Hawaiian royal family. The schools have a $6 billion endowment. The schools, operated separately for boys and girls, have been in continuous operation since the 1880s. A provision of the will providing funding for the schools requires that all teachers must be Protestants. While the schools have always been religious in the Protestant tradition, the influence of religion in the overall emphasis of the school has declined from its early years. A non-Protestant applied for a position as a part-time teacher. The application was declined on the basis of the applicant's religious affiliation. The applicant complained to the Equal Employment Opportunity Commission (EEOC). The EEOC sued the school for hiring discrimination in violation of the Civil Rights Act of 1964. The act provides an exemption from the prohibition against hiring discrimination on the basis of religion for religious organizations. EEOC contended that the Kamehameha Schools were not primarily religious and, therefore, were not entitled to the exemption. EEOC based its opinion on the fact that no religious organization had ever controlled the schools, that instruction is done from a generally secular perspective, and that only a general religious-studies course was required of all students. Students did not have to be Protestant and there was no evidence of attempts to proselyte them to the Protestant faith. A number of religious groups joined Kamehameha Schools in their argument that the court's ruling against their exemption from religious discrimination in hiring could limit the hiring practices of any religious school or college not owned or controlled by a church. The U.S. Supreme Court refused to hear the case, thereby upholding the decision of the Federal Appeals Court (*Kamehameha Schools v. EEOC*, U.S. Supreme Court, 1993). The schools are considering strengthening their religious character to reestablish their eligibility for the religious discrimination rather than drop the Protestant-only rule.

State Government

The degree of control exercised by the states over private education varies greatly. Those state government regulations and legislation that have produced problems for Christian schools have fallen into five main categories:

compulsory attendance laws, statistical reporting, standardized testing, daycare regulations, and minimum standards.

Compulsory Attendance—All fifty states have compulsory attendance laws of some kind. No two are exactly alike. Essentially, however, they require that all educable children who are physically able should attend school between certain specified ages. The problem encountered by some Christian schools is the definition of *school*. In some states this law means that one must attend a school approved by the state.

In the past some people have wanted to consider only public schools as meeting the requirements of compulsory attendance legislation. This was the issue in *Pierce v. Society of Sisters*. The state of Oregon had passed legislation requiring all normal children between ages eight and sixteen who had not completed eighth grade to be enrolled in a public school. In 1925 the U.S. Supreme Court struck down the law, thereby recognizing the "fundamental liberty of parents and guardians to direct the upbringing and education of children under their control" (Reutter, 13).

The controversy continues today; however, we have added the question "To whom do the children belong?" This was the issue in the famous *Ohio v. Whisner* case, Ohio Supreme Court, 1976. The state said that children enrolled in an unapproved school were truant and were subject to being removed from the home of their parents if they were not placed in an approved school. In considering the issue, a lower court said that "the natural rights of a parent to the custody and control of a . . . child are subordinate to power of the state; that a parent has an obligation to education not only to the child, but [also] to the state." The Supreme Court of the State of Ohio disagreed: "The compendium of minimum standards . . . taken as a whole, unduly burdens the free exercise of religion" and could result in "absolute suffocation of independent thought and educational policy and the effective retardation of religious philosophy."

State governments have reacted in varied ways. Some have shown patience and a sincere willingness to cooperate with these parents. Others have been extremely hostile, threatening parents with heavy fines, imprisonment, and even the loss of the custody of their children.

In some states, legislatures have responded sympathetically by rewriting rigid compulsory attendance laws providing considerable freedom to homeschoolers. Others have taken a wait-and-see attitude.

How long the homeschool movement will continue to grow is difficult to evaluate. One thing is certain: Christian educators must decide how they will respond to the families involved in this educational program since most Christian schools will have such children moving in and out of their programs from time to time. It seems only reasonable that Christian schools should show the same tolerant attitude toward homeschoolers that they desire others to show their institutions, regardless of their personal views of this method of education.

Statistical Reporting—Though a matter of individual conscience, there is usually no problem with the voluntary reporting of some statistical information to the state. The availability of such statistics can be beneficial to the school at times. Some states require that the names, ages, addresses, and grade levels of pupils enrolled at private schools be reported periodically to the state department of education. Likewise, reporting the numbers of administrators, teachers, counselors, and so forth should not ordinarily be a problem. Unless the requirement results in limitation of the school to operate freely or the reports are required as a condition of operating, the school should comply with the requests.

Standardized Testing—Requiring private schools to administer and report the results of standardized achievement tests is a matter of recent concern. This was a problem considered in cases in Kentucky and North Carolina. Most Christian educators do not object to administering and even reporting the results of such testing on a voluntary basis. They do object to being required to give a specific test and to maintain scores at a given level as a condition of approval. Nationwide, Christian schools boast of scoring well above the national average. Why, then, object to making minimum scores on such examinations? The objection is a philosophical one, for Christian education is inherently religious; basic "religious" presuppositions involved in any academic discipline will determine the rightness and wrongness of answers. Such presuppositions will also play a major role in determining what content is and is not important.

For the present we can use the several popular standardized achievement tests and make practical use of the scores obtained there. It may not always be so, however, and we do not want to be trapped by requirements that bind us to their results.

Daycare Regulations—For years few people thought much about licensing daycare centers that were part of a church. Many states exempted church-run daycare centers, and those that did not usually had no requirements to which churches objected. Consequently, many churches that operated daycare centers accepted licenses. Largely in conjunction with other regulatory problems affecting churches, many Christians have decided that it is not right for any church-operated ministry to accept a government license, which is an official permit to operate. This stance has resulted in numerous court actions. Several states have exempted church daycare ministries from state regulation. More recently, private daycares have challenged the legitimacy of preemptive legislation and creating unfair competition. The issue is not resolved.

Minimum Standards—The term *minimum standards* is a misnomer. Considered on the whole, they are neither minimum nor standard. In every case to date where minimum standards have been challenged in court, it has been shown that the standards have not been equitably applied to public schools. Such was the case in Ohio, where public school officials acknowledged that not all public schools met the standards being applied to the Christian schools.

Minimum standards usually attempt to consider such factors as professional employee certification; fiscal responsibility; licensing; fire, health, and safety regulations; and curriculum. It takes only cursory consideration to come to the conclusion that such control could make it impossible for a Christian school to maintain its distinctive nature. This was the conclusion of the court in *Ohio v. Whisner*, cited previously.

Regulation and legislation that govern how an organization may function can make it impossible for the organization to carry out its

God-ordained purpose. However, the requiring of approval for existence not only is an inconvenient and potential threat but also is on its very face totally unacceptable. No Christian school, whether part of a church or independent, can place its life in the hands of anyone other than the Lord and be confident that it has a future. Mandatory state approval for existence must be opposed at all costs.

Homeschools—The Christian education wave of the 1980s and 1990s may be the homeschool movement. Thousands of parents across the United States have decided to turn from public, secular private, and Christian schools to teach their own children at home. The National Center for Education in 2003 indicated that 1.5 million children were being homeschooled in the United States. Since no statistical reporting is required nation wide, the actual numbers may be much higher. This trend has caused considerable anxiety for educators who cannot understand why parents would reject all conventional educational opportunities to assume the awesome responsibility of training their own children. The potential legal problems of homeschoolers have made some conventional Christian educators nervous, fearing their problems could result in increased difficulty for them. Homeschoolers have found the government very unsympathetic to their concerns; however, in spite of some initial resistance, most states have found a way to accommodate them.

Local Government

It is at the local level that we encounter most fire, health, and safety regulations, building codes, zoning ordinances, and traffic regulations. Officials at this level are usually more friendly and more conciliatory because they often have some personal contact with patrons of the school. Local regulations and laws may be more difficult to keep up with than the state requirements, but officials carrying them out are generally easier to work with than their state counterparts.

Fire, Health, and Safety Regulations—When safety regulations are fairly constructed and equitably enforced, there is little reason to oppose them. The Word of God warns us to be mindful of the safety of our brethren. The Old Testament contains a number of such warnings.

Deuteronomy 22:8 is an example: "When thou buildest a new house, then thou shalt make a battlement for thy roof, that thou bring not blood upon thine house, if any man fall from thence."

Problems arise when unreasonable demands incur costs beyond proportionate value and when law is applied inconsistently. These matters are highly varied and must be dealt with individually.

Zoning Ordinances—Zoning laws are usually intended to restrict the use of an area to certain purposes. Problems recently encountered by churches include instances where churches were built in areas designated for residential purposes. In some cases the churches were there first, and the community was built up around them; in other cases the churches chose to locate in an existing residential neighborhood. Problems arose when the neighbors objected to the noise of hundreds of children playing in the previously quiet neighborhood. In other cases local officials objected because the increased traffic created by the existence of the school exceeded that anticipated when permission was given to build a church.

The immediate reaction of many is to say, "What right have they to prohibit me from doing what God has commanded me to do?" It is important and only fair, however, to distinguish at this point between being prohibited from building a school altogether and being prohibited from building one at a specific location. Unless there were some control of construction, we would all be in a mess. If someone purchased thirty acres of ground for a Christian school in a rural area a short distance from a community, he would be chagrined if the land immediately adjacent to the school were purchased by a steel company for a factory. When the factory began to operate, parents might readily scream, "Somebody [meaning somebody in government] should do something about this!" Fair zoning laws are for our protection. Unfair zoning laws should be opposed and changed.

Traffic Regulations—Some communities refuse to recognize private schools on the same basis as public schools for safety purposes; others will when one calls the existence of the school to their attention. Private school children deserve the same protection as public school children when walking to and from school, crossing streets, and boarding and leaving school buses. The school, however, must assume some responsibility to insure that entrances and exits from school property are safely located; bus drivers are properly trained; vehicles are properly lighted, labeled, and maintained; and students are properly trained in basic safety measures.

Many of the difficulties Christians encounter with various government agencies are of their own making if they fail to become familiar with and obey reasonable laws. Many conflicts result from failure to appreciate the legitimate concerns of government. Laws and regulations, like some of our school policies, do not always address concerns in the most effective manner. When protesting those that cause us concern, we should be alert to the real concerns of government. Often they should be our concerns as well. Together we may be able to draft laws and regulations that will be in our mutual interest.

We must also understand that not all our differences can be resolved through lobbying. The forces of Satan are opposed to what we are attempting to do through Christian schools. Sometimes he uses government to accomplish his purpose. When such is the case, we must rely on the Lord to fight for us. The battle is His, and He will win. We must seek His wisdom to separate those things we should support from those things we must oppose.

CHAPTER 27

THE CHALLENGE OF
THE EXCEPTIONAL CHILD

For who maketh thee to differ from another?
1 Corinthians 4:7

Those members of the body, which seem to be feeble are necessary. . . . For our comely parts have no need: but God hath tem-
pered the body together, having given more abundant honour
to that part which lacked: that there should be no schism in the
body; but that the members should have the same care one for
another.
1 Corinthians 12:22–25

As discussed in an earlier chapter, the typical Christian school is not
large enough to provide a curriculum broad enough to meet the
needs of all children. Consequently, most Christian schools focus on the
needs of children who are average or above average in their abilities and
have no educational problems requiring the attention of a specialized
teacher. Unfortunately, this leaves a significant portion of the population
of students whose parents want them to have the benefit of a conventional
Christian school education with no schools willing to admit them.

Any child that is unable to succeed in a conventional school setting
without assistance or accommodation represents a challenge to the classroom teacher. How such a challenge is accepted varies greatly from one
teacher to another and from one school setting to another. However, the
greater the degree of difference between such a child and the average student in the school, the less likely the school will be willing to serve him.

The typical Christian school can adequately serve students with a
range of intellectual functioning that spreads over three standard deviations. On the Wechsler model, the test mean is 100, and the standard
deviation is 15. Fifty percent of the general population has an IQ between 90 and 109. Roughly 68 percent of the population has a level of

intellectual functioning between 85 and 115. About 82 percent of the school-age population nationwide would have abilities ranging from 85 to 130. The normal curve appropriately describes the level of intellectual functioning expected in the typical school. Figure 27.1 illustrates the normal population in terms of IQ scores and the percentage of people that fall into each category.

For years Christian school leaders have taken comfort in the fact that they have been serving most of the children whose parents were interested in having them attend a Christian school. However, that provides no satisfaction whatsoever for the parents whose children are in the 18 percent that are not being served. The needs of some of those falling within this category are so severe as to require highly specialized programs; however, many within this group could definitely be served by Christian schools.

Students with IQs from 70 to 89 are classified as borderline/low average. In many Christian schools, these children could be two to three full standard deviations below the class mean. They would have a very difficult time succeeding in such a competitive academic environment. This group of students is the most underserved group of students in the entire school population, both public and private. They differ enough from most students to be unable to keep pace with the rest of the class, but they do not necessarily differ enough to qualify for special education services. Because their needs are ignored, they often develop behavior problems, and many in this group eventually drop out of school. Frequently they have very unhappy lives as adults.

An overview of the special needs areas will provide general information. However, at this time, most Christian schools will not be able to consider providing programs to serve special needs students outside the areas of slow learners, the learning disabled, and the mildly retarded. Accommodations can be made for many other categories of students that will enable those with minor disabilities to be successful in Christian schools.

Before significant accommodations are permitted, parents should be required to provide documentation of the child's learning problem based on an assessment by a competent evaluator. This evaluation should be completed by someone who is a certified or licensed psychologist or one who has completed a formal training program in educational assessment.

FIGURE 27.1

THE NORMAL CURVE

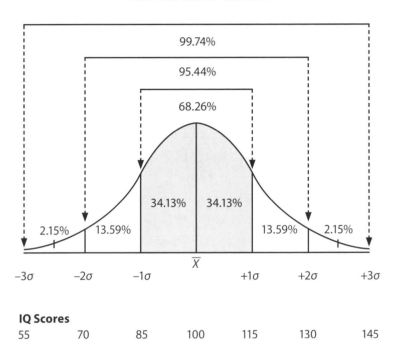

IQ SCORES AND THE WECHSLER MODEL

IQ	Classification	Percent of Normal Curve
130 & above	Very Superior	2.2
120–129	Superior	6.7
110–119	High Average	16.1
90–109	Average	50.0
80–89	Low Average	16.1
70–79	Borderline	6.7
69 & below	Intellectually Deficient	2.2

The Christian school movement has reached a level of maturity where it should now be willing to approach special education with the same pioneering spirit and degree of enthusiasm in which it addressed Christian schools as a whole a generation ago. An explanation of how this can be done will follow a discussion of the nature of the problem that is being faced.

THE SLOW LEARNER

The largest group of children that normally requires special assistance to be successful in the Christian school is those children whose IQs fall between 70 and 89 and who do not meet minimum criteria for classification as disabled. We know that nationally this group represents between 22 and 23 percent of the total school population. Their range of ability places them between the average children on the high side and the mildly retarded on the low side. There typically are no special programs for them, yet they have an extremely difficult time competing with their peers in both public and private schools. In the public schools these children are sometimes served in federally funded ECIA Title I reading and math labs.

Students in the IQ range of 70 to 89 are placed in one classification because they differ only in their degree of intellectual functioning, and there is no special program of educational services for them. Individual students in our schools vary greatly in terms of their level of motivation to succeed, degree of difference from the other students, previous educational opportunities, and amount of parental support. Not all the students in this group would be able to complete our programs even with special help, but many of them would respond positively to any encouragement from us. Few Christian schools are currently offering these students or their parents more than sympathy.

The primary difference between these students and the average student is the rate at which they are able to assimilate material and, to a lesser degree, the complexity and scope of material they can master. Most people have differing degrees of aptitude for certain cognitive areas. Consequently, some slow learners are able to perform in a manner consistent with an average level of ability in some academic areas, while being significantly below average in other academic areas.

EXCEPTIONALITIES

Leaders in the field of special education have identified eight types of exceptionalities that children may have that make it difficult for them to achieve their potential in the typical school classroom without special assistance (Hallahan & Kauffman, 1991):

- Communication (speech and language) disorders

- Emotional/behavioral disorders

- Hearing impairments

- Giftedness

- Mental retardation

- Learning disabilities

- Physical/other health impairments

- Visual impairments

The reader will quickly observe that of the eight categories of exceptionalities listed above, seven of them are negative in their impact on a child, but one—giftedness—is positive.

Communication Disorders—Children with serious speech and language impairments will usually require the services of a speech-language pathologist. These children usually receive these services from the public school speech-language pathologist or a specialist in private practice. The services are often provided while the student is enrolled in his regular school.

Emotional/Behavioral Disorders—Children who have various emotional/behavioral disorders are among the hardest to serve. Their behavior requires immense understanding and patience to reach the children and serve their needs. No doubt there is a population of students in Christian schools with legitimate emotional/behavioral disorders, but many of the students who manifest these behaviors come from homes where the parents have not done their part to train the children to practice self-control or are the product of other factors of a dysfunctional home environment.

Hearing Impairment—The needs of most hearing-impaired children can be met in our schools when teachers have been taught to understand their needs and when a school is committed to reasonable accommodations.

Giftedness—Gifted children were frequently defined as having an IQ of 130 or above and an equivalent area of academic aptitude in one or more areas. More recently the focus has become broader. Renzulli, Reis, and Smith (1981) recommend that the gifted child meet three criteria: (1) high ability, (2) high creativity, and (3) high task commitment. Since the student populations in Christian schools tend to have higher levels of ability and achievement than the overall national student population, few Christian schools will encounter students whose level of intellectual functioning and academic aptitude are so high that they cannot be accommodated in their programs. Adjustments will, of course, be required for some. Because gifted children can assimilate material so much more rapidly than average children, acceleration and enrichment will be required to keep them appropriately challenged.

Mildly Retarded—The mildly mentally disabled youngster will require that some of his formal academic work be provided in a special educational environment with other students of his ability, but he can receive the remainder of his instruction in a classroom with nondisabled peers. Typically these students receive two to three hours of special instruction in the areas of reading/language arts and math. The mildly mentally handicapped child has an IQ of 55 to 69. There is a significant difference in both the rate of learning and the degree of difficulty of academic material that can be mastered by the mildly retarded individual and the average student. They also manifest maladaptive behavior skills that make it difficult to function independently in various life and social skills. These children also typically have difficulty anticipating the normal sequence of events that a particular action will trigger. However, these students can learn and have the potential to become productive citizens and effective servants for the Lord.

Learning Disabilities—The child with a specific learning disability may face a serious challenge in the classroom of a Christian school. To be classified as a learning-disabled child, he must have average or above average ability. Consequently, he is more aware of how he is perceived by his peers and his teachers as he struggles to succeed than are those children of lesser ability or those without disabilities.

Definitions of learning disabilities will vary considerably from expert to expert and from professional organization to professional organization. The federal government has defined a learning disability as the following:

> General definition—The term "specific learning disability" means a disorder in one or more of the basic psychological processes involved in understanding or in using language, spoken or written, which disorder may manifest itself in an imperfect ability to listen, think, speak, read, write, spell, or do mathematical calculations.

> Disorders included—Such term includes such conditions as perceptual disabilities, brain injury, minimal brain dysfunction, dyslexia, and developmental aphasia.

> Disorders not included—Such term does not include a learning problem that is primarily the result of visual, hearing, or motor disabilities, of mental retardation, of emotional disturbance, or of environmental, cultural, or economic disadvantage. (Individuals with Disabilities Education Act Amendments of 1997, Sec. 602(26), 13)

Generally, it is agreed that a specific learning disability requires a level of intellectual functioning in the average range (85 or above) with an academic achievement score that is significantly lower. Currently, states and local districts have developed their own criteria, and in most public school districts a child with a discrepancy of 15 points or more will be eligible to receive services as a learning disabled student. This discrepancy is being raised to as high as 23 points in some states in a move to reduce the number of children receiving special educational services.

Some learning-disabled children are also characterized by organizational difficulties routinely associated with home and school tasks, but these problems are secondary to the psychological processing problems causing their disability.

Physical/Other Health Impairments—The physical and health related limitations experienced by some children make it difficult to meet their educational needs. Compared with other disabling conditions, this is a small group, and it is surprising how many children who would fall into this category could be served in schools that were determined to make every reasonable effort to do so.

Various building codes are now necessitating that occupants of nearly every public building consider any barriers that the building presents to the users. Newer buildings are, by the nature of their design, more accessible to the handicapped. Even when an older facility is being used, creative planning in cooperation with the student and his family can reveal ways in which the needs of the handicapped can be met with reasonable cost.

Some aspects of health-related needs present more serious challenges. Those who have incurred life-threatening communicable diseases present unusual challenges as schools seek to balance the needs of the *afflicted* with the concerns of the *affected*.

In addition to the children whose disabilities have been discussed above, there is a new category of children experiencing educational problems whose difficulties fall under other health impairments. Attention deficit disorder (ADD) or attention deficit disorder with hyperactivity (ADHD) is a problem only recently identified as a disabling condition. It is currently a very controversial area. Some people have been convinced that there is no such disorder. They believe all children identified as ADD or ADHD are simply lacking in self-control and self-discipline. Others go to the opposite extreme and want to label, without careful investigation, any child who manifests symptoms of inattention, impulsivity, or hyperactivity as ADD or ADHD.

ADD and ADHD are legitimate disabling conditions. Once a person encounters a child with a severe attention deficit problem, he will never again doubt the legitimacy of the condition. Many school psychologists and special educators would agree, however, that a very high percentage of children who have been labeled as ADD and ADHD have been incorrectly labeled. Sorting out the legitimate ADD and ADHD children from the increasingly large pool of undisciplined children enrolling in school is no simple chore. Fortunately, both the genuinely ADD and ADHD child and the undisciplined child respond well to many of the same educational intervention strategies.

Visual Impairments—To receive services as visually impaired, children must be evaluated by a licensed optometrist or ophthalmologist. Generally, to receive services as a visually impaired child, a student must have visual acuity of 20/50 or less in his best eye after correction or have visual field limitations (angle of vision) of less than 20 degrees or have progressive eye disease or binocular vision problems (double vision).

CAN OUR CHRISTIAN SCHOOLS MEET THESE NEEDS?

Few Christian schools are large enough to absorb the extra cost of providing a complete program of special education services in a Christian education framework in a conventional school setting. However, most Christian schools with complete programs offering kindergarten through the twelfth grade should be able to offer some special educational services. The provision of special educational services is an excellent area for the Christian schools in the community to address collectively.

In a community with five or six Christian schools of average enrollment, one school could agree to address the needs of children who have been identified as slow learners and as having specific learning disabilities. Another school could agree to offer a program for the mildly retarded. The remaining schools in the community could agree to support the schools with the special programs. The support could come in several ways.

Obviously, it would be important that the schools be willing to unselfishly encourage families with children requiring these services to seriously consider enrolling their children. They would have to recognize that if these families had more than one child, in many cases it would be logical for them to enroll all their children in the school offering the special services. If these schools were providing transportation for children in their schools, they could offer to provide transportation for the special education children attending the other school. They could place the schools providing special education in their budget and support them financially on a regular basis.

Children who are slow learners and those that have specific learning disabilities respond well to similar instructional intervention. One special education teacher can work with eight to ten mildly handicapped students requiring special help at the same time. When the student load is in the upper limits of this range, an aide should be provided. Typically, schools set up a resource room in which children come from their regular classes to receive special help in various subjects. The teacher works at the same time with all children who have weaknesses in the same cognitive areas and are functioning at the same level of proficiency.

The cost of offering resource room assistance to your students is less than many would think. There is, of course, the salary of the teacher who works full-time or part-time (depending on your student load), the need for special educational resources, and a classroom equipped with appropriately sized furniture. Overall, the expense of providing the students in your school with special educational assistance would be similar to adding another section of a grade with 40 to 50 percent of the number of students you would normally serve. Part of the expense could be borne by making a monthly surcharge for each student of 25 to 50 percent of the regular tuition. The balance of the expense could be covered by the general budget in much the same way that you presently cover the cost of offering other low enrollment classes such as second year language classes, chemistry, and physics or as you provide for certain extracurricular activities such as intramural athletics and fine arts programs. Based on the current salary structure in our Christian schools, the upper limits of the cost to start a program for the slow learner and the learning disabled would be $30,000 the first year. This would be reduced by the amount of surcharges that would be collected from students in the program. It would probably take two years for the program to enroll the maximum number of students that could be handled. At that time the school could anticipate the need to continue supplementing the program in the amount of $12,000 to $15,000 annually.

Another option that could be considered would be for one school to contract a full-time special education teacher and parcel that teacher's services out to other Christian schools with special-needs children and thus share the expense of the teacher. This approach would be similar to the itinerant model that was used in the beginning of special education in public schools and continues to be used in such specialty areas as speech pathology.

Most Christian educators have examined the secular educational options available to Christian parents and have concluded that some form of Christian education is needed. If Christian education is a need, is it a need for all children or just "normal" children? The answer is, of course, very obvious. If any child has a "need" for Christian education, all children share that need.

We need an attitude change toward those God has seen fit to have enter this world with less than average potential for academic success. The next time someone with a special needs child approaches your school, instead of saying, *"I'm sorry, but we can't help you,"* why not say, *"I would very much like to help you; let's see if we can find a way to do it."*

STRATEGIES FOR HELPING SPECIAL-NEEDS CHILDREN IN THE REGULAR CLASSROOM

There are a number of steps that can be taken to provide reasonable accommodations to students in your school that are experiencing difficulty without taking away from the academic integrity of your program. The practices mentioned below are currently being used successfully in many schools.

The Attention Deficit Disorder Child/the Learning Disabled Child

1. Maintain good communication with the parents to insure their awareness of the child's progress.

2. Emphasize quality rather than quantity of work.

3. Provide good classroom structure and clearly defined limits and expectations. Do not accept unsatisfactory work.

4. Seat the student in the classroom to minimize distractions.

5. Examinations may be given orally for those known to be auditory learners.

6. Provide extended time to take quizzes and unlimited time for examinations.

7. Provide a proctor to clarify test items.

8. Audiotape tests so students can listen to the test on a recorder.

9. Permit students to take an essay exam rather than a multiple choice, true-false, and so on.

10. Permit students to take a multiple choice, true-false test instead of an essay test.

11. Permit students to respond to tests orally.

12. Permit students with a disability in spelling to use a Franklin speller.

13. Permit students with a disability in math to use a calculator to check their work and to take exams. Provide students with multiplication tables for use in class work, homework, and tests.

14. Provide reading material on audio cassettes for the auditory learner. Older students and adult volunteers can be used to record material.

15. Provide volunteer readers to help auditory learners. Consider using other students and parent/grandparent volunteer readers.

16. Provide written assignments to insure parental understanding of what the teacher expects from the child.

17. Permit students to copy the notes of other students.

18. Permit students to dictate assignments to others for word processing.

19. Use peers for tutors.

20. Correct reversals and transpositions of letters and numbers but do not count these against the student's grade.

21. Take class participation into consideration in the overall assessment of the child.

22. Modify assignments as needed to properly consider the student's disability. Permit some students to substitute oral presentations for written projects or written projects for oral.

HELPING THE FACULTY UNDERSTAND SPECIAL-NEEDS CHILDREN

It is important for Christian school administrators to understand the frustration that classroom teachers face when confronted with an exceptional child in a regular classroom of 25 to 30 children, having no prior experience or training to prepare them for the task. Most teachers who have completed their teacher education program since 1991 will have had a course in the characteristics of the exceptional child, and some will even have had an introductory methods course giving some direction in teaching exceptional children. For those who have not been fortunate enough to have received such instruction, the school must provide in-service training to prepare the faculty.

In-service programs dealing with the following subjects would be very helpful to all classroom teachers (NJCLD, 1993, 330–32):

1. Child and adolescent development

2. Individual differences

3. Spoken and written language development disorders

4. Cognitive development and learning theory

5. Social and emotional development

6. Nature of learning disabilities

7. Informal assessment

8. Instructional strategies

9. Adaptation of instructional materials and teaching techniques

10. Classroom management

Meeting the needs of children thrills the heart of every school administrator and classroom teacher. There is, however, something very special about seeing a child who has struggled be able to succeed, finally tasting success. Working with exceptional children opens an entirely new avenue of opportunity for ministry.

Christian educators will find the following books to be excellent resources in working with exceptional children:

Sutton, Joe P., ed. *Special Education: A Biblical Approach.* Greenville, SC: Hidden Treasure Publications, 1993.

A CHRISTIAN PHILOSOPHY OF EDUCATION

AN ADMINISTRATOR'S PERSPECTIVE

Every school needs a statement of philosophy that will keep the ministry in focus with the emphasis the governing body has determined to be its direction. For a Christian school, this philosophy statement must have a distinctly biblical foundation reflecting what the institution believes the Bible requires for it to honor God and achieve its objectives. The following areas must be addressed by a typical Christian school offering academic programs at the elementary and secondary levels.

The Responsibility for Christian Education

1. The state?

2. The church?

3. Their parents?

The Purpose of Christian Education

1. To help parents satisfy the state's requirements for compulsory education without compromising their own biblical convictions.

2. To assist parents in the development of their children in the image of Christ.

3. To offer children a quality program of general education consistent with the truth revealed in the Word of God.

4. To provide structured opportunities for young people to practice Christian principles they have learned.

5. To provide young people appropriate opportunities for social and recreational activities consistent with their chronological age and biblical standards.

The Recipient of Christian Education

1. Only Christians can benefit fully from a Christian education.

2. Christian education can lead lost people who are open to Him to a knowledge of Him.

3. The presence of large numbers of unsaved children from homes where parents are unsaved is detrimental to the true purpose of Christian education.

4. Schools organized primarily as an evangelistic outreach of their church will not normally be able to do as good a job of developing Christlikeness in their Christian young people.

Admissions Policies

1. Admissions standards will limit enrollment of students to reflect the purpose of the school.

2. Enrollment in the school will be limited to students whose spiritual and educational needs can be met by the school.

3. Admissions standards will take into consideration the chronological age, spiritual interests, intellectual capacity, previous educational experiences, and disabling conditions of the applicants.

Program of the School

1. Will provide instructional and educational experiences appropriate to the attainment of the spiritual development of its students.

2. Will include instructional and educational experiences appropriate to the attainment of the academic development of its students.

3. Will provide instructional and educational experiences appropriate to the cultural, physical, and social development of its students.

Financial Policies

1. Believing that the provision of educational opportunities is the primary responsibility of parents, the school will provide children educational opportunities at the lowest possible cost consistent with maintaining its own obligations to those making Christian education possible.

2. Financial planning will insure that sufficient revenues are on hand to pay school financial obligations in a timely manner.

3. Appropriate salaries and benefits will be provided to the faculty and staff and will be paid in a timely manner.

4. The church will supplement the cost of operating the school in the interest of making Christian education available to as many young people as possible.

5. The school will seek to make financial assistance available to families unable to pay for the educational needs of their children.

6. Children whose financial obligations are not satisfied in a timely manner will not be retained in school.

7. Recognizing its accountability to God and man, the school will conduct its business in accordance with all legal requirements and generally accepted business practices. All financial records will be subject to the review of the appropriate personnel within the organization and will be audited regularly by an accounting firm.

School Personnel

1. They must be appropriate spiritual role models for its students.

2. They must have adequate training and/or experience to perform their assigned duties.

3. They must have strong convictions about the importance of the Christian education of young people.

Supervision of Personnel

1. Because the school recognizes its accountability to God for the instructional program it provides for its constituents, there must be supervision of the work of all personnel, involving both direct and indirect observation, to insure that the ministry is conducted in a manner consistent with biblical principles and the goals and objectives of the school.

2. Faculty and staff will be given written and/or oral reviews of the evaluations of their performance, which will include specific suggestions to remediate any areas of concern.

3. The school will provide staff development programs to remediate general areas of concern and to develop the full potential of the faculty and staff.

Behavioral Standards

1. Enrollment in the school will be limited to students whose parents support the goals and objectives of the school.

2. Enrollment in the school will be limited to students agreeing to submit themselves to the authority of the school and to cooperate in their own educational process.

3. Parents and students must be willing to allow the school to define the limits of acceptable behavior, recognizing that in doing so the school is not passing judgment on individual family values or seeking to subordinate the authority of the family.

4. Acceptable behavior will edify the body of Christ and bring honor to His name.

Academic Standards

1. Since the enrollment of children in the Christian school satisfies the parents' legal obligation for educating their children under the state's compulsory education laws, the curriculum of the school must generally be consistent with the academic

programs offered by public and private schools in terms of academic content and levels of achievement expected.

2. Records of academic progress will reflect accurately subjects studied, dates of enrollment, teacher evaluation of progress, standardized measures of progress, and standardized measures of ability.

Program Completion Standards

1. As a Christian educational institution we consider Christian character an integral component of the requirements for graduation.

2. Units of credit and diplomas awarded will be granted on the basis of generally accepted educational standards.

Physical Facilities and Grounds

1. The school will provide adequate physical facilities and resources consistent with the educational programs it has committed itself to provide.

2. Physical facilities, equipment, and grounds will be maintained in a manner that reflects the institution's commitment to quality Christian education.

3. Faculty, staff, and students will be expected to respect the resources God has provided and to do everything possible to maintain them and extend their usefulness.

THE *ABC*S OF A *GOOD*
CHRISTIAN SCHOOL

Every Christian school is unique to some degree; however, all good schools will have a number of common characteristics. A good Christian school will do the following:

A. Seek to identify and meet the spiritual needs of its students.

B. Have a philosophy statement that provides direction for every function.

C. Have a board that determines general policies for the educational program. Because the board will be unable to administer the school on a day-to-day basis, it will delegate authority to administrative personnel who will assist the board in achieving the goals of the school.

D. Have an administrator who has the professional training and/ or experience necessary to direct the school toward the development and achievement of Christ-honoring academic and spiritual objectives.

E. Be staffed by personnel who possess the academic credentials and/or experience necessary to fulfill their responsibilities. A good school will not place a professional employee in a position for which he has little or no opportunity for success. Nonprofessional employees should also have training and/or experience necessary to fulfill their duties.

F. Be concerned about the spiritual condition of all its employees, recognizing that all of them have the potential to influence students for or against God's purpose in their lives.

G. Have a continuous program of supervision with follow-up conferences, whereby employees are made aware of their weaknesses and are provided direction and encouragement to overcome them.

H. Have a continuous program of in-service training, designed to help all employees refine and update their knowledge and skills.

I. Have a curriculum that will insure that each student is exposed to the spiritual and academic subject matter appropriate for his age and grade placement.

J. Make appropriate charges for services rendered so that the school will be able to offer an adequate spiritual and academic program. Fees should be established in such a manner that those receiving benefit from the services are bearing their share of the cost.

K. Have a budget that reflects the objectives of the educational program and includes adequate income and cooperatively planned expenditures.

L. Operate in a businesslike manner, making provision for the payment of salaries and bills when they are due.

M. Have a salary and fringe-benefit program that is adequate for its faculty and staff, with annual consideration for experience and additional training. Unless the school periodically provides increases that at least equal the increases in the cost of living, it is actually reducing its employees' pay.

N. Have a grant and/or loan program to assist professional employees in continuing their education.

O. Provide its students with the best textbooks and educational resources available. Every effort should be made to include materials that are distinctly Christian and to exclude and/or replace those that have philosophies contradictory to that of Christian education.

P. Have a library containing reference materials and other books that will supplement the textbooks used in the classrooms. The materials in the library must take into account the needs of all the students. A regular amount per child should be budgeted each year for the purchase of additional books and the replacement of worn-out and obsolete books.

Q. Have physical facilities that will enable students to receive their education in a safe, comfortable environment that is conducive to learning. The physical facilities should reflect a level of quality and refinement consistent with the housing of the school's constituency.

R. Have an admissions policy that reflects its educational goals.

S. Have standards of conduct that reflect a Christian philosophy of character development.

T. Develop policies that take into account differences in the ability and behavior of students, realizing that it may not be able to accept or retain some students without jeopardizing the remainder of the student body.

U. Have a program of standardized testing to measure pupil progress, using both mental aptitude and achievement examinations. The results of these tests should be properly interpreted to teachers, parents, and pupils.

V. Keep records of the child's academic progress, physical welfare, mental ability, and spiritual development. These records, properly interpreted, should be made available to and used by all school personnel who can use them.

W. Have an easily understood system of reporting pupil progress in academic and spiritual areas—one that will encourage parent cooperation and participation in promoting this progress.

X. Have a promotion policy based on objective criteria.

Y. Have a program of extracurricular activities that complement the educational philosophy and objectives of the school.

Z. Structure its program so that it complements rather than competes with the program of its sponsoring church.

CHART OF ACCOUNTS WITH NARRATIVE DESCRIPTION OF EACH CATEGORY

INCOME

Tuition, fees, and other charges for student services—All tuition income and fees charged to students.

Unearned tuition, fees, and other charges for student services—All income received for prepaid tuition, fees, and so on for subsequent year.

Food service—All income from sale of food and drinks except income from concessions sales at athletic events.

Interest—All interest income, regardless of source.

Sale of promotional materials—All income from sale of items designed to generate income.

Loan proceeds—All income for loans incurred for any reason.

Sale of school assets—All income from sale of school assets.

Gifts and pledges—All gifts and promises of gifts.

Athletic activities—All game receipts and money received from athletes for reimbursement for equipment or uniforms purchased on their behalf; any money received from participation in tournaments.

Fine arts activities—All receipts and incomes received from participants in fine arts activities for reimbursement for equipment or uniforms purchased on their behalf; any income received as a result of fine arts activities.

Yearbook—All yearbook fees and income from yearbook advertising.

Other student activities—This account is for bookkeeping to handle income received that will be paid out for some student expense not to be borne by the school such as field-trip admission fees, class activities, and so on.

EXPENSES

Administration

Payroll—All salaries and wages for administrators and office employees and their payroll taxes.

Administrative travel—All expenses for administrative travel and entertainment, except in-service and educational expenses.

Legal service—All fees paid for legal counsel.

Office expense—All expenses related to office maintenance except equipment purchases and repair. Does not include supplies for teacher-related activities even though processed through the school office.

Advertising—All printed materials designed to recruit students, such as yellow-page advertising, all media advertising, and so on.

Promotional materials—All expenses related to the generation of income through student sales for a profit for school or student activities. Includes wearing apparel, bumper stickers, decals, school pictures, and similar fundraising and promotional materials not directly related to some curricular or extracurricular activity.

Recruiting—All expenses incurred while attempting to recruit professional or nonprofessional faculty/staff, including transportation and entertainment.

Office equipment—All office equipment costing less than $100. Equipment costing more than $100 should be charged to capital outlay.

Office equipment repair—All expenses related to office equipment maintenance including maintenance contracts.

Membership in professional organizations—Dues and fees for institutional memberships in professional organizations.

Instruction

Payroll—All salaries and wages for instructional personnel and their payroll taxes.

Textbooks—All books and workbooks, standardized tests, and instructional materials not consumed in use.

Library—All books, periodicals, library supplies, media materials, and equipment. Equipment costing $100 or more should be placed under capital outlay.

Teaching supplies—All paper, pencils, chalk, paper clips, and similar materials purchased for instructional use that are consumed in use or cost $100 or less per item.

Educational grants/loans—All money made available to current employees to further their formal education exclusive of in-service activities.

In-service training—All expenses for informal faculty/staff development.

Membership in professional organizations—Dues and related expenses for memberships for faculty/staff requested by the school.

Health service—All expenses for nonprescription medication and first aid items for faculty/staff and students.

Extracurricular Activities

Payroll—Salaries and wages for all personnel involved in extracurricular activities who receive special remuneration (i.e., coaches, yearbook sponsors, etc.), and their payroll taxes.

Athletics—All expenses for athletics except salaries for personnel on the school payroll. Athletic equipment costing more than $100 should be charged to capital outlay.

Extension ministries—All expenses for extension ministries. All equipment costing more than $100 should be charged to capital outlay.

Fine arts—All expenses for art and music activities outside the classroom such as student participation in school competitions, awards, band uniforms for which the school will pay, music, and supplies. Fine arts equipment costing more than $100 should be charged to capital outlay.

Yearbook—All yearbook-related expenses.

Other student activities—All expenses for student activities for which you will be directly reimbursed by the students such as field trips, uniforms to be paid for by students, and so on.

Food Service

Payroll—Salaries and wages for food preparation personnel and their payroll taxes.

Food—All expenses for food.

Equipment—All expenses for food preparation equipment costing less than $100. Equipment costing more than $100 should be charged to capital outlay.

Maintenance and Operation

Payroll—Salaries and wages for all maintenance and operation personnel and their payroll taxes.

Maintenance of buildings—All expenses relating to building maintenance, except cleaning, modernization, and remodeling.

Maintenance of equipment—All expenses related to maintaining equipment except office equipment and transportation.

Utilities—All expenses for water, sewage, electricity, telephone, natural gas, garbage collection, and so on.

Custodial supplies—All supplies necessary for the care and cleaning of the building, paper products, sanitary supplies, exterminator services, and so on, and equipment costing $100 or less.

Maintenance and operational equipment—All equipment used in maintaining the buildings and grounds such as lawn mowers, scrub buckets, buffers, hand and power tools, and so on, costing $100 or less. Equipment costing more than $100 should be charged to capital outlay.

Transportation

Payroll—Salaries and wages for all transportation employees and their payroll taxes.

Purchase of vehicles—All expenses relating to the purchase of vehicles, including taxes and fees incurred at the time of purchase.

Lease of vehicles—All monthly lease payments, deposits, and other lease-related expenses.

Maintenance of vehicles—All expenses related to vehicle maintenance except fuel and lubrication.

Fuel and lubricants—All expenses for fuel and lubricants.

Fixed Charges

Employee insurance—All expenses related to insurance for employees to be paid by the school or from money withheld from the employees' salary.

Student insurance—All student-related insurance, school accident insurance, insurance for participation in athletic programs, and travel insurance for trips.

Property/liability insurance—All insurance to protect property owned by the school and to protect the school from suits against negligence through acts of the organization, the existence of the organization, or for acts of the employees or officers of the organization.

Taxes and licenses—All expenses for taxes except payroll or those incurred through purchase of equipment and supplies; all licenses for which the school may be responsible.

Employee expenses—Expenses for housing, utilities, and so on, for employees eligible for tax-exempt compensation.

Capital Outlay

Site improvements—Any expense related to alteration of the landscape or the installation of sidewalks, driveways, and so on.

Remodeling/modernization of facilities—Any expense related to the alteration or updating of existing facilities.

Equipment (other than transportation)—Expenses for the acquisition of new or replacement equipment costing more than $100.

Debt service

Payments on all loans (does not include lease payments)

Depreciation (for those on accrual basis)

REPRESENTATIVE JOB DESCRIPTION FOR THE FINANCIAL ADMINISTRATOR OF A CHURCH

IMMEDIATE SUPERVISOR

Although the financial administrator will work with several staff members and lay leaders, he is responsible to the pastor.

JOB OBJECTIVE

The financial administrator's objective is to assist the pastor and lay leadership by managing the financial operations of all the church's ministries and related subsidiaries, to establish and maintain sound accounting procedures and controls, to prepare regular financial reports on which financial decisions can be based, and to work closely with all facets of the organization to achieve maximum spiritual impact compatible with the resources the Lord provides.

QUALIFICATIONS FOR POSITION

1. He should be a mature Christian who is an example to others in personal conduct and Christian walk, giving offense to no man and being careful not to bring reproach on the church or the cause of Christ.

2. He should have a servant's heart; he should be faithful and dependable; and he should be willing to participate wholeheartedly in the entire spiritual ministry of the church, encouraging others to do so as well.

3. He should have the ability to organize, to work quickly, to handle details accurately, to work harmoniously with others, and to keep confidences.

4. He should have the ability to follow instructions and to work with a minimum of supervision.

NATURE AND SCOPE

He performs all financially related tasks except those assigned to other church members for the purpose of internal control. The following are the duties which should be delegated to someone other than the financial advisor:

1. Counting and depositing all regular church offerings and gifts.

2. Counting, depositing, and posting all accounts receivable.

3. Reconciling monthly bank statements with records.

The financial administrator coordinates the short- and long-term budgeting for the church, issues control reports, and takes approved steps for the correction of adverse variances. In helping subsidiary ministries establish sound financial controls, he works closely with all organizations in the church and with the finance committee. He must perform all his duties so that the spiritual ministry of the church is enhanced and the sound financial operation is not compromised. The financial administrator must frequently evaluate insurance needs, make recommendations for changes, and insure that maximum benefit is received for minimum cost. In addition, he must take appropriate actions for the security of the church assets. As the ministries of the church expand and become more diversified, the importance of this greatly increases. This is a spiritual ministry. The financial administrator is responsible for the wise handling of all funds the Lord provides for the ministry of the church.

PRIMARY ACCOUNTABILITIES

1. To coordinate short- and long-term budgeting for the church and to update the five-year master plan that incorporates all the plans, goals, and financial objectives of the church.

2. To prepare stewardship programs and other financial programs that fit the personality of the church and that are compatible with the Scriptures.

3. To see that all financial records of the church are kept accurately and currently in line with acceptable accounting procedures.

4. To render regular revenue and expense reports for the leadership of the church.

5. To render control reports on revenue and expenses and initiate approved corrective measures when adverse variances are reported.

6. To prepare the payroll in accordance with church-approved salaries.

7. To be financial advisor to the pastor, principal, and other staff members, keeping them well informed of anticipated cash needs.

8. To plan for effective utilization of cash on hand, making wise investment of cash not in immediate use.

9. To establish sound internal controls over all money coming into the church and to work with subsidiary organizations within the church in establishing sound financial controls.

10. To assure that all obligations of the church are paid on time.

11. To handle all correspondence and reports of a tax nature and to keep informed of local, state, and federal laws and regulatory agencies' demands that affect the financial operation of the church.

12. To evaluate all aspects of the insurance program and assure that maximum benefit is received for minimum cost, to constantly evaluate needs for coverage and make recommendations for change, to make sure the church does everything feasible to protect its property and facilities.

13. To provide all records necessary for an annual audit of the church records and take corrective action for any audit exceptions.

14. To prepare cost analyses of programs or ministries needed.

15. To make recommendations for cost savings.

16. To perform other duties as assigned.

SUBORDINATE PERSONNEL

The financial administrator is responsible for the supervision of the bookkeeper and related clerical personnel. He is responsible for the supervision of the activities of lay leaders with responsibility for financial affairs. He is an ex officio member of the Finance Committee and the School Committee (School Board). All financial proposals are subject to his review before they are presented to the congregation for approval.

Adapted from the job description of the financial administrator, Hampton Park Baptist Church, Greenville, S.C. Used with permission.

APPENDIX E

HAMPTON PARK BAPTIST CHURCH MINISTRIES
COMPENSATION AND EMPLOYEE BENEFITS PHILOSOPHY

Philosophy: Hampton Park Baptist Church Ministries seeks to provide for its full-time employees as follows:

A wage level that provides a reasonable standard of living in the Greenville area; and

A workplace environment that is clean, maintained, and conducive to performing one's responsibilities enjoyably; and

A workplace environment that is free from harassment, both internally and externally; and

A work environment that provides time with one's family; and

Employee benefits that reduce the potential financial disaster from catastrophic experiences; and

Employee benefits that provide an opportunity to enjoy life after a normal work cycle.

Application: Hampton Park Baptist Church Ministries will accomplish the above philosophy through the following programs:

Wages will be reviewed against other not-for-profit organizations, both in the Greenville area and on a national level every three years. School faculty wages will be compared to the Greenville County School System every three years; and

Wages will be adjusted annually for the effect of inflation (cost-of-living), for merit in performing one's responsibilities, and for the increase in one's responsibilities; and

Our workplace will be maintained on a daily basis for cleanliness, orderliness and supplies that enable our employees to efficiently perform their responsibilities; and

We will monitor the work environment to minimize/eliminate adversarial situations. We will strive to make Hampton Park a pleasant, enjoyable, and desirable place to minister for the Lord Jesus Christ; and

We will provide our team members with proper tools to carry out their responsibilities; and

We will provide our team members' immediate family with education as they go through school, providing these needs are met within the normal offerings of Hampton Park Christian School; and

We encourage our employees to continue their education and will assist them within reasonable measures. Teachers are rewarded with additional compensation upon satisfactory completion of advance degree programs as well as partial reimbursement for tuition costs. The Pastoral staff members are given an annual stipend. Other employees are encouraged to seek approval for programs that will help them better use their talents in our ministry; and

We will provide reasonable vacation and holiday benefits to enable our employees to enjoy time with their families, have time for rest and relaxation away from our ministry and to recharge their batteries. We will encourage employees to take at least two consecutive weeks of vacation each year for personal refreshment; and

We will provide benefits or make benefits available that will give our employees peace of mind concerning potential catastrophic financial situations. These will include, but not be limited to the following:

- Life insurance that will provide the employee's family the approximate net earnings of that employee for the next two years; and

- Life insurance on a non–Hampton Park employed spouse that will provide adequate funds for final arrangements; and

- Long-term disability insurance to provide approximate net earnings of an employee for their normal working years which we are assuming is age 65; and

- Health insurance that provides for major medical expenses while the employee assumes the routine costs. The exposure per family should not exceed $6,000 in a year.

- We will provide a retirement program that encourages our employees to provide for their retirement years. This program will have a Hampton Park match, which, when combined with an employee's participation, should enable one to retire without major financial concerns.

By John Yessa, Business Manager, Hampton Park Baptist Church, Greenville, S.C. Used with permission.

SAMPLE EMPLOYMENT APPLICATION

THUNDER MOUNTAIN CHRISTIAN SCHOOL ANYTOWN • CO 76432 123-555-4567	**For Official Use Only** Date _____ By _____ Attn. of _____ Attn. to _____ Checked _____

Application for Employment

Personal

Date _____

Name _____ Social Security Number _____
      Last   First   Middle

Address _____ Phone (____) ____

City _____ State ____ Zip ____ E-mail ____

How long have you been at this address? _____ Do you have the legal right to work in the United States? ☐ yes ☐ no

If your application is considered favorably, on what date will you be available for work? _____

Previously employed by TMCS? ☐ yes ☐ no   If yes, when? _____   On what basis? ☐ faculty ☐ staff ☐ student

What prompted you to seek employment at Thunder Mountain Christian School? _____

Briefly describe why you feel you could be an asset to Thunder Mountain Christian School: _____

What do you consider to be the single most important event in your life? _____

What do you consider the second most important event in your life? _____

Have you ever been convicted of a felony? ☐ yes ☐ no

Education

High school: _____ Graduated? ☐ yes ☐ no

College or technical training:

Degree held	School name and address	Major(s) & number of hours	Minor(s) & number of hours

If applying for a teaching position, please have official transcripts of all college work sent to TMCS, Attn: Administrator.

List any special work toward a degree or other special training (indicate school where taken): _____

Honors Received: _____

List any Professional Certificates or Licenses that you hold: (If teaching certificate, indicate level and subjects)

Type of Certificate or License _____ Issuing State ____ Number ____

Type of Certificate or License _____ Issuing State ____ Number ____

Work Preference/Job Skills

What type of work do you prefer? 1 _____ 2 _____

Please list proficient job skills: 1 _____ 2 _____ 3 _____

over

Work Experience

If you are presently employed, may we contact your employer? ☐ yes ☐ no

List all employers you have had during the **past five years**, starting with present or most recent employer:

■ 1. Firm _____ Address _____
City _____ State _____ Zip _____
Phone ( ) _____ Fax ( ) _____ E-mail _____
Position/Responsibilities _____
Supervisor _____ Contact Person _____
Reason for leaving _____ Dates employed _____

■ 2. Firm _____ Address _____
City _____ State _____ Zip _____
Phone ( ) _____ Fax ( ) _____ E-mail _____
Position/Responsibilities _____
Supervisor _____ Contact Person _____
Reason for leaving _____ Dates employed _____

■ 3. Firm _____ Address _____
City _____ State _____ Zip _____
Phone ( ) _____ Fax ( ) _____ E-mail _____
Position/Responsibilities _____
Supervisor _____ Contact Person _____
Reason for leaving _____ Dates employed _____

References

Name of present church _____ Present pastor's name _____
Address _____ City _____ State _____ Zip _____
Phone ( ) _____ Fax ( ) _____ E-mail _____ Attended since _____

If you have attended your present church less than one year, list your previous church:

Name of previous church _____ Previous pastor's name _____
Address _____ City _____ State _____ Zip _____
Phone ( ) _____ Fax ( ) _____ E-mail _____ Period attended _____

List three persons who are well acquainted with you, not including relatives, former teachers, or anyone listed above:

■ 1. Name _____ Phone ( ) _____ E-mail _____
Address _____ City _____ State _____ Zip _____

■ 2. Name _____ Phone ( ) _____ E-mail _____
Address _____ City _____ State _____ Zip _____

■ 3. Name _____ Phone ( ) _____ E-mail _____
Address _____ City _____ State _____ Zip _____

No employee other than the Administrator of Thunder Mountain Christian School or his authorized representative has the authority to enter into an employment contract with any employee, and any employment contract entered into must be in writing.

The facts set forth in my application for employment are true and complete. I understand that if I am employed, any false statement on this application may result in my dismissal. I further understand that this application is not, and is not intended to be, a contract of employment, nor does this application obligate Thunder Mountain Christian School in any way if they decide to employ me. I understand and agree that my employment is on an at-will basis.

I authorize Thunder Mountain Christian School to make such investigations and inquiries of my personal employment, and other related matters as may be necessary, in arriving at an employment decision. I hereby release employers, schools, or persons from all liability in responding to inquiries in connection with my application.

Signed: _____ Date _____

SAMPLE CONTRACTS

CONTRACT A:

Employment Agreement between XYZ Christian School, a ministry of XYZ Church, and

I. Church Relationship

XYZ Christian School is a ministry of the XYZ Church. All employees of XYZ Christian School are employees of XYZ Church.

Every teacher must regularly attend and be an active member of XYZ Church or a church of like faith and practice.

Teachers not members of a church of like faith and practice in the area on the date of acceptance of employment will be required to become members of XYZ Church.

Teachers who are members of a local church of like faith and practice in the area upon acceptance of employment may remain members of that church; however, if that church ceases to be a church of like faith and practice or if the teacher decides to move his/her membership from that church, he/she will be required to become a member of XYZ Church.

II. Purpose of the School

The primary purpose of XYZ Christian School is to give each student a maximum knowledge of secular subjects and the essentials of culture, in the light of God's Word, "that in all things he might have the preeminence" (Col. 1:18). Even though knowledge is factually the same for believer and unbeliever, no subject can be taught in its truth if its Originator is ignored. Because spiritual truths are spiritually discerned, only teachers who have personally accepted Jesus Christ as their Savior and Lord can teach in a manner pleasing to God. Consequently, only a Christian school with born-again teachers can give a child the education God expects in keeping with His instruction in Proverbs 22:6, "Train up a child in the way he should go: and when he is old, he will not depart from it." Our entire school program is designed to help parents fulfill this command of God.

III. Biblical Position

The Word of God is the ultimate source of our instruction in spiritual matters. XYZ Christian School has a twofold Bible emphasis: to show each student his need of Jesus Christ as his personal Savior and to present the Bible as God's absolute standard for moral conduct. Only the King James Version of the Bible may be used for classroom instruction and for preaching in chapel.

IV. Standards of Conduct

All members of XYZ Christian School's faculty and staff are required to abstain from the use of tobacco, dancing, card playing, the use of liquor in any form, and attendance at movie theaters and at meetings of secret societies. We believe that these practices do not contribute to spiritual growth and development and are a poor testimony for Christian leaders.

V. Personal Life

All teachers are expected to exemplify Christ in their daily lives in such a manner that others will know that they are born-again Christians. Details of the dress code for students and faculty are included in the Student-Parent Handbook and the Faculty Handbook.

VI. Administrative Policies

Principal—The duties of the principal will differ from those of the faculty. The principal is not responsible to the faculty; on the contrary, the faculty members are responsible to the principal or to his appointed representative. The final word on major matters rests entirely in the hands of the principal, the school board, and the church body, who reserve the right to make any changes that seem necessary for the general welfare of the school.

Faculty and staff—If a teacher is worthy of teaching at this school, then he/she is due the respect of his/her office. It is expected that the same attitude will be shown the administration by each member of the faculty. No teacher or member of the staff should criticize the policies of the administration publicly or to the parents of the school children. Criticism of the administration or school program by any staff member is grounds for immediate dismissal. All employees are encouraged to discuss with the administration policies they do not understand.

VII. Salary and Allowances for Teachers
      Gross annual salary: _____

All salaries are paid as above, less deductions for federal and state taxes and deductions made at the request of the employee for insurance, retirement, and so forth. A private retirement program is available to full-time employees on September 1 following completion of three years' service as a full-time employee. Details of the program are included in the Faculty Handbook.

Group insurance is provided for all full-time employees. Coverage is also available for employees' dependents. Dependents' coverage is paid for by the employee. Details of the group insurance program are included in the Faculty Handbook.

An educational grant program is available to encourage teachers and administrators to continue their professional development; $ _____ per course is available to teachers who satisfactorily complete approved courses. Details of the program are included in the Faculty Handbook.

XYZ Christian School shall provide such additional benefits as the board shall approve from time to time. Details of these benefits are provided in the Faculty Handbook.

VIII. The Contract Period

The contract year is from _____ through _____

Teachers are expected to be available throughout this entire period. Teachers normally receive several days off at Thanksgiving, Christmas, and Easter.

The normal workday while school is in session is from 8:00 A.M. to 4:00 P.M. The normal workday during preplanning and postplanning sessions is from 9:00 AM to 4:00 P.M. Teachers are expected to be present during these times. Teachers are also expected to be present for faculty meetings, faculty prayer meetings, Parent Teacher Fellowship meetings, school programs, and school social functions where children they normally teach are present. Teachers are expected to make themselves available for conferences with students, parents, and the school administration upon receipt of reasonable notice.

IX. Leave

Paid sick leave is authorized on the following basis:

First year of employment	5 days
Second year of employment	10 days
Third and subsequent years	15 days

Unused sick leave may be carried over from one year to the next.

A maximum of 30 days may be accrued. If an employee exceeds the maximum allowable sick leave, the cost of a substitute teacher (not to exceed the regular teacher's normal daily rate) will be deducted from his/her salary.

Personal leave will be made available to teachers when it can be done without hindering the daily operation of the school. It may be authorized on the following basis:

First year of employment	none
Second year of employment	1 day

Third year of employment   2 days

Fourth and subsequent years   3 days

Personal days may not be accrued. Permission to use personal days must be obtained from the principal in advance.

X. Termination of Contract

Either party may terminate the terms of this contract for any reason by giving thirty days' written notice of such intent. The school may give thirty days' salary in lieu of thirty days' notice of termination.

XI. Statement of Acceptance

I have read my contract, and it has been sufficiently explained. I realize that violation of this contract may result in immediate termination of my employment. I will do everything in my power, with God's help, to make this school year fruitful. With my signature, I commit myself to teach for the _____ year.

Signatures:

_____   _____
Teacher   Date

_____   _____
Pastor/Board Chairman   Date

_____   _____
School Administrator   Date

CONTRACT B:

By Attorney John McLario, General Counsel

Christian Legal Defense and Education Foundation

CONTRACTUAL AGREEMENT FOR EMPLOYMENT AND ACKNOWLEDGEMENT OF ORDINATION FOR SERVICE

By

_____

(Name of Church)

_____

(Address)

_____

(City & State)

IT IS HEREBY AGREED by and between the Church located in _____ County, State of _____ (herein called the Church) and _____ (hereinafter called the Teacher, Employee, Principal, etc.);

WITNESSETH:

THAT WHEREAS, the Teacher (or said employee) agrees to perform the duties of ___[Position]___ in the Church for one school year, the first day being on or about the _____ day of _____, 20_____, in addition to approximately _____ days of in-service training during 20_____;

That, in consideration of a salary in the sum of _____ dollars ($_____) payable _____, said employee agrees to perform faithfully the duties of ___[Position]___ in the Church.

That throughout the terms of this contract the Teacher shall be subject to discharge for good and just causes, provided that he/she shall have the right to service of written charges, and a hearing before the Church Board if requested in writing within five (5) days after receipt of the charges. If the Teacher chooses to be accompanied by legal counsel at the hearing, said legal expenses will be incurred by the Teacher. Continued unsatisfactory work or conduct, after written warning, shall be considered justifiable grounds for discharge (e.g., inability to teach, inability to control or discipline the class or classes, inefficiency, physical disability, absenteeism, unreasonable tardiness, unprofessional attitude, inability to deal with students or parents, conduct not in keeping with Christian principles, or conduct detrimental to the Church).

That the first sixty (60) teaching days of a teacher's initial contract with the Church is a probationary period and the contract can be terminated by the Church with or without cause during such period.

That the Teacher will give _____ weeks'[1] written notice to the Church Board in the event that he/she is unable for any reason to continue to faithfully fulfill such duties as are agreed upon in this contract.

That the Teacher will teach classes and perform any other Church services as directed by the Church Board or its authorized representative. The Teacher hereby agrees to devote his/her full time, skill, labor, and attention to said employment during the term of this contract.

That this contract is subject to all the rules and regulations that the Church Board has adopted or adopts hereafter in the operation of this Church Ministry, and that the failure of the Teacher to abide by said rules and regulations shall be deemed sufficient cause for termination of this contract by the Church Board. The Teacher is responsible for being familiar with the Church Rules and Regulations, the Teacher Manual, and the Parent-Student Handbook.

That the Teacher shall receive without loss of pay _____ days' absence each school year for personal illness or serious illness or death in the Teacher's immediate family. The Church Board will provide a substitute Teacher during such sick leave. The Church Board will also permit _____ days' absence for personal reasons. For such absences, the Teacher will consult the administration for written approval.

That the Teacher will be entitled to such other fringe benefits as may be provided by the Church Board, including [2]

_____

_____

_____

_____

That in signing this contract the Teacher acknowledges full agreement with the doctrinal statement of the Church and agrees to become a member in good standing of the Church, supporting the Church with regular attendance at all services (Sunday school, Sunday morning and evening services, Wednesday midweek service, and all special services), and with tithes and offerings. In addition, the signing of this contract signifies agreement with the following: "I acknowledge Jesus Christ as my personal Lord and Savior, believing the Bible to be the inspired Word of God without contradiction or error in its original languages. I believe that every Christian should be separated from worldly habits such as smoking, drinking, dancing, and other such unacceptable activities, and I believe that a Christian should conduct himself/herself at all times in a manner that will reflect a sound Christian testimony. With God giving me the strength, I shall endeavor to walk in such holiness and temperance as will be an example to the youth."

That said employee acknowledges that this position is ordained by God, and that his/her dedication and ordination is of God. That the principal activity of the Church rests in the instruction, advancement, and propagation of its religious beliefs. Its primary purpose is religious, but it also serves educational purposes.

IN WITNESS WHEREOF, the Teacher shall fulfill all aspects of this contract, any exception thereto being by mutual consent of the Church and the Teacher in writing. Failure to fulfill the obligations agreed to in this contract will be viewed as a violation.

Dated this _____ day of _____, 20_____

_____

Teacher

_____

Pastor

_____

Principal

_____

Chairman of the Church Board

[1]The contract should require minimum notice. Unhappy teachers often violate it anyway, and those who do not are often ineffective during the time they stay.

[2]The contract here should either state the specific benefits given or state "None."

SAMPLE FACULTY HANDBOOK FORMAT

I. Introduction
   A. Philosophy of education
   B. Introduction to the school
      1. History
      2. Purpose
      3. Organization (including church-school relationship)
      4. Doctrinal position

II. Employment Policies
   A. Basis for employment
   B. Financial arrangements
   C. Benefits
      1. Insurance
      2. Educational grants
      3. Retirement program

III. Personnel Regulations
   A. Standards
      1. Personal appearance
      2. Promptness
   B. Schedule
      1. Hours
      2. Prayer meeting
      3. Other meetings
      4. Tutoring
   C. Paid time off
      1. Breaks
      2. Absences (including responsibilities when absent)

3. Special requests

IV. Academic Policy
  A. Accreditation and certification
  B. Admissions
    1. Admissions policy
    2. Testing
    3. Scholarships
  C. Curricula
    1. Elementary
    2. Junior high
    3. Senior high
  D. Reporting
    1. Report card
    2. Promotion
    3. Graduation

V. Parent-Student Relationships
  A. Meetings
    1. Grade-level meetings
    2. Parent-teacher fellowships
    3. Parent-teacher conferences
  B. Discipline
    1. Minor disciplinary action
    2. Suspension
    3. Expulsion

VI. Spiritual Responsibilities
  A. Character training schedule
  B. Character traits
  C. Personal testimony
  D. Soulwinning

VII. Teaching Policies and Suggestions
  A. Daily schedule
    1. Class schedule

2. Preparation for the day

3. Lesson plans

4. Arrival/Late arrival

5. Beginning the day

6. Pledges

7. Attendance records

    a. Excused absences

    b. Unexcused absences

    c. Tardiness

8. Recess and physical education

9. Ending the day

10. Early dismissal

11. Departure

B. Building policies

    1. Classroom rules

    2. Moving in the building

    3. Restrooms

    4. Food service

    5. Safety precautions

    6. Mailboxes

    7. Hall bulletin board

    8. General maintenance

    9. Library

    10. Study hall

C. Supplies and equipment

    1. Requesting supplies

    2. Purchasing supplies

    3. Using supplies

        a. Audiovisuals

        b. Bulletin boards

        c. Copying service

        d. Books

        e. Computers

D. Special activities
1. Scheduled
    a. First day
    b. Getting to know the students
    c. Classroom checklist (beginning of the year)
    d. Field trips
    e. Parties
    f. Checkout list (end of the year)
    g. Ads
2. Unscheduled
    a. Fire and tornado drills
    b. Illness and accidents

SAMPLE STUDENT APPLICATION

THUNDER MOUNTAIN CHRISTIAN SCHOOL
ANYTOWN • CO 76432
123-555-4567

FOR OFFICE USE ONLY
ID no.
AK no.
Reg. fee paid ☐ yes ☐ no
TR request ☐ yes ☐ no
PR _____ AP
BK _____ SEC
FM (f)
FM (m)

Application for Admission

Application date: _____ Grade to enter: _____ For school year: _____ Pay Plan: ☐ 10 months ☐ 12 months

Legal name: _____
Last _____ First _____ Middle _____ Name child goes by

Sex: _____ Age: _____ Birthdate: / / _____ Social Security Number: _____

Country of birth: _____ Country of citizenship: _____

Which best describes your race? ☐ White ☐ Black ☐ Hispanic ☐ Asian or Pacific Islander ☐ American Indian or Alaskan Native

Father's name or legal guardian if other than parents: _____
Last _____ First _____ Middle

Current address: _____
Street _____ City _____ State _____ Zip

Home phone: _____ Social Security Number: _____

Place of employment: _____ Work phone: _____

Mother's name or legal guardian if other than parents: _____
Last _____ First _____ Maiden

Current address: _____
Street _____ City _____ State _____ Zip

Home phone: _____ Social Security Number: _____

Place of employment: _____ Work phone: _____

Parental status:

	Father	Mother		Father	Mother	
	☐	☐	Married	☐	☐	Divorced
	☐	☐	Separated	☐	☐	Divorced, Remarried
	☐	☐	Adoptive	☐	☐	Widowed, Remarried
	☐	☐	Foster	☐	☐	Deceased

Sibling information:

First name	Age	Sex	Grade	Name of school attending

Child lives with: ☐ Mr. ☐ Mrs. ☐ Rev. ☐ Dr.

_____
Last name | First name and middle initial of father or person having paternal authority | First name and middle initial of mother or person having maternal authority | (Maiden name)

Do you attend church regularly? ☐ Yes ☐ No   If yes, name of church: _____

Pastor's name: _____ Church phone: _____

Please indicate your reason for selecting this school: _____

If applicable, indicate grades of previous attendance at Thunder Mountain Christian School: ☐K4 ☐K5 ☐1 ☐2 ☐3 ☐4 ☐5 ☐6 ☐7 ☐8 ☐9 ☐10 ☐11

Has child repeated any grade? ☐ Yes ☐ No   If yes, indicate grade: _____

If child has been homeschooled, indicate grade(s): ☐K4 ☐K5 ☐1 ☐2 ☐3 ☐4 ☐5 ☐6 ☐7 ☐8 ☐9 ☐10 ☐11

Has child been treated for a nervous, mental, or emotional disorder? ☐ Yes ☐ No

If yes, please explain: _____

Has child ever been expelled, dropped, or suspended by any school? ☐ Yes ☐ No

Complete the information below for other schools attended:

Name of school	Address	Phone/Fax	Dates of attendance

Statement of Cooperation

I understand that my child's attendance at Thunder Mountain Christian School is a privilege and not a right; and that if at any time his/her conduct, academic progress, or cooperation with the school's authorities is not in keeping with the school's requirements, the school reserves the right to terminate **at its discretion** my child's enrollment.

I give permission for my child to take part in all school activities including sports programs and school-sponsored trips away from the school premises. I absolve the school from all liability in the event my child is injured at school or during any school activity. I agree with the school's efforts to train my child in the Bible and will encourage my child in this and in all other phases of the curriculum.

I pledge not to interfere with the school in its efforts to administer discipline to my child in accordance with the standards the school sets for itself. If my child voluntarily withdraws or is requested to withdraw by the school, I understand and accept that no refund of registration fee nor monthly tuition will be made.

Signature of parent or guardian: _____

Financial Responsibility

I understand that I am responsible for all tuition and fees, as well as miscellaneous charges, that accrue on the above student's account. Payments are due the 5th of each month: beginning June 5 for those electing the 12-payment plan and beginning August 5 for those on the 10-payment plan. A 10-day grace period will be allowed from the day the payment is due, after which a late charge of 1½% will be assessed on all past-due account balances. Should the past-due balance on any account become more than $500 ($350 for K4 and K5), the student's enrollment will be temporarily suspended until all past-due amounts are paid. If a student's enrollment is suspended for more than two weeks for financial reasons, the enrollment will be terminated for that school year. Any outstanding charges referred to a collection agency will have the agency fees added to the balance due.

Printed name of parents (or one assuming financial responsibility): _____

Signature	Relationship	Social Security Number of person assuming financial responsibility

Give complete name and address of person to whom the statement should be sent (if other than parent or guardian):

Name	Street	City	State	Zip

Withdrawal date: _____   Reason for withdrawal: _____

STUDENT-PARENT HANDBOOK FORMAT

I. Introduction
   A. History of the school
   B. Purpose of the school

II. Admissions
   A. Statement of nondiscrimination
   B. Testing

III. Academics
   A. Accreditation
   B. Curriculum
   C. Homework
   D. Grading/promotion
   E. Scholarship

IV. Conduct and discipline
   A. Dress and hair codes
   B. Conduct rules
   C. Disciplinary penalties

V. Services
   A. Bus
      1. Schedules
      2. Rules
      3. Patrol guards
   B. Food

VI. Fees

VII. General policies and information
   A. Hours

       1. School hours

       2. Office hours

   B. Attendance

   C. Parent involvement

       1. Parent-teacher fellowships

       2. Parent-teacher conferences

       3. Visiting hours

   D. Use of telephone

   E. Student drivers

   F. Sickness, injury, and medication

   G. Cancellation days

   H. School colors

VIII. Agreement clause

SAMPLE ASSESSMENT PROGRAM

I. Entrance Examinations for New Students

   A. Four- and five-year kindergarten

      1. Conduct a personal interview with parents or guardians and child.

      2. Administer a readiness test if there appears to be a question about the child's readiness for school.

   B. Grades one through seven

      1. Administer the group IQ (school ability) test in general use for this grade level.

      2. Administer the reading and mathematics portion of the standardized achievement test in use at the school for this grade level.

      3. If there is a question about the child's overall level of intellectual functioning or if the child appears to be ADD, ADHD, or have specific learning disabilities, he should be referred to a specialist for an individualized evaluation before admission.

   C. Grades eight through twelve

      1. Most schools are no longer testing all students entering at the eighth grade and above. Admissions decisions are usually made on the basis of the students' grades and/or achievement and mental ability test scores that accompany their transcripts. Where grades are marginal, and/or there is no standardized test data available, step two should be followed.

2. Administer the group IQ (school ability) test in general use for this grade level. Administer the reading and mathematics portion of the standardized achievement test in general use in the appropriate grade level.

II. Continuous Evaluation

A. Intelligence and achievement should be monitored continuously throughout the years of the student's enrollment in the school. The same tests used in the admissions process should be used.

B. Intelligence tests do not need to be administered every year. The following schedule would usually provide the comparison needed with achievement scores: grades one, four, eight, and eleven.

C. Achievement tests should be routinely administered every year. The results of achievement testing should be compared with the previous year's achievement scores and the most recent intelligence test results. Students should achieve in a manner consistent with their ability.

D. Students whose achievement test results are not generally consistent with their level of ability should be referred for further testing in an attempt to pinpoint their problems and recommend remediation.

E. Telebinocular vision testing should be done in grades one, three, and five, and on the basis of the teacher's recommendation.

F. Audiometer testing should be done in grades one, three, and five, and on the basis of the teacher's recommendation.

III. Aptitude Testing

A. Senior high school students need to take the ACT or SAT as a measure of their potential for success in higher education and to help the school monitor the progress of its students.

B. Students planning to enroll in some form of higher education will normally be required to take either the ACT or the SAT. Most Christian colleges prefer the ACT.

IV. Interest Testing

A. Interest tests should be administered routinely to senior high school students beginning in grade nine.

B. Interest tests help students identify types of work that are consistent with their interests and frequently make them aware of good vocational options they had not considered previously.

THUNDER MOUNTAIN CHRISTIAN SCHOOL

Grades 1-8

STUDENT _____ TEACHER _____ YEAR _____

	Quarters				
	1	2	3	4	Final
Bible					
Conduct					
Reading					
Spelling/Phonics (Grade 1)					
Spelling (Grades 2–6)					
Penmanship					
Math					
English					
U.S. History					
World History					
Civics					

	Quarters				
	1	2	3	4	Final
Colorado History					
U.S. Geography					
World Geography					
Biological Science					
Elementary Science					
Earth Science					
Music					
Physical Education					
Chorus (Grades 7–8)					
Band (Grades 7–8)					

Explanation of Grading

A	93–100	Superior
B	85–92	Excellent
C	75–84	Above Average
D	70–74	Average
F	69–below	Below Average

	1	2	3	4
Days Tardy				
Days Absent				
Days Present				
Days on Roll				

Date Enrolled _____

Date Withdrawn _____

Finished School Year?   Yes _____   No _____

Assigned to _____ Grade for Next School Year

Conference Requested?   Yes _____   No _____

Achievement Test Percentile _____

CASE SUMMARY

DONALD T. REGAN, Secretary of Treasury,
et al., Appellants
v.
TAXATION WITH REPRESENTATION OF
WASHINGTON (No. 81-2338)
TAXATION WITH REPRESENTATION OF
WASHINGTON, Appellant
v.
DONALD T. REGAN, Secretary of Treasury,
et al. (Not. 82-134)
–US–, 76 L Ed 2d 129, 103 S Ct–
(Nos. 81-2338 and 82-134)
Argued March 22, 1983. May 23, 1983

Decision: Prohibition against lobbying for tax-exempt status under 26 USCS § 501(c)(3) held constitutional

SUMMARY

A non-profit corporation organized to promote certain interests in the field of federal taxation applied for tax-exempt status under 26 USCS § 501(c)(3). The Internal Revenue Service denied the application because it appeared that a substantial part of the corporation's activities would consist of attempting to influence legislation, which is not permitted by § 501(c)(3). The corporation sued federal officials in the United States District Court for the District of Columbia, challenging the prohibition against substantial lobbying as violative of the First Amendment and the equal protection component of the Fifth Amendment's due process clause. The District Court granted summary judgment against the corporation. On appeal, the en banc United States Court of Appeals for the District of Columbia reversed, holding that § 501(c)(3) did not violate the First Amendment but did violate the Fifth Amendment (676 F2d 715).

On appeal, the United States Supreme Court reversed. In an opinion by REHNQUIST, expressing the unanimous view of the court, it was held that (1) the prohibition against lobbying in § 501(c)(3) did not violate the First Amendment, since Congress, pursuant to § 501(c)(3), had not infringed on any First Amendment rights or regulated any First Amendment activity, and (2) the prohibition against lobbying in § 501(c)(3) did not violate the equal protection component of the Fifth Amendment, even though veterans' organizations were allowed under § 501(c)(19) to carry on substantial lobbying and still qualify to receive tax-deductible contributions, regardless of the content of the speech they used, and it was not irrational for Congress to decide that taxpayers should not subsidize the lobbying of tax exempt charities, or to decide that although it would not subsidize lobbying by charities in general, it would subsidize the lobbying of veterans' organizations.

BLACKMUN, J., joined by BRENNAN and MARSHALL J. J., concurred expressing the view that while he joined the court's opinion, the holding that § 501(c)(3) did not violate the First Amendment depended entirely on the court's necessary assumption that the Internal Revenue Service, in enforcing the lobbying restrictions, required an organization qualified under § 501(c)(3) and its lobbying affiliate with tax exempt status under § 501(c)(4), only to be separately incorporated and to keep records adequate to show that the tax deductible contributions were not used to pay for lobbying.

Following are significant quotations from the text of the decision:

Both tax exemption and tax-deductibility are a form of subsidy that is administered through the tax system. A tax exemption has much the same effect as a cash grant to the organization of the amount of tax it would have to pay on its income. Deductible contributions are similar to cash grants of the amount of a portion of the individual's contributions. The system Congress has enacted provides this kind of subsidy to nonprofit civic welfare organizations generally, and an additional subsidy to those charitable organizations that do not engage in substantial lobbying. In short, Congress chose not to subsidize lobbying as extensively as it chose to subsidize other activities that nonprofit organizations undertake to promote the public welfare.

We again reject the "notion that First Amendment rights are somehow not fully realized unless they are subsidized by the state." Id., at 515 3 L Ed 2d 462, 79 S Ct 524 (Douglas; J., concurring). . . .

Congress has not violated TWR's First Amendment Rights by declining to subsidize its First Amendment activities. The case would be different if Congress were to discriminate invidiously in its subsidies in such a way as to "'aim[] at the suppression of dangerous ideas.'" Cammarrano, supra, at 513 3 L Ed 2d 462, 79 S Ct 524, quoting Speiser, supra, at 519 2 L Ed 2d 1460, 78 5 Ct 1332. But the veterans' organizations that qualify under § 501(c)(19) are entitled to receive tax-deductible contributions regardless of the content of any speech they may use, including lobbying. We find no indication that the statute was intended to suppress any ideas or any demonstration that it has had that effect. The sections of the Internal Revenue Code here at issue do not employ any suspect classification. The distinction between veterans' organizations and other charitable organizations is not at all like distinction based on race or national origin. . . .

Congressional selection of particular entities or persons for entitlement to this sort of largesse "is obviously a matter of policy and discretion not open to judicial review unless in circumstances which here we are not able to find." United States v Realty Co. [163 US 427] 444 [41 L Ed 215, 16 S Ct 1120][(1896)]. Cincinnati Soap Co. v United States 301 US 308, 317, 81 L Ed 1122, 57 5 Ct 524 (1937). See also, id., at 313, 81 L Ed 1122, 57 S Ct 76; Alabama v Texas, 347 US 272, 98 L Ed 689, 74 S Ct 481 (1954). For the purposes of this case appropriations are comparable to tax exemptions and deductions, which are also "a matter of grace

[that] Congress can, of course, disallow . . . as it chooses," Commissioner v Sullivan 386 US 27, 2 L Ed 2d 559, 78 S Ct 512 (1958). . . .

The reasoning of the decisions is simple: "although government may not place obstacles in the path of a [person's] exercise of freedom of [speech], it need not remove those not of its own creation." Harris, supra, at 316 65 L Ed 2d 784, 100 S Ct 2671. Although TWR does not have as much money as it wants, and thus cannot exercise its freedom of speech as much as it would like, the Constitution "does not confer an entitlement of funds as may be necessary to realize all the advantages of that freedom," Id., at 316 65 L Ed 2d 784, 100 S Ct 2671. As we said in Maher, "[c]onstitutional concerns are greatest when the State attempts to impose its will by force of law. . . ." 432 US, at 476, 53 L Ed 2d 484, 97 S Ct 2376. Where governmental provision of subsidies is not "aimed at the suppression of dangerous ideas," Cammarrano, supra, at 513 3 L Ed 2d 462, 79 S Ct 524, its "power to encourage actions deemed to be in the public interest is necessarily far broader." Maher, supra, at 476, 53 L Ed 2d 484, 97 S Ct 2376. . . .

The issue in this case is not whether TWR must be permitted to lobby, but whether Congress is required to provide it with public money with which to lobby. For the reasons stated above, we hold that it is not. Accordingly, the judgment of the Court of Appeals is reversed. . . .

CASE SUMMARY

Syllabus
BOB JONES UNIVERSITY
v.
UNITED STATES
CERTIORARI TO THE UNITED STATES
COURT OF APPEALS FOR
THE FOURTH CIRCUIT

No. 81-3 Argued October 12, 1982—Decided May 24, 1983*

Section 501(c)(3) of the Internal Revenue Code of 1954 (IRC) provides that "[c]orporations . . . organized and operated exclusively for religious, charitable . . . or educational purposes" are entitled to tax exemption. Until 1970, the Internal Revenue Service (IRS) granted tax-exempt status under § 501(c)(3) to private schools, independent of racial admissions policies, and granted charitable deductions for contributions to such schools under § 170 of the IRC. But in 1970, the IRS concluded that it could no longer justify allowing tax-exempt status under § 501(c)(3) to private schools that practiced racial discrimination, and in 1971 issued Revenue Ruling 71-447 providing that a private school not having a racially nondiscriminatory policy as to students is not "charitable" within the common law concepts reflected in §§ 170 and 501(c)(3). In No. 81-3, petitioner Bob Jones University, while permitting unmarried Negroes to enroll as students, denies admission to applicants engaged in an interracial marriage or known to advocate interracial marriage or dating. Because of this admission policy, the IRS revoked the University's tax-exempt status. After paying a portion of the federal unemployment taxes for a certain taxable year, the University filed a refund action in Federal District Court, and the Government counterclaimed for unpaid taxes for that and other taxable years. Holding that the IRS exceeded its powers in revoking the University's tax-exempt status and violated the University's rights under the Religion Clauses of the First Amendment, the District Court ordered the IRS to refund the taxes paid and rejected the counterclaim. The Court of Appeals reversed. In No. 81-1, petitioner Goldsboro Christian Schools maintains a racially discriminatory admissions policy based on its interpretation of the Bible, accepting for the most part only Caucasian students. The IRS determined that Goldsboro was not an organization described in § 501(c)(3) and hence was required to pay federal, social security, and unemployment taxes. After paying a portion of such taxes for certain years, Goldsboro filed a refund suit in Federal District Court, and the IRS counterclaimed for unpaid taxes. The District Court entered summary judgment for the Government, rejecting Goldsboro's claim to tax-exempt status under § 501(c)(3) and also its claim that the denial of such status violated the Religion Clauses of the First Amendment. The Court of Appeals affirmed.

Held: Neither petitioner qualifies as a tax-exempt organization under § 501(c)(3). Pp. 9-29.

(a) An examination of the IRC's framework and the background of congressional purposes reveals unmistakable evidence that underlying all relevant parts of the IRC is the intent that the entitlement to tax-exemption depends on meeting certain common-law standards of charity—namely, that an institution seeking tax-exempt status must serve a public purpose and not be contrary to established public policy. Thus, to warrant exemption under § 501(c)(3), an institution must fall within a category specified in that section and must demonstrably serve and be in harmony with the public interest, and the institution's purpose must not be so at odds with the common community conscience as to undermine any public benefit that might otherwise be conferred. Pp. 9-16.

(b) The IRS's 1970 interpretation of § 501(c)(3) was correct. It would be wholly incompatible with the concepts underlying tax exemption to grant tax-exempt status to racially discriminatory private educational entities. Whatever may be the rationale for such private schools' policies, racial discrimination in education is contrary to public policy. Racially discriminatory educational institutions cannot be viewed as conferring a public benefit within the above "charitable" concept or within the congressional intent underlying § 501(c)(3). Pp. 16-19.

(c) The IRS did not exceed its authority when it announced its interpretation of § 501(c)(3) in 1970 and 1971. Such interpretation is wholly consistent with what Congress, the Executive, and the courts had previously declared. And the actions of Congress since 1970 leave no doubt that the IRS reached the correct conclusion in exercising its authority. Pp. 20-25.

(d) The Government's fundamental, overriding interest in eradicating racial discrimination in education substantially outweighs whatever burden denial of tax benefits places on petitioners' exercise of their religious beliefs. Petitioners' asserted interests cannot be accommodated with compelling governmental interest, and no less restrictive means are available to achieve the governmental interest. Pp. 26-27.

(e) The IRS properly applied its policy to both petitioners. Goldsboro admits that it maintains racially discriminatory policies, and, contrary to Bob Jones University's contention that it is not racially discriminatory, discrimination on the basis of racial affiliation and association is a form of racial discrimination. Pp. 28-29.

No. 81-1, 644 F. 2d 870, and No. 81-3, 639 F. 2d 147, affirmed.

BURGER, C. J., delivered the opinion of the Court, in which BRENNAN, WHITE, MARSHALL, BLACKMUN, STEVENS, and O'CONNOR, J. J. joined, and in Part III of which POWELL, J. joined. POWELL, J., filed an opinion concurring in part and concurring in the judgment. REHNQUIST, J., filed a dissenting opinion.

Following are significant quotations from the text of the decision:

Tax exemptions for certain institutions thought beneficial to the social order of the country as a whole, or to a particular community, are deeply rooted in our history, as in that of England. The origins of such exemptions lie in the special privileges that have long been extended to charitable trusts. . . .

In enacting the Revenue Act of 1938, ch. 289, 52 Stat. 447 (1938), Congress expressly reconfirmed this view with respect to the charitable deduction provision:

"The exemption from taxation of money and property, devoted to charitable and other purposes is based on the theory that the Government is compensated for the loss of revenue by its relief from financial burdens which would otherwise have to be met by appropriations from other public funds and by the benefits resulting from the promotion of the general welfare." H. R. Rep. No. 1860, 75th Cong., 3d Sess. 19 (1938).

A corollary to the public benefit principle is the requirement, long recognized in the law of trusts, that the purpose of a charitable trust may not be illegal or violate established public policy. In 1861, this Court stated that a public charitable use must be "consistent with local laws and public policy. . . ."

When the Government grants exemptions or allows deductions, all taxpayers are affected; the very fact of the exemption or deduction for the donor means that other taxpayers can be said to be indirect or vicarious "donors." Charitable exemptions are justified on the basis that the exempt entity confers a public benefit—a benefit which the society or the community may not itself choose or be able to provide, or which supplements and advances the work of public institutions already supported by tax revenues. History buttresses logic to make clear that, to warrant exemptions under § 501(c)(3), an institution must fall within a category specified in that section and must demonstrably serve and be in harmony with the public interest. The institution's purpose must not be so at odds with the common community conscience as to undermine any public benefit that might otherwise be conferred. . . .

We are bound to approach these questions with full awareness that determinations of public benefit and public policy are sensitive matters with serious implications for the institutions affected; a declaration that a given institution is not "charitable" should be made only where there can be no doubt that the activity involved is contrary to a fundamental public policy. But there can no longer be any doubt that racial discrimination in education violates deeply and widely accepted views of elementary justice.

Whatever may be the rationale for such private schools' policies, and however sincere the rationale may be, racial discrimination in education is contrary to public policy. Racially discriminatory educational institutions cannot be viewed as conferring a public benefit within the "charitable" concept discussed earlier, or within the Congressional intent underlying 170 and 501(c)(3). . . .

On the record before us, there can be no doubt as to the national policy. In 1970, when the IRS first issued the ruling challenged here, the position of all three branches of the Federal Government was unmistakably clear. The correctness of the Commissioner's conclusion that a racially discriminatory private school "is not 'charitable' within the common law concepts reflected in . . . the Code," Rev. Rul. 71-477, 1972-2 Cum. Bull., at 231, is wholly consistent with what Congress, the Executive, and the courts had repeatedly declared before 1970. Indeed, it would be anomalous for the Executive, Legislative, and Judicial Branches to reach conclusions that add up to a firm public policy on racial discrimination, and at the same time have the IRS blissfully ignore what all three branches of the Federal Government had declared. Clearly an educational institution engaging in practices affirmatively at odds with this declared position of the whole government cannot be seen as exercising a "beneficial and stabilizing influenc[e] in community life," *Walz v. Tax Comm'n supra*, 397 U.S., at 673, and is not "charitable," within the meaning of § 170 and § 501(c)(3) in 1970 and 1971. . . .

Petitioners contend that, even if the Commissioner's policy is valid as to nonreligious private schools, that policy cannot constitutionally be applied to schools that engage in racial discrimination on the basis of sincerely held religious beliefs. . . . As to such schools, it is argued that the IRS construction of § 170 and § 501(c)(3) violates their free exercise rights under the Religion Clauses of the First Amendment. This contention presents claims not heretofore considered by this Court in precisely this context.

This Court has long held the Free Exercise Clause of the First Amendment an absolute prohibition against governmental regulation of religious beliefs, *Wisconsin v. Yoder* 406 U.S. 205, 219 (1972); *Sherbert v. Vernei* 374 U.S. 398, 402 (1963); *Cantwell v. Connecticut*, 310 U.S. 296, 303 (1940). As interpreted by this Court, moreover, the Free Exercise Clause provides substantial protection for lawful conduct grounded in religious belief, see *Wisconsin v. Yoder supra*, 406 U.S., at 220; *Thomas v. Review Board of the Indiana Emp. Security Div.*, 450, U.S. 707 (1981); *Sherbert v. Verner supra*, 374 U.S., at 402-403. However, "[n]ot all burdens on religion are unconstitutional. . . . The state may justify a limitation on religious liberty by showing that it is essential to accomplish an overriding governmental interest." *United States v. Lee*, 455, U.S. 252, 257-258 (1982) (citations omitted). See e. g., *McDaniel v. Paty*, 435 U.S. 618, 628 and n. 8 (1978); *Wisconsin v. Yoder, supra*, 406 U.S., at 215; *Gillette v. United States*, 401 U.S. 437 (1971).

On occasion this Court has found certain governmental interests so compelling as to allow even regulations prohibiting religiously based conduct. In *Prince v. Massachusetts*, 321 U.S. 158 (1944), for example, the Court held that neutrally cast child labor laws prohibiting sale of printed material on public streets could be applied to prohibit children from dispensing religious literature. The Court found no constitutional infirmity in "excluding [Jehovah's Witness children] from doing there what no other children may do." *Id.*, at 170. See also *Reynolds v. United States*, 98 U.S. 145 (1878); *United States v. Lee, supra; Gillette v. United States, supra*. Denial of tax benefits will inevitably have a substantial impact on the operation of private religious schools, but will not prevent those schools from observing their religious tenets.

The governmental interest at stake here is compelling. As discussed in Part II(B), *supra*, the Government has a fundamental, overriding interest in eradicating racial discrimination in education—discrimination that prevailed, with official approval, for the first 165 years of this Nation's history. That governmental interest substantially outweighs whatever burden denial of tax benefits places on petitioners' exercise of their religious beliefs. The interests asserted by petitioners cannot be accommodated with that compelling governmental interest, see *United States v. Less*, 455 U. S., at 259-260; and no "less restrictive means," see *Thomas v. Review Board, supra*, 450 U.S., at 718, are able to achieve the governmental interest.

BIBLIOGRAPHY

Adams, B. K., et al. *Principles of Public School Accounting.* Washington, DC: U.S. Government Printing Office, 1967.

Adams, J. E. *The Christian Counselor Manual.* Grand Rapids: Zondervan, 1973.

Bloss, J. L. *The Church Guide to Employment Law.* Matthews, NC: Christian Ministry Resources, 1993.

Blumenfeld, S. L. *Is Public Education Necessary?* Old Greenwich, CT: Devin-Adair, 1981.

Boydston, J. A., ed. *The Early Works of John Dewey.* 5 vols. Carbondale, IL: Southern Illinois Univ. Press, 1972.

Cubberly, E. P. *The History of Education.* Boston: Houghton Mifflin, 1920.

DeBruyn, R. L. *Causing Others to Want Your Leadership.* Manhattan, KS: DeBruyn, 1976.

DeJong, N. *Education in the Truth.* Nutley, NJ: Presbyterian and Reformed Publishing, 1969.

Deuink J. W. *Charting the Course: Pupil Personnel Services in the Christian School.* Greenville, SC: BJU Press, 2003.

Deuink J. W., ed. A *Fresh Look at Christian Education.* Greenville, SC: BJU Press, 1988.

Deuink, J. W., ed. *Preparing the Christian School for the Twenty-first Century.* Greenville, SC: BJU Press, 1991.

Deuink, J. W., ed. *Some Light on Christian Education.* Greenville, SC: BJU Press, 1984.

Drucker, P. F. *The Effective Executive.* New York: Harper and Row, 1974.

"Fundamentalist Colleges Must Be Wary of Governmental Strings." *American Association of Christian Colleges Newsletter* (spring 1985).

Furst, L. G., and C. J. Russo. *The Legal Aspects of Nonpublic Schools.* Berrien Springs, MI: Andrews Univ., 1993.

Gaebelein, F. E. *The Pattern of God's Truth.* New York: Oxford Univ. Press, 1954.

Gregory, J. M. *A Twenty-first Century Perspective of the Seven Laws of Teaching.* Edited by C. E. Walker & B. E. Walker. East Ridge, TN: TAKE TENN Publications, 2006.

Gross, M. J., Jr., J. H. McCarthy., and R. F. Larkin. *Financial and Accounting Guide for Not-for-Profit Organizations.* 4th ed. New York: John Wiley, 2000.

Grover, A. N. *Ohio's Trojan Horse.* Greenville, SC: BJU Press, 1977.

Hadik, W. *The Distinctives of Christian Textbooks.* In J. W. Deuink (Ed.) *Some Light on Christian Education* (pp. 109–14). Greenville, SC: Bob Jones University Press, 1984.

Hallahan, D. P., and J. M. Kauffman. *Exceptional Children: Introduction to Special Education.* 5th ed. Englewood Cliffs, NJ: Prentice Hall, 1991.

Hammer, R. R., S. W. Klipowicz, and J. F. Cobble, Jr. *Reducing the Risk* of *Child Sexual Abuse in Your Church.* Matthews, NC: Christian Ministry Resources, 1993.

Hammer, R. R. *Church and Clergy Tax Guide.* (revised annually) Carol Stream, IL: Christianity Today International, 2006.

Hefley, J. C. *Textbooks on Trial.* Wheaton, IL: Victor, 1976.

Hodge, A. A. *Popular Lectures on Theological Themes.* Philadelphia: Presbyterian Board of Publication and Sabbath-School Work, 1887.

Horton, R. A., ed. *Christian Education: Its Mandate and Mission.* Greenville, SC: BJU Press, 1992.

Johns, R. L., E. L. Morphet, and K. Alexander. *The Economics and Financing of Education.* 4th ed. Englewood Cliffs, NJ: Prentice-Hall, 1983.

Kelly, K. *State of North Carolina vs. Christian Liberty.* Southern Pines, NC: Calvary Press, n.d.

Kienel, P. A. *A History of Christian School Education.* (Vols. 1 & 2). Colorado Springs, CO: Association of Christian Schools International (1998, 2005).

Kienel, P. A. *The Christian School: Why It Is Right for Your Child.* Wheaton, IL: Victor, 1974.

Kienel, P. A., ed. *The Philosophy of Christian School Education.* Whittier, CA: Western Association of Christian Schools, n.d.

Lowrie, R. W., Jr. *To Those Who Teach in Christian Schools.* Whittier, CA: Association of Christian Schools International, 1978.

McLario, J. J. "Basic Legal Problems Encountered by a Pastor or Administrator." *The Administrator* (winter 1982): 15–18.

McLario, J. J. *Legal Problems.* Pamphlet available from the Christian Legal Defense and Educational Foundation, n.d.

Metts, W. C. *Your Faith on Trial.* Greenville, SC: BJU Press, 1979.

Morris, H. M. *Education for the Real World.* San Diego: CreationLife Publishers, 1977.

National Joint Committee on Learning Disabilities. "Providing Appropriate Education for Students with Learning Disabilities in Regular Education Classrooms." *Journal of Learning Disabilities,* (1993) 26 (5), 330–32.

Page, W. H. *The School That Built a Town.* New York: Harper and Row, 1952.

Private School Law in America. 6th ed. Rosemount, MN: Data Research, 1995.

Publication 557, Tax-exempt Status for Your Organization. (March 2005). Internal Revenue Service, Department of the Treasury. Washington, DC: U.S. Government Printing Office.

Renzulli, J. S., S. M. Reis, and L. H. Smith. *The Revolving Door* Identification Model. Mansfield Center, CT: Creative Learning Press, 1981.

Rushdoony, R. J. *The Messianic Character of American Education.* Philadelphia: Presbyterian and Reformed Publishing, 1963.

Sanders, J. O. *Spiritual Leadership.* Chicago: Moody, 1982.

Stoops, E., M. Rafferty, and R. L. Johnson. *Handbook of Educational Administration.* Boston: Allyn and Bacon, 1981.

Standard no. 17., Highway Safety Program, Department of Transportation. Washington, DC: U.S. Government Printing Office, 1972.

Sutton, Joe P., ed. *Special Education: A Biblical Approach.* Greenville, SC: Hidden Treasure Publications, 1993.

U.S. Supreme Court Education Cases. 3rd ed. Rosemount, MN: Data Research, 1993.

Vargo, R. J. *Effective Church Accounting.* San Francisco: HarperCollins, 1989.

Vargo, R. J. *The Church Guide to Financial Reporting.* Matthews, NC: Christian Ministries Resource, 1995.

Vargo, R. J. *The Church Guide to Internal Controls.* Matthews, NC: Christian Ministry Resources, 1995.

Vargo, R. J. *The Church Guide to Planning and Budgeting.* Matthews, NC: Christian Ministries Resources, 1995.